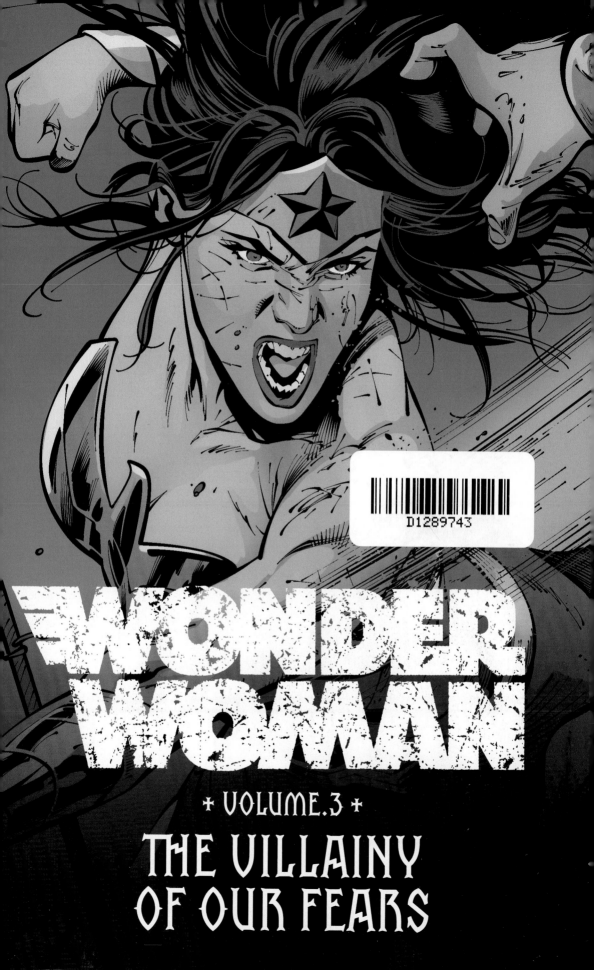

WONDER WOMAN

✦ VOLUME.3 ✦

THE VILLAINY OF OUR FEARS

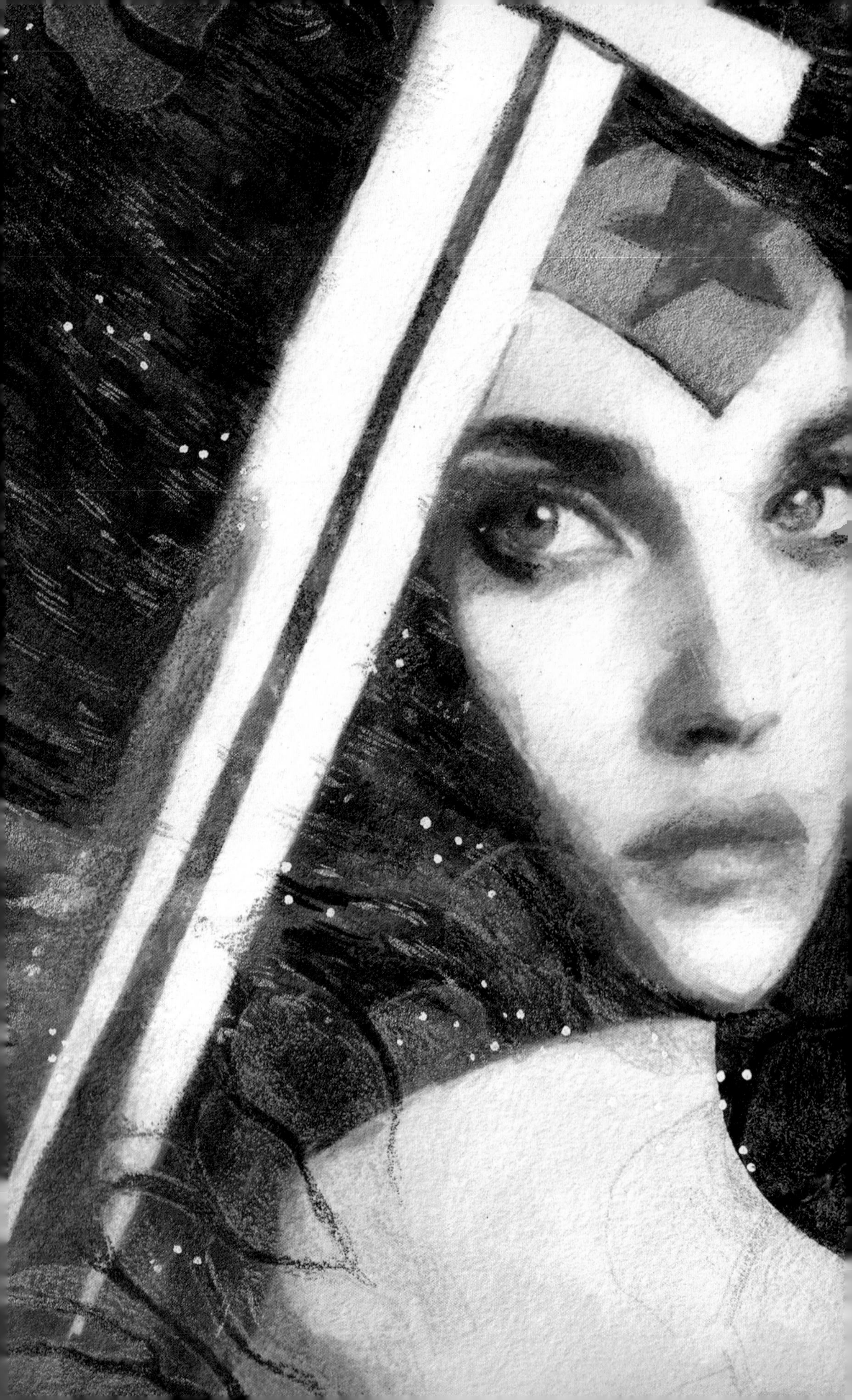

WONDER WOMAN

✦ VOLUME.3 ✦

THE VILLAINY OF OUR FEARS

BECKY CLOONAN, MICHAEL W. CONRAD

writers

EMANUELA LUPACCHINO, MARGUERITE SAUVAGE, EDUARDO PANSICA, AND JOSÉ LUÍS

pencillers

WADE VON GRAWBADGER, MARGUERITE SAUVAGE, AND JÚLIO FERREIRA

inkers

TAMRA BONVILLAIN, MARGUERITE SAUVAGE, AND JORDIE BELLAIRE

colorists

PAT BROSSEAU

letterer

YANICK PAQUETTE AND NATHAN FAIRBAIRN

collection cover artists

WONDER WOMAN created by WILLIAM MOULTON MARSTON.

SUPERMAN created by JERRY SIEGEL and JOE SHUSTER.
By special arrangement with the JERRY SIEGEL family.

Brittany Holzherr Editor – Original Series & Collected Edition
Chris Rosa Associate Editor – Original Series
Steve Cook Design Director – Books
& Publication Design
Emily Elmer Publication Production

Marie Javins Editor-in-Chief, DC Comics

Anne DePies Senior VP – General Manager
Jim Lee Publisher & Chief Creative Officer
Don Falletti VP – Manufacturing Operations & Workflow Management
Lawrence Ganem VP – Talent Services
Alison Gill Senior VP – Manufacturing & Operations
Jeffrey Kaufman VP – Editorial Strategy & Programming
Nick J. Napolitano VP – Manufacturing Administration & Design
Nancy Spears VP – Revenue

WONDER WOMAN VOL.3: THE VILLAINY OF OUR FEARS

DC Comics, 4000 Warner Blvd., Bldg. 700, 2nd Floor, Burbank, CA 91522
Printed by Solisco Printers, Scott, QC, Canada. 1/6/23. First Printing.
ISBN: 978-1-77951-984-9

Library of Congress Cataloging-in-Publication Data is available.

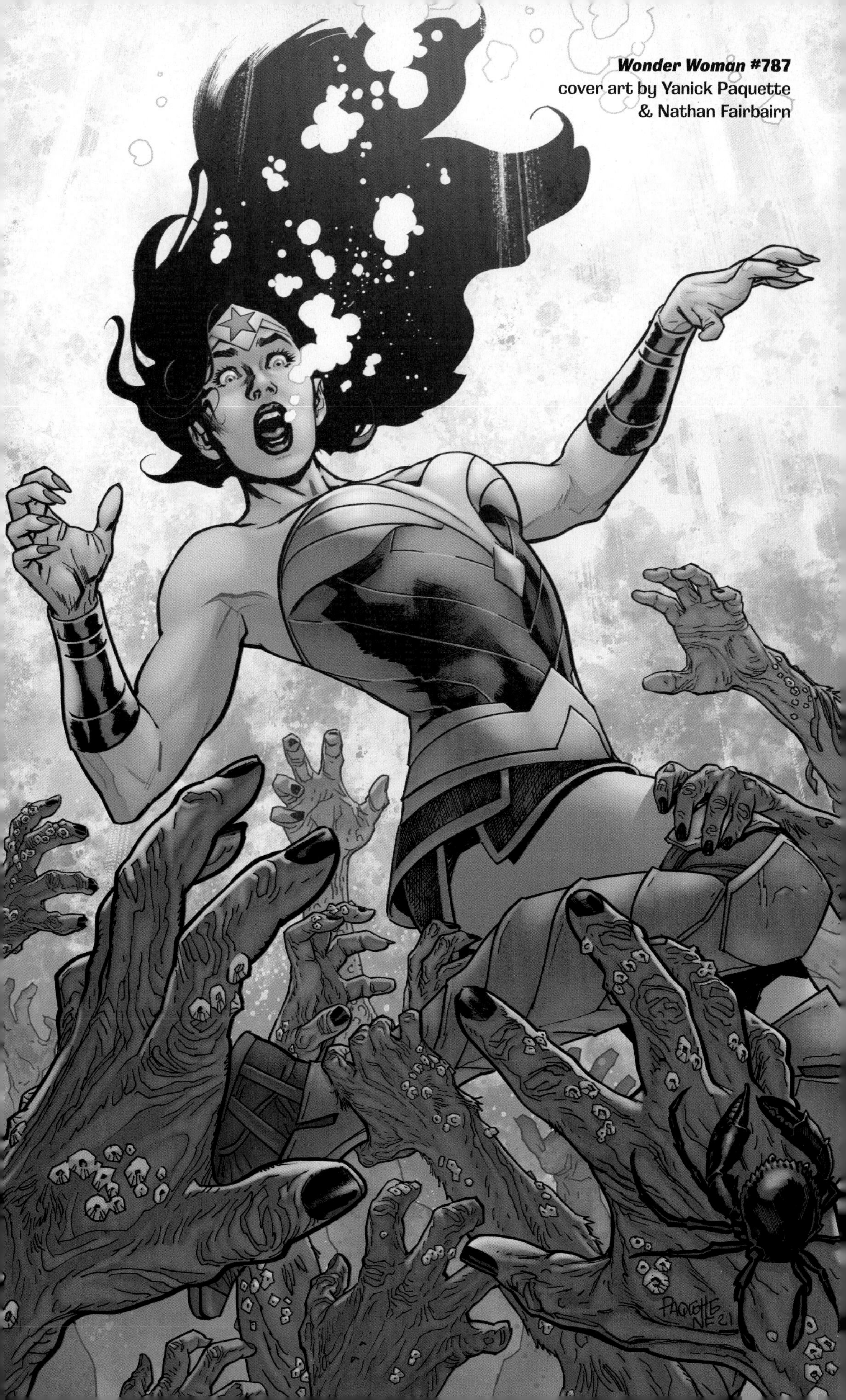

***Wonder Woman* #787**
cover art by Yanick Paquette
& Nathan Fairbairn

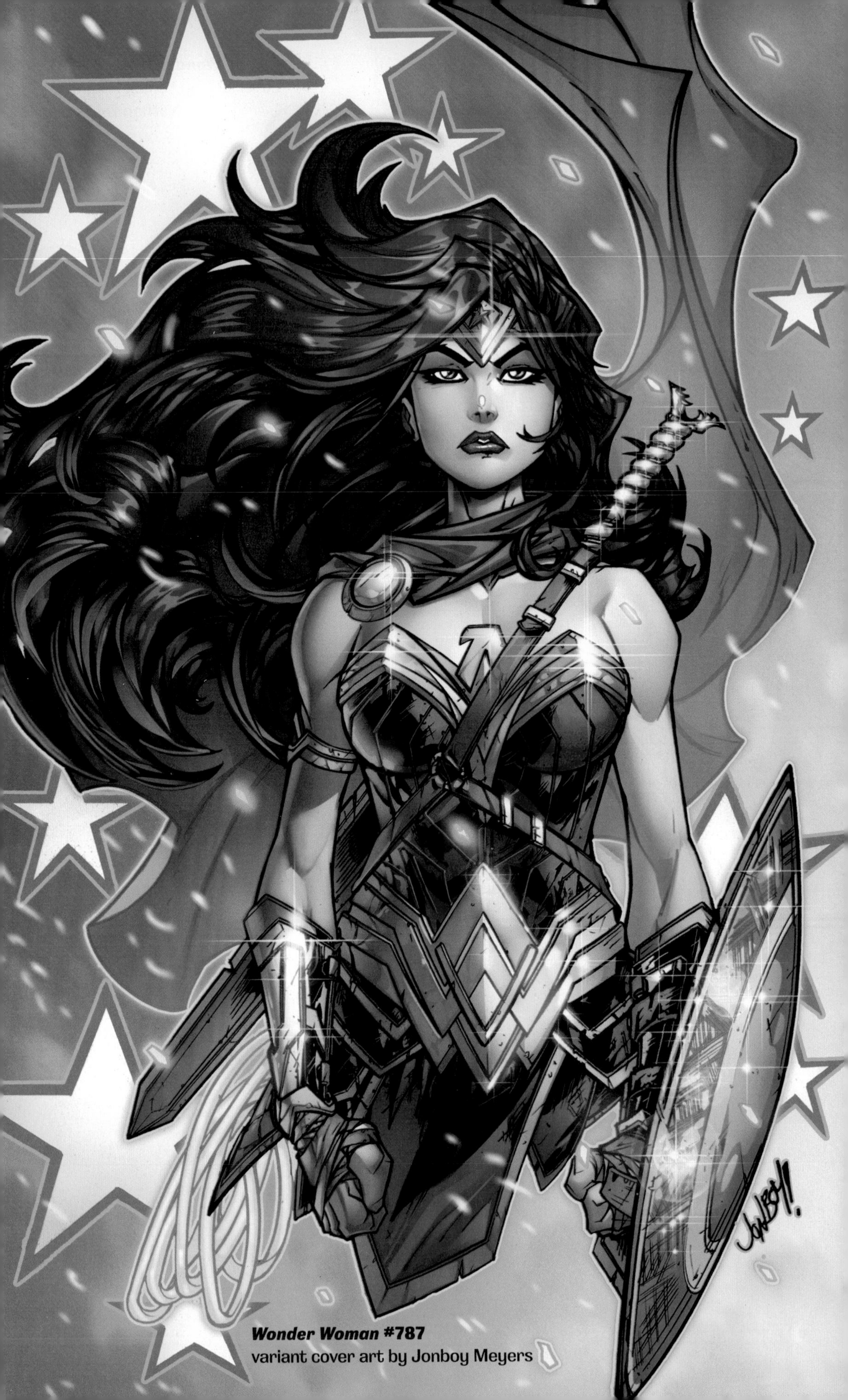

***Wonder Woman* #787**
variant cover art by Jonboy Meyers

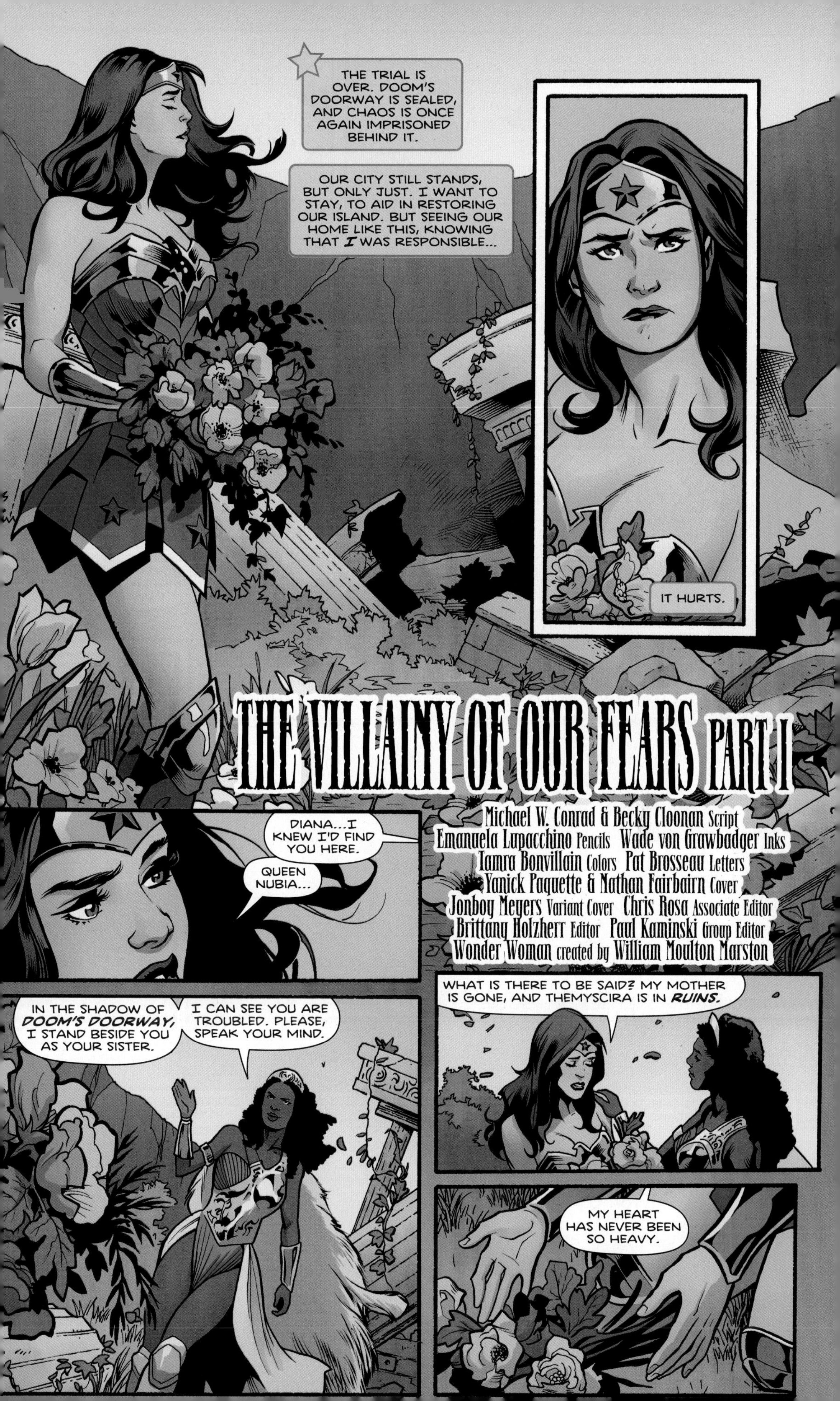

THE TRIAL IS OVER. DOOM'S DOORWAY IS SEALED, AND CHAOS IS ONCE AGAIN IMPRISONED BEHIND IT.
OUR CITY STILL STANDS, BUT ONLY JUST. I WANT TO STAY, TO AID IN RESTORING OUR ISLAND. BUT SEEING OUR HOME LIKE THIS, KNOWING THAT *I* WAS RESPONSIBLE...
IT HURTS.
THE VILLAINY OF OUR FEARS PART I
Michael W. Conrad & Becky Cloonan Script
Emanuela Lupacchino Pencils Wade von Grawbadger Inks
Tamra Bonvillain Colors Pat Brosseau Letters
Yanick Paquette & Nathan Fairbairn Cover
Jonboy Meyers Variant Cover Chris Rosa Associate Editor
Brittany Holzherr Editor Paul Kaminski Group Editor
Wonder Woman created by William Moulton Marston
DIANA...I KNEW I'D FIND YOU HERE.
QUEEN NUBIA...
IN THE SHADOW OF ***DOOM'S DOORWAY,*** I STAND BESIDE YOU AS YOUR SISTER.
I CAN SEE YOU ARE TROUBLED. PLEASE, SPEAK YOUR MIND.
WHAT IS THERE TO BE SAID? MY MOTHER IS GONE, AND THEMYSCIRA IS IN ***RUINS.***
MY HEART HAS NEVER BEEN SO HEAVY.

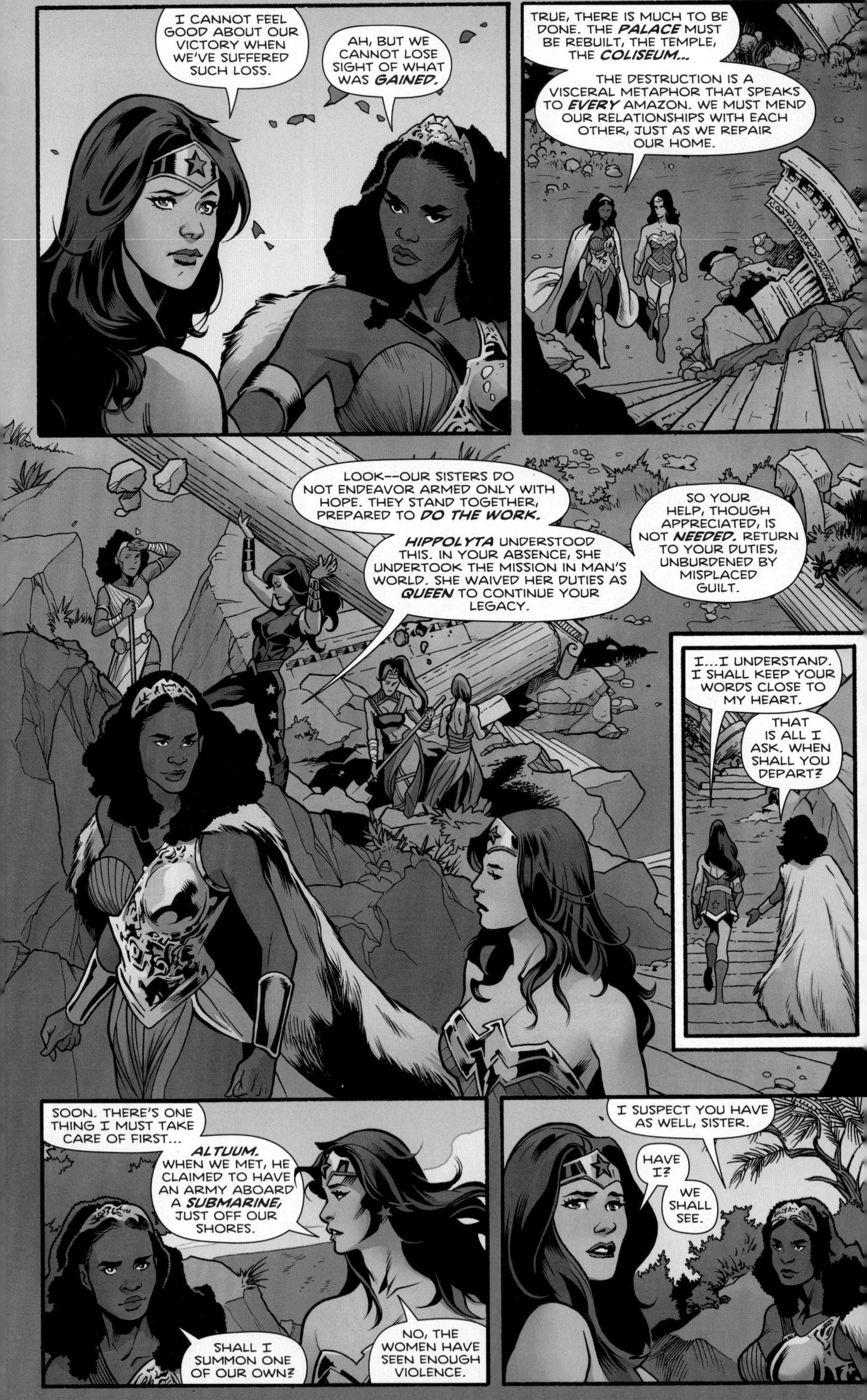
I CANNOT FEEL GOOD ABOUT OUR VICTORY WHEN WE'VE SUFFERED SUCH LOSS.
AH, BUT WE CANNOT LOSE SIGHT OF WHAT WAS GAINED.
TRUE, THERE IS MUCH TO BE DONE. THE PALACE MUST BE REBUILT, THE TEMPLE, THE COLISEUM...
THE DESTRUCTION IS A VISCERAL METAPHOR THAT SPEAKS TO EVERY AMAZON. WE MUST MEND OUR RELATIONSHIPS WITH EACH OTHER, JUST AS WE REPAIR OUR HOME.
LOOK--OUR SISTERS DO NOT ENDEAVOR ARMED ONLY WITH HOPE. THEY STAND TOGETHER, PREPARED TO DO THE WORK.
HIPPOLYTA UNDERSTOOD THIS. IN YOUR ABSENCE, SHE UNDERTOOK THE MISSION IN MAN'S WORLD. SHE WAIVED HER DUTIES AS QUEEN TO CONTINUE YOUR LEGACY.
SO YOUR HELP, THOUGH APPRECIATED, IS NOT NEEDED. RETURN TO YOUR DUTIES, UNBURDENED BY MISPLACED GUILT.
I...I UNDERSTAND. I SHALL KEEP YOUR WORDS CLOSE TO MY HEART.
THAT IS ALL I ASK. WHEN SHALL YOU DEPART?
SOON. THERE'S ONE THING I MUST TAKE CARE OF FIRST...
ALTUUM. WHEN WE MET, HE CLAIMED TO HAVE AN ARMY ABOARD A SUBMARINE, JUST OFF OUR SHORES.
SHALL I SUMMON ONE OF OUR OWN?
NO, THE WOMEN HAVE SEEN ENOUGH VIOLENCE.
I SUSPECT YOU HAVE AS WELL, SISTER.
HAVE I?
WE SHALL SEE.

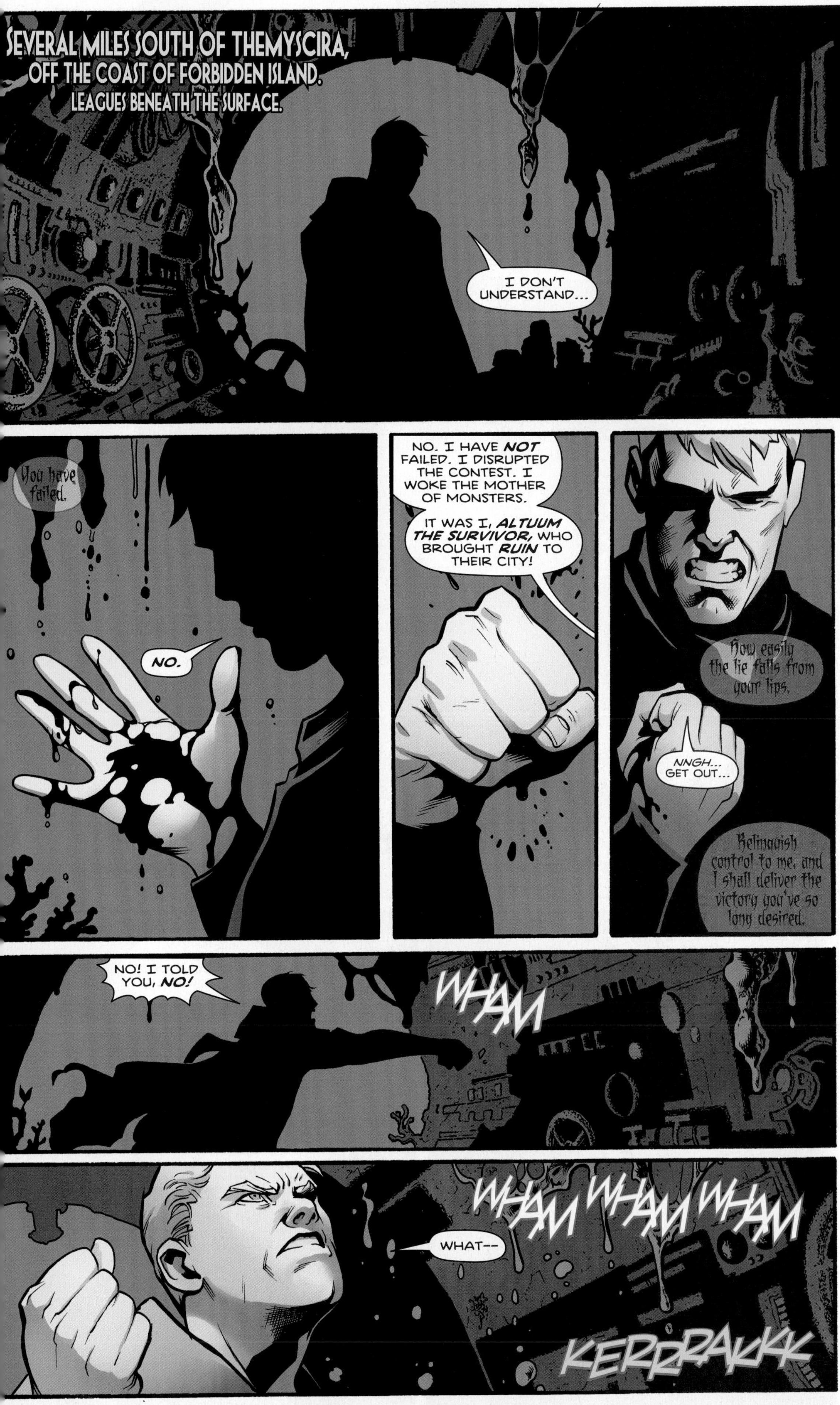
SEVERAL MILES SOUTH OF THEMYSCIRA,
OFF THE COAST OF FORBIDDEN ISLAND.
LEAGUES BENEATH THE SURFACE.
I DON'T UNDERSTAND...
You have failed.
NO.
NO. I HAVE NOT FAILED. I DISRUPTED THE CONTEST. I WOKE THE MOTHER OF MONSTERS.
IT WAS I, ALTUUM THE SURVIVOR, WHO BROUGHT RUIN TO THEIR CITY!
How easily the lie falls from your lips.
NNGH... GET OUT...
Relinquish control to me, and I shall deliver the victory you've so long desired.
NO! I TOLD YOU, NO!
WHAM
WHAM WHAM WHAM
WHAT--
KERRRAKKK

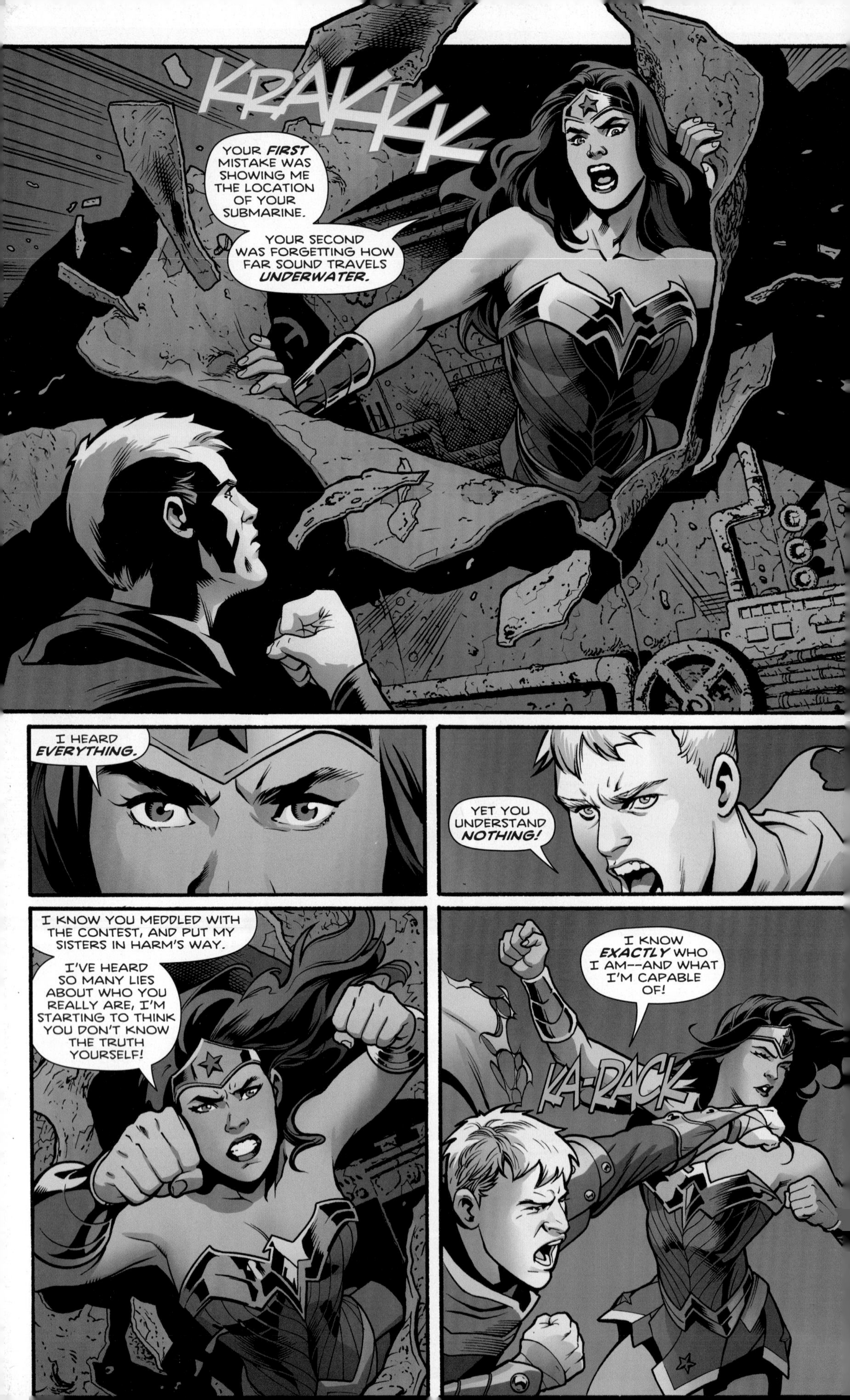
KRAKKK
YOUR FIRST MISTAKE WAS SHOWING ME THE LOCATION OF YOUR SUBMARINE.
YOUR SECOND WAS FORGETTING HOW FAR SOUND TRAVELS UNDERWATER.
I HEARD EVERYTHING.
YET YOU UNDERSTAND NOTHING!
I KNOW YOU MEDDLED WITH THE CONTEST, AND PUT MY SISTERS IN HARM'S WAY.
I'VE HEARD SO MANY LIES ABOUT WHO YOU REALLY ARE, I'M STARTING TO THINK YOU DON'T KNOW THE TRUTH YOURSELF!
I KNOW EXACTLY WHO I AM--AND WHAT I'M CAPABLE OF!
KA-RACK

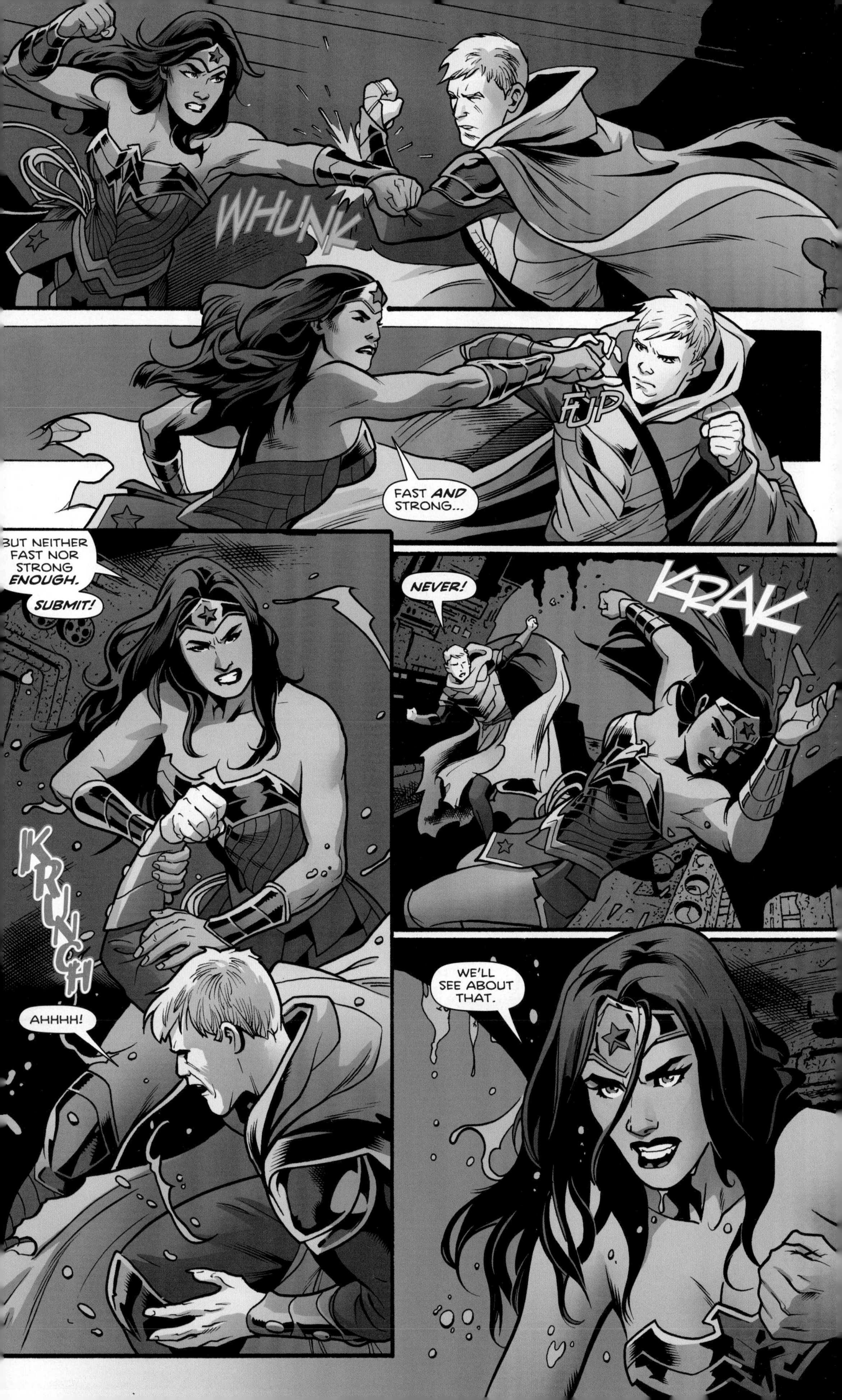

WHUNK
FUP
FAST AND STRONG...
BUT NEITHER FAST NOR STRONG ENOUGH.
SUBMIT!
KRUNCH
AHHHH!
NEVER!
KRAK
WE'LL SEE ABOUT THAT.

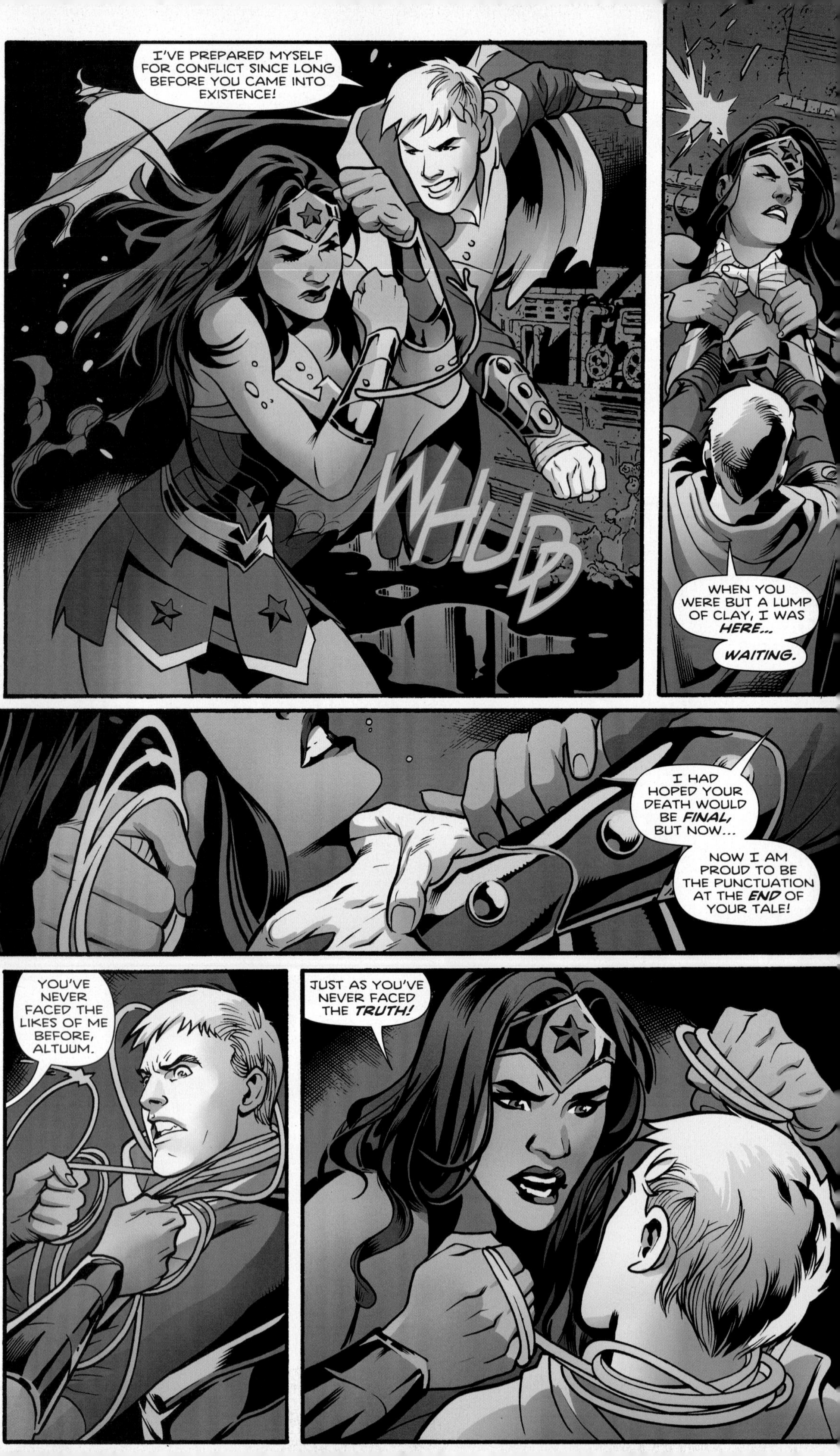
I'VE PREPARED MYSELF FOR CONFLICT SINCE LONG BEFORE YOU CAME INTO EXISTENCE!
WHUDD
WHEN YOU WERE BUT A LUMP OF CLAY, I WAS *HERE...*
WAITING.
I HAD HOPED YOUR DEATH WOULD BE *FINAL,* BUT NOW...
NOW I AM PROUD TO BE THE PUNCTUATION AT THE *END* OF YOUR TALE!
YOU'VE NEVER FACED THE LIKES OF ME BEFORE, ALTUUM.
JUST AS YOU'VE NEVER FACED THE *TRUTH!*

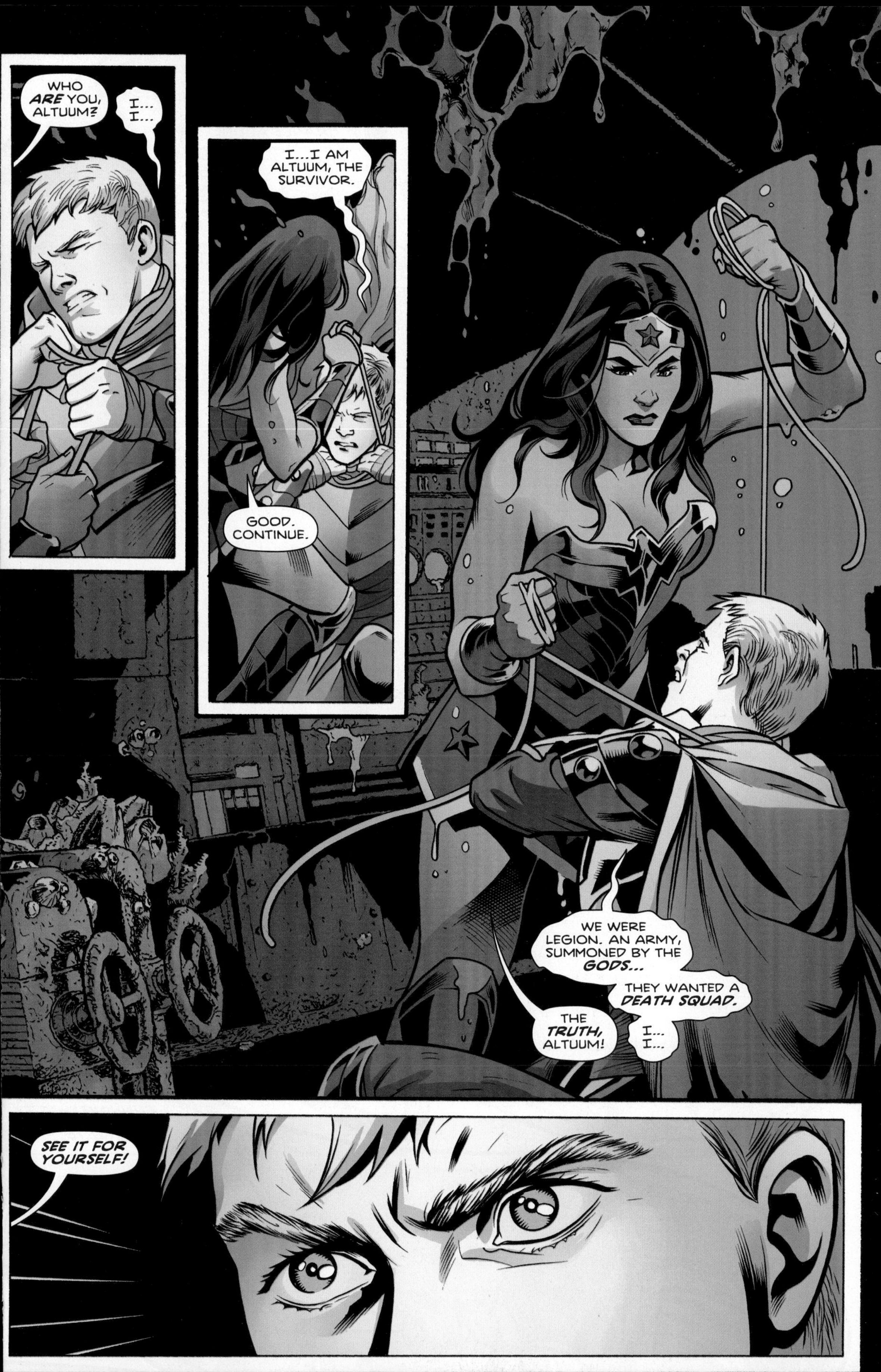
WHO ARE YOU, ALTUUM?
I... I...
I...I AM ALTUUM, THE SURVIVOR.
GOOD. CONTINUE.
WE WERE LEGION. AN ARMY, SUMMONED BY THE GODS...
THEY WANTED A DEATH SQUAD.
THE TRUTH, ALTUUM!
I... I...
SEE IT FOR YOURSELF!

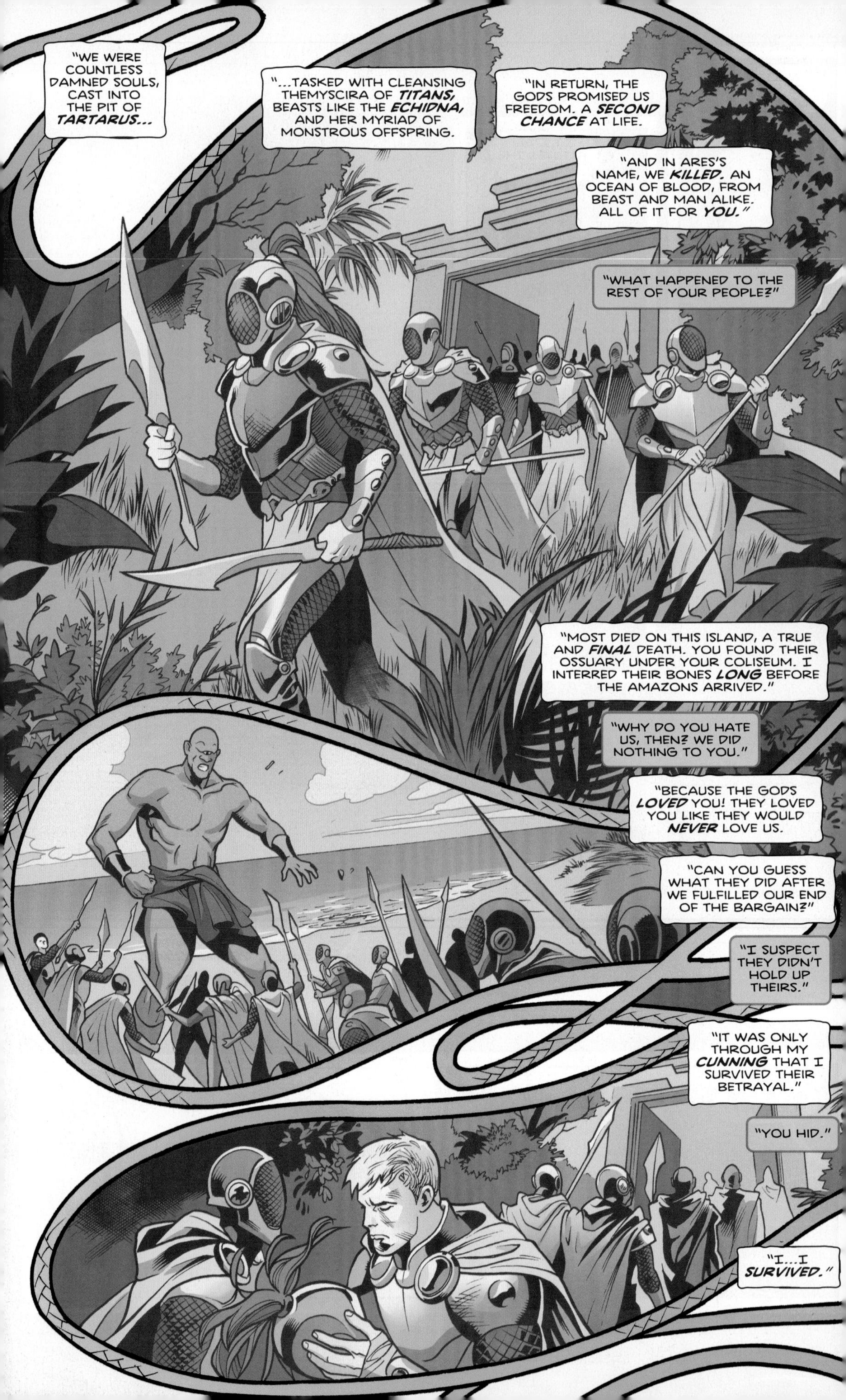
"WE WERE COUNTLESS DAMNED SOULS, CAST INTO THE PIT OF *TARTARUS...*
"...TASKED WITH CLEANSING THEMYSCIRA OF *TITANS,* BEASTS LIKE THE *ECHIDNA,* AND HER MYRIAD OF MONSTROUS OFFSPRING.
"IN RETURN, THE GODS PROMISED US FREEDOM. A *SECOND CHANCE* AT LIFE.
"AND IN ARES'S NAME, WE *KILLED.* AN OCEAN OF BLOOD, FROM BEAST AND MAN ALIKE. ALL OF IT FOR *YOU.*"
"WHAT HAPPENED TO THE REST OF YOUR PEOPLE?"
"MOST DIED ON THIS ISLAND, A TRUE AND *FINAL* DEATH. YOU FOUND THEIR OSSUARY UNDER YOUR COLISEUM. I INTERRED THEIR BONES *LONG* BEFORE THE AMAZONS ARRIVED."
"WHY DO YOU HATE US, THEN? WE DID NOTHING TO YOU."
"BECAUSE THE GODS *LOVED* YOU! THEY LOVED YOU LIKE THEY WOULD *NEVER* LOVE US.
"CAN YOU GUESS WHAT THEY DID AFTER WE FULFILLED OUR END OF THE BARGAIN?"
"I SUSPECT THEY DIDN'T HOLD UP THEIRS."
"IT WAS ONLY THROUGH MY *CUNNING* THAT I SURVIVED THEIR BETRAYAL."
"YOU HID."
"I...I *SURVIVED.*"

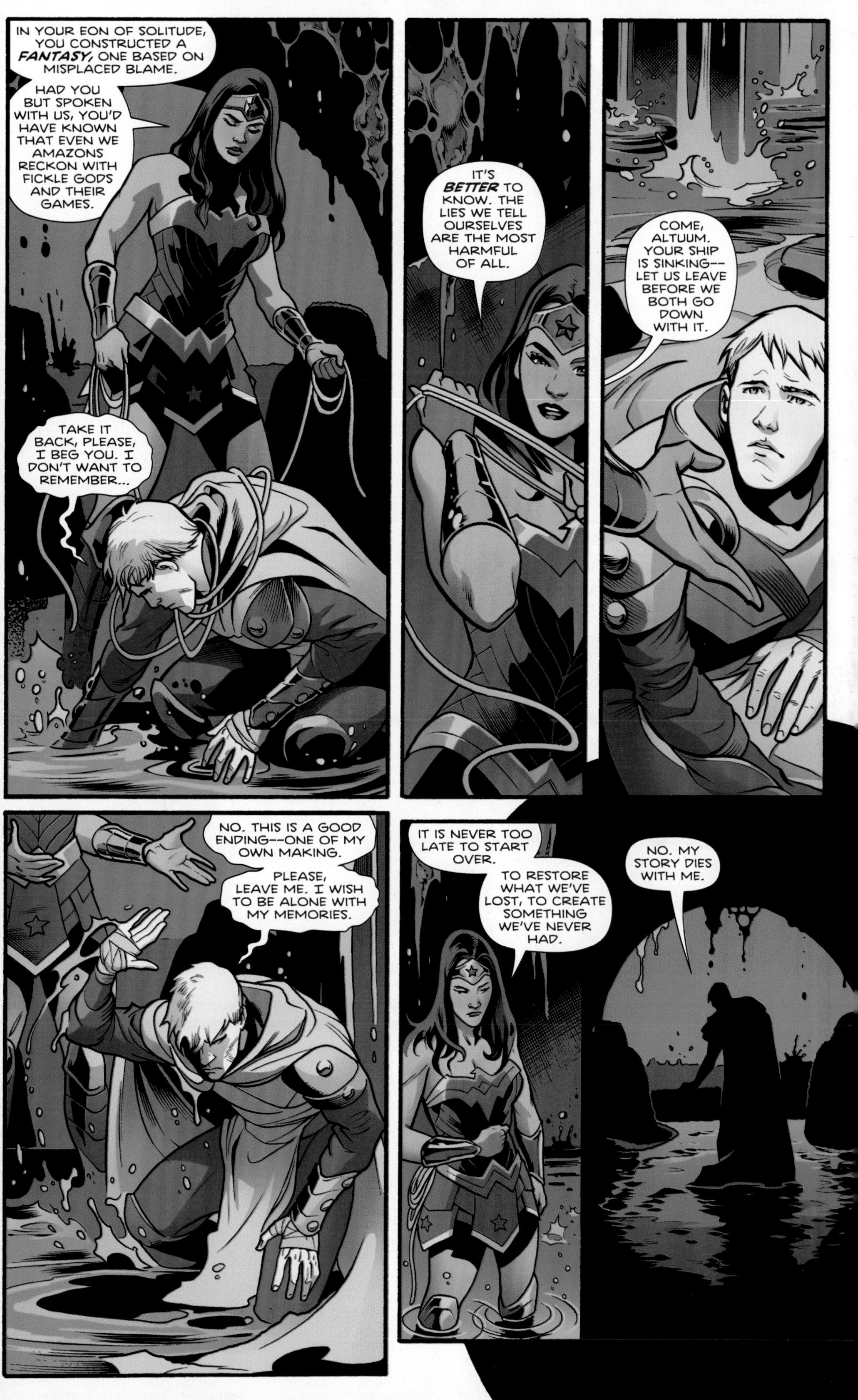
IN YOUR EON OF SOLITUDE, YOU CONSTRUCTED A *FANTASY,* ONE BASED ON MISPLACED BLAME.
HAD YOU BUT SPOKEN WITH US, YOU'D HAVE KNOWN THAT EVEN WE AMAZONS RECKON WITH FICKLE GODS AND THEIR GAMES.
TAKE IT BACK, PLEASE, I BEG YOU. I DON'T WANT TO REMEMBER...
IT'S *BETTER* TO KNOW. THE LIES WE TELL OURSELVES ARE THE MOST HARMFUL OF ALL.
COME, ALTUUM. YOUR SHIP IS SINKING-- LET US LEAVE BEFORE WE BOTH GO DOWN WITH IT.
NO. THIS IS A GOOD ENDING--ONE OF MY OWN MAKING.
PLEASE, LEAVE ME. I WISH TO BE ALONE WITH MY MEMORIES.
IT IS NEVER TOO LATE TO START OVER.
TO RESTORE WHAT WE'VE LOST, TO CREATE SOMETHING WE'VE NEVER HAD.
NO. MY STORY DIES WITH ME.

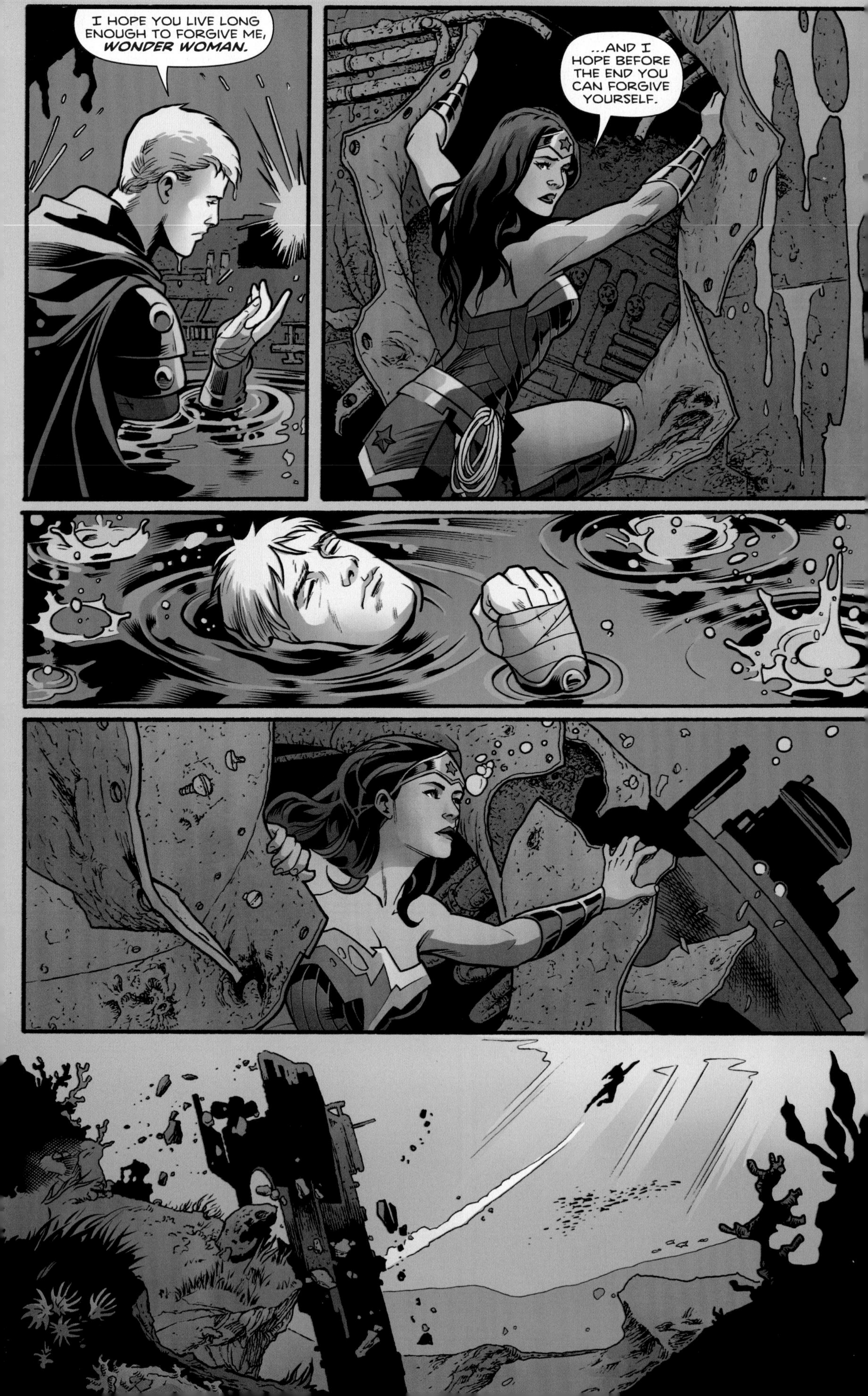
I HOPE YOU LIVE LONG ENOUGH TO FORGIVE ME, WONDER WOMAN.
...AND I HOPE BEFORE THE END YOU CAN FORGIVE YOURSELF.

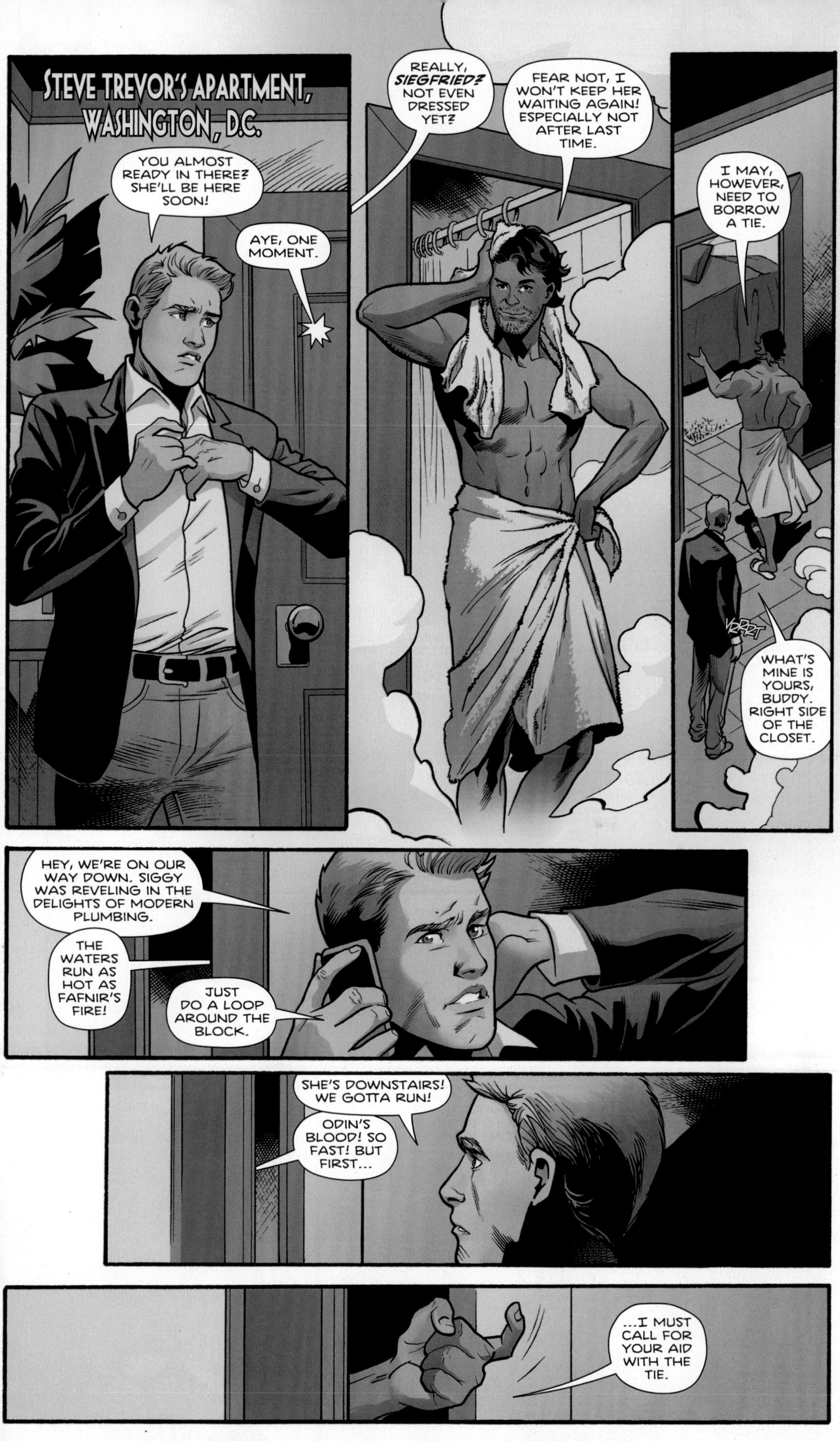
STEVE TREVOR'S APARTMENT, WASHINGTON, D.C.
YOU ALMOST READY IN THERE? SHE'LL BE HERE SOON!
AYE, ONE MOMENT.
REALLY, SIEGFRIED? NOT EVEN DRESSED YET?
FEAR NOT, I WON'T KEEP HER WAITING AGAIN! ESPECIALLY NOT AFTER LAST TIME.
I MAY, HOWEVER, NEED TO BORROW A TIE.
VRRRT
WHAT'S MINE IS YOURS, BUDDY. RIGHT SIDE OF THE CLOSET.
HEY, WE'RE ON OUR WAY DOWN. SIGGY WAS REVELING IN THE DELIGHTS OF MODERN PLUMBING.
THE WATERS RUN AS HOT AS FAFNIR'S FIRE!
JUST DO A LOOP AROUND THE BLOCK.
SHE'S DOWNSTAIRS! WE GOTTA RUN!
ODIN'S BLOOD! SO FAST! BUT FIRST...
...I MUST CALL FOR YOUR AID WITH THE TIE.

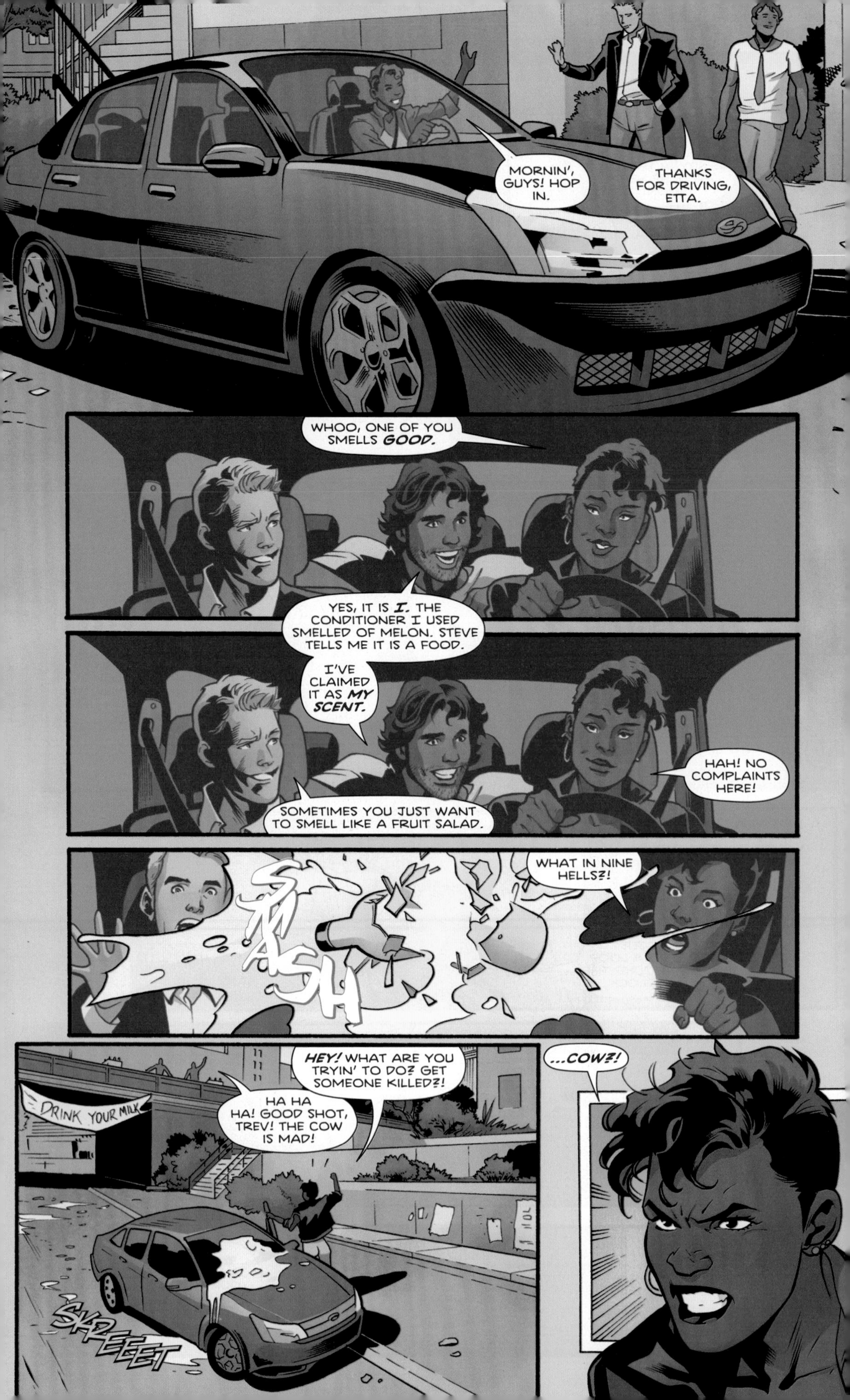

MORNIN', GUYS! HOP IN.
THANKS FOR DRIVING, ETTA.
WHOO, ONE OF YOU SMELLS GOOD.
YES, IT IS I. THE CONDITIONER I USED SMELLED OF MELON. STEVE TELLS ME IT IS A FOOD.
I'VE CLAIMED IT AS MY SCENT.
SOMETIMES YOU JUST WANT TO SMELL LIKE A FRUIT SALAD.
HAH! NO COMPLAINTS HERE!
SMASH
WHAT IN NINE HELLS?!
DRINK YOUR MILK
HEY! WHAT ARE YOU TRYIN' TO DO? GET SOMEONE KILLED?!
HA HA HA! GOOD SHOT, TREV! THE COW IS MAD!
SKREEEET
...COW?!

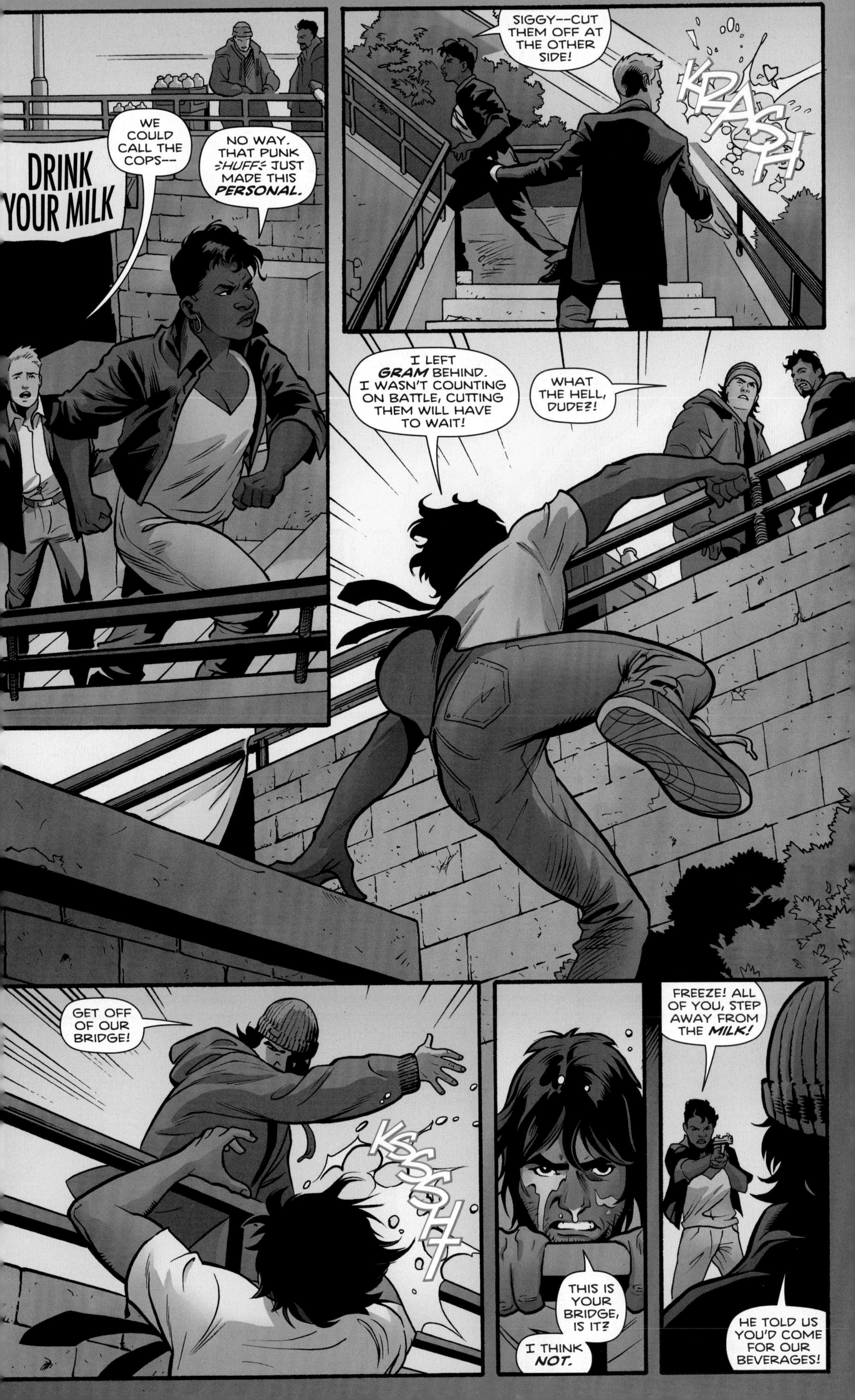
DRINK YOUR MILK
WE COULD CALL THE COPS--
NO WAY. THAT PUNK *HUFF* JUST MADE THIS PERSONAL.
SIGGY--CUT THEM OFF AT THE OTHER SIDE!
KRASH
I LEFT GRAM BEHIND. I WASN'T COUNTING ON BATTLE, CUTTING THEM WILL HAVE TO WAIT!
WHAT THE HELL, DUDE?!
GET OFF OF OUR BRIDGE!
KSSSH
THIS IS YOUR BRIDGE, IS IT?
I THINK NOT.
FREEZE! ALL OF YOU, STEP AWAY FROM THE MILK!
HE TOLD US YOU'D COME FOR OUR BEVERAGES!

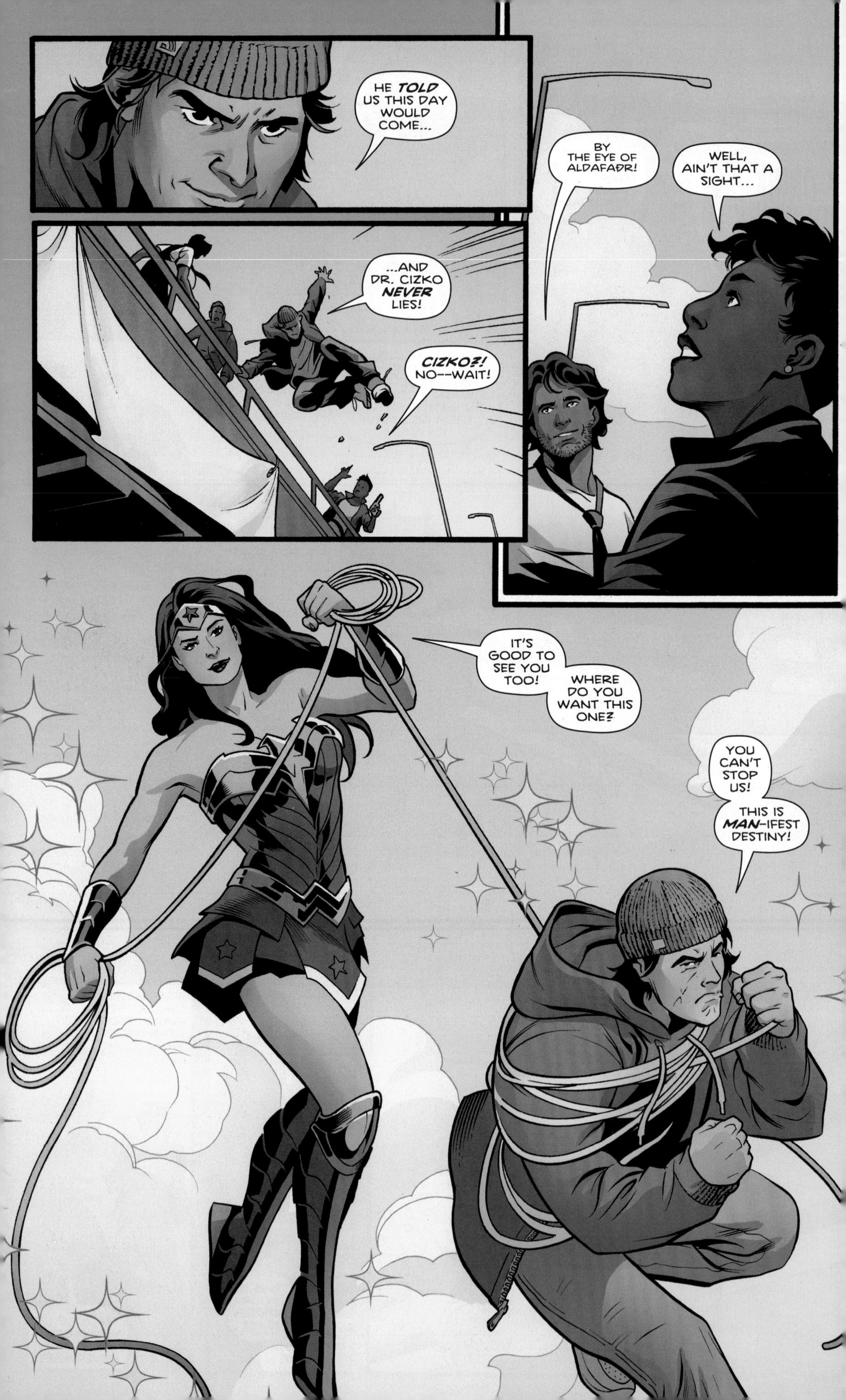
HE TOLD US THIS DAY WOULD COME...
...AND DR. CIZKO NEVER LIES!
CIZKO?! NO--WAIT!
BY THE EYE OF ALDAFADR!
WELL, AIN'T THAT A SIGHT...
IT'S GOOD TO SEE YOU TOO!
WHERE DO YOU WANT THIS ONE?
YOU CAN'T STOP US!
THIS IS MAN-IFEST DESTINY!

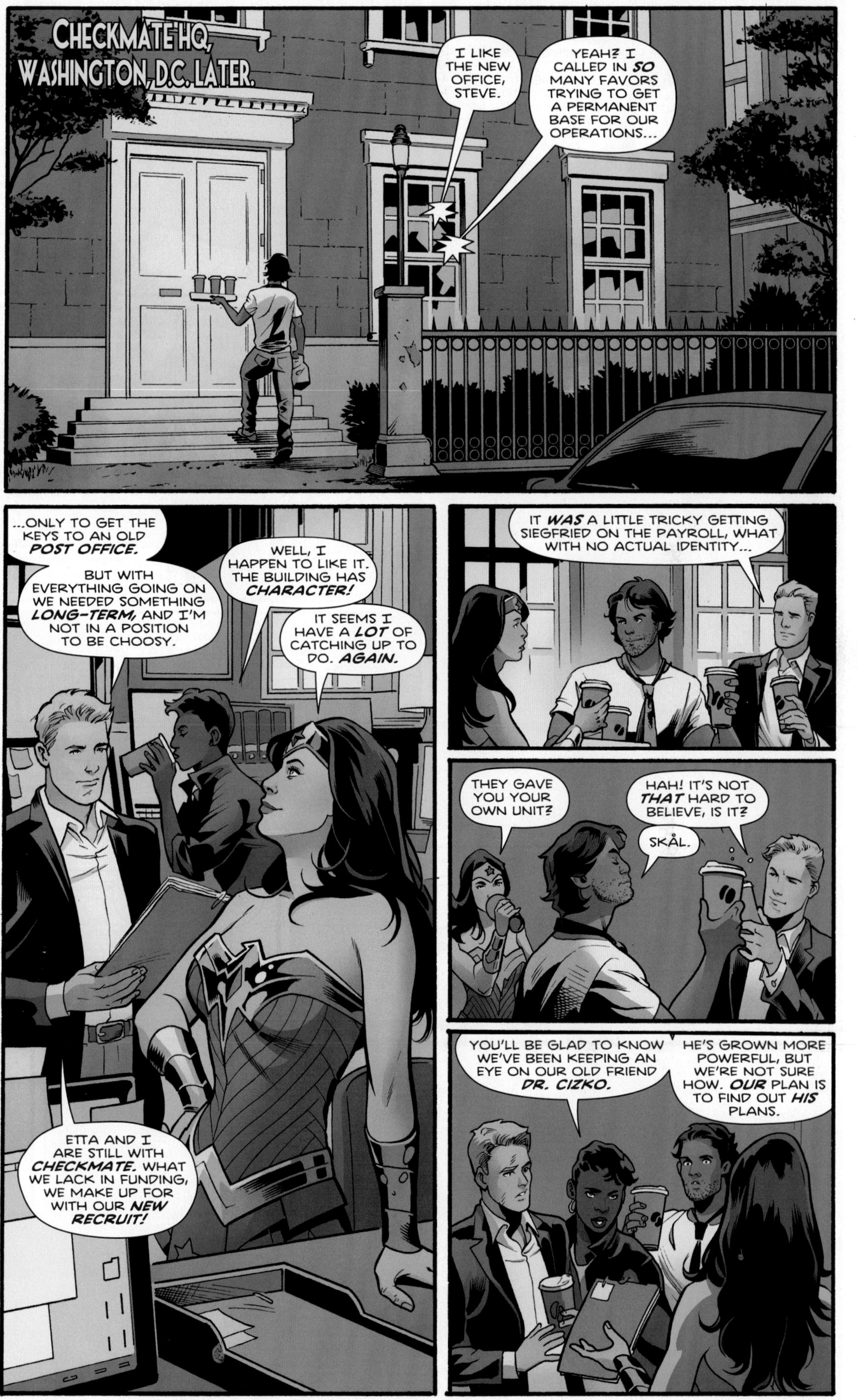

CHECKMATE HQ, WASHINGTON, D.C. LATER.
I LIKE THE NEW OFFICE, STEVE.
YEAH? I CALLED IN SO MANY FAVORS TRYING TO GET A PERMANENT BASE FOR OUR OPERATIONS...
...ONLY TO GET THE KEYS TO AN OLD POST OFFICE.
BUT WITH EVERYTHING GOING ON WE NEEDED SOMETHING LONG-TERM, AND I'M NOT IN A POSITION TO BE CHOOSY.
WELL, I HAPPEN TO LIKE IT. THE BUILDING HAS CHARACTER!
IT SEEMS I HAVE A LOT OF CATCHING UP TO DO. AGAIN.
ETTA AND I ARE STILL WITH CHECKMATE. WHAT WE LACK IN FUNDING, WE MAKE UP FOR WITH OUR NEW RECRUIT!
IT WAS A LITTLE TRICKY GETTING SIEGFRIED ON THE PAYROLL, WHAT WITH NO ACTUAL IDENTITY...
THEY GAVE YOU YOUR OWN UNIT?
HAH! IT'S NOT THAT HARD TO BELIEVE, IS IT?
SKÅL.
YOU'LL BE GLAD TO KNOW WE'VE BEEN KEEPING AN EYE ON OUR OLD FRIEND DR. CIZKO.
HE'S GROWN MORE POWERFUL, BUT WE'RE NOT SURE HOW. OUR PLAN IS TO FIND OUT HIS PLANS.

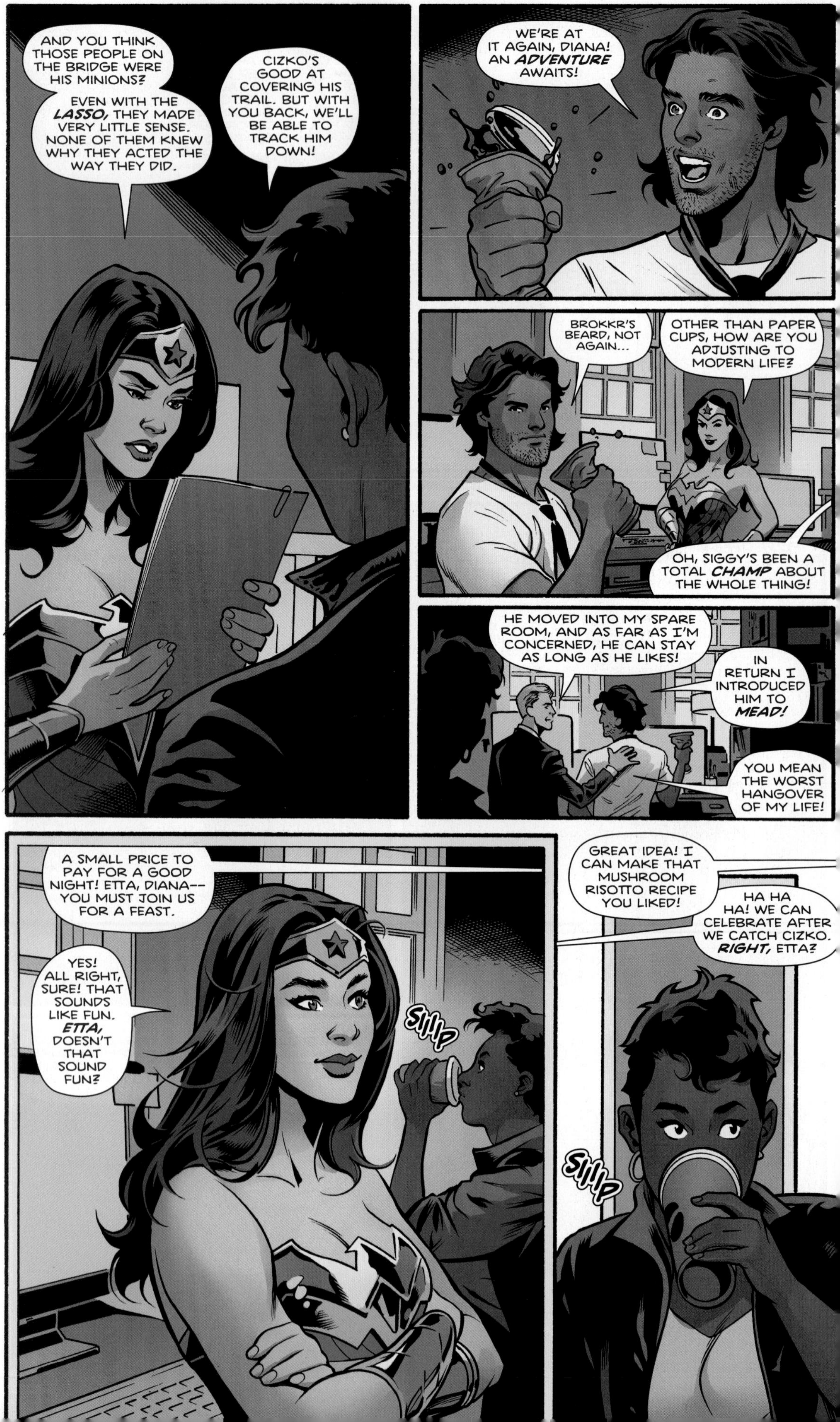
AND YOU THINK THOSE PEOPLE ON THE BRIDGE WERE HIS MINIONS?
EVEN WITH THE LASSO, THEY MADE VERY LITTLE SENSE. NONE OF THEM KNEW WHY THEY ACTED THE WAY THEY DID.
CIZKO'S GOOD AT COVERING HIS TRAIL. BUT WITH YOU BACK, WE'LL BE ABLE TO TRACK HIM DOWN!
WE'RE AT IT AGAIN, DIANA! AN ADVENTURE AWAITS!
BROKKR'S BEARD, NOT AGAIN...
OTHER THAN PAPER CUPS, HOW ARE YOU ADJUSTING TO MODERN LIFE?
OH, SIGGY'S BEEN A TOTAL CHAMP ABOUT THE WHOLE THING!
HE MOVED INTO MY SPARE ROOM, AND AS FAR AS I'M CONCERNED, HE CAN STAY AS LONG AS HE LIKES!
IN RETURN I INTRODUCED HIM TO MEAD!
YOU MEAN THE WORST HANGOVER OF MY LIFE!
A SMALL PRICE TO PAY FOR A GOOD NIGHT! ETTA, DIANA-- YOU MUST JOIN US FOR A FEAST.
YES! ALL RIGHT, SURE! THAT SOUNDS LIKE FUN. ETTA, DOESN'T THAT SOUND FUN?
SIIIP
GREAT IDEA! I CAN MAKE THAT MUSHROOM RISOTTO RECIPE YOU LIKED!
HA HA HA! WE CAN CELEBRATE AFTER WE CATCH CIZKO. RIGHT, ETTA?
SIIIP

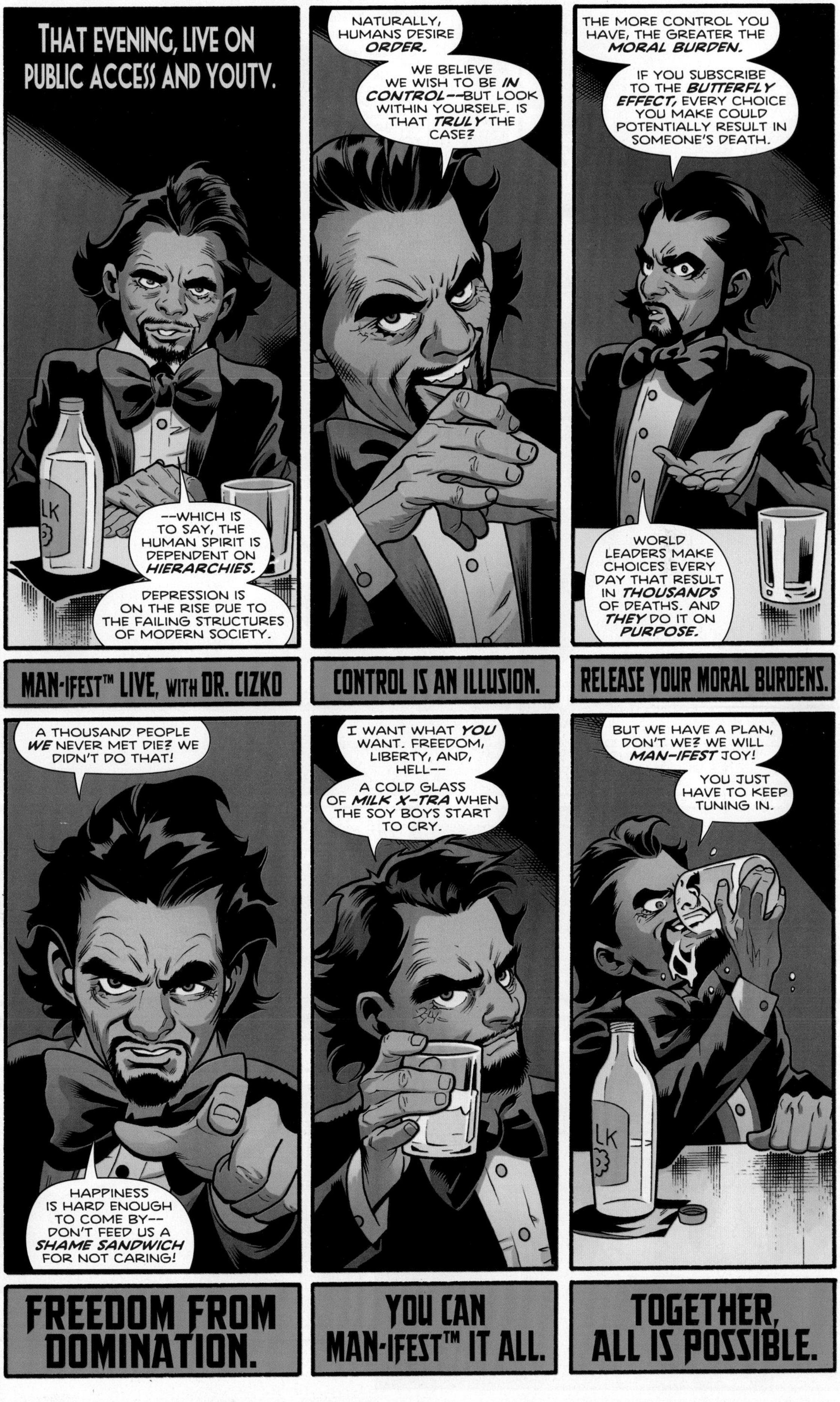

THAT EVENING, LIVE ON PUBLIC ACCESS AND YOUTV.
--WHICH IS TO SAY, THE HUMAN SPIRIT IS DEPENDENT ON HIERARCHIES.
DEPRESSION IS ON THE RISE DUE TO THE FAILING STRUCTURES OF MODERN SOCIETY.
MAN-IFEST™ LIVE, WITH DR. CIZKO
NATURALLY, HUMANS DESIRE ORDER.
WE BELIEVE WE WISH TO BE IN CONTROL--BUT LOOK WITHIN YOURSELF. IS THAT TRULY THE CASE?
CONTROL IS AN ILLUSION.
THE MORE CONTROL YOU HAVE, THE GREATER THE MORAL BURDEN.
IF YOU SUBSCRIBE TO THE BUTTERFLY EFFECT, EVERY CHOICE YOU MAKE COULD POTENTIALLY RESULT IN SOMEONE'S DEATH.
WORLD LEADERS MAKE CHOICES EVERY DAY THAT RESULT IN THOUSANDS OF DEATHS. AND THEY DO IT ON PURPOSE.
RELEASE YOUR MORAL BURDENS.
A THOUSAND PEOPLE WE NEVER MET DIE? WE DIDN'T DO THAT!
HAPPINESS IS HARD ENOUGH TO COME BY--DON'T FEED US A SHAME SANDWICH FOR NOT CARING!
FREEDOM FROM DOMINATION.
I WANT WHAT YOU WANT. FREEDOM, LIBERTY, AND, HELL--
A COLD GLASS OF MILK X-TRA WHEN THE SOY BOYS START TO CRY.
YOU CAN MAN-IFEST™ IT ALL.
BUT WE HAVE A PLAN, DON'T WE? WE WILL MAN-IFEST JOY!
YOU JUST HAVE TO KEEP TUNING IN.
TOGETHER, ALL IS POSSIBLE.

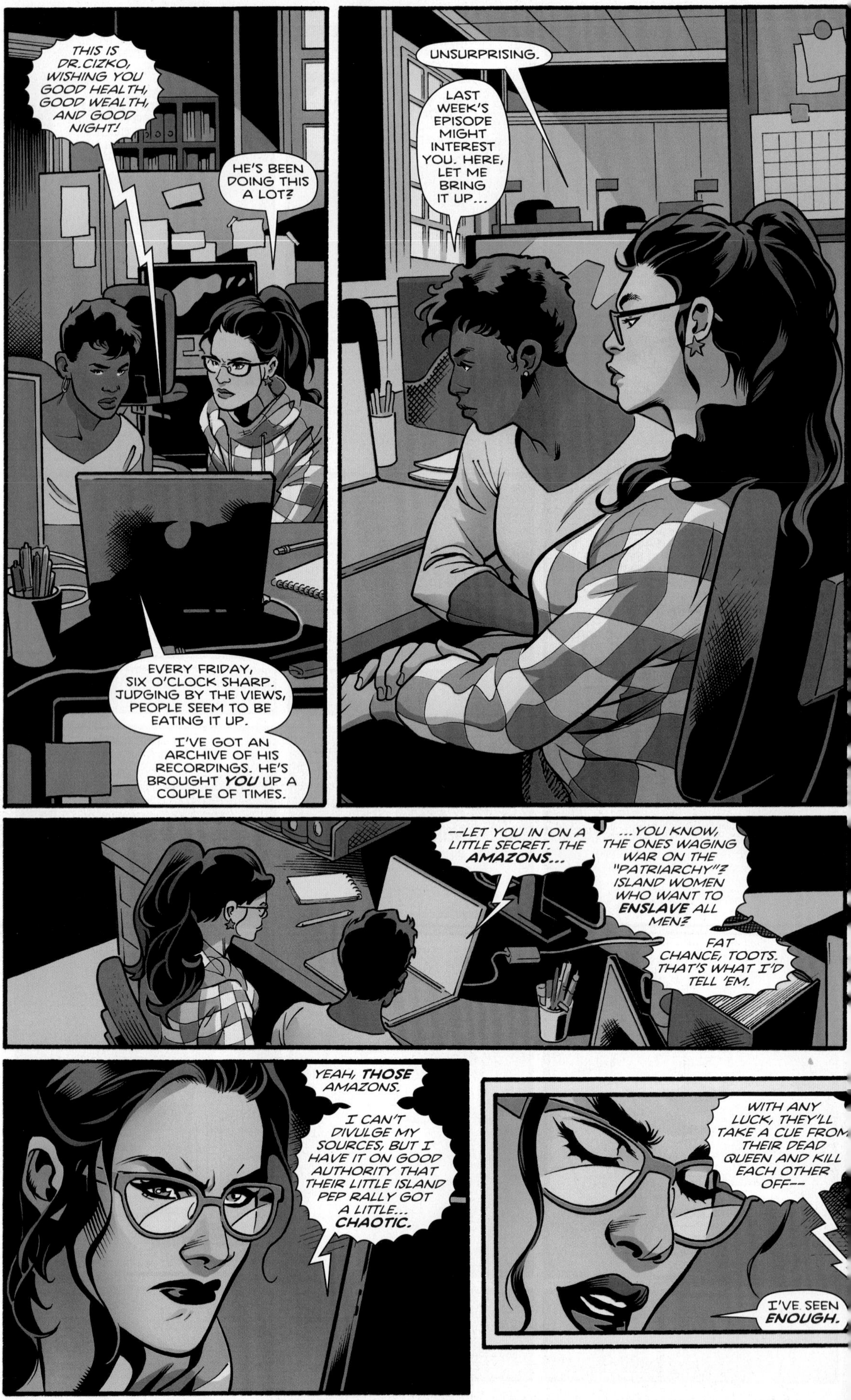
THIS IS DR.CIZKO, WISHING YOU GOOD HEALTH, GOOD WEALTH, AND GOOD NIGHT!
HE'S BEEN DOING THIS A LOT?
EVERY FRIDAY, SIX O'CLOCK SHARP. JUDGING BY THE VIEWS, PEOPLE SEEM TO BE EATING IT UP.
I'VE GOT AN ARCHIVE OF HIS RECORDINGS. HE'S BROUGHT YOU UP A COUPLE OF TIMES.
UNSURPRISING.
LAST WEEK'S EPISODE MIGHT INTEREST YOU. HERE, LET ME BRING IT UP...
--LET YOU IN ON A LITTLE SECRET. THE AMAZONS...
...YOU KNOW, THE ONES WAGING WAR ON THE "PATRIARCHY"? ISLAND WOMEN WHO WANT TO ENSLAVE ALL MEN?
FAT CHANCE, TOOTS. THAT'S WHAT I'D TELL 'EM.
YEAH, THOSE AMAZONS.
I CAN'T DIVULGE MY SOURCES, BUT I HAVE IT ON GOOD AUTHORITY THAT THEIR LITTLE ISLAND PEP RALLY GOT A LITTLE... CHAOTIC.
WITH ANY LUCK, THEY'LL TAKE A CUE FROM THEIR DEAD QUEEN AND KILL EACH OTHER OFF--
I'VE SEEN ENOUGH.

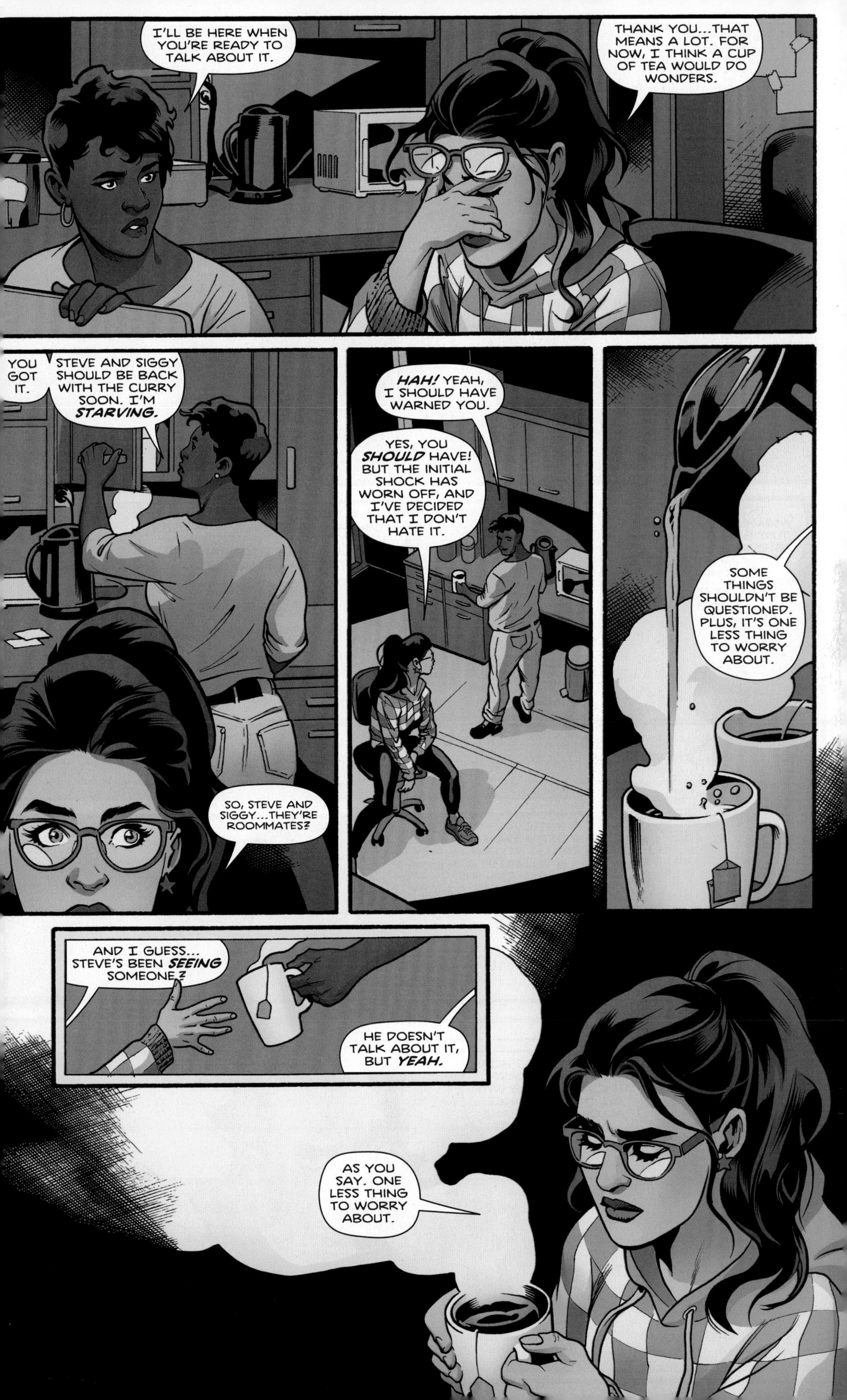

I'LL BE HERE WHEN YOU'RE READY TO TALK ABOUT IT.
THANK YOU...THAT MEANS A LOT. FOR NOW, I THINK A CUP OF TEA WOULD DO WONDERS.
YOU GOT IT.
STEVE AND SIGGY SHOULD BE BACK WITH THE CURRY SOON. I'M STARVING.
SO, STEVE AND SIGGY...THEY'RE ROOMMATES?
HAH! YEAH, I SHOULD HAVE WARNED YOU.
YES, YOU SHOULD HAVE! BUT THE INITIAL SHOCK HAS WORN OFF, AND I'VE DECIDED THAT I DON'T HATE IT.
SOME THINGS SHOULDN'T BE QUESTIONED. PLUS, IT'S ONE LESS THING TO WORRY ABOUT.
AND I GUESS... STEVE'S BEEN SEEING SOMEONE?
HE DOESN'T TALK ABOUT IT, BUT YEAH.
AS YOU SAY. ONE LESS THING TO WORRY ABOUT.

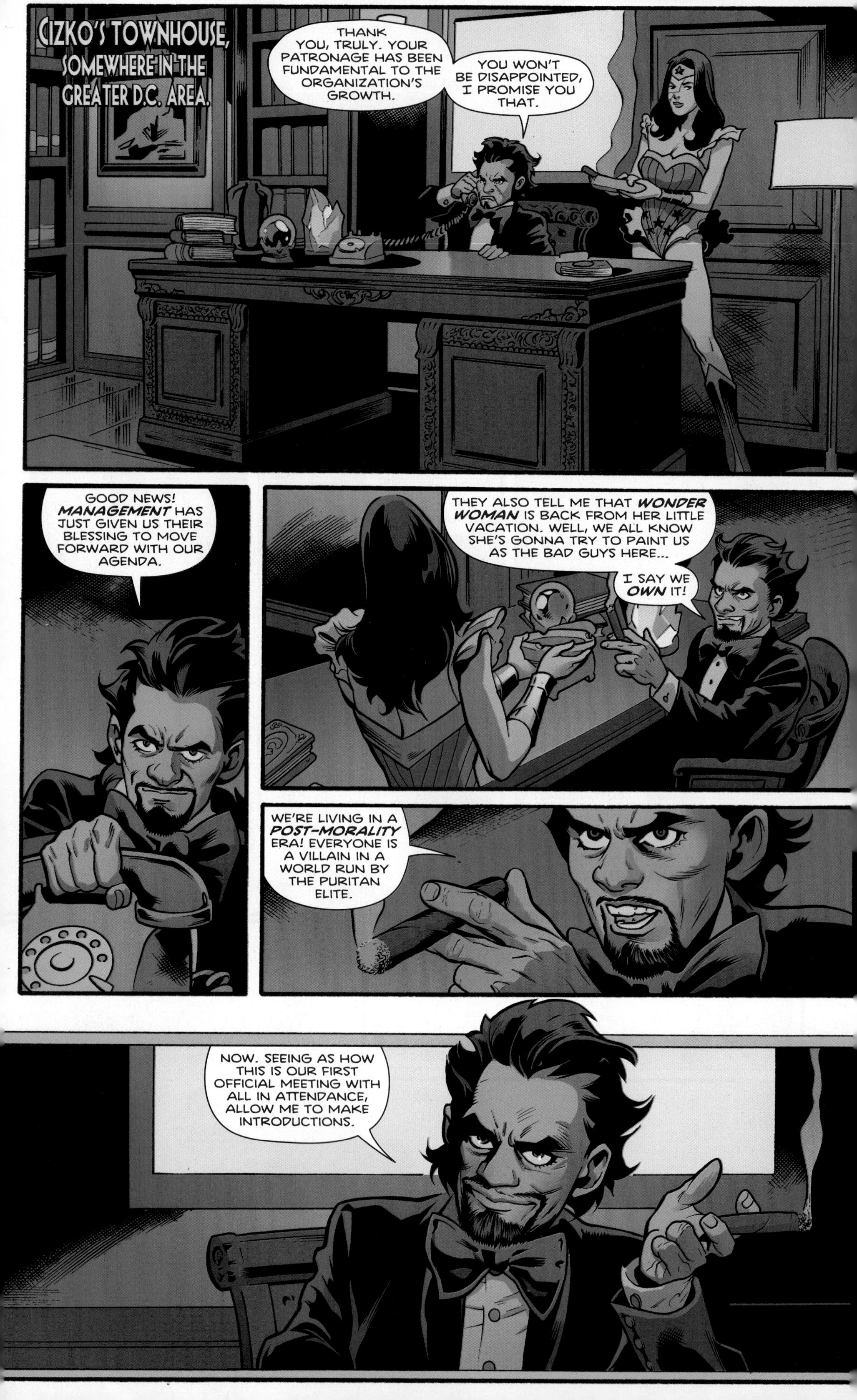
CIZKO'S TOWNHOUSE, SOMEWHERE IN THE GREATER D.C. AREA.
THANK YOU, TRULY. YOUR PATRONAGE HAS BEEN FUNDAMENTAL TO THE ORGANIZATION'S GROWTH.
YOU WON'T BE DISAPPOINTED, I PROMISE YOU THAT.
GOOD NEWS! MANAGEMENT HAS JUST GIVEN US THEIR BLESSING TO MOVE FORWARD WITH OUR AGENDA.
THEY ALSO TELL ME THAT WONDER WOMAN IS BACK FROM HER LITTLE VACATION. WELL, WE ALL KNOW SHE'S GONNA TRY TO PAINT US AS THE BAD GUYS HERE...
I SAY WE OWN IT!
WE'RE LIVING IN A POST-MORALITY ERA! EVERYONE IS A VILLAIN IN A WORLD RUN BY THE PURITAN ELITE.
NOW. SEEING AS HOW THIS IS OUR FIRST OFFICIAL MEETING WITH ALL IN ATTENDANCE, ALLOW ME TO MAKE INTRODUCTIONS.

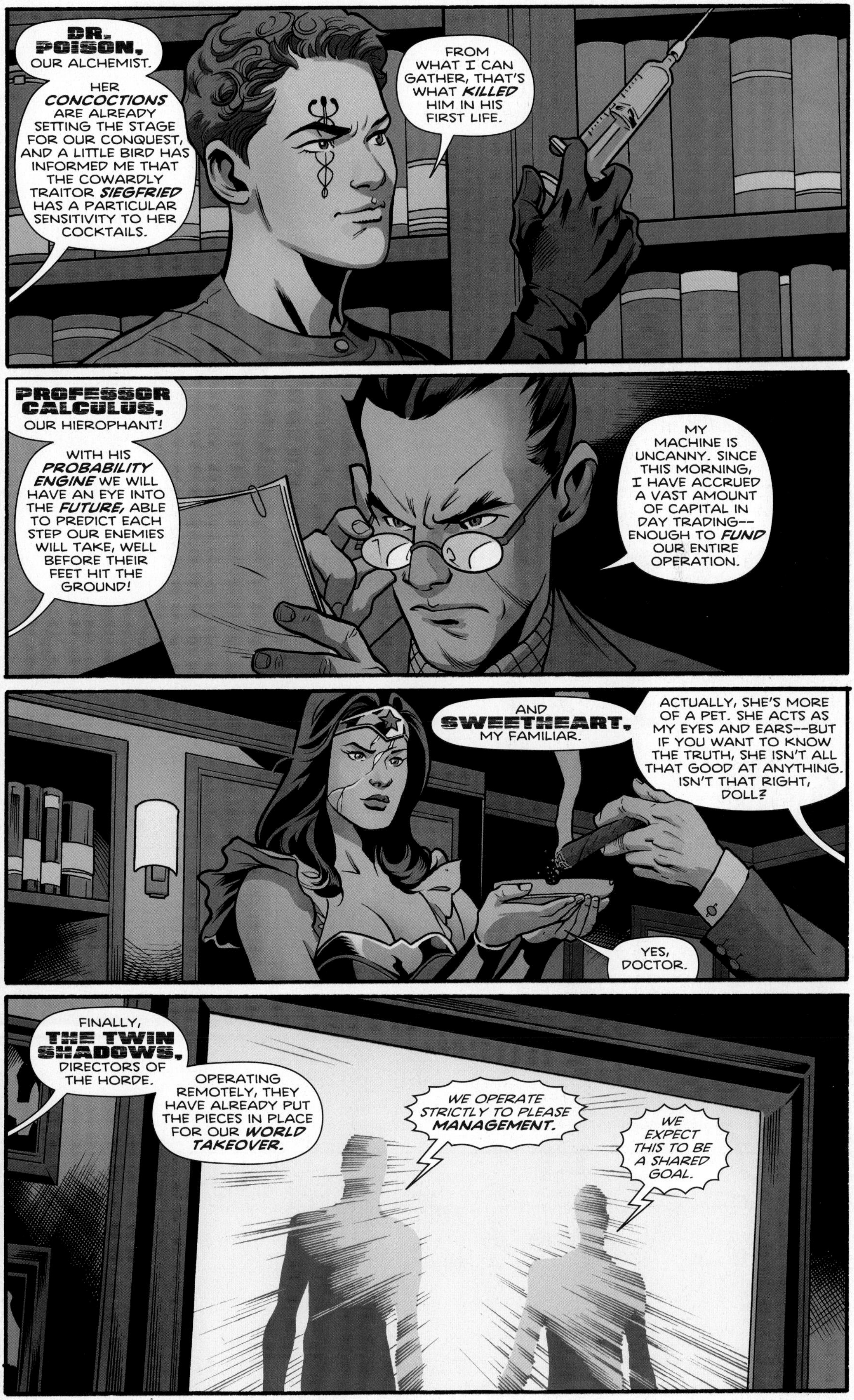
DR. POISON, OUR ALCHEMIST.
HER CONCOCTIONS ARE ALREADY SETTING THE STAGE FOR OUR CONQUEST, AND A LITTLE BIRD HAS INFORMED ME THAT THE COWARDLY TRAITOR SIEGFRIED HAS A PARTICULAR SENSITIVITY TO HER COCKTAILS.
FROM WHAT I CAN GATHER, THAT'S WHAT KILLED HIM IN HIS FIRST LIFE.
PROFESSOR CALCULUS, OUR HIEROPHANT!
WITH HIS PROBABILITY ENGINE WE WILL HAVE AN EYE INTO THE FUTURE, ABLE TO PREDICT EACH STEP OUR ENEMIES WILL TAKE, WELL BEFORE THEIR FEET HIT THE GROUND!
MY MACHINE IS UNCANNY. SINCE THIS MORNING, I HAVE ACCRUED A VAST AMOUNT OF CAPITAL IN DAY TRADING-- ENOUGH TO FUND OUR ENTIRE OPERATION.
AND SWEETHEART, MY FAMILIAR.
ACTUALLY, SHE'S MORE OF A PET. SHE ACTS AS MY EYES AND EARS--BUT IF YOU WANT TO KNOW THE TRUTH, SHE ISN'T ALL THAT GOOD AT ANYTHING. ISN'T THAT RIGHT, DOLL?
YES, DOCTOR.
FINALLY, THE TWIN SHADOWS, DIRECTORS OF THE HORDE.
OPERATING REMOTELY, THEY HAVE ALREADY PUT THE PIECES IN PLACE FOR OUR WORLD TAKEOVER.
WE OPERATE STRICTLY TO PLEASE MANAGEMENT.
WE EXPECT THIS TO BE A SHARED GOAL.

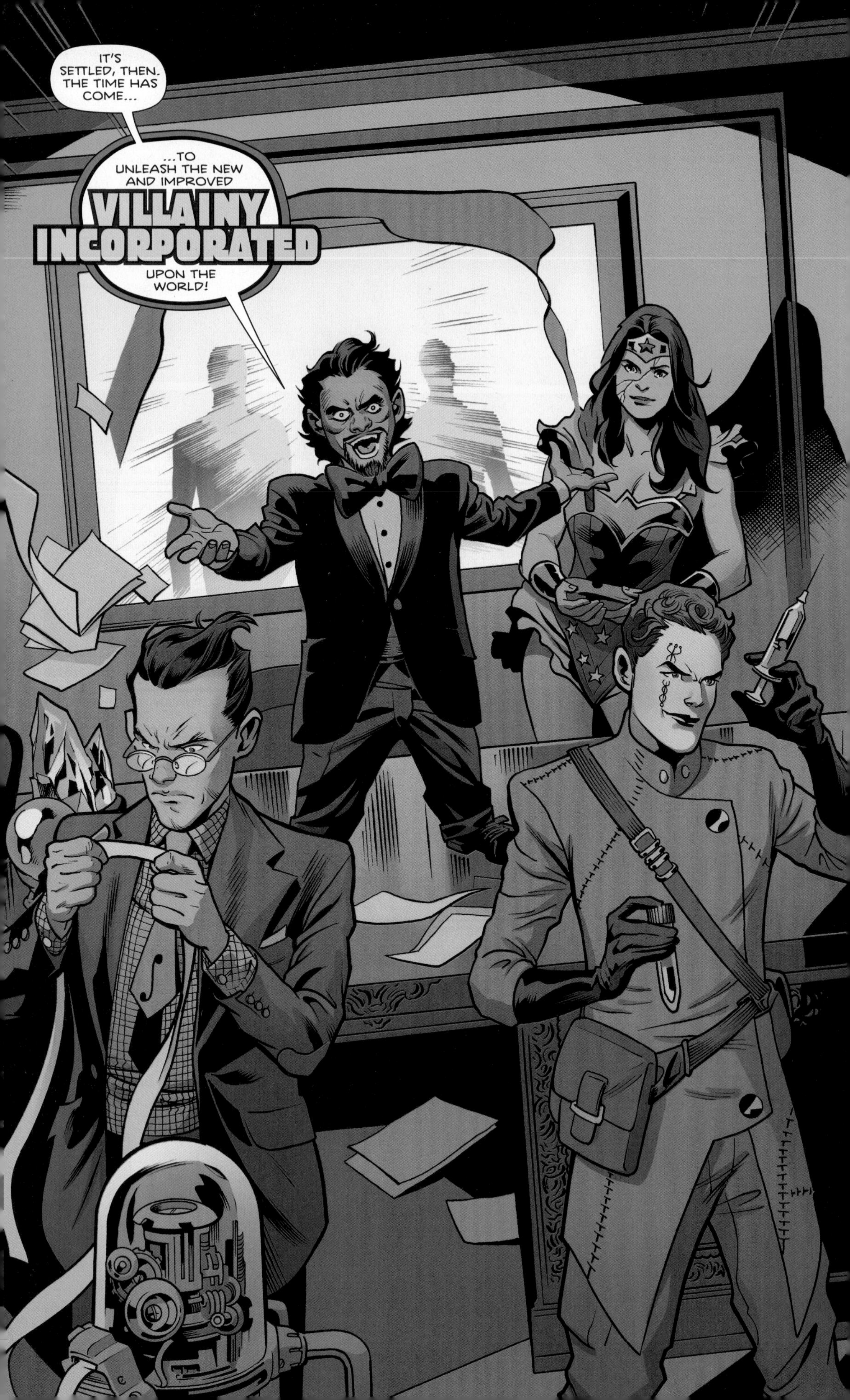
IT'S SETTLED, THEN. THE TIME HAS COME...
...TO UNLEASH THE NEW AND IMPROVED
VILLAINY INCORPORATED
UPON THE WORLD!

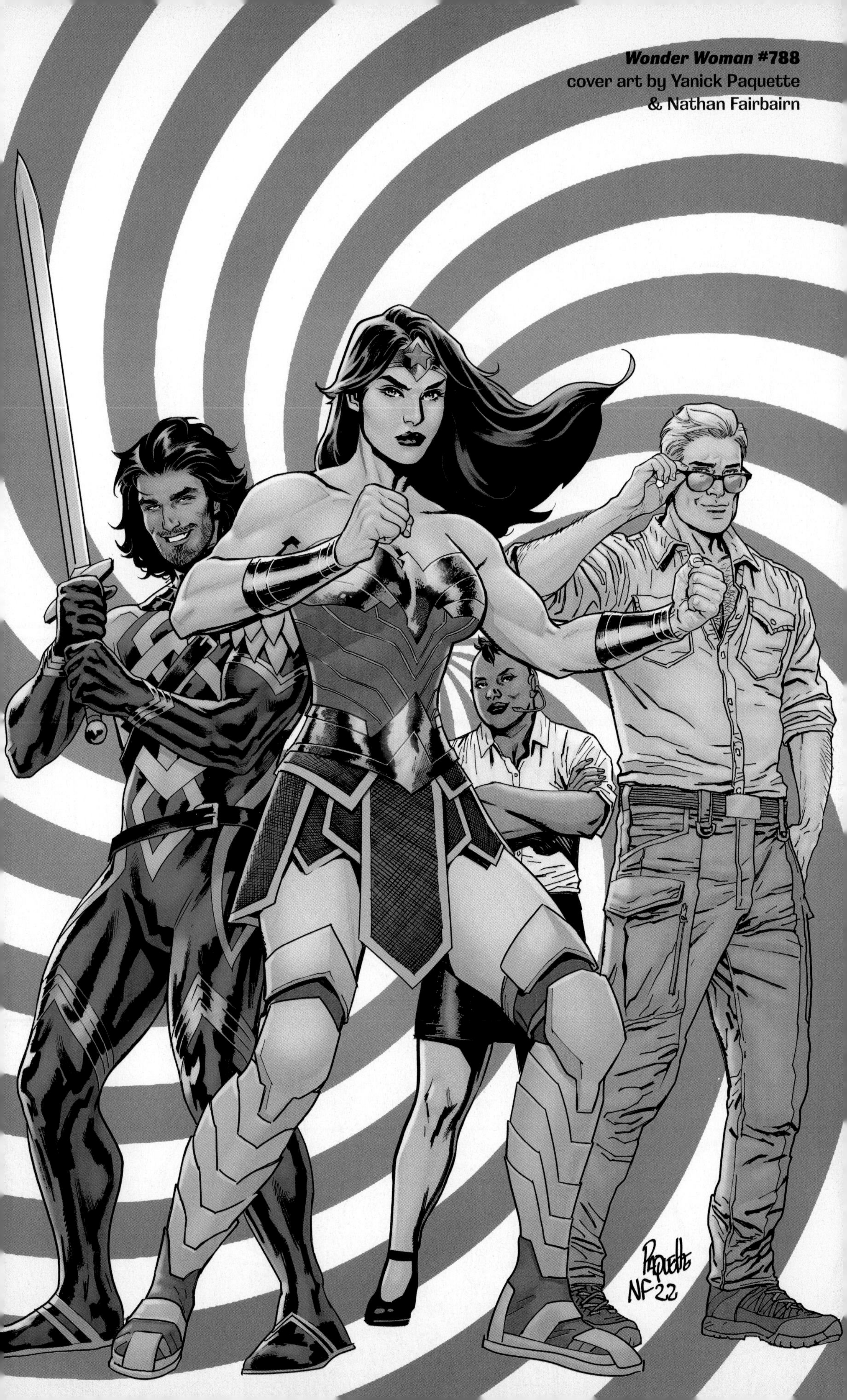

***Wonder Woman* #788**
cover art by Yanick Paquette
& Nathan Fairbairn

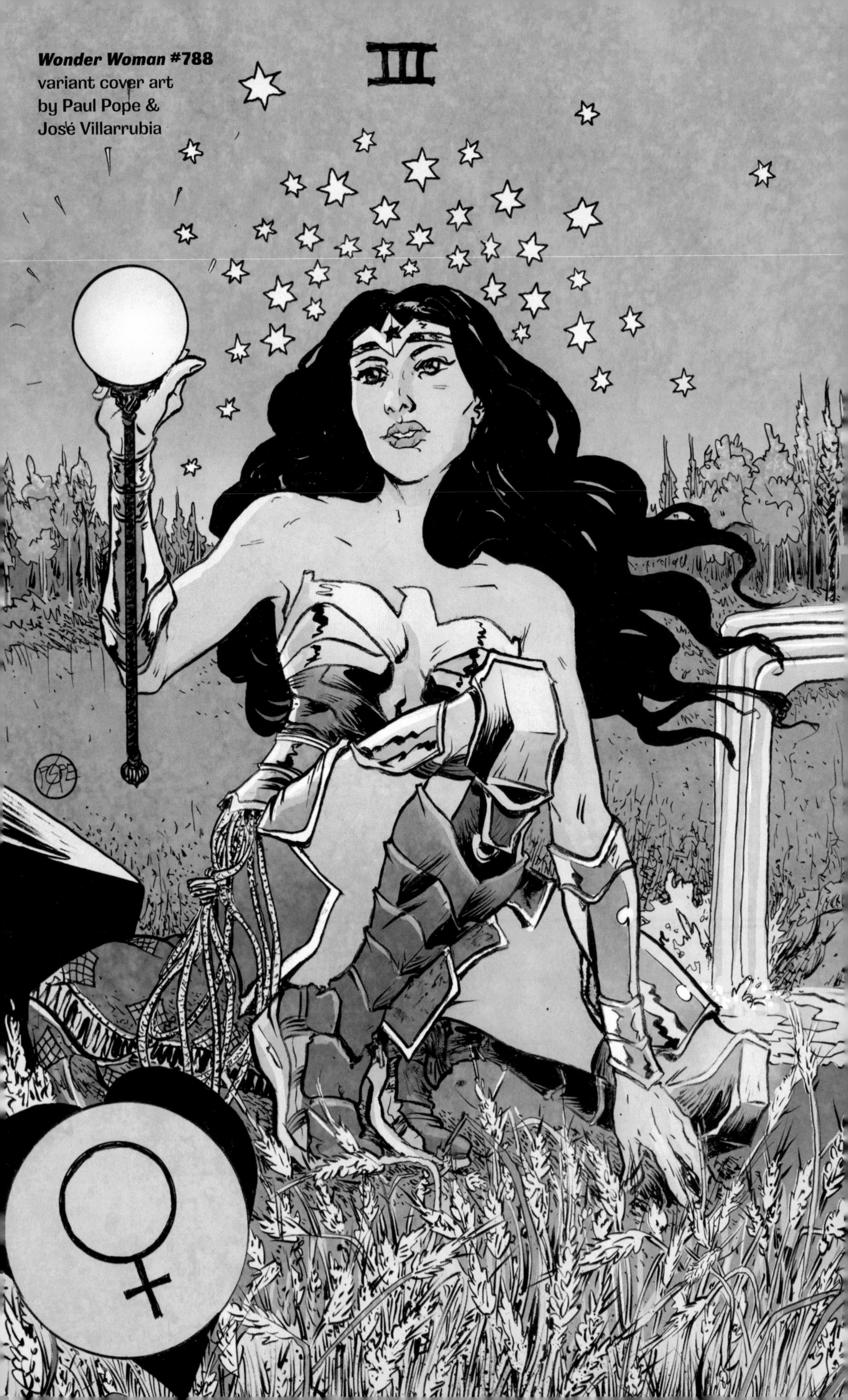
III
POPE

***Wonder Woman* #788**
variant cover art
by Paul Pope &
José Villarrubia

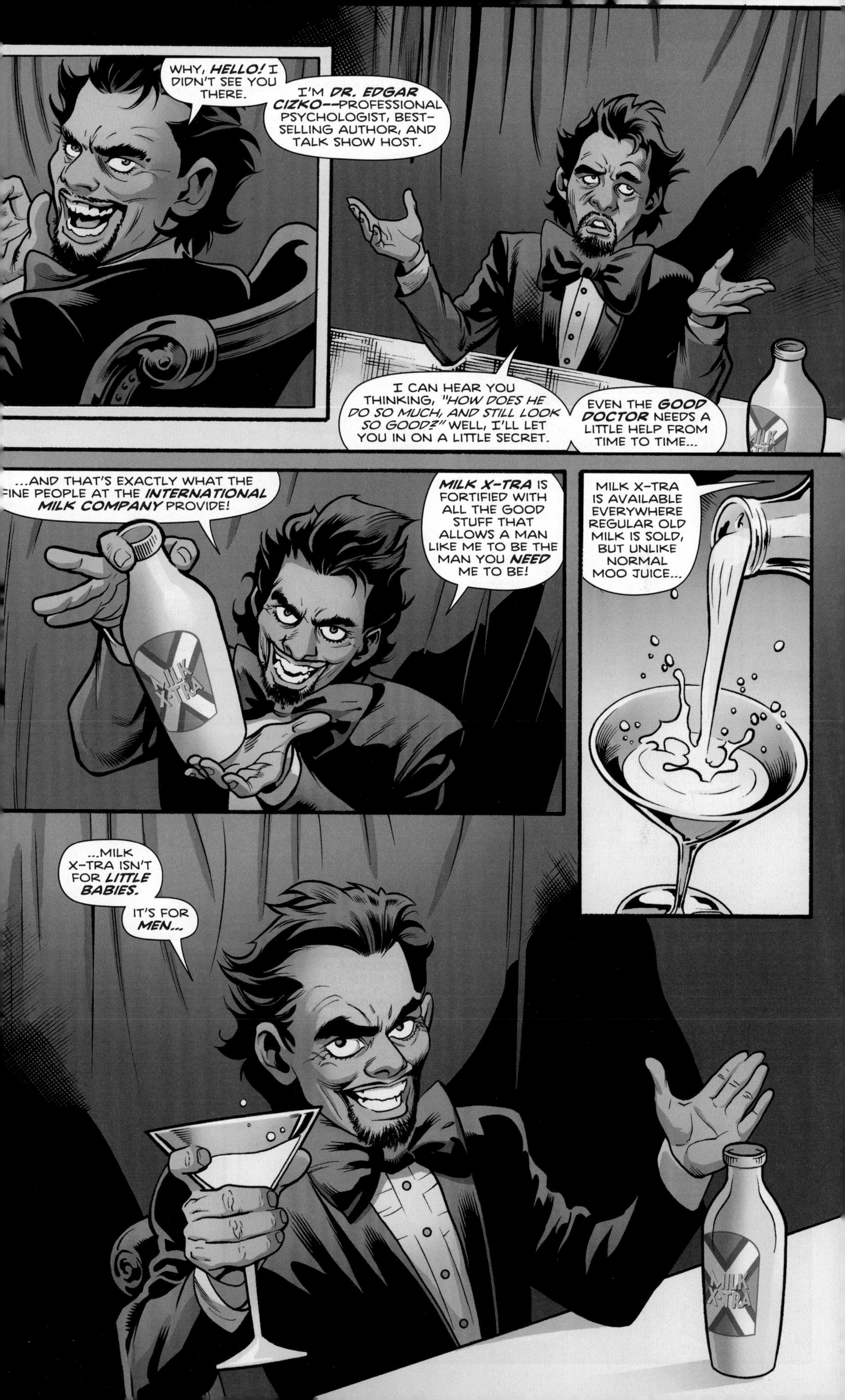
WHY, HELLO! I DIDN'T SEE YOU THERE.
I'M DR. EDGAR CIZKO--PROFESSIONAL PSYCHOLOGIST, BEST-SELLING AUTHOR, AND TALK SHOW HOST.
I CAN HEAR YOU THINKING, "HOW DOES HE DO SO MUCH, AND STILL LOOK SO GOOD?" WELL, I'LL LET YOU IN ON A LITTLE SECRET.
EVEN THE GOOD DOCTOR NEEDS A LITTLE HELP FROM TIME TO TIME...
MILK X-TRA
...AND THAT'S EXACTLY WHAT THE FINE PEOPLE AT THE INTERNATIONAL MILK COMPANY PROVIDE!
MILK X-TRA IS FORTIFIED WITH ALL THE GOOD STUFF THAT ALLOWS A MAN LIKE ME TO BE THE MAN YOU NEED ME TO BE!
MILK X-TRA
MILK X-TRA IS AVAILABLE EVERYWHERE REGULAR OLD MILK IS SOLD, BUT UNLIKE NORMAL MOO JUICE...
...MILK X-TRA ISN'T FOR LITTLE BABIES.
IT'S FOR MEN...
MILK X-TRA

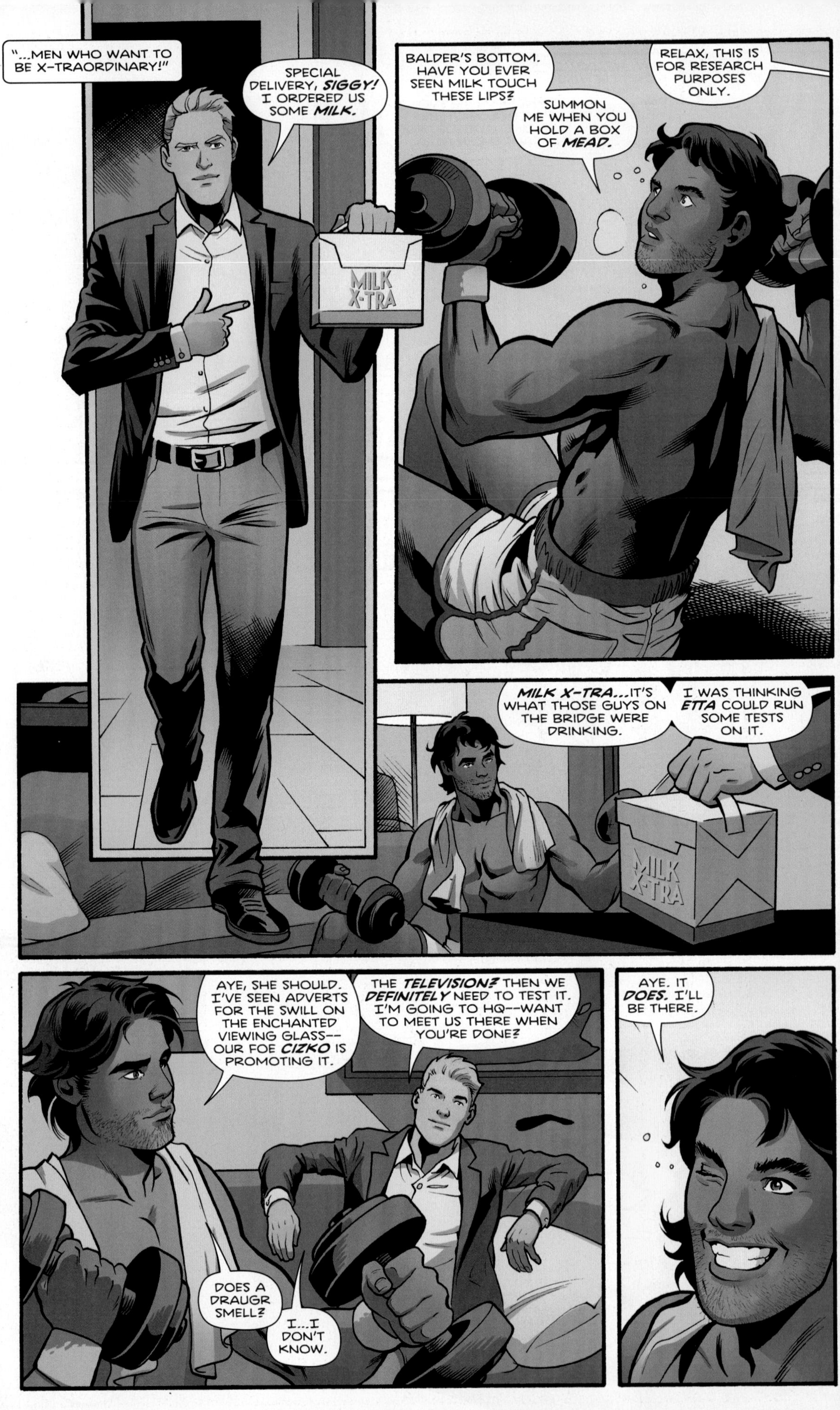
"...MEN WHO WANT TO BE X-TRAORDINARY!"
SPECIAL DELIVERY, SIGGY! I ORDERED US SOME MILK.
MILK X-TRA
BALDER'S BOTTOM. HAVE YOU EVER SEEN MILK TOUCH THESE LIPS?
SUMMON ME WHEN YOU HOLD A BOX OF MEAD.
RELAX, THIS IS FOR RESEARCH PURPOSES ONLY.
MILK X-TRA...IT'S WHAT THOSE GUYS ON THE BRIDGE WERE DRINKING.
I WAS THINKING ETTA COULD RUN SOME TESTS ON IT.
MILK X-TRA
AYE, SHE SHOULD. I'VE SEEN ADVERTS FOR THE SWILL ON THE ENCHANTED VIEWING GLASS--OUR FOE CIZKO IS PROMOTING IT.
THE TELEVISION? THEN WE DEFINITELY NEED TO TEST IT. I'M GOING TO HQ--WANT TO MEET US THERE WHEN YOU'RE DONE?
DOES A DRAUGR SMELL?
I...I DON'T KNOW.
AYE. IT DOES. I'LL BE THERE.

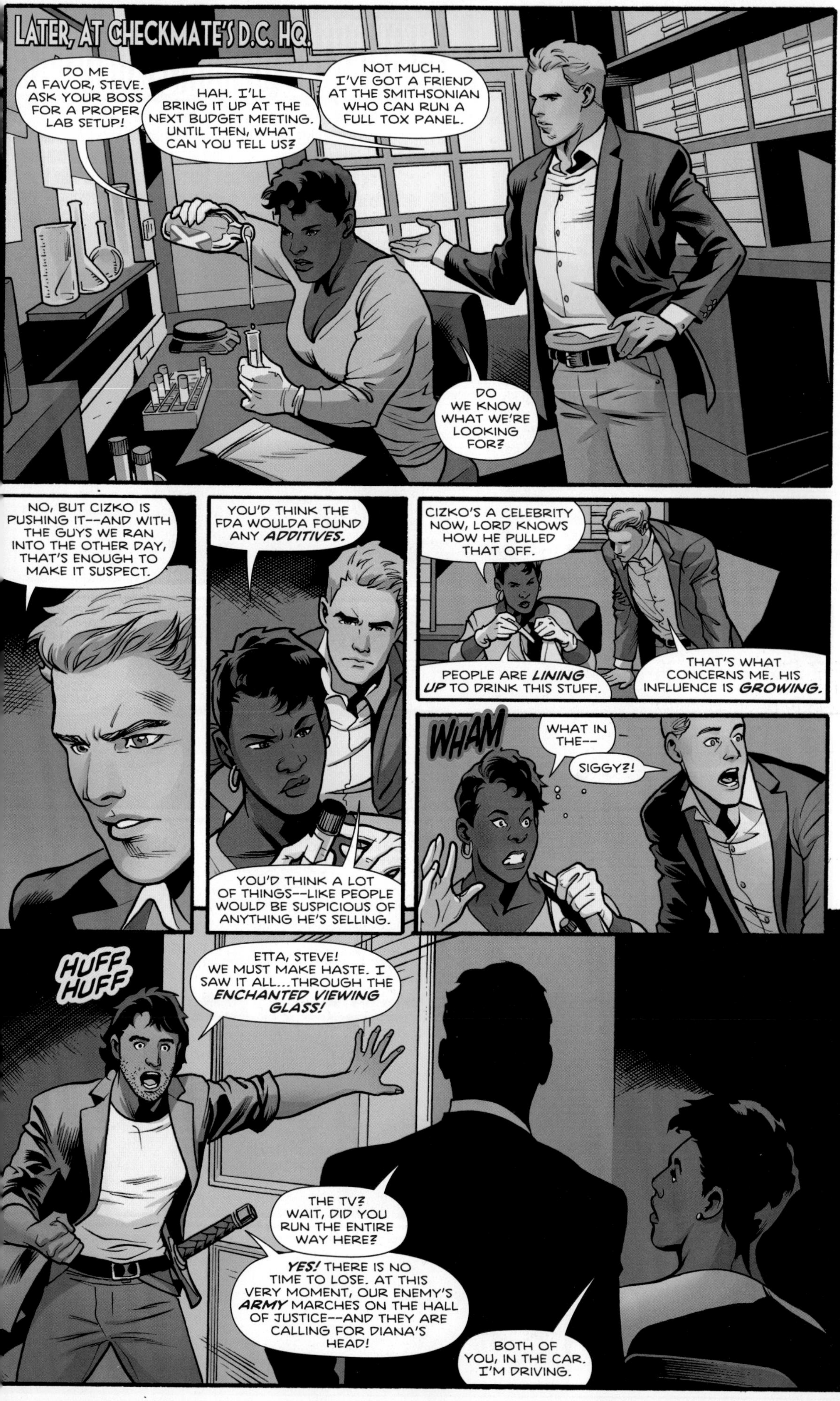

LATER, AT CHECKMATE'S D.C. HQ.
DO ME A FAVOR, STEVE. ASK YOUR BOSS FOR A PROPER LAB SETUP!
HAH. I'LL BRING IT UP AT THE NEXT BUDGET MEETING. UNTIL THEN, WHAT CAN YOU TELL US?
NOT MUCH. I'VE GOT A FRIEND AT THE SMITHSONIAN WHO CAN RUN A FULL TOX PANEL.
DO WE KNOW WHAT WE'RE LOOKING FOR?
NO, BUT CIZKO IS PUSHING IT--AND WITH THE GUYS WE RAN INTO THE OTHER DAY, THAT'S ENOUGH TO MAKE IT SUSPECT.
YOU'D THINK THE FDA WOULDA FOUND ANY ADDITIVES.
YOU'D THINK A LOT OF THINGS--LIKE PEOPLE WOULD BE SUSPICIOUS OF ANYTHING HE'S SELLING.
CIZKO'S A CELEBRITY NOW, LORD KNOWS HOW HE PULLED THAT OFF.
PEOPLE ARE LINING UP TO DRINK THIS STUFF.
THAT'S WHAT CONCERNS ME. HIS INFLUENCE IS GROWING.
WHAM
WHAT IN THE--
SIGGY?!
HUFF HUFF
ETTA, STEVE! WE MUST MAKE HASTE. I SAW IT ALL...THROUGH THE ENCHANTED VIEWING GLASS!
THE TV? WAIT, DID YOU RUN THE ENTIRE WAY HERE?
YES! THERE IS NO TIME TO LOSE. AT THIS VERY MOMENT, OUR ENEMY'S ARMY MARCHES ON THE HALL OF JUSTICE--AND THEY ARE CALLING FOR DIANA'S HEAD!
BOTH OF YOU, IN THE CAR. I'M DRIVING.

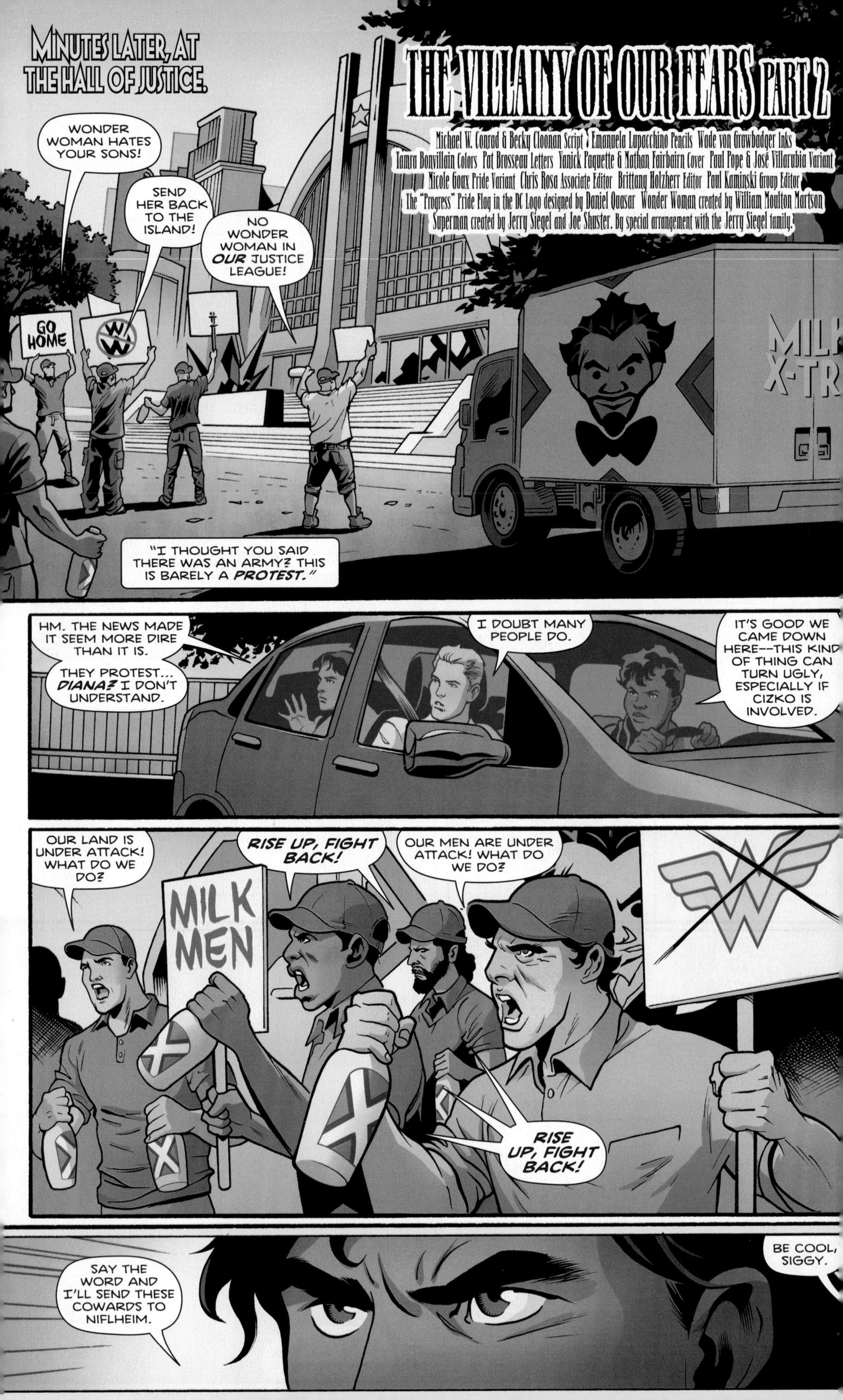
MINUTES LATER, AT THE HALL OF JUSTICE.
THE VILLAINY OF OUR FEARS PART 2
Michael W. Conrad & Becky Cloonan Script / Emanuela Lupacchino Pencils Wade von Grawbadger Inks
Tamra Bonvillain Colors Pat Brosseau Letters Yanick Paquette & Nathan Fairbairn Cover Paul Pope & José Villarubia Variant
Nicole Goux Pride Variant Chris Rosa Associate Editor Brittany Holzherr Editor Paul Kaminski Group Editor
The "Progress" Pride Flag in the DC Logo designed by Daniel Quasar Wonder Woman created by William Moulton Martson
Superman created by Jerry Siegel and Joe Shuster. By special arrangement with the Jerry Siegel family.
WONDER WOMAN HATES YOUR SONS!
SEND HER BACK TO THE ISLAND!
NO WONDER WOMAN IN OUR JUSTICE LEAGUE!
GO HOME
"I THOUGHT YOU SAID THERE WAS AN ARMY? THIS IS BARELY A PROTEST."
HM. THE NEWS MADE IT SEEM MORE DIRE THAN IT IS.
THEY PROTEST... DIANA? I DON'T UNDERSTAND.
I DOUBT MANY PEOPLE DO.
IT'S GOOD WE CAME DOWN HERE--THIS KIND OF THING CAN TURN UGLY, ESPECIALLY IF CIZKO IS INVOLVED.
OUR LAND IS UNDER ATTACK! WHAT DO WE DO?
RISE UP, FIGHT BACK!
OUR MEN ARE UNDER ATTACK! WHAT DO WE DO?
MILK MEN
RISE UP, FIGHT BACK!
SAY THE WORD AND I'LL SEND THESE COWARDS TO NIFLHEIM.
BE COOL, SIGGY.

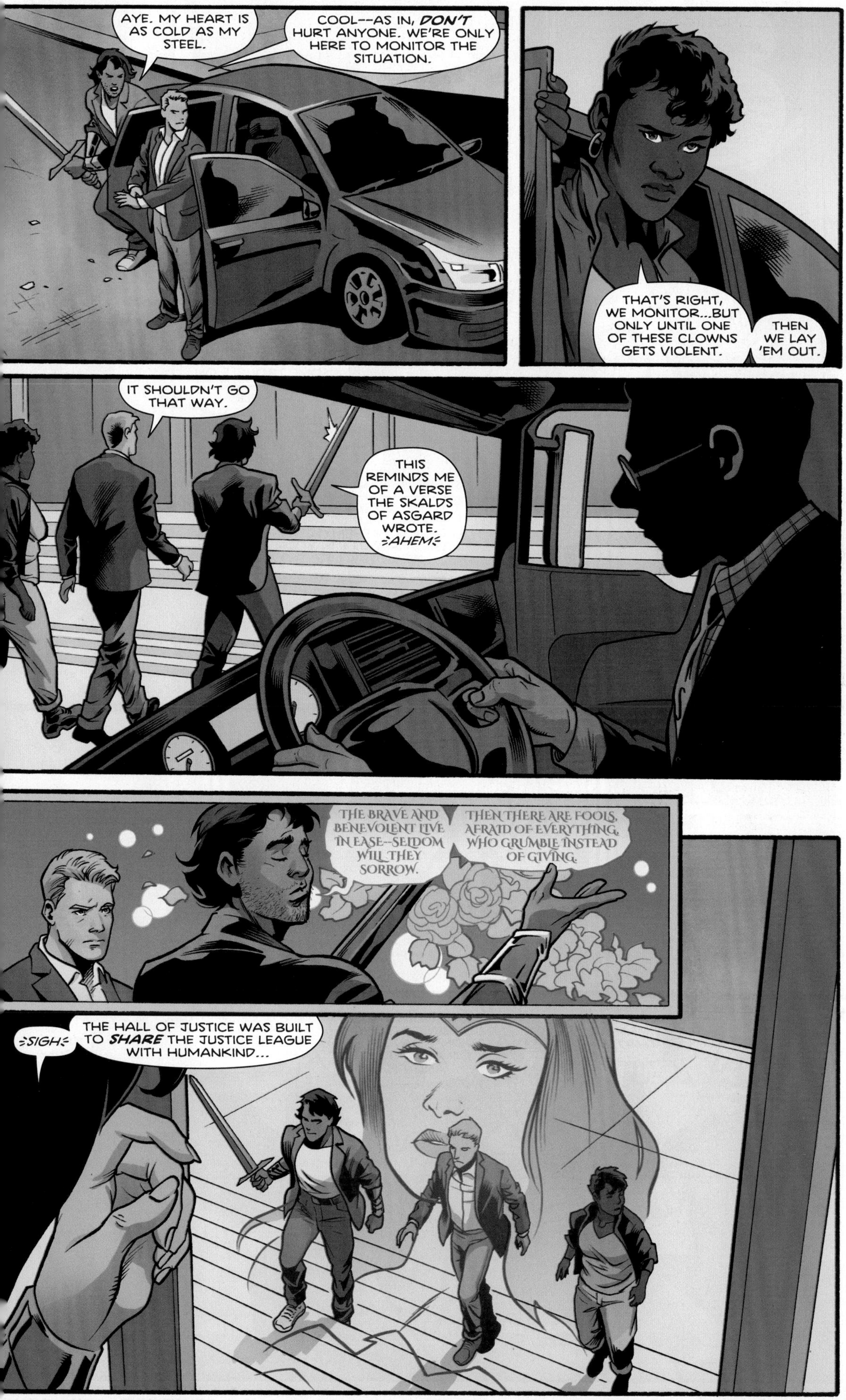
AYE. MY HEART IS AS COLD AS MY STEEL.
COOL--AS IN, DON'T HURT ANYONE. WE'RE ONLY HERE TO MONITOR THE SITUATION.
THAT'S RIGHT, WE MONITOR...BUT ONLY UNTIL ONE OF THESE CLOWNS GETS VIOLENT.
THEN WE LAY 'EM OUT.
IT SHOULDN'T GO THAT WAY.
THIS REMINDS ME OF A VERSE THE SKALDS OF ASGARD WROTE. AHEM
THE BRAVE AND BENEVOLENT LIVE IN EASE--SELDOM WILL THEY SORROW.
THEN THERE ARE FOOLS, AFRAID OF EVERYTHING, WHO GRUMBLE INSTEAD OF GIVING.
SIGH
THE HALL OF JUSTICE WAS BUILT TO SHARE THE JUSTICE LEAGUE WITH HUMANKIND...

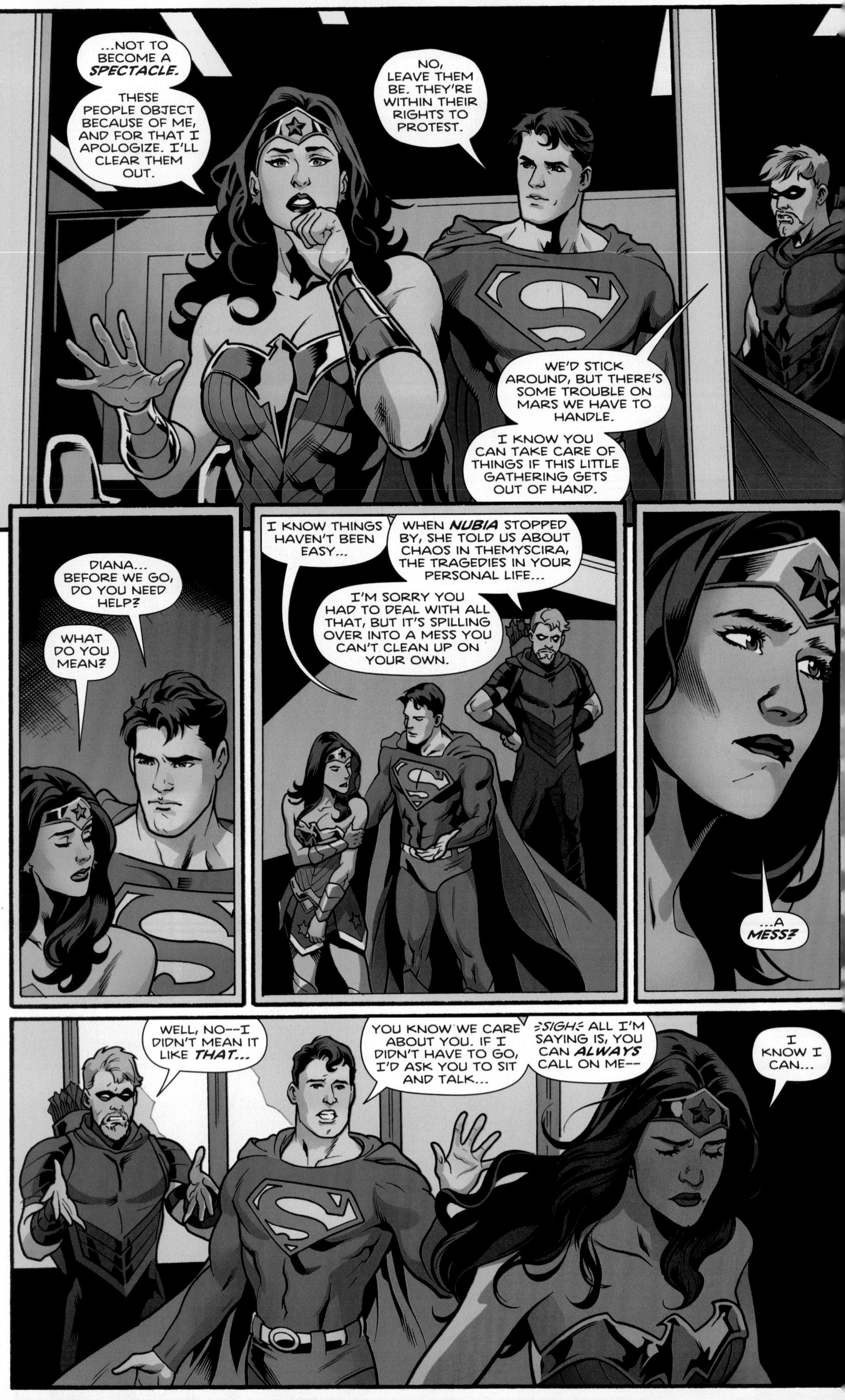

...NOT TO BECOME A SPECTACLE.
THESE PEOPLE OBJECT BECAUSE OF ME, AND FOR THAT I APOLOGIZE. I'LL CLEAR THEM OUT.
NO, LEAVE THEM BE. THEY'RE WITHIN THEIR RIGHTS TO PROTEST.
WE'D STICK AROUND, BUT THERE'S SOME TROUBLE ON MARS WE HAVE TO HANDLE.
I KNOW YOU CAN TAKE CARE OF THINGS IF THIS LITTLE GATHERING GETS OUT OF HAND.
DIANA... BEFORE WE GO, DO YOU NEED HELP?
WHAT DO YOU MEAN?
I KNOW THINGS HAVEN'T BEEN EASY...
WHEN NUBIA STOPPED BY, SHE TOLD US ABOUT CHAOS IN THEMYSCIRA, THE TRAGEDIES IN YOUR PERSONAL LIFE...
I'M SORRY YOU HAD TO DEAL WITH ALL THAT, BUT IT'S SPILLING OVER INTO A MESS YOU CAN'T CLEAN UP ON YOUR OWN.
...A MESS?
WELL, NO--I DIDN'T MEAN IT LIKE THAT...
YOU KNOW WE CARE ABOUT YOU. IF I DIDN'T HAVE TO GO, I'D ASK YOU TO SIT AND TALK...
=SIGH= ALL I'M SAYING IS, YOU CAN ALWAYS CALL ON ME--
I KNOW I CAN...

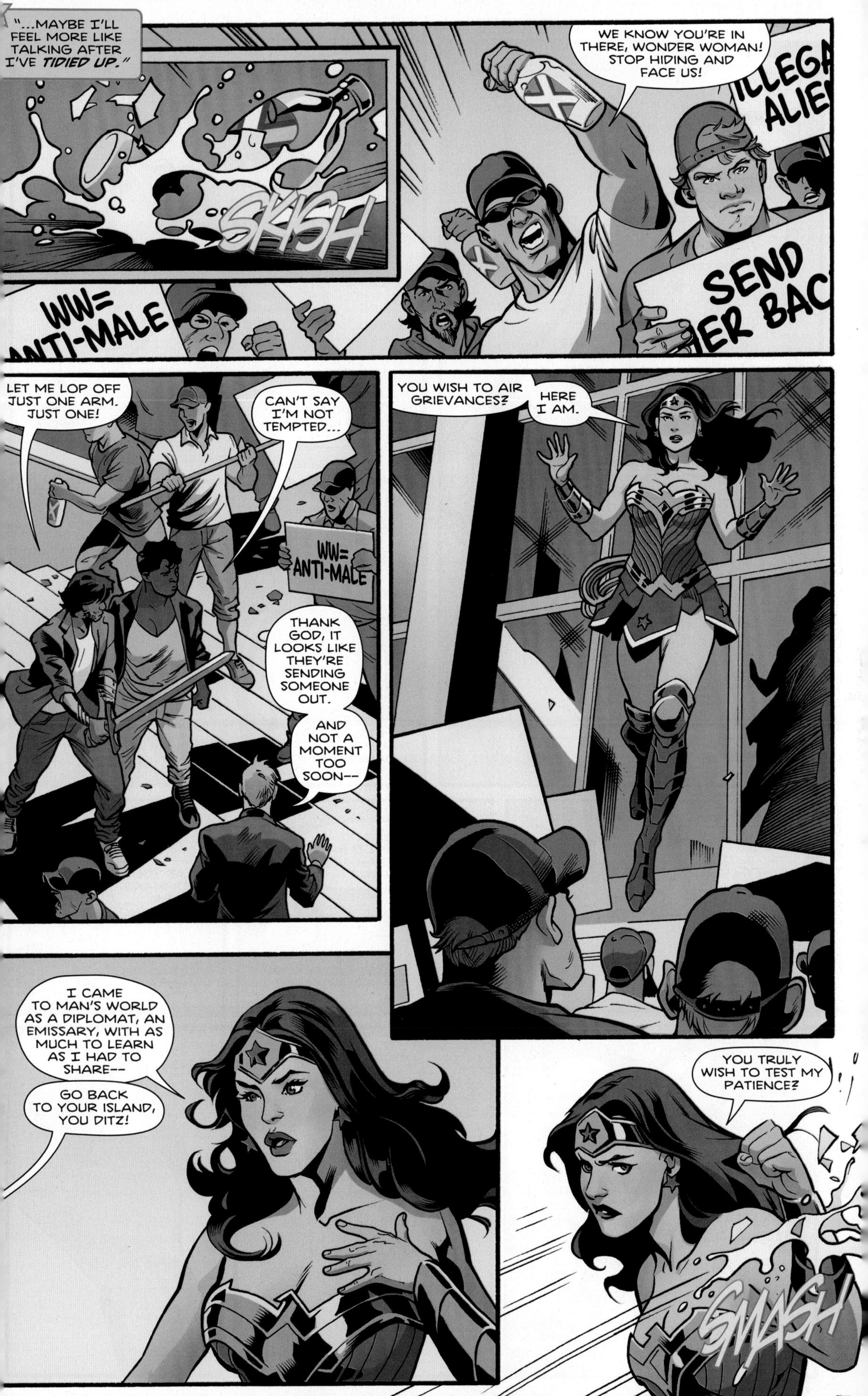
"...MAYBE I'LL FEEL MORE LIKE TALKING AFTER I'VE TIDIED UP."
SKISH
WE KNOW YOU'RE IN THERE, WONDER WOMAN! STOP HIDING AND FACE US!
ILLEGA ALIEN
SEND HER BAC
WW= ANTI-MALE
LET ME LOP OFF JUST ONE ARM. JUST ONE!
CAN'T SAY I'M NOT TEMPTED...
WW= ANTI-MALE
THANK GOD, IT LOOKS LIKE THEY'RE SENDING SOMEONE OUT.
AND NOT A MOMENT TOO SOON--
YOU WISH TO AIR GRIEVANCES?
HERE I AM.
I CAME TO MAN'S WORLD AS A DIPLOMAT, AN EMISSARY, WITH AS MUCH TO LEARN AS I HAD TO SHARE--
GO BACK TO YOUR ISLAND, YOU DITZ!
YOU TRULY WISH TO TEST MY PATIENCE?
SMASH

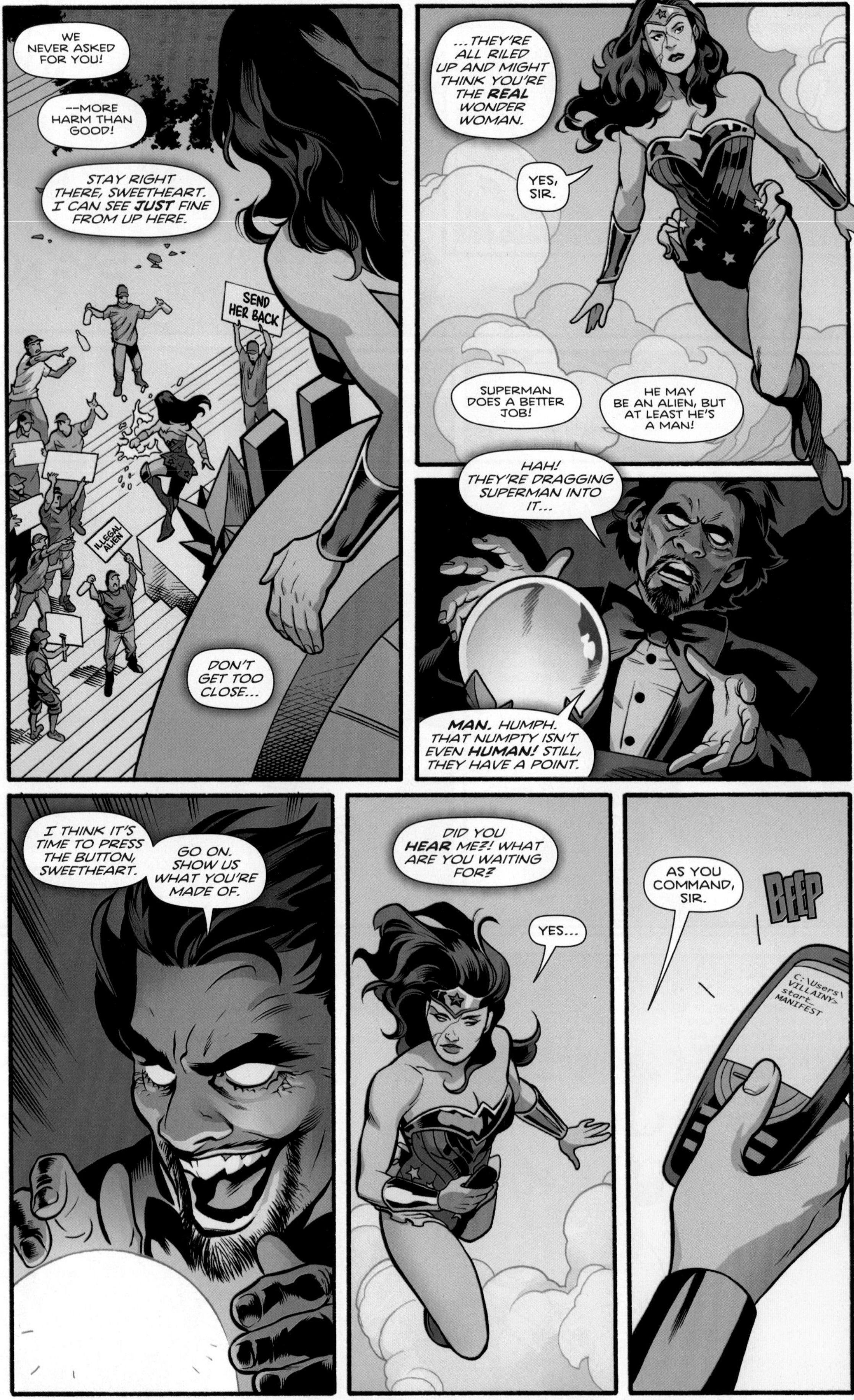
WE NEVER ASKED FOR YOU!
--MORE HARM THAN GOOD!
STAY RIGHT THERE, SWEETHEART. I CAN SEE JUST FINE FROM UP HERE.
SEND HER BACK
ILLEGAL ALIEN
DON'T GET TOO CLOSE...
...THEY'RE ALL RILED UP AND MIGHT THINK YOU'RE THE REAL WONDER WOMAN.
YES, SIR.
SUPERMAN DOES A BETTER JOB!
HE MAY BE AN ALIEN, BUT AT LEAST HE'S A MAN!
HAH! THEY'RE DRAGGING SUPERMAN INTO IT...
MAN. HUMPH. THAT NUMPTY ISN'T EVEN HUMAN! STILL, THEY HAVE A POINT.
I THINK IT'S TIME TO PRESS THE BUTTON, SWEETHEART.
GO ON. SHOW US WHAT YOU'RE MADE OF.
DID YOU HEAR ME?! WHAT ARE YOU WAITING FOR?
YES...
AS YOU COMMAND, SIR.
BEEP
C:\Users\VILLAINY> start_MANIFEST

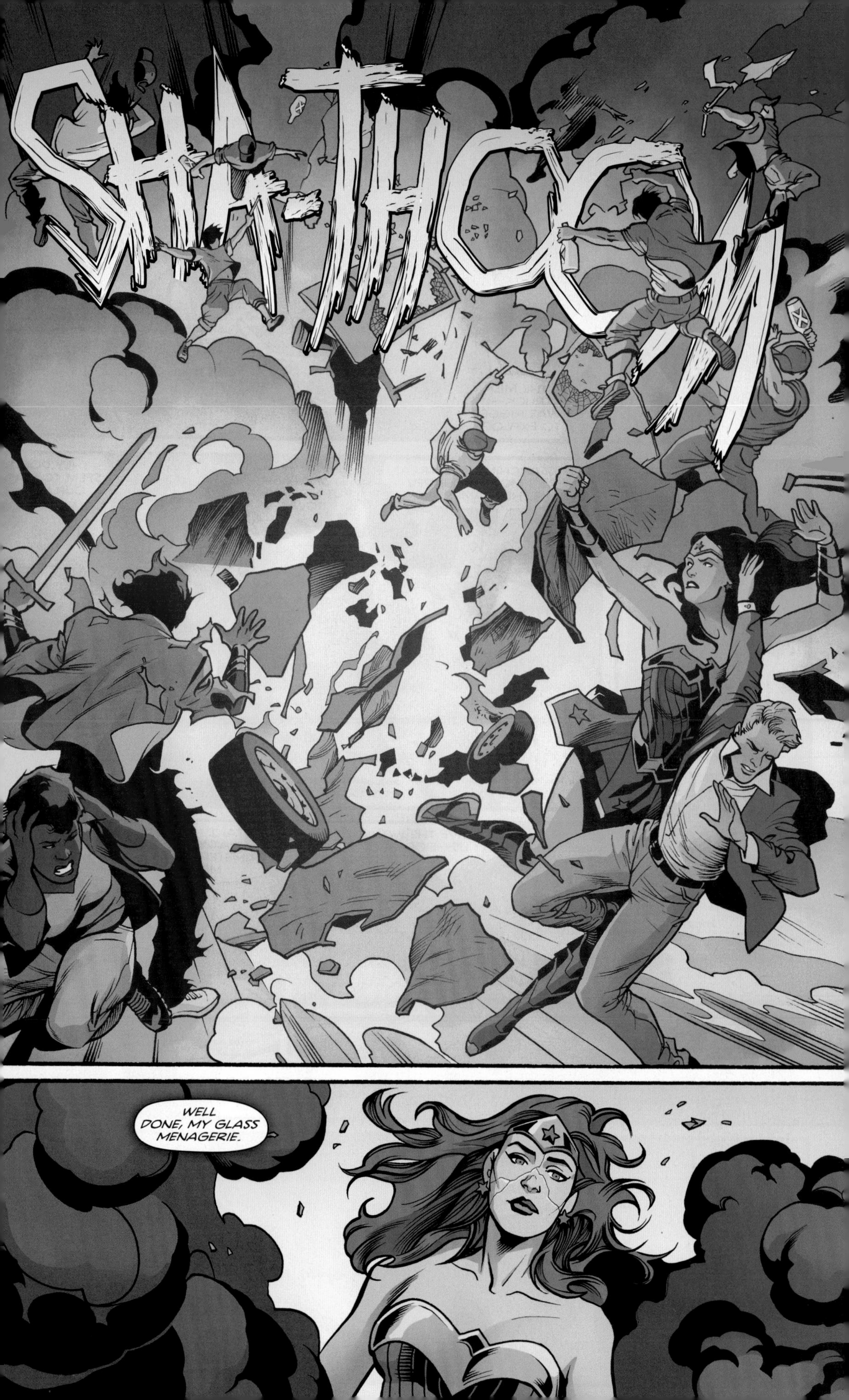
SHATHOOM
WELL DONE, MY GLASS MENAGERIE.

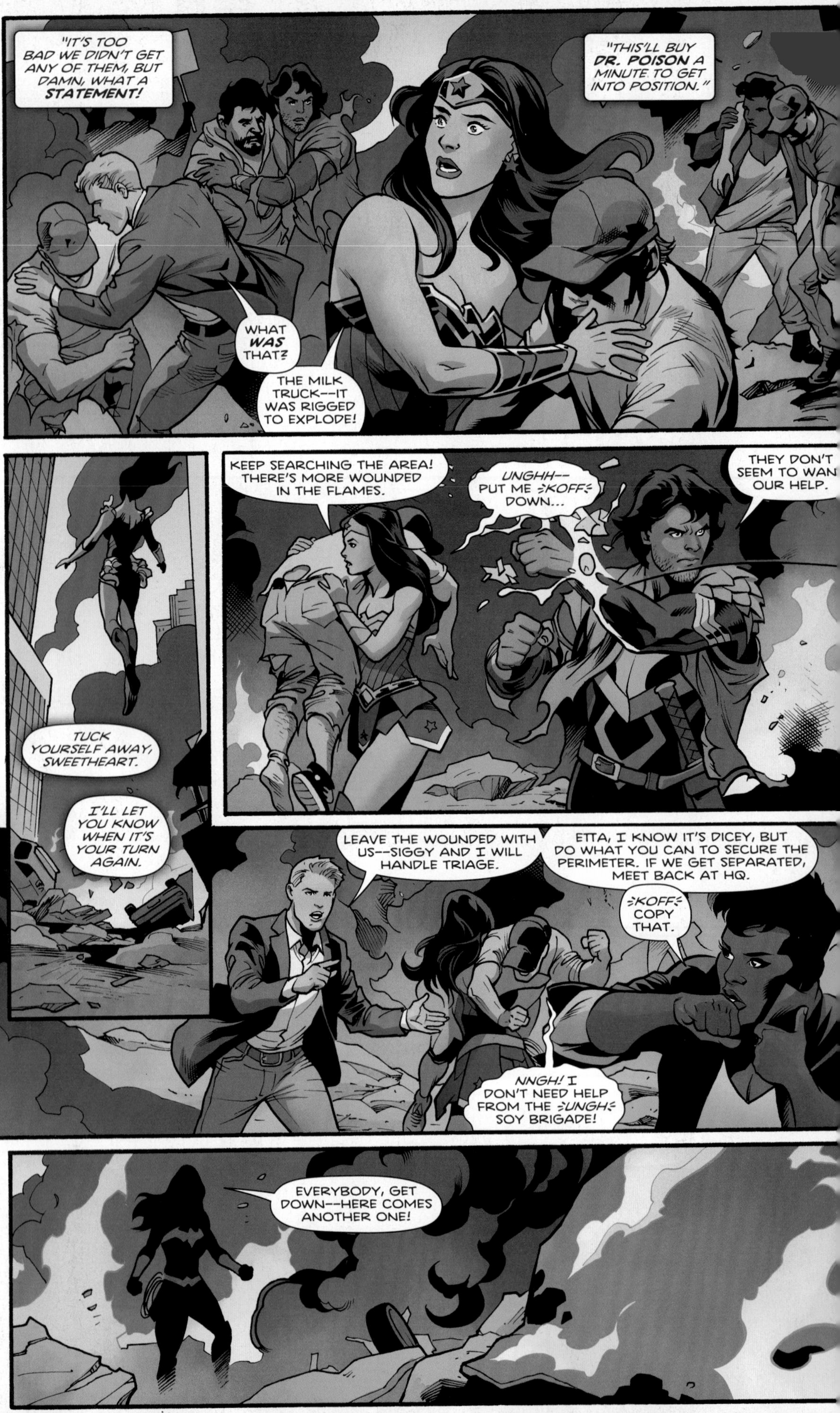
"IT'S TOO BAD WE DIDN'T GET ANY OF THEM, BUT DAMN, WHAT A STATEMENT!
"THIS'LL BUY DR. POISON A MINUTE TO GET INTO POSITION."
WHAT WAS THAT?
THE MILK TRUCK--IT WAS RIGGED TO EXPLODE!
TUCK YOURSELF AWAY, SWEETHEART.
I'LL LET YOU KNOW WHEN IT'S YOUR TURN AGAIN.
KEEP SEARCHING THE AREA! THERE'S MORE WOUNDED IN THE FLAMES.
UNGHH-- PUT ME KOFF DOWN...
THEY DON'T SEEM TO WAN OUR HELP.
LEAVE THE WOUNDED WITH US--SIGGY AND I WILL HANDLE TRIAGE.
ETTA, I KNOW IT'S DICEY, BUT DO WHAT YOU CAN TO SECURE THE PERIMETER. IF WE GET SEPARATED, MEET BACK AT HQ.
KOFF COPY THAT.
NNGH! I DON'T NEED HELP FROM THE UNGH SOY BRIGADE!
EVERYBODY, GET DOWN--HERE COMES ANOTHER ONE!

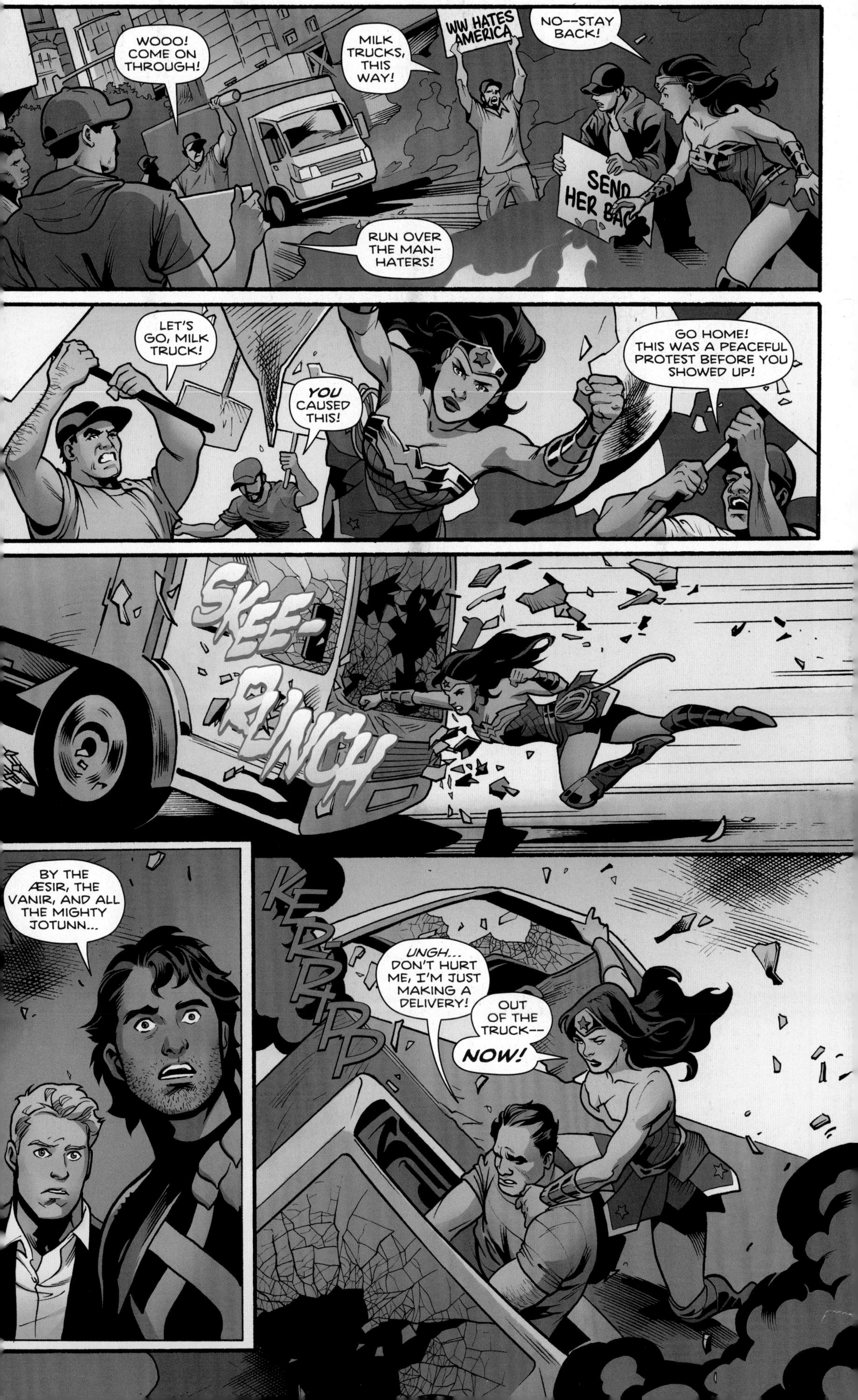
WOOO! COME ON THROUGH!
MILK TRUCKS, THIS WAY!
WW HATES AMERICA
NO--STAY BACK!
SEND HER BACK
RUN OVER THE MAN-HATERS!
LET'S GO, MILK TRUCK!
YOU CAUSED THIS!
GO HOME! THIS WAS A PEACEFUL PROTEST BEFORE YOU SHOWED UP!
SKEE-RUNCH
BY THE ÆSIR, THE VANIR, AND ALL THE MIGHTY JOTUNN...
KERRRIPP
UNGH... DON'T HURT ME, I'M JUST MAKING A DELIVERY!
OUT OF THE TRUCK--
NOW!

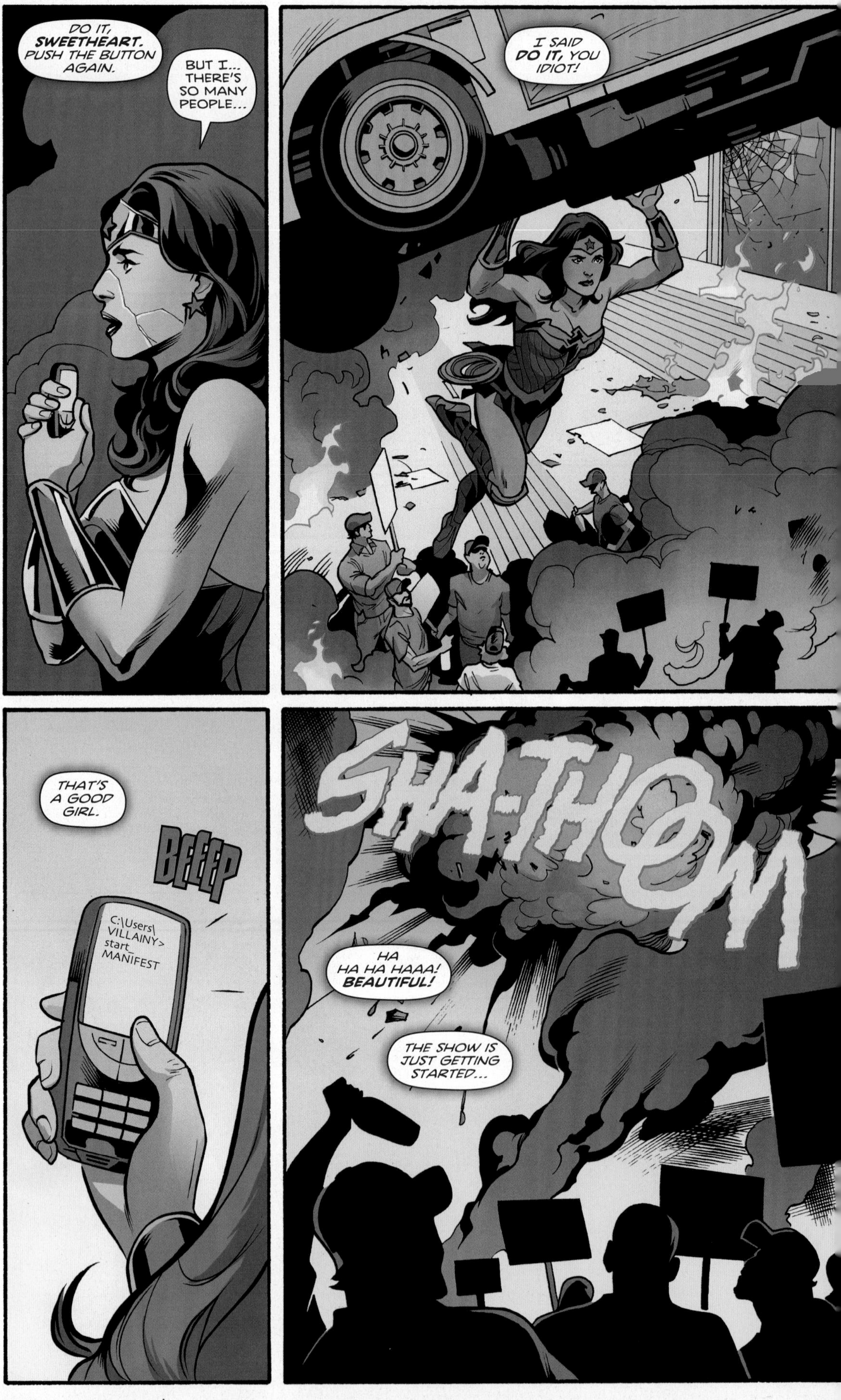
DO IT, **SWEETHEART.** PUSH THE BUTTON AGAIN.
BUT I... THERE'S SO MANY PEOPLE...
I SAID **DO IT,** YOU IDIOT!
THAT'S A GOOD GIRL.
BEEEP
C:\Users\ VILLAINY> start_ MANIFEST
SHA-THOOM
HA HA HA HAAA! **BEAUTIFUL!**
THE SHOW IS JUST GETTING STARTED...

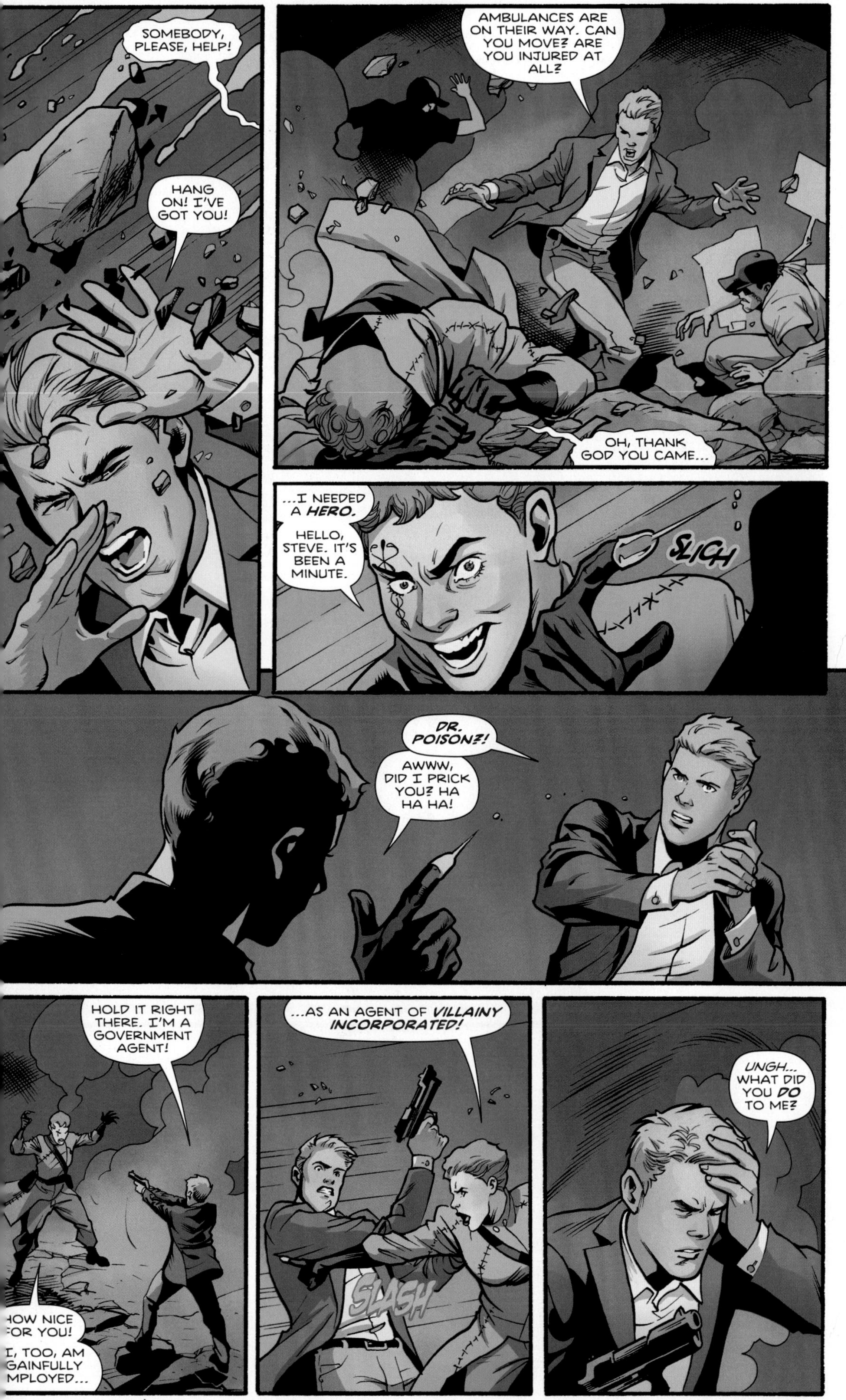
SOMEBODY, PLEASE, HELP!
HANG ON! I'VE GOT YOU!
AMBULANCES ARE ON THEIR WAY. CAN YOU MOVE? ARE YOU INJURED AT ALL?
OH, THANK GOD YOU CAME...
...I NEEDED A HERO.
HELLO, STEVE. IT'S BEEN A MINUTE.
SLICH
DR. POISON?!
AWWW, DID I PRICK YOU? HA HA HA!
HOLD IT RIGHT THERE. I'M A GOVERNMENT AGENT!
HOW NICE FOR YOU!
I, TOO, AM GAINFULLY MPLOYED...
...AS AN AGENT OF VILLAINY INCORPORATED!
SLASH
UNGH... WHAT DID YOU DO TO ME?

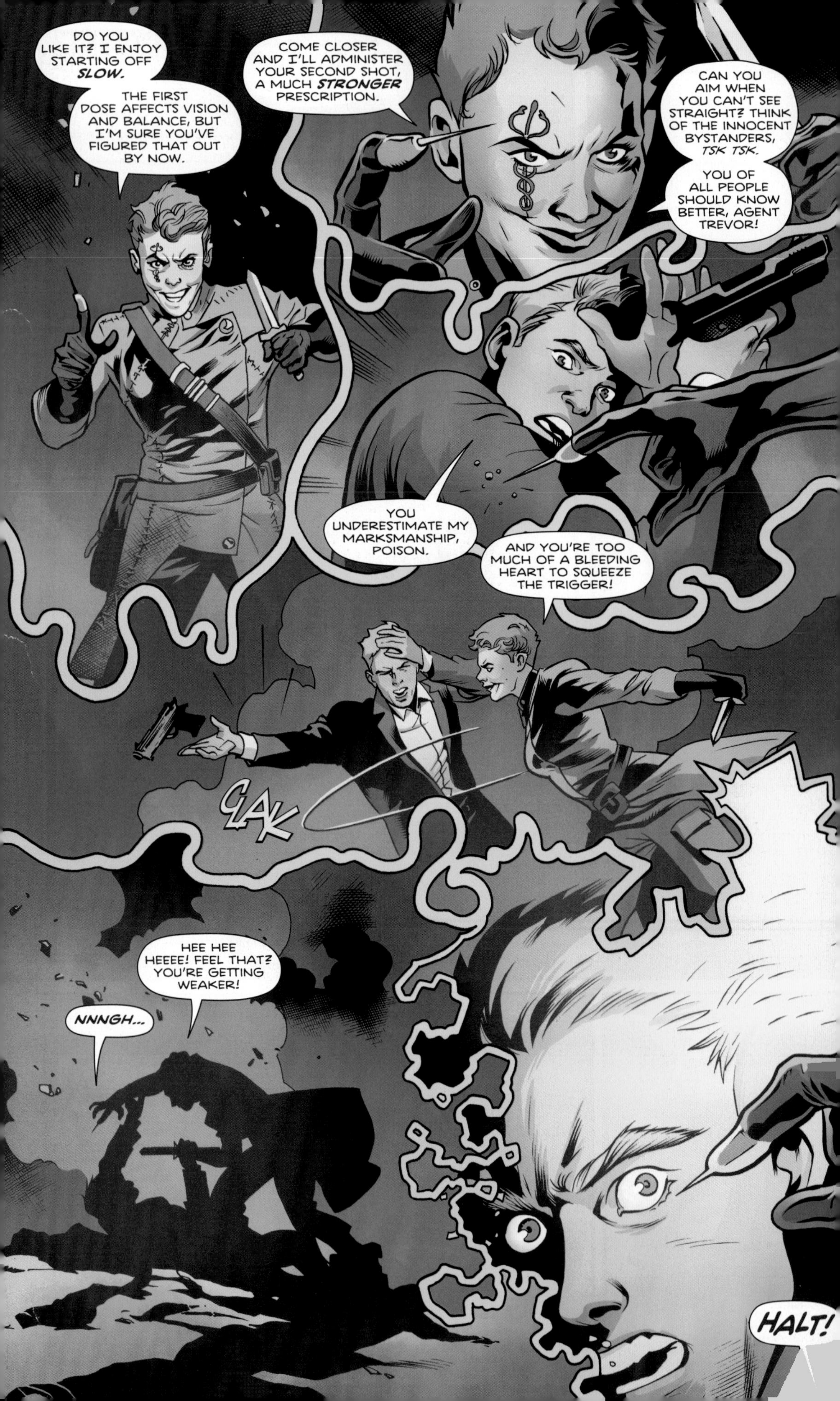
DO YOU LIKE IT? I ENJOY STARTING OFF SLOW.
THE FIRST DOSE AFFECTS VISION AND BALANCE, BUT I'M SURE YOU'VE FIGURED THAT OUT BY NOW.
COME CLOSER AND I'LL ADMINISTER YOUR SECOND SHOT, A MUCH STRONGER PRESCRIPTION.
CAN YOU AIM WHEN YOU CAN'T SEE STRAIGHT? THINK OF THE INNOCENT BYSTANDERS, TSK TSK.
YOU OF ALL PEOPLE SHOULD KNOW BETTER, AGENT TREVOR!
YOU UNDERESTIMATE MY MARKSMANSHIP, POISON.
AND YOU'RE TOO MUCH OF A BLEEDING HEART TO SQUEEZE THE TRIGGER!
CLAK
HEE HEE HEEEE! FEEL THAT? YOU'RE GETTING WEAKER!
NNNGH...
HALT!

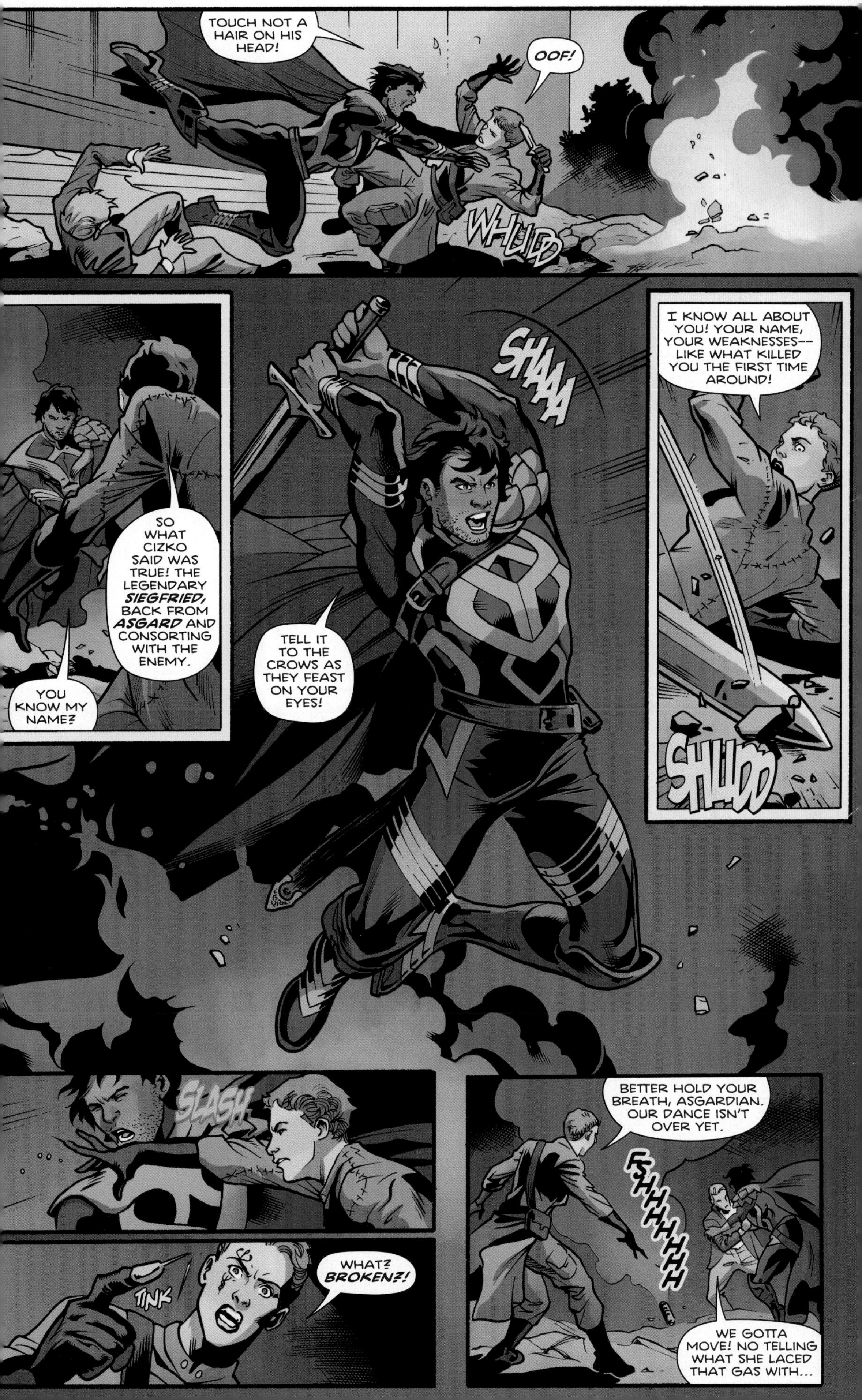
TOUCH NOT A HAIR ON HIS HEAD!
OOF!
WHUDD
SO WHAT CIZKO SAID WAS TRUE! THE LEGENDARY SIEGFRIED, BACK FROM ASGARD AND CONSORTING WITH THE ENEMY.
YOU KNOW MY NAME?
SHAAA
TELL IT TO THE CROWS AS THEY FEAST ON YOUR EYES!
I KNOW ALL ABOUT YOU! YOUR NAME, YOUR WEAKNESSES-- LIKE WHAT KILLED YOU THE FIRST TIME AROUND!
SHUDD
SLASH
TINK
WHAT? BROKEN?!
BETTER HOLD YOUR BREATH, ASGARDIAN. OUR DANCE ISN'T OVER YET.
FSHHHHHH
WE GOTTA MOVE! NO TELLING WHAT SHE LACED THAT GAS WITH...

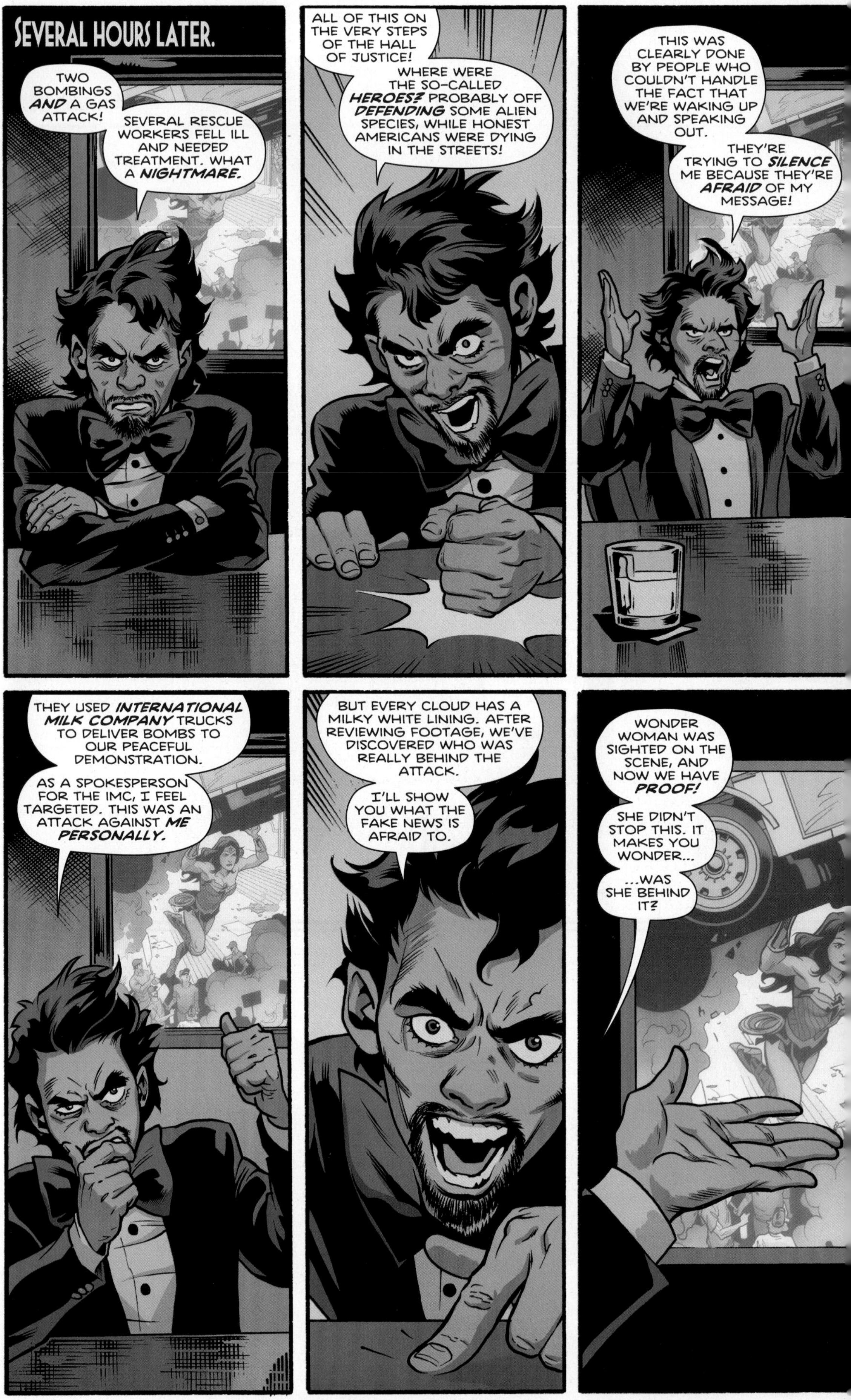
SEVERAL HOURS LATER.
TWO BOMBINGS AND A GAS ATTACK!
SEVERAL RESCUE WORKERS FELL ILL AND NEEDED TREATMENT. WHAT A NIGHTMARE.
ALL OF THIS ON THE VERY STEPS OF THE HALL OF JUSTICE!
WHERE WERE THE SO-CALLED HEROES? PROBABLY OFF DEFENDING SOME ALIEN SPECIES, WHILE HONEST AMERICANS WERE DYING IN THE STREETS!
THIS WAS CLEARLY DONE BY PEOPLE WHO COULDN'T HANDLE THE FACT THAT WE'RE WAKING UP AND SPEAKING OUT.
THEY'RE TRYING TO SILENCE ME BECAUSE THEY'RE AFRAID OF MY MESSAGE!
THEY USED INTERNATIONAL MILK COMPANY TRUCKS TO DELIVER BOMBS TO OUR PEACEFUL DEMONSTRATION.
AS A SPOKESPERSON FOR THE IMC, I FEEL TARGETED. THIS WAS AN ATTACK AGAINST ME PERSONALLY.
BUT EVERY CLOUD HAS A MILKY WHITE LINING. AFTER REVIEWING FOOTAGE, WE'VE DISCOVERED WHO WAS REALLY BEHIND THE ATTACK.
I'LL SHOW YOU WHAT THE FAKE NEWS IS AFRAID TO.
WONDER WOMAN WAS SIGHTED ON THE SCENE, AND NOW WE HAVE PROOF!
SHE DIDN'T STOP THIS. IT MAKES YOU WONDER...
...WAS SHE BEHIND IT?

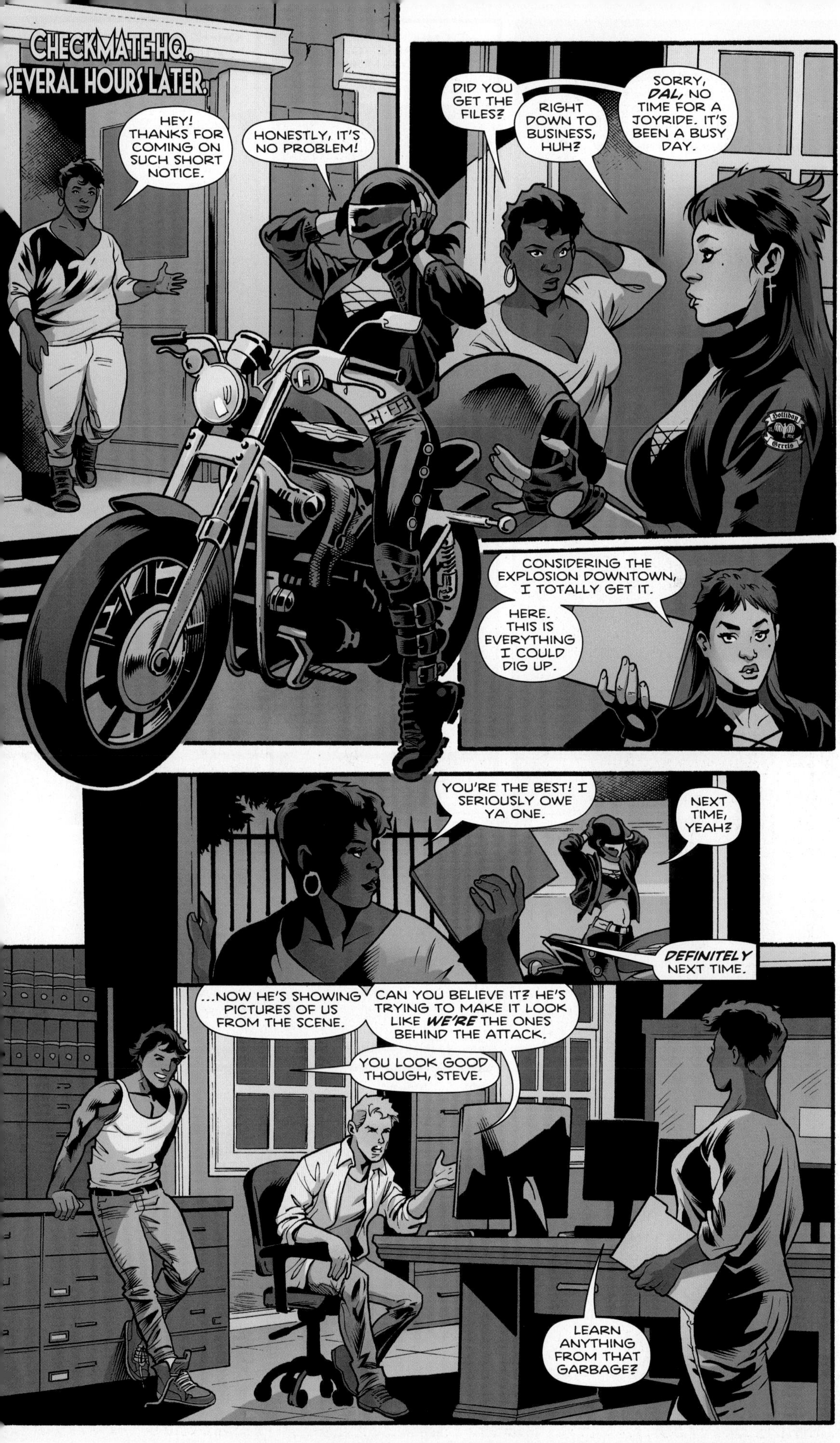
CHECKMATE HQ. SEVERAL HOURS LATER.
HEY! THANKS FOR COMING ON SUCH SHORT NOTICE.
HONESTLY, IT'S NO PROBLEM!
DID YOU GET THE FILES?
RIGHT DOWN TO BUSINESS, HUH?
SORRY, DAL, NO TIME FOR A JOYRIDE. IT'S BEEN A BUSY DAY.
CONSIDERING THE EXPLOSION DOWNTOWN, I TOTALLY GET IT.
HERE. THIS IS EVERYTHING I COULD DIG UP.
YOU'RE THE BEST! I SERIOUSLY OWE YA ONE.
NEXT TIME, YEAH?
DEFINITELY NEXT TIME.
...NOW HE'S SHOWING PICTURES OF US FROM THE SCENE.
CAN YOU BELIEVE IT? HE'S TRYING TO MAKE IT LOOK LIKE WE'RE THE ONES BEHIND THE ATTACK.
YOU LOOK GOOD THOUGH, STEVE.
LEARN ANYTHING FROM THAT GARBAGE?

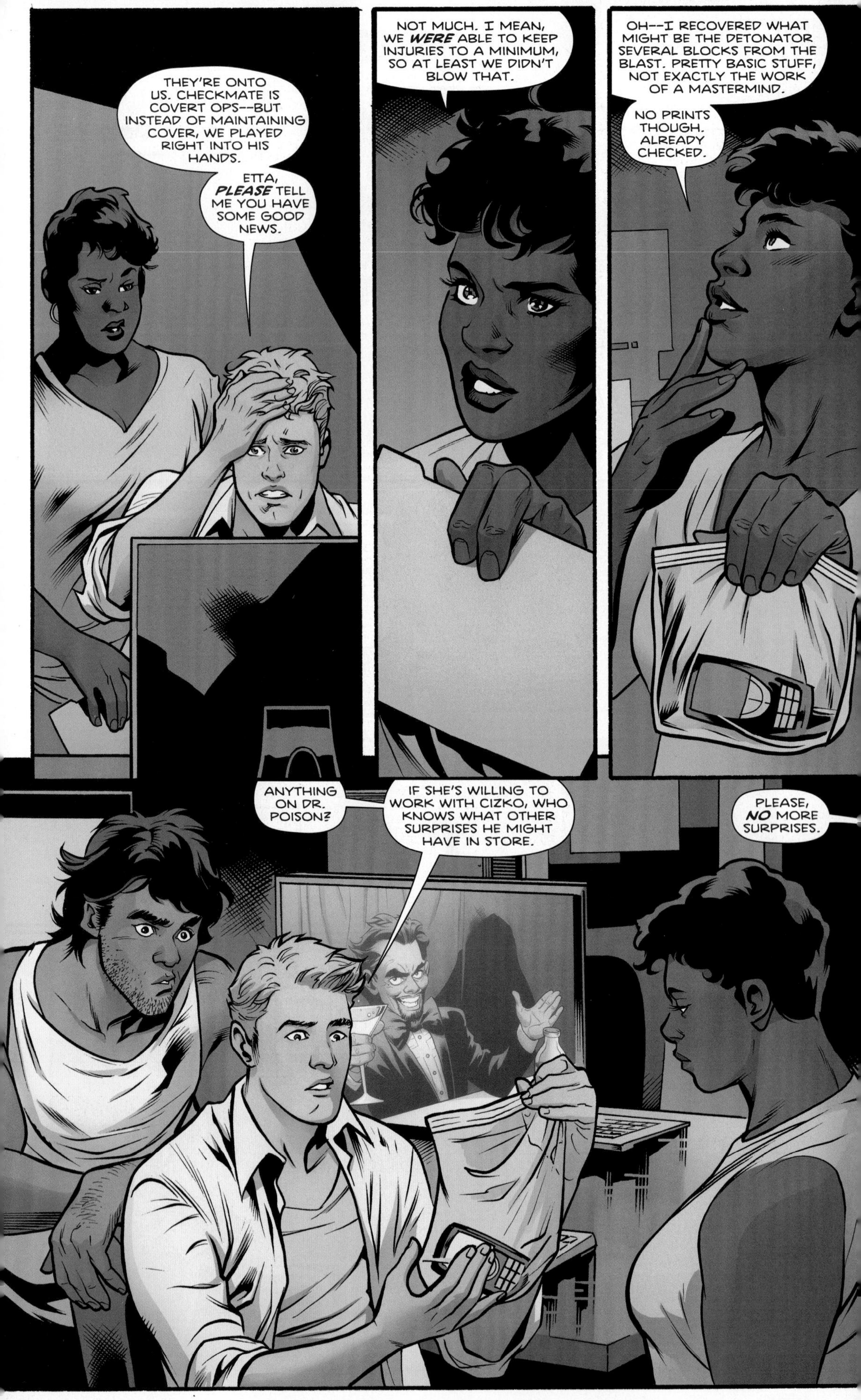
THEY'RE ONTO US. CHECKMATE IS COVERT OPS--BUT INSTEAD OF MAINTAINING COVER, WE PLAYED RIGHT INTO HIS HANDS.
ETTA, PLEASE TELL ME YOU HAVE SOME GOOD NEWS.
NOT MUCH. I MEAN, WE WERE ABLE TO KEEP INJURIES TO A MINIMUM, SO AT LEAST WE DIDN'T BLOW THAT.
OH--I RECOVERED WHAT MIGHT BE THE DETONATOR SEVERAL BLOCKS FROM THE BLAST. PRETTY BASIC STUFF, NOT EXACTLY THE WORK OF A MASTERMIND.
NO PRINTS THOUGH. ALREADY CHECKED.
ANYTHING ON DR. POISON?
IF SHE'S WILLING TO WORK WITH CIZKO, WHO KNOWS WHAT OTHER SURPRISES HE MIGHT HAVE IN STORE.
PLEASE, NO MORE SURPRISES.

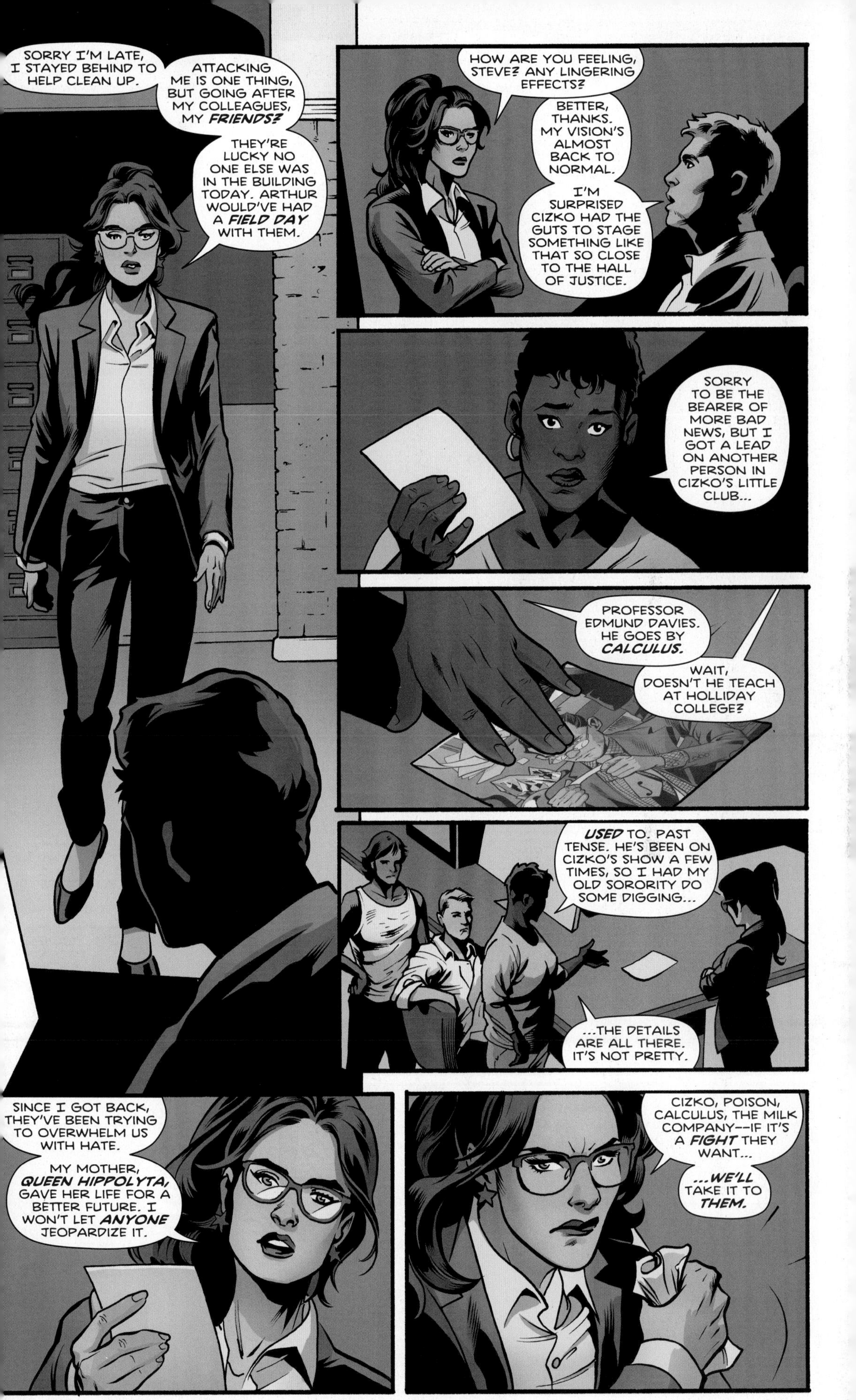
SORRY I'M LATE, I STAYED BEHIND TO HELP CLEAN UP.
ATTACKING ME IS ONE THING, BUT GOING AFTER MY COLLEAGUES, MY *FRIENDS?*
THEY'RE LUCKY NO ONE ELSE WAS IN THE BUILDING TODAY. ARTHUR WOULD'VE HAD A *FIELD DAY* WITH THEM.
HOW ARE YOU FEELING, STEVE? ANY LINGERING EFFECTS?
BETTER, THANKS. MY VISION'S ALMOST BACK TO NORMAL.
I'M SURPRISED CIZKO HAD THE GUTS TO STAGE SOMETHING LIKE THAT SO CLOSE TO THE HALL OF JUSTICE.
SORRY TO BE THE BEARER OF MORE BAD NEWS, BUT I GOT A LEAD ON ANOTHER PERSON IN CIZKO'S LITTLE CLUB...
PROFESSOR EDMUND DAVIES. HE GOES BY *CALCULUS.*
WAIT, DOESN'T HE TEACH AT HOLLIDAY COLLEGE?
USED TO. PAST TENSE. HE'S BEEN ON CIZKO'S SHOW A FEW TIMES, SO I HAD MY OLD SORORITY DO SOME DIGGING...
...THE DETAILS ARE ALL THERE. IT'S NOT PRETTY.
SINCE I GOT BACK, THEY'VE BEEN TRYING TO OVERWHELM US WITH HATE.
MY MOTHER, *QUEEN HIPPOLYTA,* GAVE HER LIFE FOR A BETTER FUTURE. I WON'T LET *ANYONE* JEOPARDIZE IT.
CIZKO, POISON, CALCULUS, THE MILK COMPANY--IF IT'S A *FIGHT* THEY WANT...
...WE'LL TAKE IT TO *THEM.*

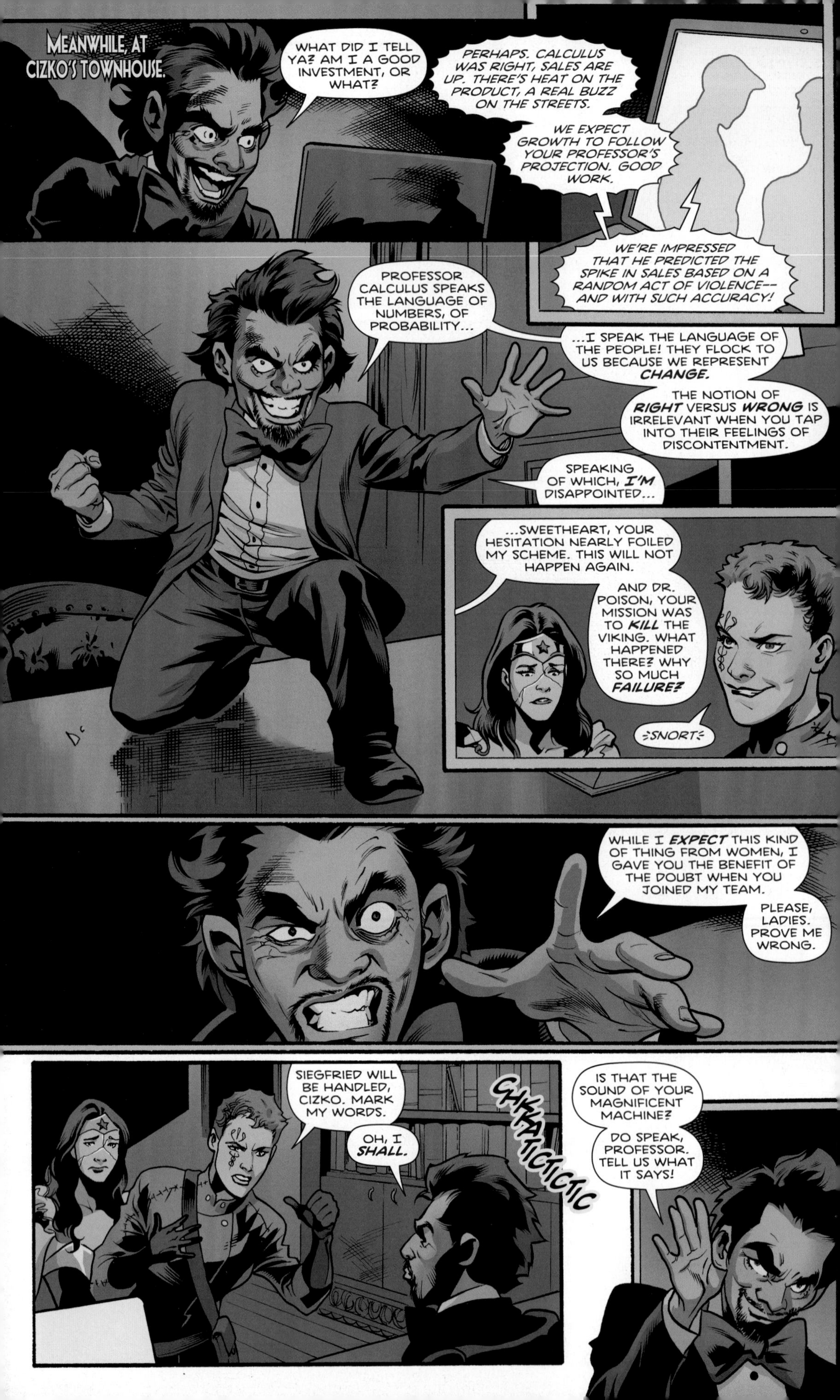
MEANWHILE, AT CIZKO'S TOWNHOUSE.
WHAT DID I TELL YA? AM I A GOOD INVESTMENT, OR WHAT?
PERHAPS. CALCULUS WAS RIGHT, SALES ARE UP. THERE'S HEAT ON THE PRODUCT, A REAL BUZZ ON THE STREETS.
WE EXPECT GROWTH TO FOLLOW YOUR PROFESSOR'S PROJECTION. GOOD WORK.
WE'RE IMPRESSED THAT HE PREDICTED THE SPIKE IN SALES BASED ON A RANDOM ACT OF VIOLENCE-- AND WITH SUCH ACCURACY!
PROFESSOR CALCULUS SPEAKS THE LANGUAGE OF NUMBERS, OF PROBABILITY...
...I SPEAK THE LANGUAGE OF THE PEOPLE! THEY FLOCK TO US BECAUSE WE REPRESENT CHANGE.
THE NOTION OF RIGHT VERSUS WRONG IS IRRELEVANT WHEN YOU TAP INTO THEIR FEELINGS OF DISCONTENTMENT.
SPEAKING OF WHICH, I'M DISAPPOINTED...
...SWEETHEART, YOUR HESITATION NEARLY FOILED MY SCHEME. THIS WILL NOT HAPPEN AGAIN.
AND DR. POISON, YOUR MISSION WAS TO KILL THE VIKING. WHAT HAPPENED THERE? WHY SO MUCH FAILURE?
SNORT
WHILE I EXPECT THIS KIND OF THING FROM WOMEN, I GAVE YOU THE BENEFIT OF THE DOUBT WHEN YOU JOINED MY TEAM.
PLEASE, LADIES. PROVE ME WRONG.
SIEGFRIED WILL BE HANDLED, CIZKO. MARK MY WORDS.
OH, I SHALL.
CHKATICTICTIC
IS THAT THE SOUND OF YOUR MAGNIFICENT MACHINE?
DO SPEAK, PROFESSOR. TELL US WHAT IT SAYS!

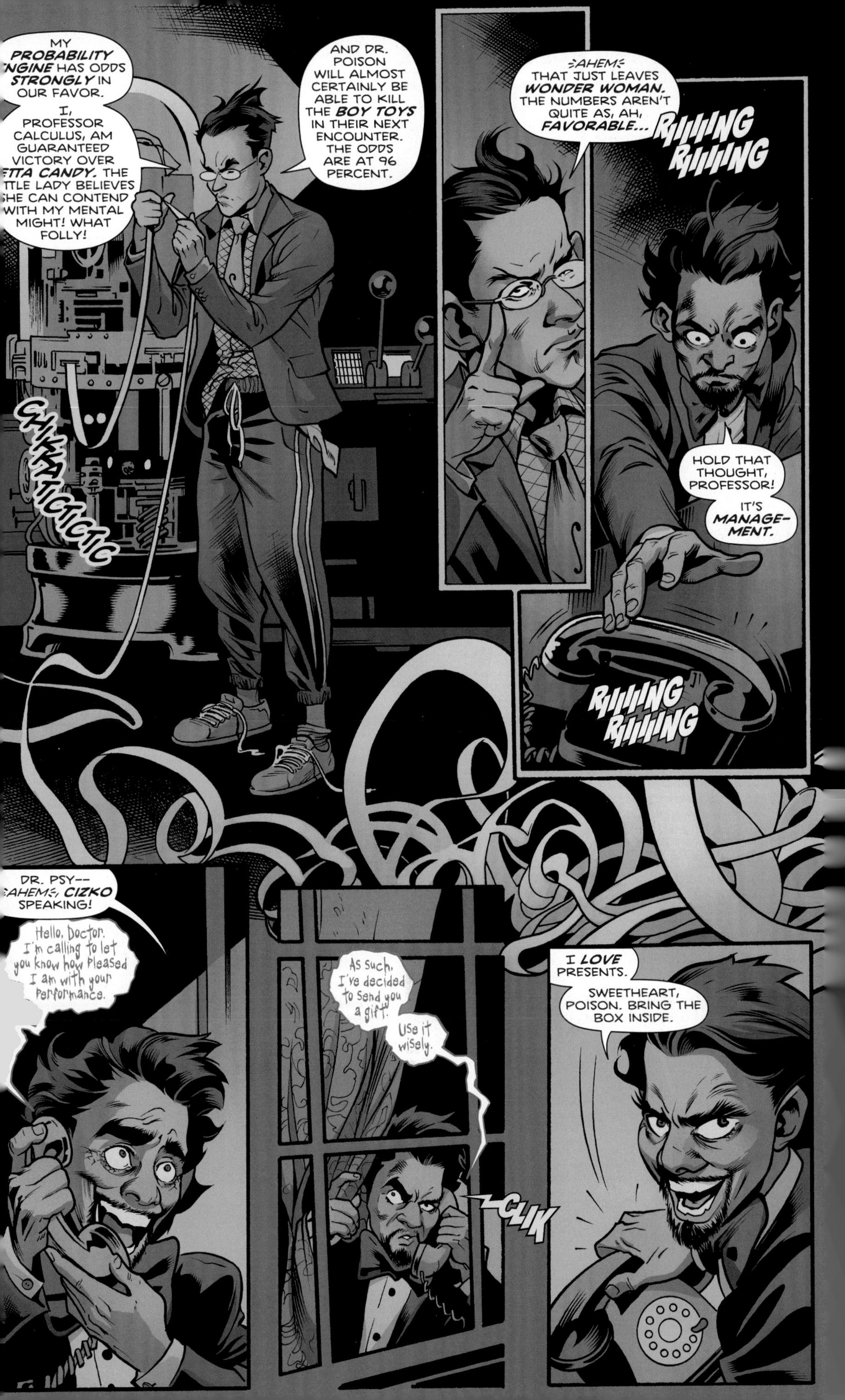
MY PROBABILITY ENGINE HAS ODDS STRONGLY IN OUR FAVOR.
I, PROFESSOR CALCULUS, AM GUARANTEED VICTORY OVER ETTA CANDY. THE LITTLE LADY BELIEVES SHE CAN CONTEND WITH MY MENTAL MIGHT! WHAT FOLLY!
AND DR. POISON WILL ALMOST CERTAINLY BE ABLE TO KILL THE BOY TOYS IN THEIR NEXT ENCOUNTER. THE ODDS ARE AT 96 PERCENT.
CHKKATICTICTIC
AHEM THAT JUST LEAVES WONDER WOMAN. THE NUMBERS AREN'T QUITE AS, AH, FAVORABLE...
RIIIING RIIIING
HOLD THAT THOUGHT, PROFESSOR!
IT'S MANAGE-MENT.
RIIIING RIIIING
DR. PSY-- AHEM, CIZKO SPEAKING!
Hello, Doctor. I'm calling to let you know how pleased I am with your performance.
As such, I've decided to send you a gift.
Use it wisely.
CLIK
I LOVE PRESENTS.
SWEETHEART, POISON. BRING THE BOX INSIDE.

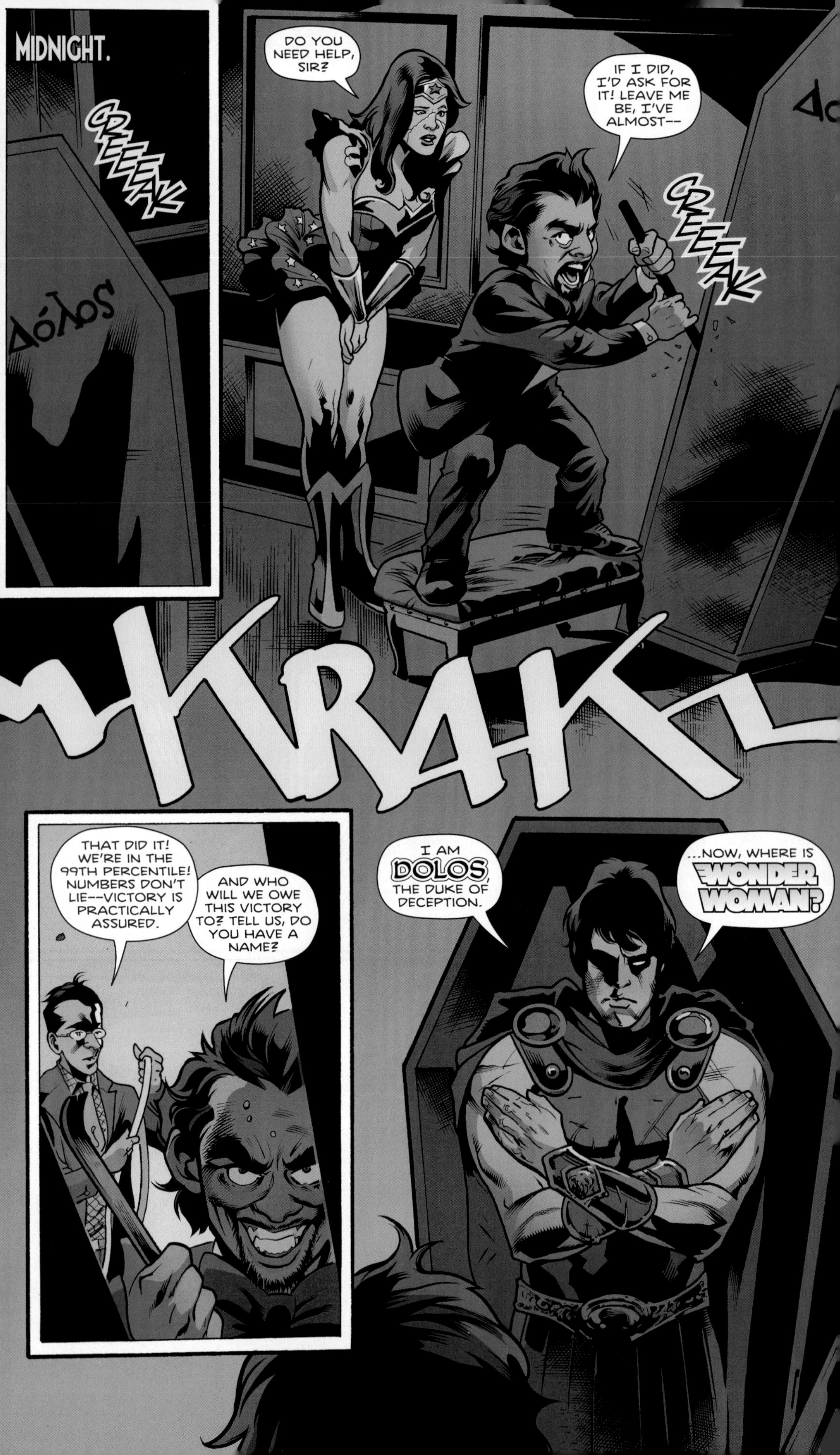
MIDNIGHT.
CREEEAK
Δόλος
DO YOU NEED HELP, SIR?
IF I DID, I'D ASK FOR IT! LEAVE ME BE, I'VE ALMOST--
CREEEAK
Δο
KRAK
THAT DID IT! WE'RE IN THE 99TH PERCENTILE! NUMBERS DON'T LIE--VICTORY IS PRACTICALLY ASSURED.
AND WHO WILL WE OWE THIS VICTORY TO? TELL US, DO YOU HAVE A NAME?
I AM DOLOS, THE DUKE OF DECEPTION.
...NOW, WHERE IS WONDER WOMAN?

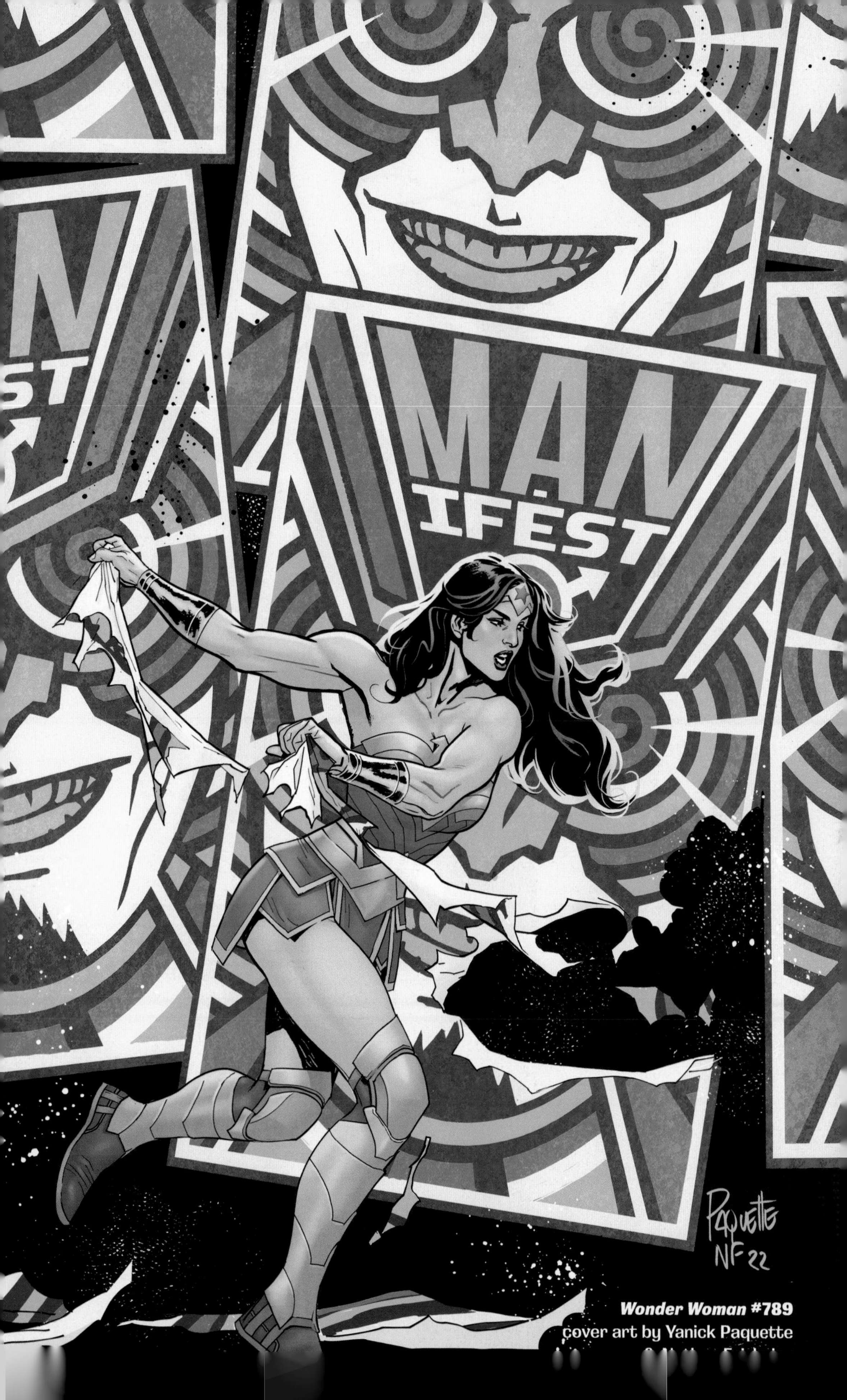
MAN
IFÉST

***Wonder Woman* #789**
cover art by Yanick Paquette

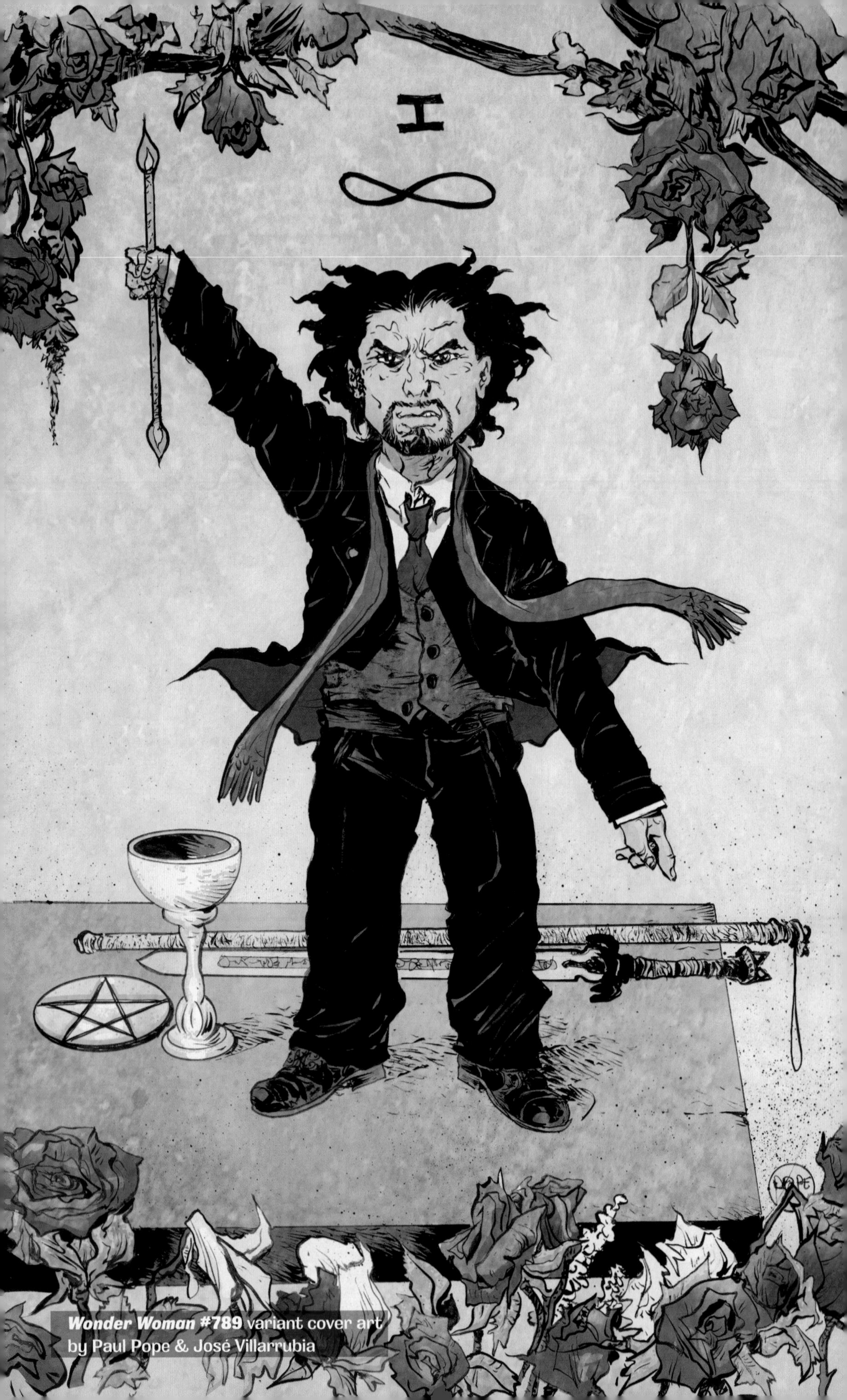
I

***Wonder Woman* #789** variant cover art
by Paul Pope & José Villarrubia

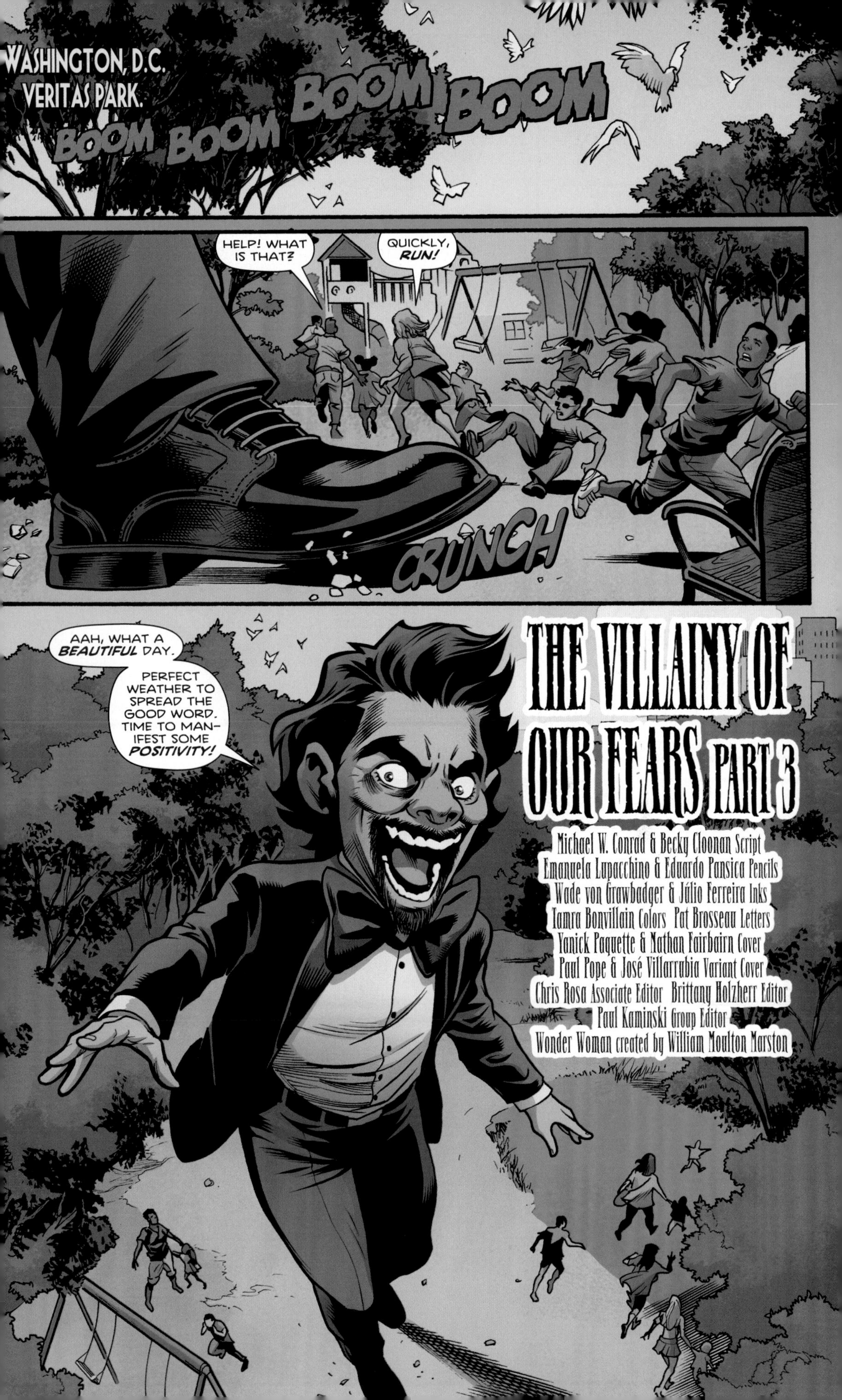
WASHINGTON, D.C. VERITAS PARK.
BOOM BOOM BOOM BOOM
HELP! WHAT IS THAT?
QUICKLY, RUN!
CRUNCH
AAH, WHAT A BEAUTIFUL DAY.
PERFECT WEATHER TO SPREAD THE GOOD WORD. TIME TO MANIFEST SOME POSITIVITY!
THE VILLAINY OF OUR FEARS PART 3
Michael W. Conrad & Becky Cloonan Script
Emanuela Lupacchino & Eduardo Pansica Pencils
Wade von Grawbadger & Júlio Ferreira Inks
Tamra Bonvillain Colors Pat Brosseau Letters
Yanick Paquette & Nathan Fairbairn Cover
Paul Pope & José Villarrubia Variant Cover
Chris Rosa Associate Editor Brittany Holzherr Editor
Paul Kaminski Group Editor
Wonder Woman created by William Moulton Marston

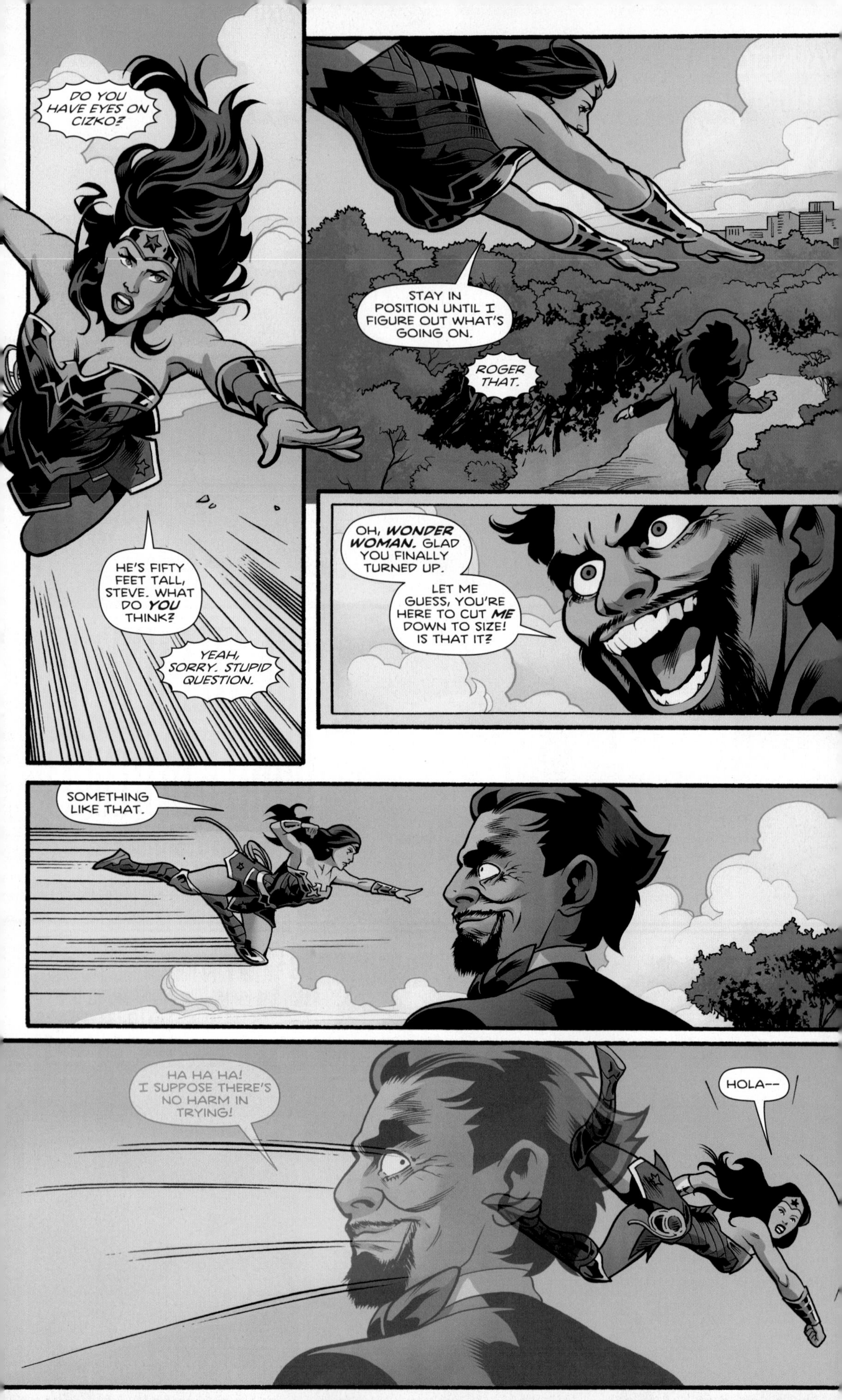
DO YOU HAVE EYES ON CIZKO?
HE'S FIFTY FEET TALL, STEVE. WHAT DO YOU THINK?
YEAH, SORRY. STUPID QUESTION.
STAY IN POSITION UNTIL I FIGURE OUT WHAT'S GOING ON.
ROGER THAT.
OH, WONDER WOMAN. GLAD YOU FINALLY TURNED UP.
LET ME GUESS, YOU'RE HERE TO CUT ME DOWN TO SIZE! IS THAT IT?
SOMETHING LIKE THAT.
HA HA HA! I SUPPOSE THERE'S NO HARM IN TRYING!
HOLA--

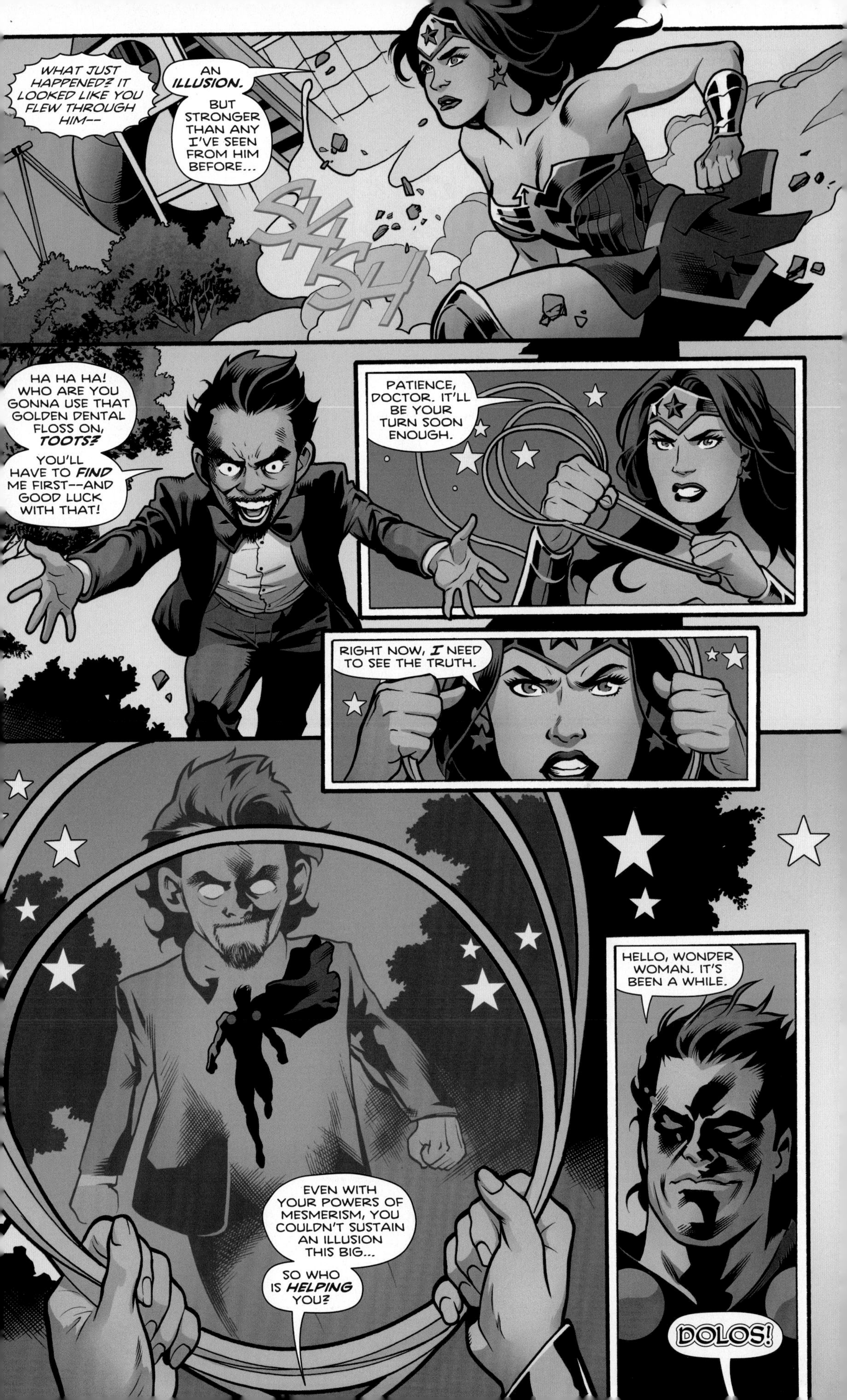
WHAT JUST HAPPENED? IT LOOKED LIKE YOU FLEW THROUGH HIM--
AN *ILLUSION.*
BUT STRONGER THAN ANY I'VE SEEN FROM HIM BEFORE...
SHASH
HA HA HA! WHO ARE YOU GONNA USE THAT GOLDEN DENTAL FLOSS ON, *TOOTS?*
YOU'LL HAVE TO *FIND* ME FIRST--AND GOOD LUCK WITH THAT!
PATIENCE, DOCTOR. IT'LL BE YOUR TURN SOON ENOUGH.
RIGHT NOW, *I* NEED TO SEE THE TRUTH.
EVEN WITH YOUR POWERS OF MESMERISM, YOU COULDN'T SUSTAIN AN ILLUSION THIS BIG...
SO WHO IS *HELPING* YOU?
HELLO, WONDER WOMAN. IT'S BEEN A WHILE.
DOLOS!

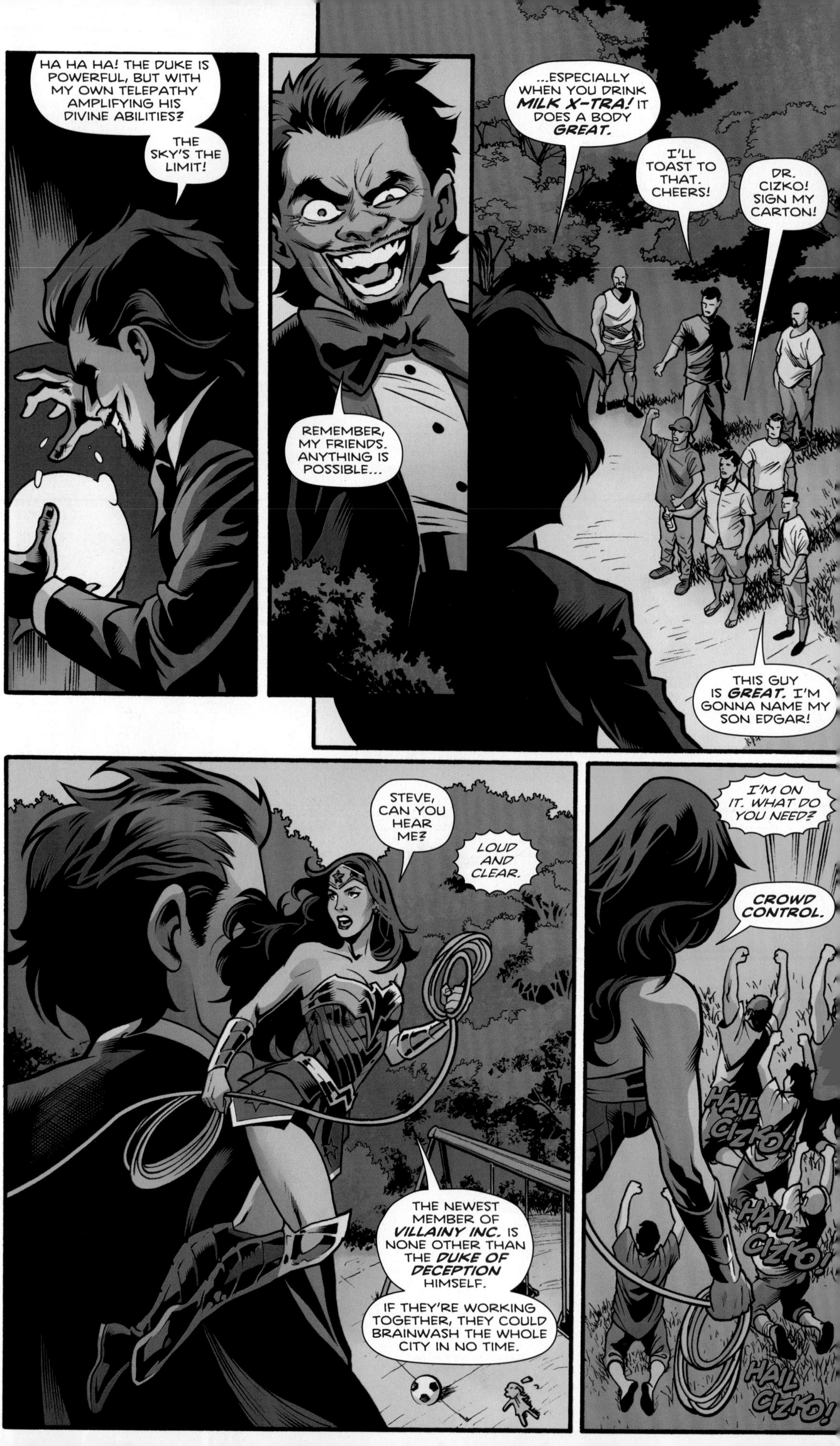
HA HA HA! THE DUKE IS POWERFUL, BUT WITH MY OWN TELEPATHY AMPLIFYING HIS DIVINE ABILITIES?
THE SKY'S THE LIMIT!
REMEMBER, MY FRIENDS. ANYTHING IS POSSIBLE...
...ESPECIALLY WHEN YOU DRINK MILK X-TRA! IT DOES A BODY GREAT.
I'LL TOAST TO THAT. CHEERS!
DR. CIZKO! SIGN MY CARTON!
THIS GUY IS GREAT. I'M GONNA NAME MY SON EDGAR!
STEVE, CAN YOU HEAR ME?
LOUD AND CLEAR.
THE NEWEST MEMBER OF VILLAINY INC. IS NONE OTHER THAN THE DUKE OF DECEPTION HIMSELF.
IF THEY'RE WORKING TOGETHER, THEY COULD BRAINWASH THE WHOLE CITY IN NO TIME.
I'M ON IT. WHAT DO YOU NEED?
CROWD CONTROL.
HAIL CIZKO!
HAIL CIZKO!
HAIL CIZKO!

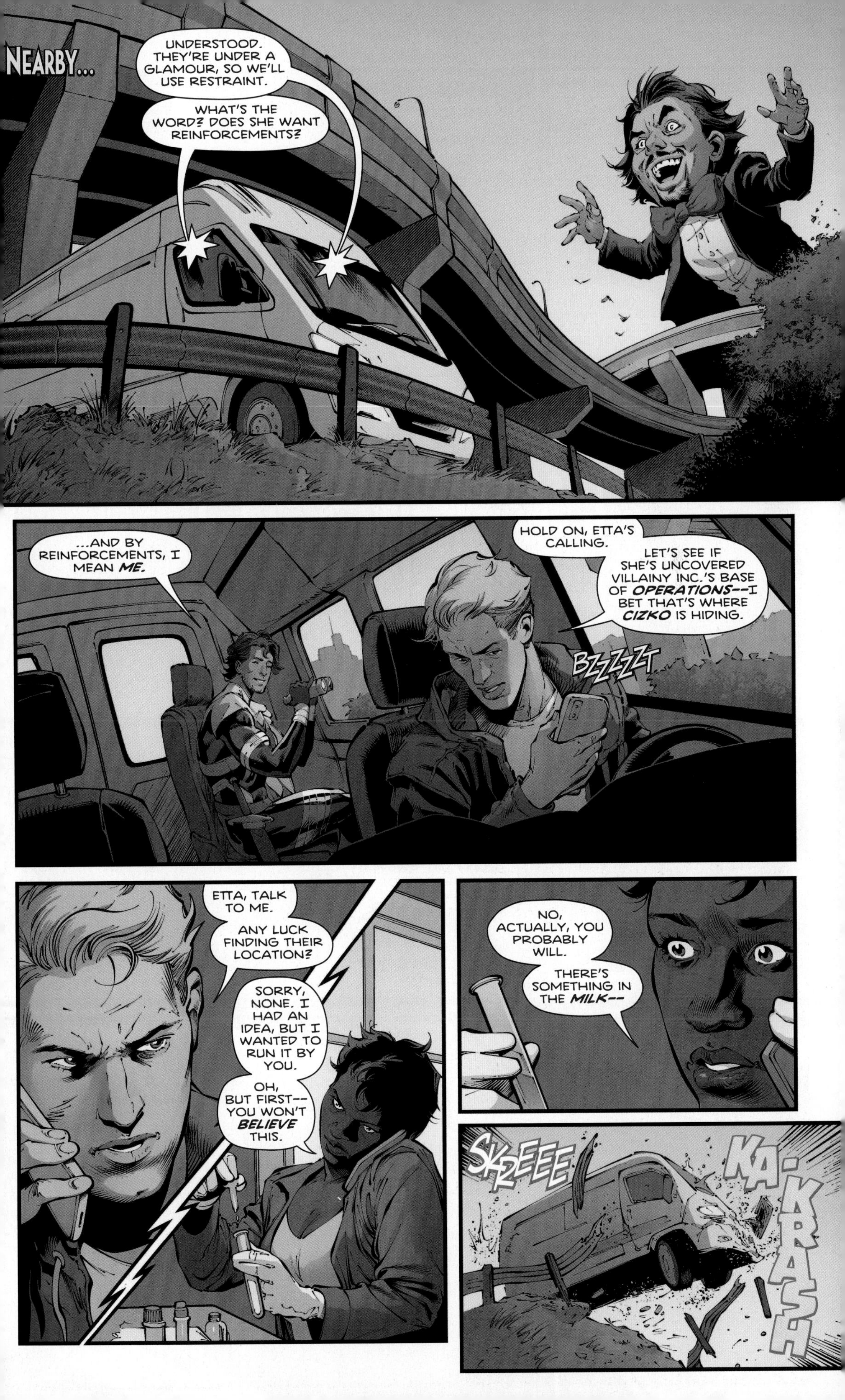
NEARBY...
UNDERSTOOD. THEY'RE UNDER A GLAMOUR, SO WE'LL USE RESTRAINT.
WHAT'S THE WORD? DOES SHE WANT REINFORCEMENTS?
...AND BY REINFORCEMENTS, I MEAN ME.
HOLD ON, ETTA'S CALLING.
LET'S SEE IF SHE'S UNCOVERED VILLAINY INC.'S BASE OF OPERATIONS--I BET THAT'S WHERE CIZKO IS HIDING.
BZZZZZT
ETTA, TALK TO ME.
ANY LUCK FINDING THEIR LOCATION?
SORRY, NONE. I HAD AN IDEA, BUT I WANTED TO RUN IT BY YOU.
OH, BUT FIRST-- YOU WON'T BELIEVE THIS.
NO, ACTUALLY, YOU PROBABLY WILL.
THERE'S SOMETHING IN THE MILK--
SKREEEE
KA-KRASH

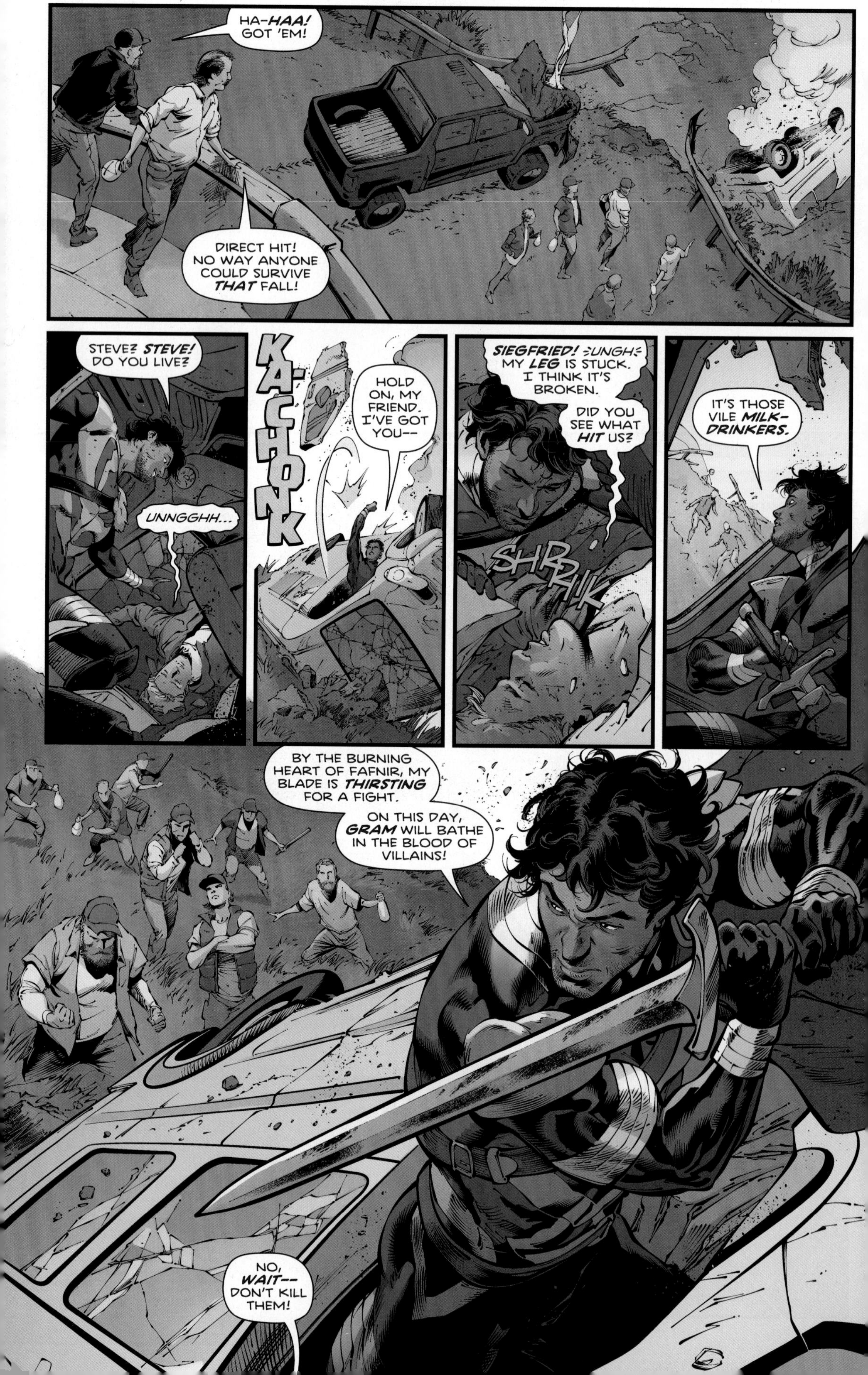
HA-HAA! GOT 'EM!
DIRECT HIT! NO WAY ANYONE COULD SURVIVE THAT FALL!
STEVE? STEVE! DO YOU LIVE?
UNNGGHH...
KA-CHONK
HOLD ON, MY FRIEND. I'VE GOT YOU--
SIEGFRIED! UNGH MY LEG IS STUCK. I THINK IT'S BROKEN.
DID YOU SEE WHAT HIT US?
SHRRIIK
IT'S THOSE VILE MILK-DRINKERS.
BY THE BURNING HEART OF FAFNIR, MY BLADE IS THIRSTING FOR A FIGHT.
ON THIS DAY, GRAM WILL BATHE IN THE BLOOD OF VILLAINS!
NO, WAIT-- DON'T KILL THEM!

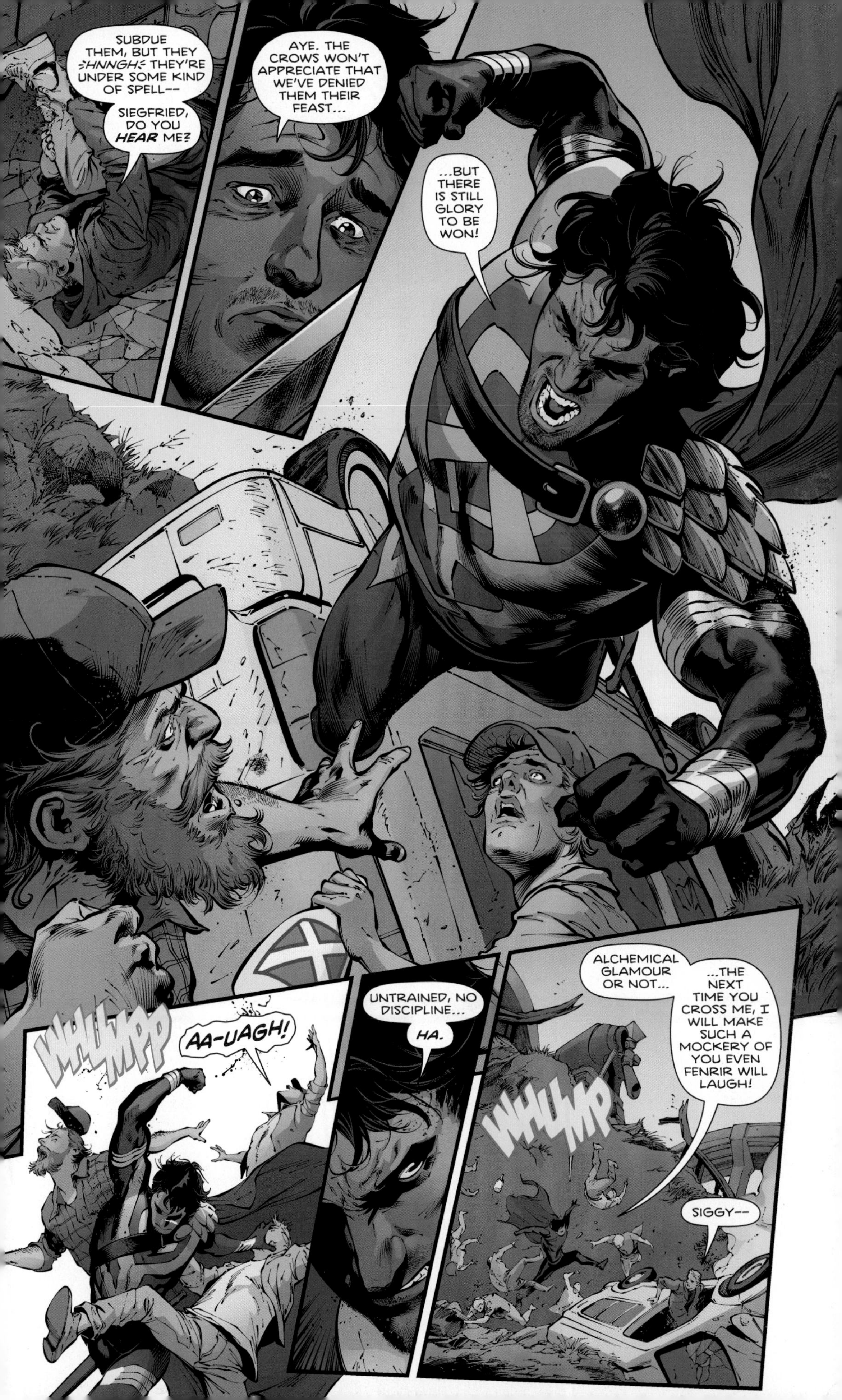
SUBDUE THEM, BUT THEY *HNNGH* THEY'RE UNDER SOME KIND OF SPELL--
SIEGFRIED, DO YOU **HEAR** ME?
AYE. THE CROWS WON'T APPRECIATE THAT WE'VE DENIED THEM THEIR FEAST...
...BUT THERE IS STILL GLORY TO BE WON!
WHUMPP
AA-UAGH!
UNTRAINED, NO DISCIPLINE...
HA.
ALCHEMICAL GLAMOUR OR NOT...
...THE NEXT TIME YOU CROSS ME, I WILL MAKE SUCH A MOCKERY OF YOU EVEN FENRIR WILL LAUGH!
WHUMP
SIGGY--

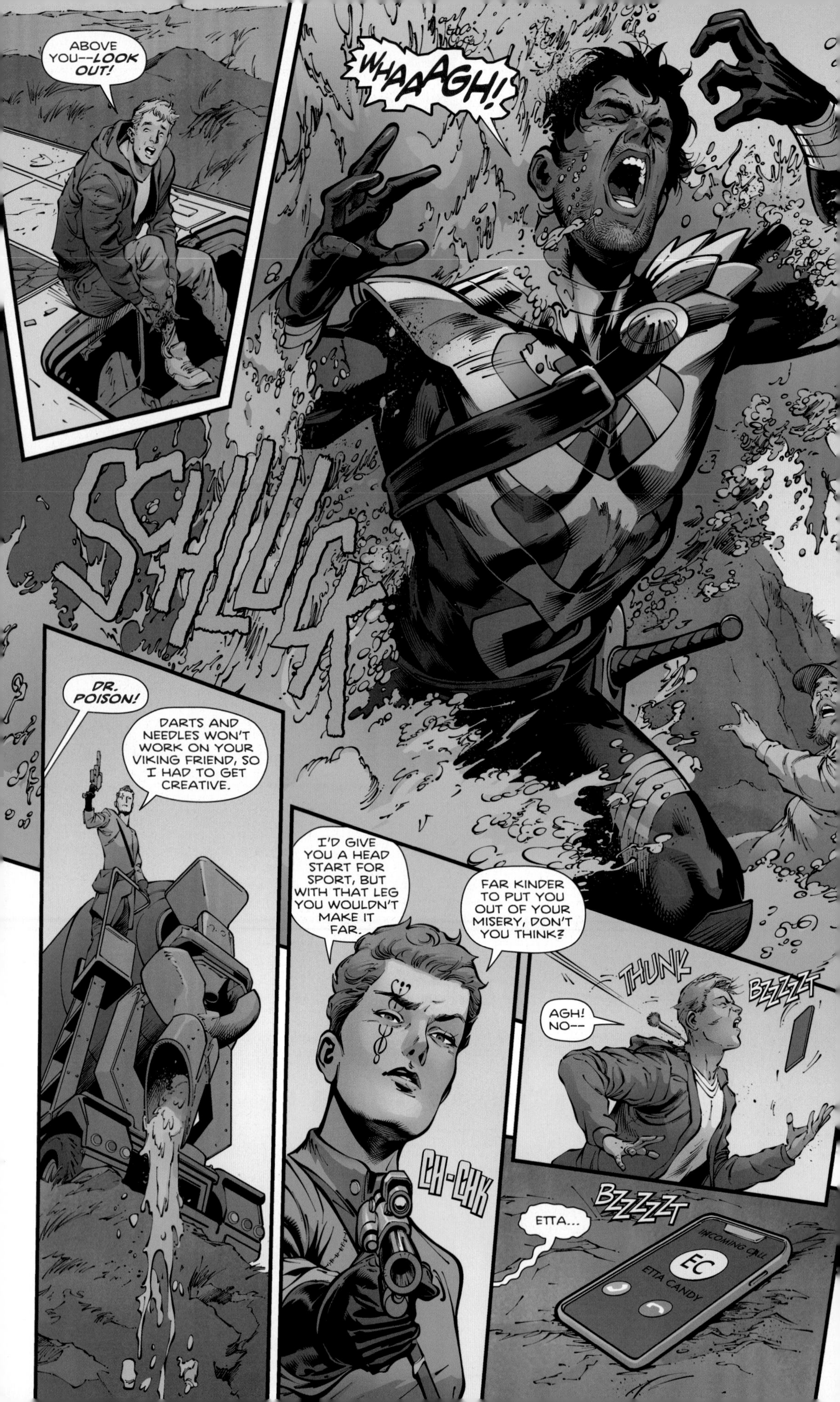
ABOVE YOU--LOOK OUT!
WHAAAGH!
SCHLUK
DR. POISON!
DARTS AND NEEDLES WON'T WORK ON YOUR VIKING FRIEND, SO I HAD TO GET CREATIVE.
I'D GIVE YOU A HEAD START FOR SPORT, BUT WITH THAT LEG YOU WOULDN'T MAKE IT FAR.
CH-CHK
FAR KINDER TO PUT YOU OUT OF YOUR MISERY, DON'T YOU THINK?
THUNK
BZZZZZT
AGH! NO--
BZZZZZT
ETTA...
INCOMING CALL
EC
ETTA CANDY

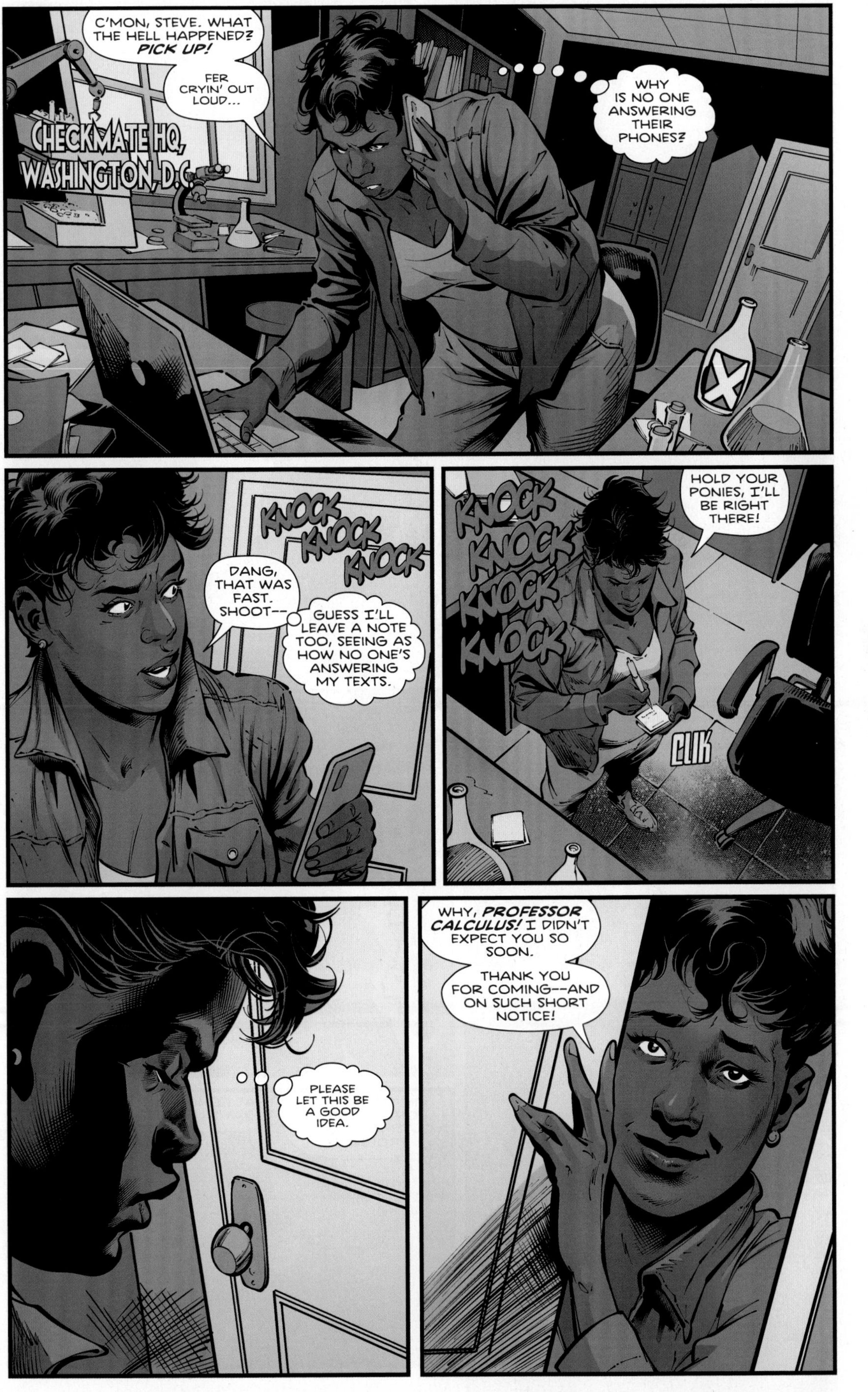
CHECKMATE HQ, WASHINGTON, D.C.
C'MON, STEVE. WHAT THE HELL HAPPENED? PICK UP!
FER CRYIN' OUT LOUD...
WHY IS NO ONE ANSWERING THEIR PHONES?
KNOCK KNOCK KNOCK
DANG, THAT WAS FAST. SHOOT--
GUESS I'LL LEAVE A NOTE TOO, SEEING AS HOW NO ONE'S ANSWERING MY TEXTS.
KNOCK KNOCK KNOCK KNOCK
HOLD YOUR PONIES, I'LL BE RIGHT THERE!
CLIK
PLEASE LET THIS BE A GOOD IDEA.
WHY, PROFESSOR CALCULUS! I DIDN'T EXPECT YOU SO SOON.
THANK YOU FOR COMING--AND ON SUCH SHORT NOTICE!

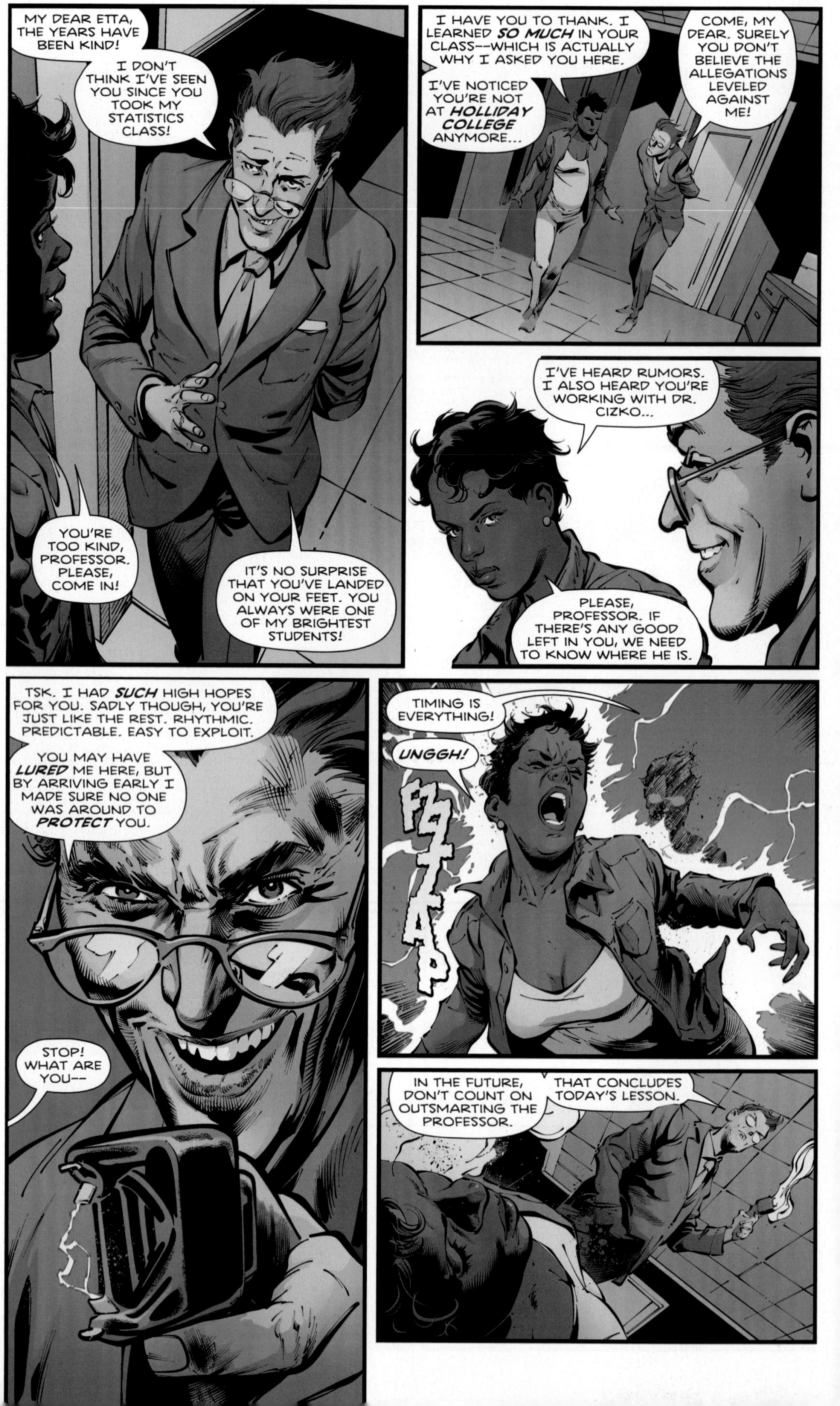
MY DEAR ETTA, THE YEARS HAVE BEEN KIND!
I DON'T THINK I'VE SEEN YOU SINCE YOU TOOK MY STATISTICS CLASS!
YOU'RE TOO KIND, PROFESSOR. PLEASE, COME IN!
IT'S NO SURPRISE THAT YOU'VE LANDED ON YOUR FEET. YOU ALWAYS WERE ONE OF MY BRIGHTEST STUDENTS!
I HAVE YOU TO THANK. I LEARNED SO MUCH IN YOUR CLASS--WHICH IS ACTUALLY WHY I ASKED YOU HERE.
I'VE NOTICED YOU'RE NOT AT HOLLIDAY COLLEGE ANYMORE...
COME, MY DEAR. SURELY YOU DON'T BELIEVE THE ALLEGATIONS LEVELED AGAINST ME!
I'VE HEARD RUMORS. I ALSO HEARD YOU'RE WORKING WITH DR. CIZKO...
PLEASE, PROFESSOR. IF THERE'S ANY GOOD LEFT IN YOU, WE NEED TO KNOW WHERE HE IS.
TSK. I HAD SUCH HIGH HOPES FOR YOU. SADLY THOUGH, YOU'RE JUST LIKE THE REST. RHYTHMIC. PREDICTABLE. EASY TO EXPLOIT.
YOU MAY HAVE LURED ME HERE, BUT BY ARRIVING EARLY I MADE SURE NO ONE WAS AROUND TO PROTECT YOU.
STOP! WHAT ARE YOU--
TIMING IS EVERYTHING!
UNGGH!
FZZZAP
IN THE FUTURE, DON'T COUNT ON OUTSMARTING THE PROFESSOR.
THAT CONCLUDES TODAY'S LESSON.

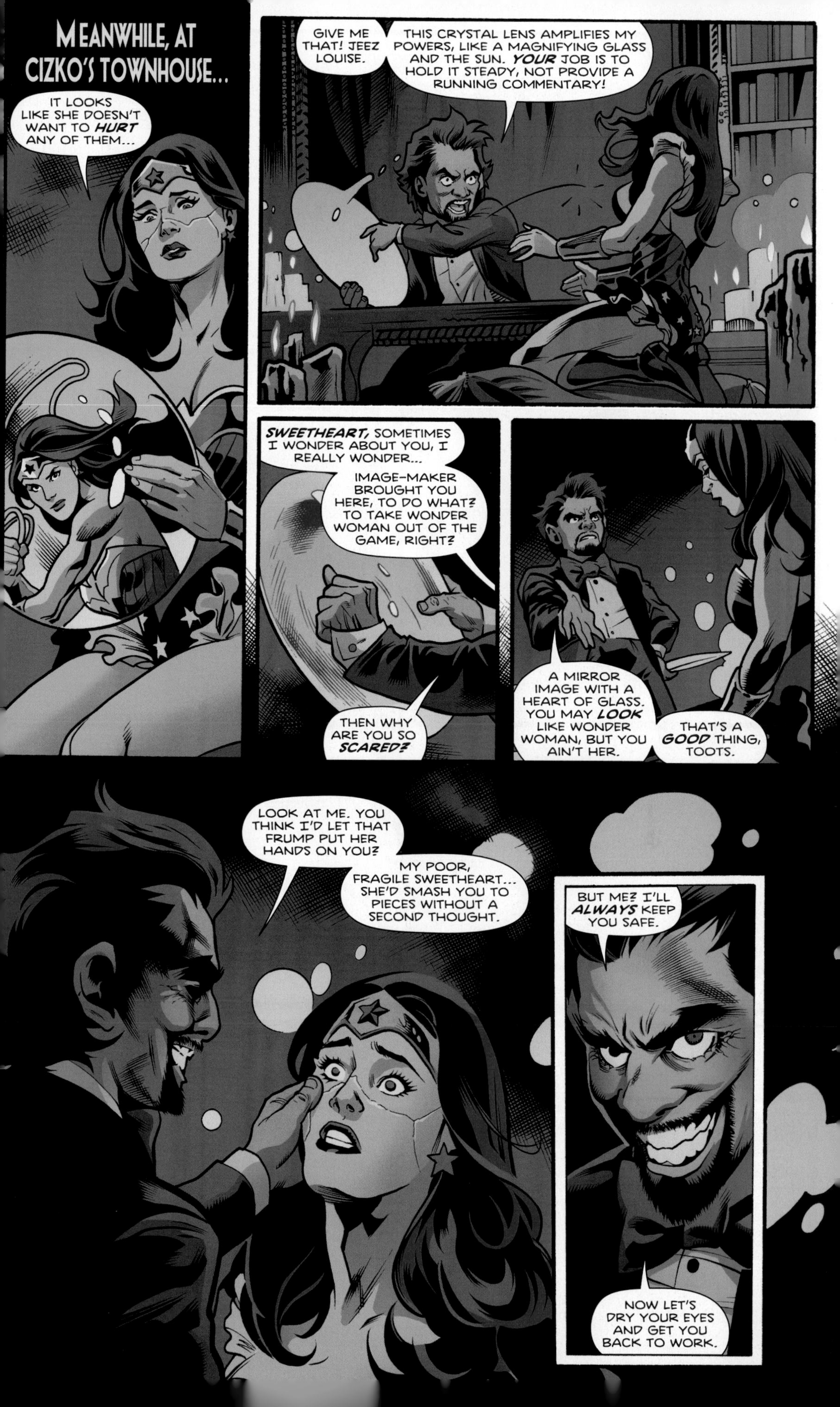
MEANWHILE, AT CIZKO'S TOWNHOUSE...
IT LOOKS LIKE SHE DOESN'T WANT TO HURT ANY OF THEM...
GIVE ME THAT! JEEZ LOUISE.
THIS CRYSTAL LENS AMPLIFIES MY POWERS, LIKE A MAGNIFYING GLASS AND THE SUN. YOUR JOB IS TO HOLD IT STEADY, NOT PROVIDE A RUNNING COMMENTARY!
SWEETHEART, SOMETIMES I WONDER ABOUT YOU, I REALLY WONDER...
IMAGE-MAKER BROUGHT YOU HERE, TO DO WHAT? TO TAKE WONDER WOMAN OUT OF THE GAME, RIGHT?
THEN WHY ARE YOU SO SCARED?
A MIRROR IMAGE WITH A HEART OF GLASS. YOU MAY LOOK LIKE WONDER WOMAN, BUT YOU AIN'T HER.
THAT'S A GOOD THING, TOOTS.
LOOK AT ME. YOU THINK I'D LET THAT FRUMP PUT HER HANDS ON YOU?
MY POOR, FRAGILE SWEETHEART... SHE'D SMASH YOU TO PIECES WITHOUT A SECOND THOUGHT.
BUT ME? I'LL ALWAYS KEEP YOU SAFE.
NOW LET'S DRY YOUR EYES AND GET YOU BACK TO WORK.

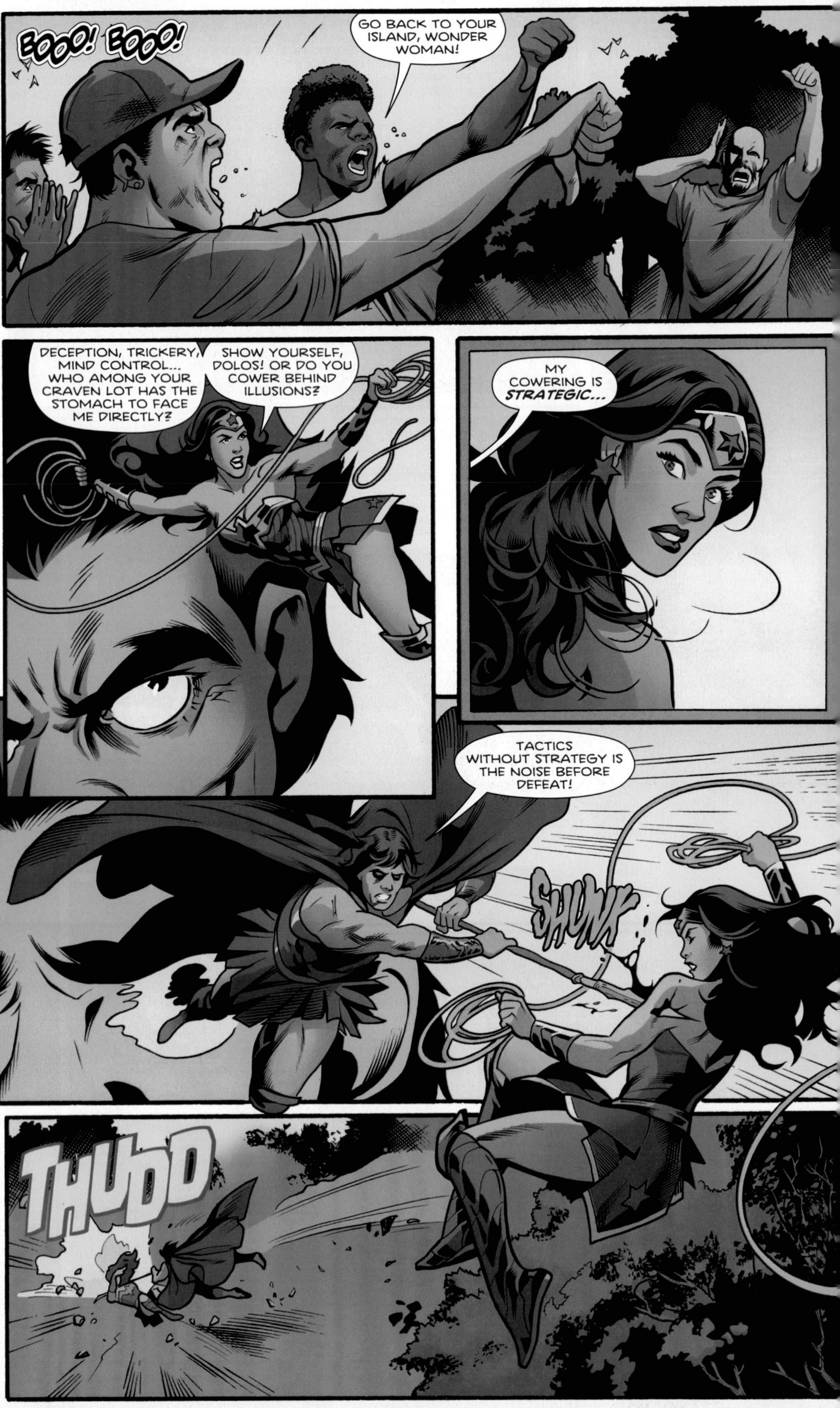
BOOO! BOOO!
GO BACK TO YOUR ISLAND, WONDER WOMAN!
DECEPTION, TRICKERY, MIND CONTROL... WHO AMONG YOUR CRAVEN LOT HAS THE STOMACH TO FACE ME DIRECTLY?
SHOW YOURSELF, DOLOS! OR DO YOU COWER BEHIND ILLUSIONS?
MY COWERING IS *STRATEGIC...*
TACTICS WITHOUT STRATEGY IS THE NOISE BEFORE DEFEAT!
SHUNK
THUDD

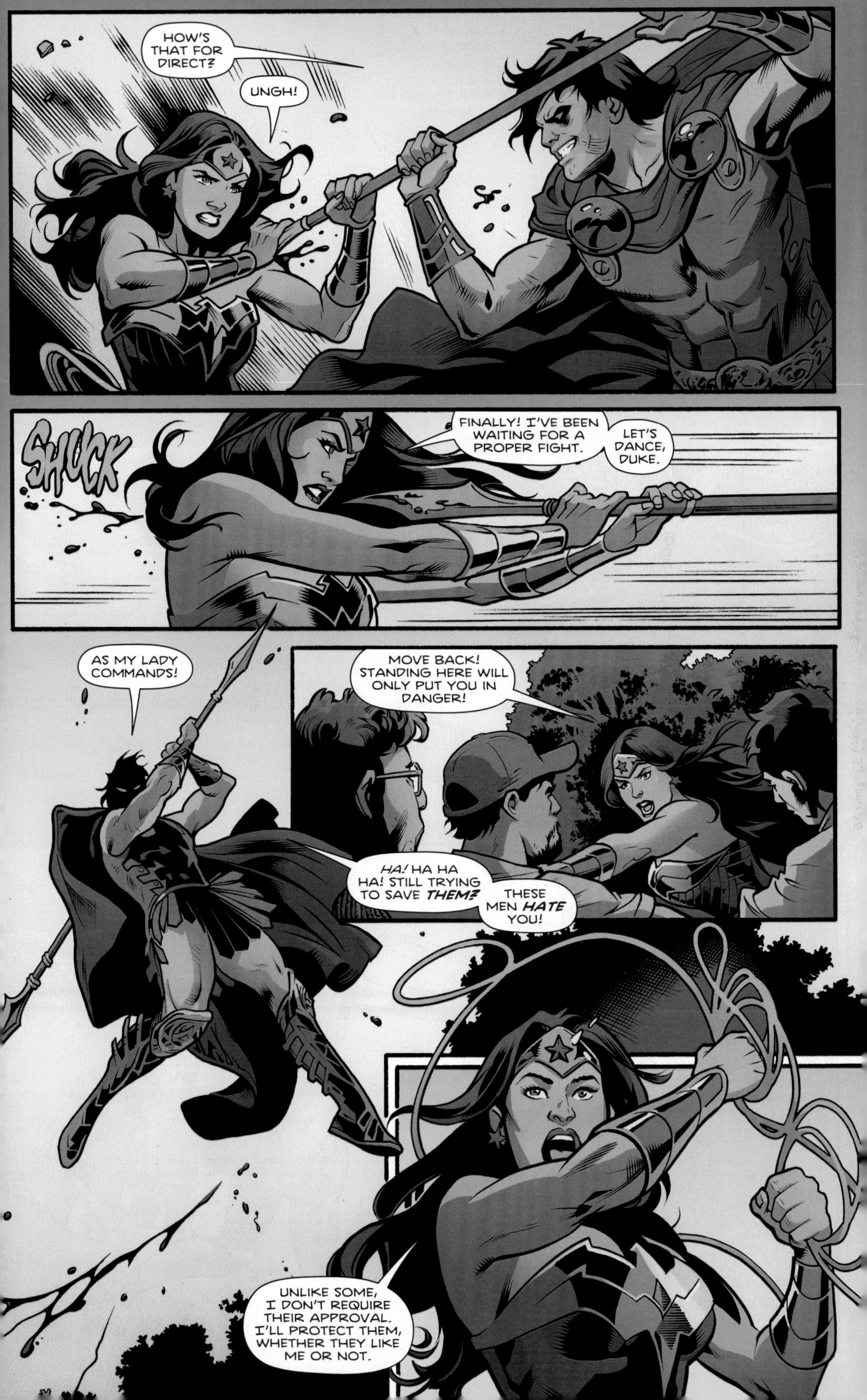
HOW'S THAT FOR DIRECT?
UNGH!
SHUCK
FINALLY! I'VE BEEN WAITING FOR A PROPER FIGHT.
LET'S DANCE, DUKE.
AS MY LADY COMMANDS!
MOVE BACK! STANDING HERE WILL ONLY PUT YOU IN DANGER!
HA! HA HA HA! STILL TRYING TO SAVE THEM?
THESE MEN HATE YOU!
UNLIKE SOME, I DON'T REQUIRE THEIR APPROVAL. I'LL PROTECT THEM, WHETHER THEY LIKE ME OR NOT.

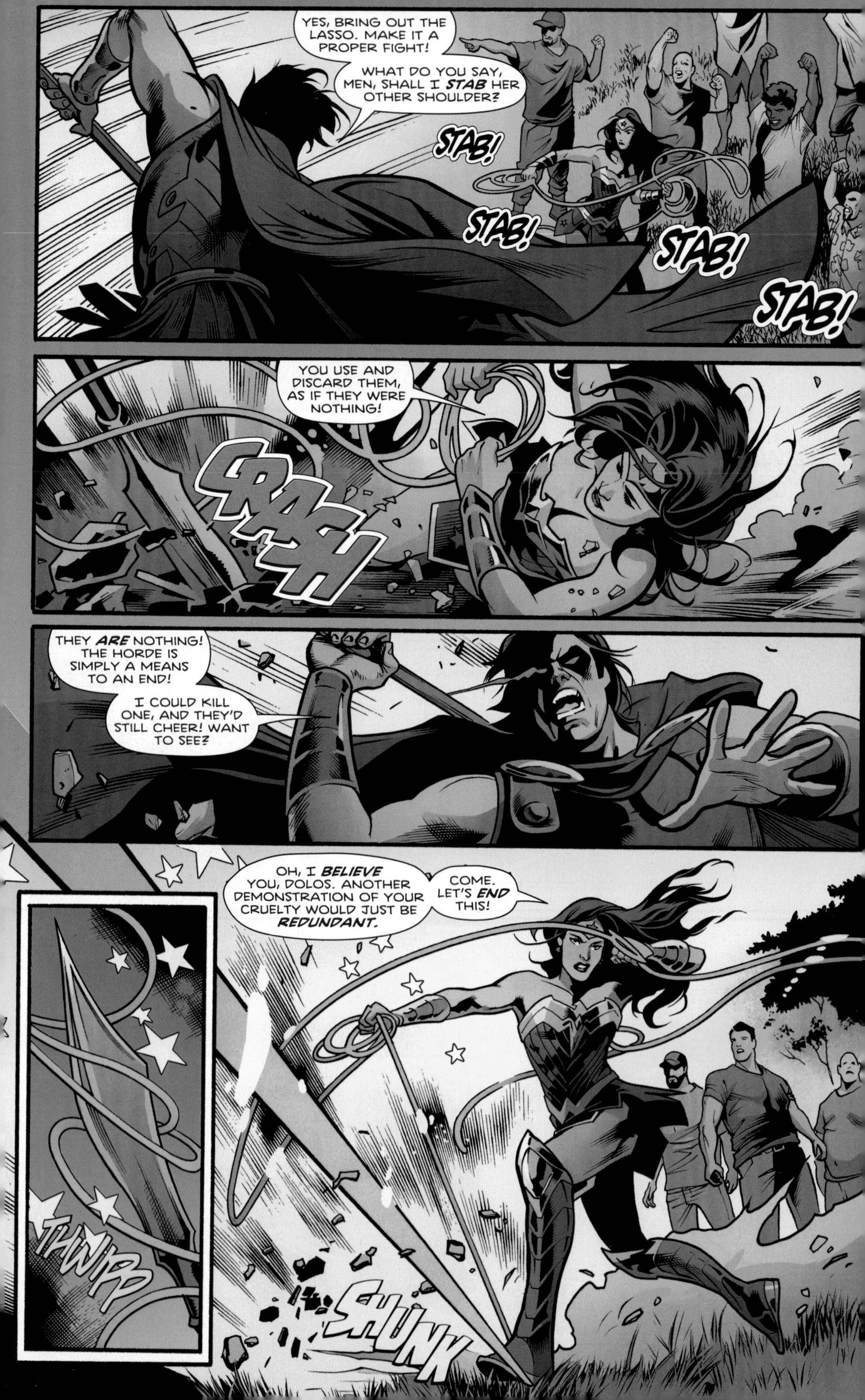
YES, BRING OUT THE LASSO. MAKE IT A PROPER FIGHT!
WHAT DO YOU SAY, MEN, SHALL I STAB HER OTHER SHOULDER?
STAB!
STAB!
STAB!
STAB!
YOU USE AND DISCARD THEM, AS IF THEY WERE NOTHING!
CRASH
THEY ARE NOTHING! THE HORDE IS SIMPLY A MEANS TO AN END!
I COULD KILL ONE, AND THEY'D STILL CHEER! WANT TO SEE?
OH, I BELIEVE YOU, DOLOS. ANOTHER DEMONSTRATION OF YOUR CRUELTY WOULD JUST BE REDUNDANT.
COME. LET'S END THIS!
THWIPP
SHUNK

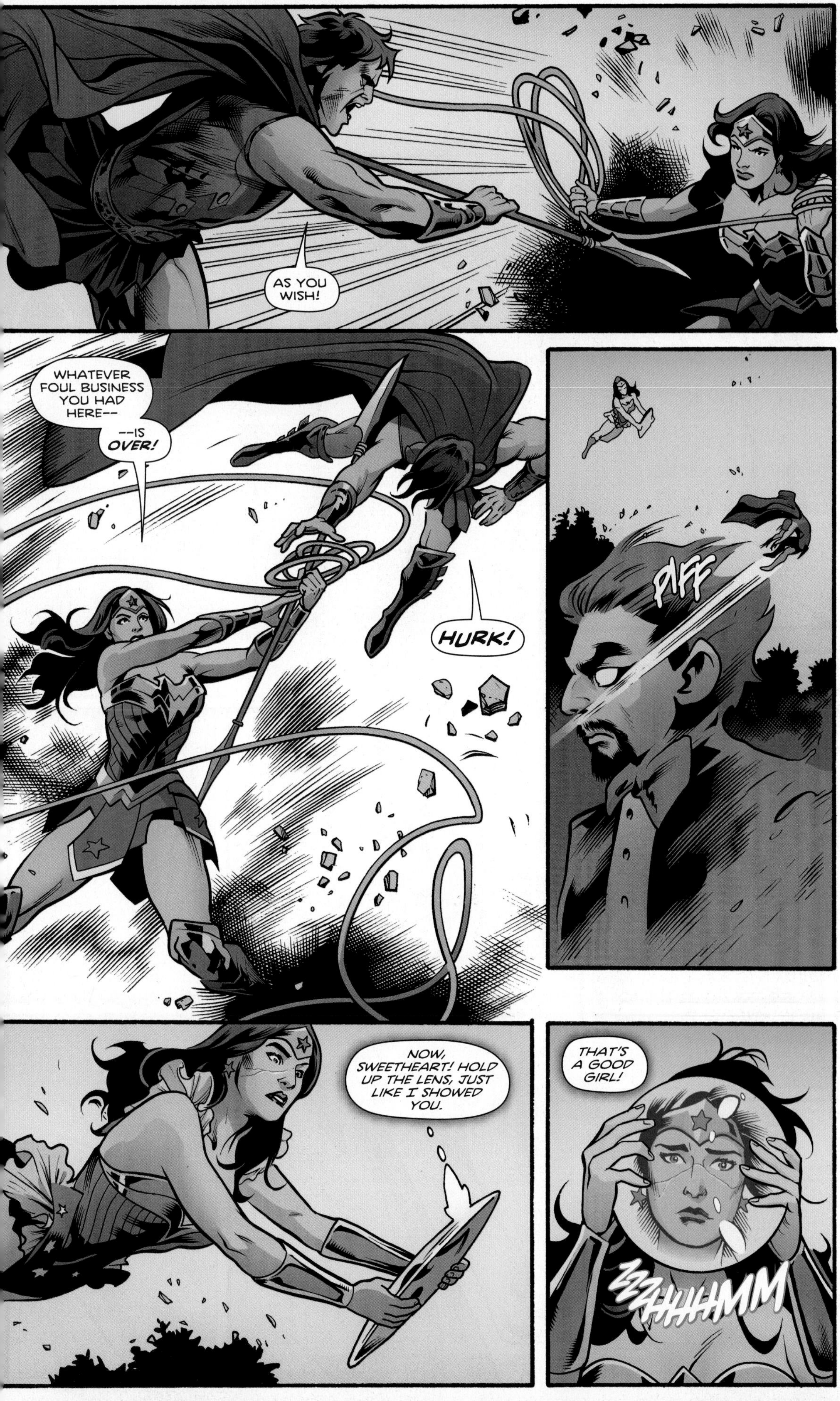
AS YOU WISH!
WHATEVER FOUL BUSINESS YOU HAD HERE--
--IS *OVER!*
HURK!
PIFF
NOW, SWEETHEART! HOLD UP THE LENS, JUST LIKE I SHOWED YOU.
THAT'S A GOOD GIRL!
ZZZHHHHMM

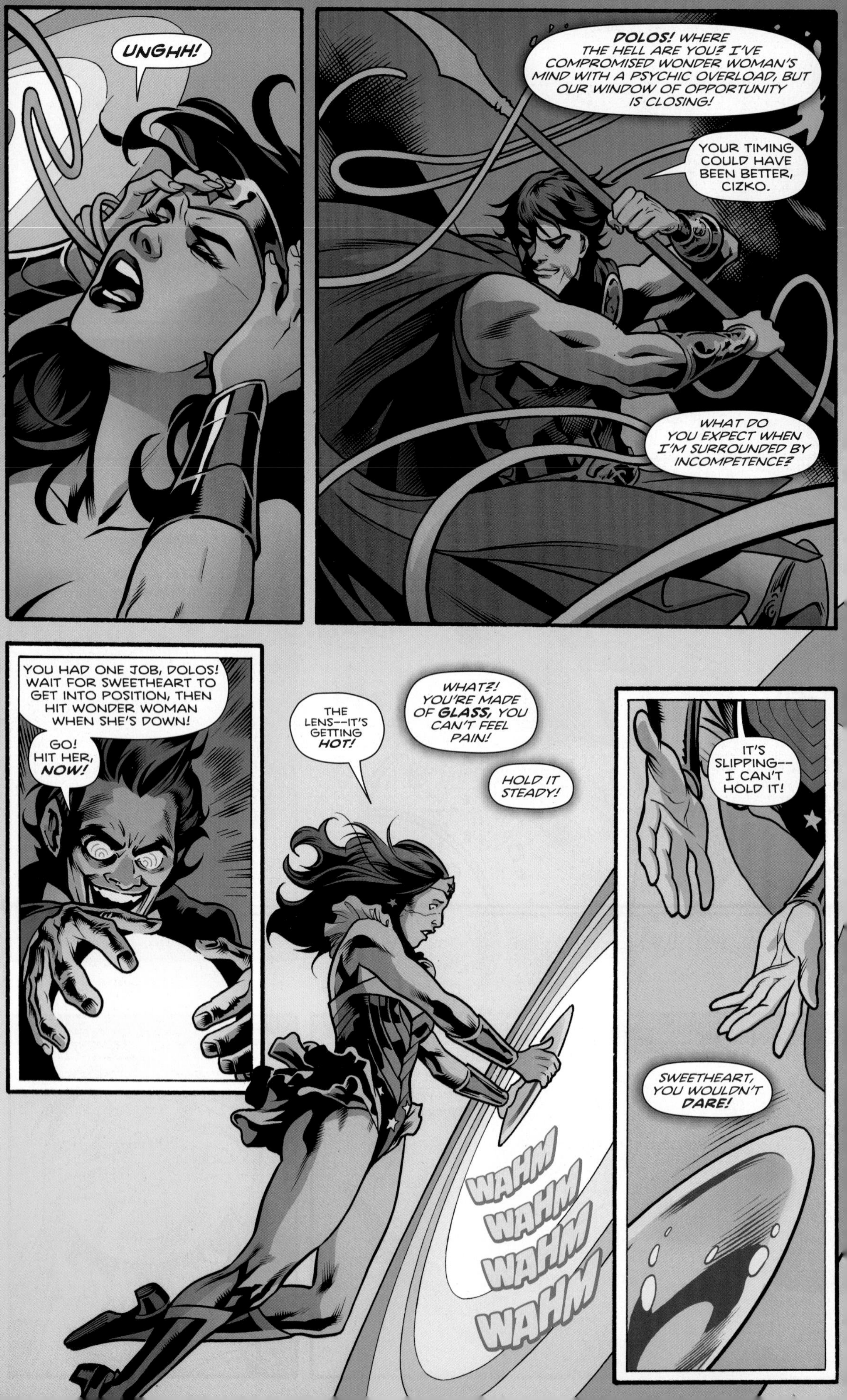
UNGHH!
DOLOS! WHERE THE HELL ARE YOU? I'VE COMPROMISED WONDER WOMAN'S MIND WITH A PSYCHIC OVERLOAD, BUT OUR WINDOW OF OPPORTUNITY IS CLOSING!
YOUR TIMING COULD HAVE BEEN BETTER, CIZKO.
WHAT DO YOU EXPECT WHEN I'M SURROUNDED BY INCOMPETENCE?
YOU HAD ONE JOB, DOLOS! WAIT FOR SWEETHEART TO GET INTO POSITION, THEN HIT WONDER WOMAN WHEN SHE'S DOWN!
GO! HIT HER, NOW!
THE LENS--IT'S GETTING HOT!
WHAT?! YOU'RE MADE OF GLASS, YOU CAN'T FEEL PAIN!
HOLD IT STEADY!
WAHM WAHM WAHM WAHM WAHM
IT'S SLIPPING-- I CAN'T HOLD IT!
SWEETHEART, YOU WOULDN'T DARE!

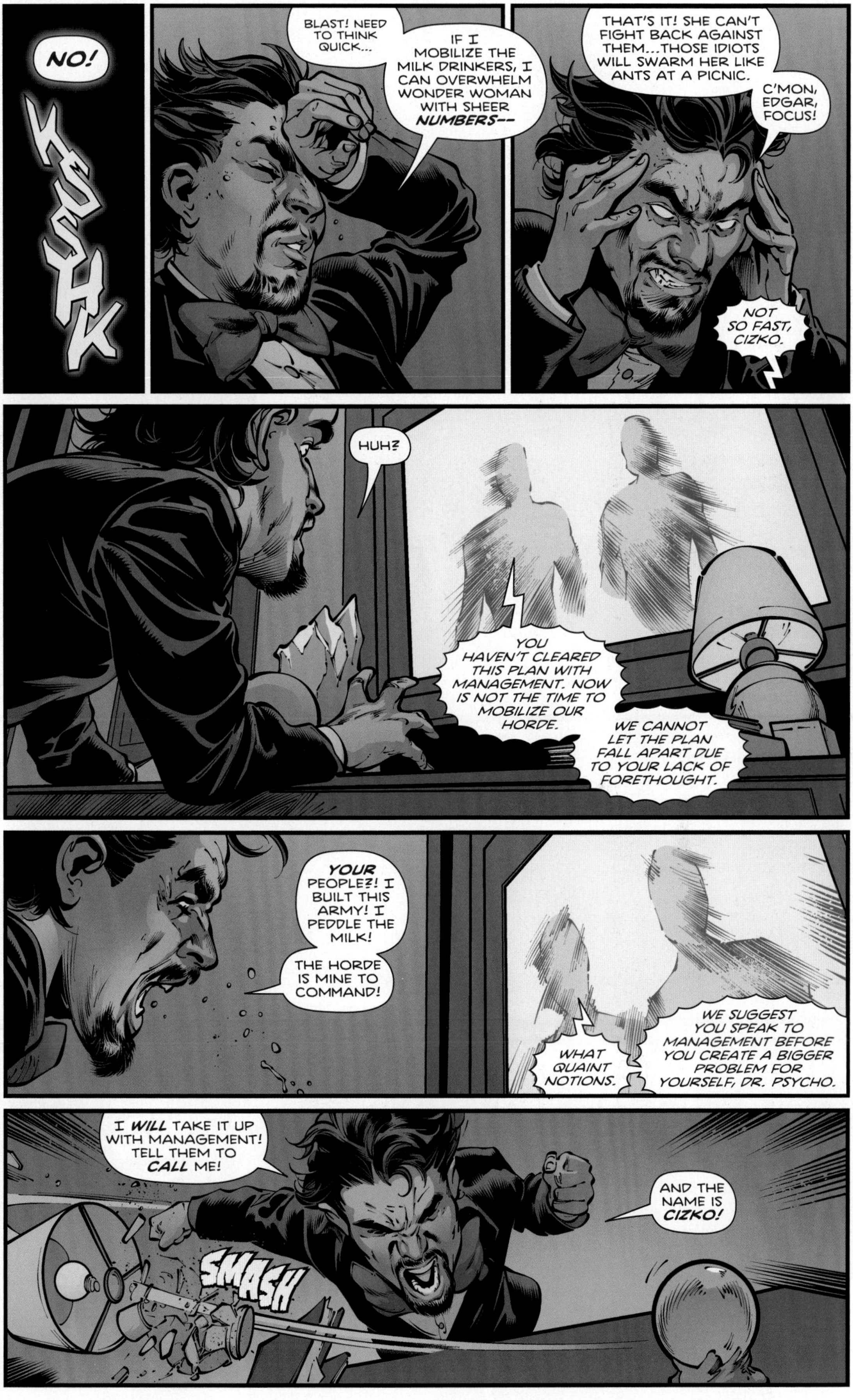
NO!
KSSHK
BLAST! NEED TO THINK QUICK...
IF I MOBILIZE THE MILK DRINKERS, I CAN OVERWHELM WONDER WOMAN WITH SHEER NUMBERS--
THAT'S IT! SHE CAN'T FIGHT BACK AGAINST THEM...THOSE IDIOTS WILL SWARM HER LIKE ANTS AT A PICNIC.
C'MON, EDGAR, FOCUS!
NOT SO FAST, CIZKO.
HUH?
YOU HAVEN'T CLEARED THIS PLAN WITH MANAGEMENT. NOW IS NOT THE TIME TO MOBILIZE OUR HORDE.
WE CANNOT LET THE PLAN FALL APART DUE TO YOUR LACK OF FORETHOUGHT.
YOUR PEOPLE?! I BUILT THIS ARMY! I PEDDLE THE MILK!
THE HORDE IS MINE TO COMMAND!
WHAT QUAINT NOTIONS.
WE SUGGEST YOU SPEAK TO MANAGEMENT BEFORE YOU CREATE A BIGGER PROBLEM FOR YOURSELF, DR. PSYCHO.
I WILL TAKE IT UP WITH MANAGEMENT! TELL THEM TO CALL ME!
AND THE NAME IS CIZKO!
SMASH

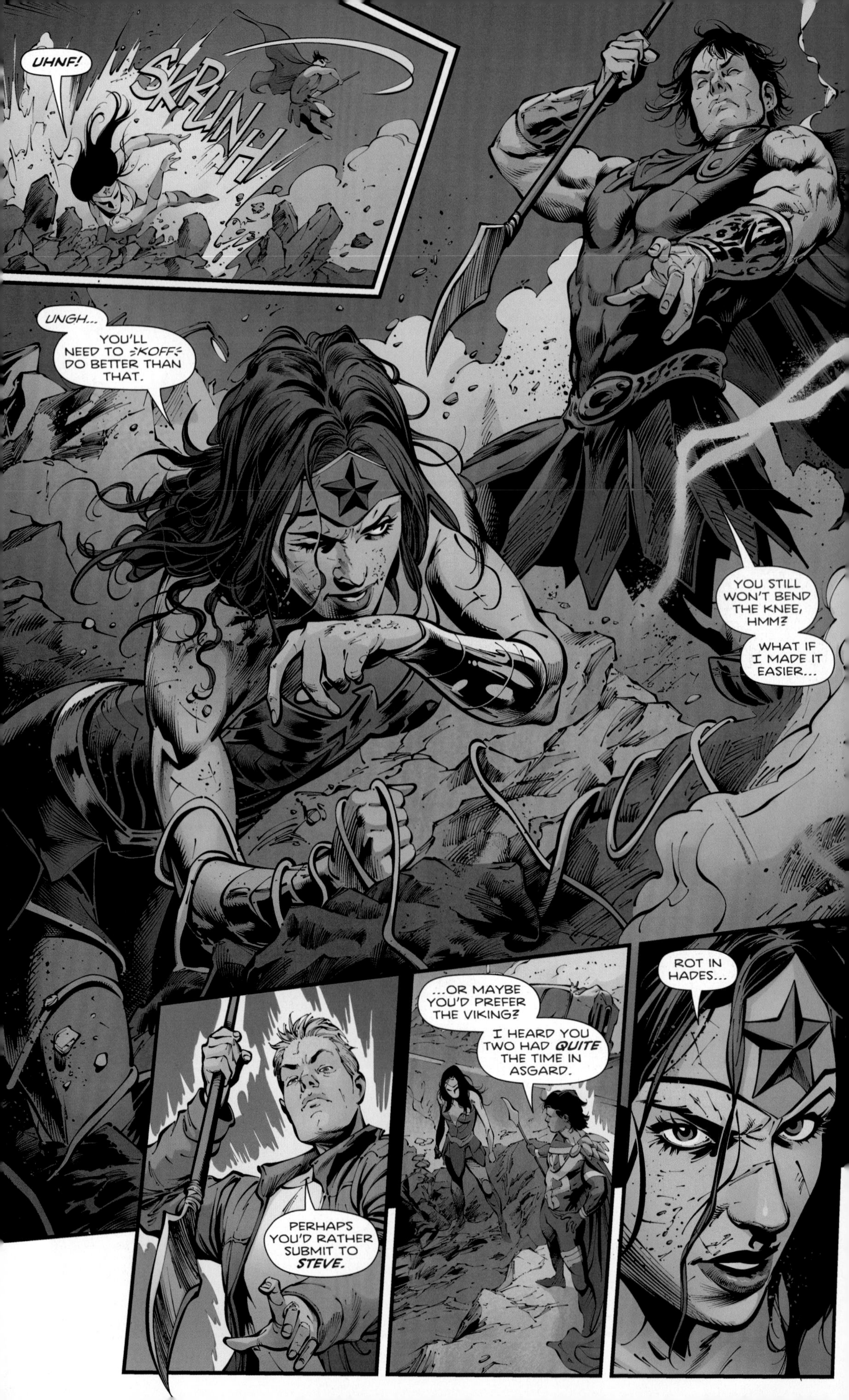
UHNF!
SKRUNH
UNGH...
YOU'LL NEED TO ⸗KOFF⸗ DO BETTER THAN THAT.
YOU STILL WON'T BEND THE KNEE, HMM?
WHAT IF I MADE IT EASIER...
PERHAPS YOU'D RATHER SUBMIT TO STEVE.
...OR MAYBE YOU'D PREFER THE VIKING?
I HEARD YOU TWO HAD QUITE THE TIME IN ASGARD.
ROT IN HADES...

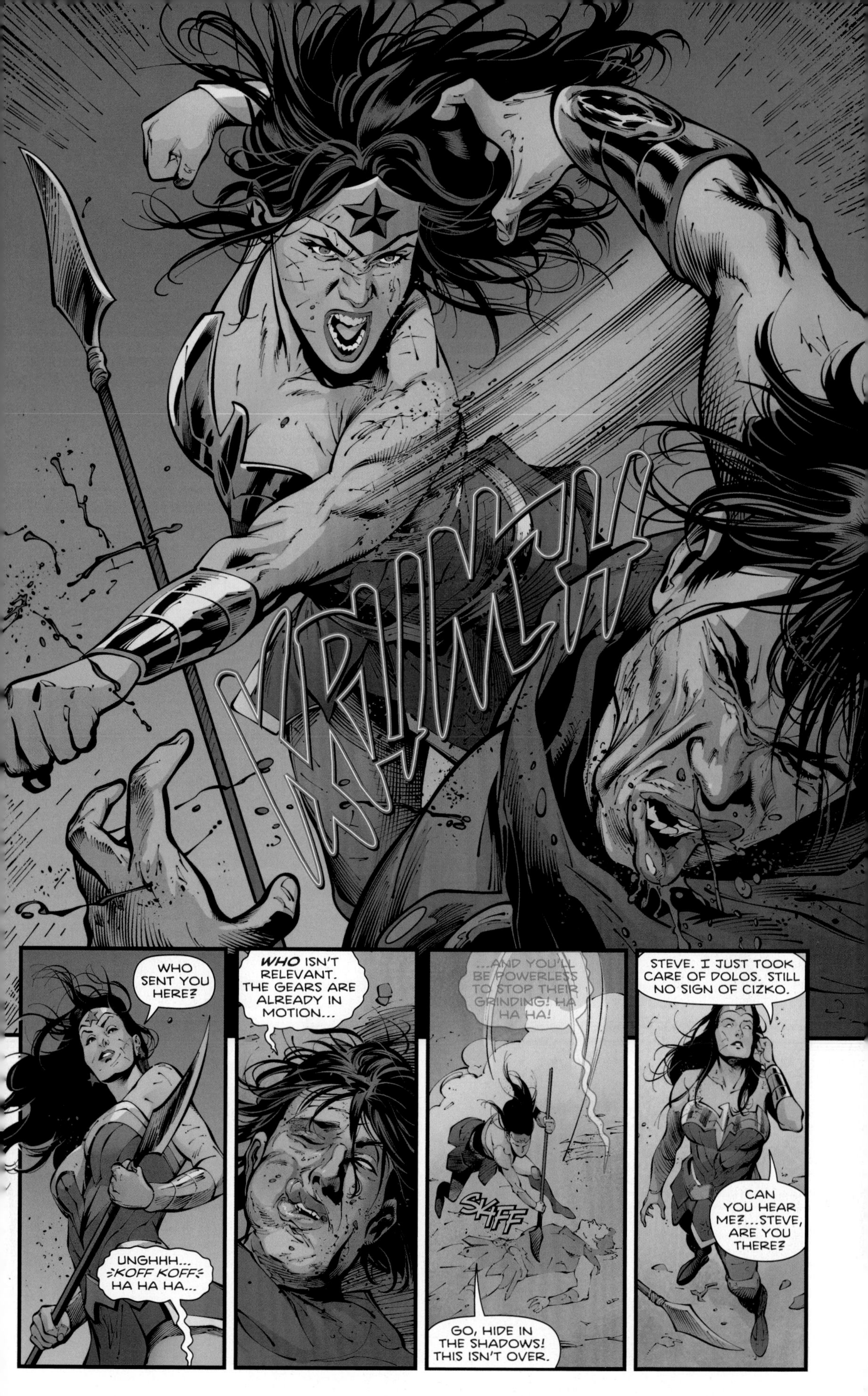
KRUNCH
WHO SENT YOU HERE?
UNGHHH... KOFF KOFF HA HA HA...
WHO ISN'T RELEVANT. THE GEARS ARE ALREADY IN MOTION...
...AND YOU'LL BE POWERLESS TO STOP THEIR GRINDING! HA HA HA!
SKFF
GO, HIDE IN THE SHADOWS! THIS ISN'T OVER.
STEVE. I JUST TOOK CARE OF DOLOS. STILL NO SIGN OF CIZKO.
CAN YOU HEAR ME?...STEVE, ARE YOU THERE?

SPIRITS, YOU KNOW I DON'T ASK FOR MUCH. AND I'VE ALWAYS SERVED YOU, ASK ANYONE.

NOW, IN MY HOUR OF NEED, SURROUNDED BY FAILURES LIKE SWEETHEART HERE, I BEG FOR GUIDANCE.

REVEAL TO ME THE PATH-- SITUATION, OBSTACLE, AND OUTCOME.

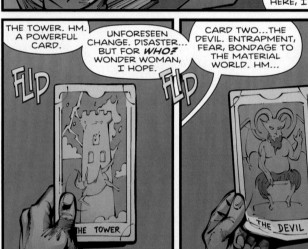

THE TOWER. HM. A POWERFUL CARD.

UNFORESEEN CHANGE. DISASTER... BUT FOR *WHO?* WONDER WOMAN, I HOPE.

FLIP

FLIP

THE TOWER

CARD TWO...THE DEVIL. ENTRAPMENT, FEAR, BONDAGE TO THE MATERIAL WORLD. HM...

THE DEVIL

AND THE FINAL CARD...

RIIIING

H-HELLO?

AH, MANAGEMENT. YES, I WANTED TO SPEAK TO YOU. THANK YOU FOR GETTING BACK TO ME.

AS A MATTER OF FACT...

THE TOWER

DEATH

THE DEVIL

"...I *DO* HAVE GOOD NEWS."

MEANWHILE...

CRKKRTKTKTK

AAAH, YOU'RE FINALLY AWAKE. GOOD, CLASS IS ABOUT TO START.

WHAT IN THE...

YOU TIED ME UP TO GIVE ME A LECTURE? *SERIOUSLY?* WHAT'S THE MEANING OF THIS?

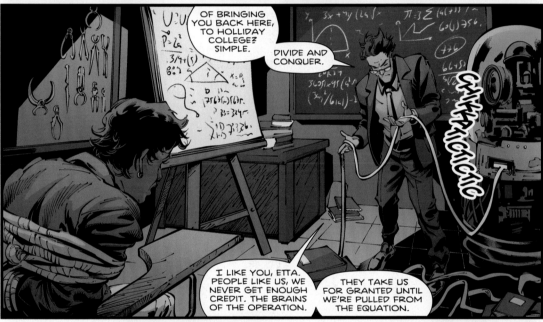

OF BRINGING YOU BACK HERE, TO HOLLIDAY COLLEGE? SIMPLE.

DIVIDE AND CONQUER.

CRKKRTKTKTK

I LIKE YOU, ETTA. PEOPLE LIKE US, WE NEVER GET ENOUGH CREDIT. THE BRAINS OF THE OPERATION.

THEY TAKE US FOR GRANTED UNTIL WE'RE PULLED FROM THE EQUATION.

SEE THIS? THE MOMENT I CAPTURED YOU, OUR CHANCES OF SUCCESS IMPROVED *IMMENSELY!*

THAT'S A GOOD THING! IT MEANS YOU'RE *IMPORTANT.*

I SUPPOSE THE ONLY THING LEFT IS TO DECIDE WHAT TO DO WITH YOU.

OH, AND DON'T WORRY ABOUT YOUR LITTLE FRIENDS...

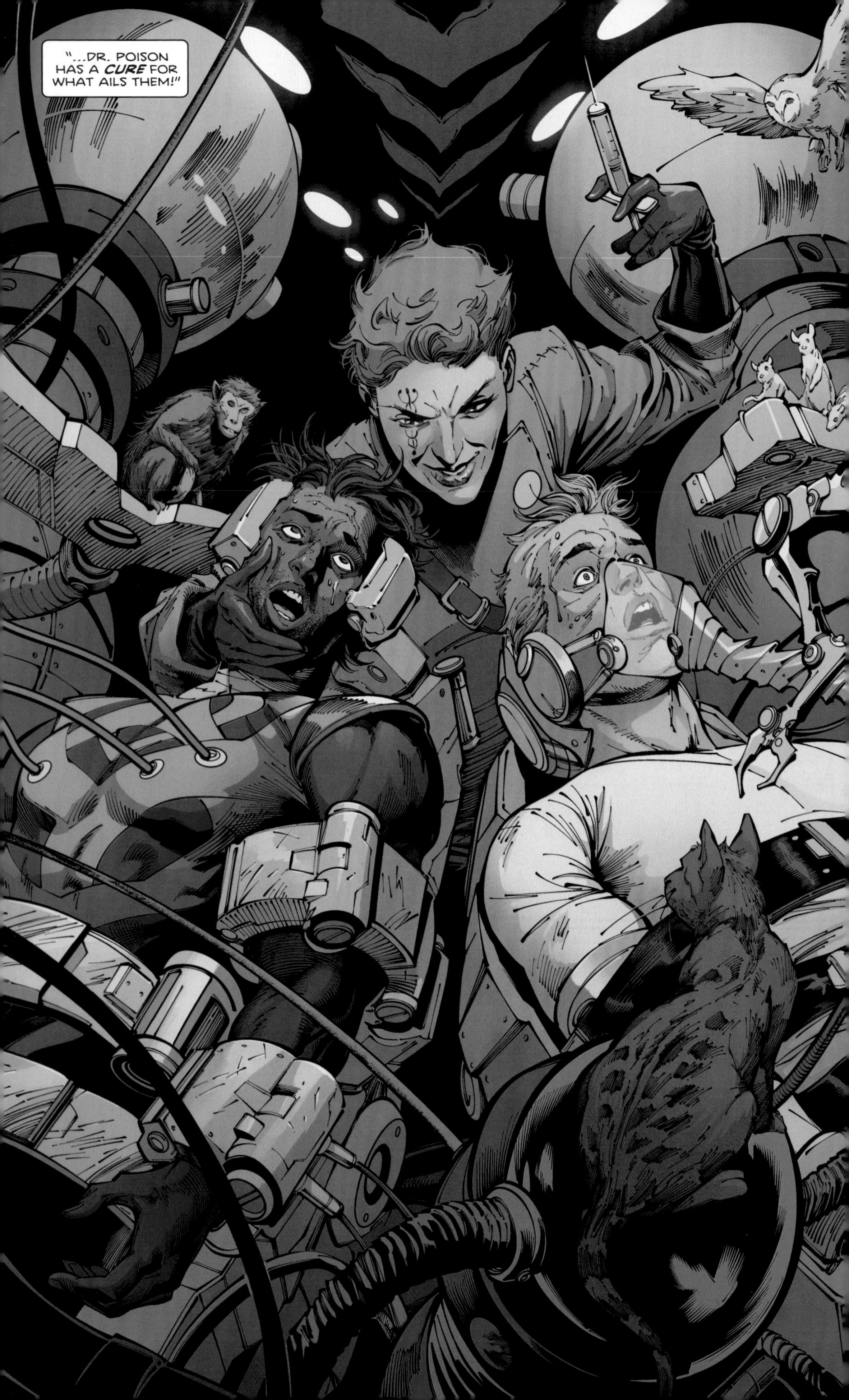
"...DR. POISON HAS A CURE FOR WHAT AILS THEM!"

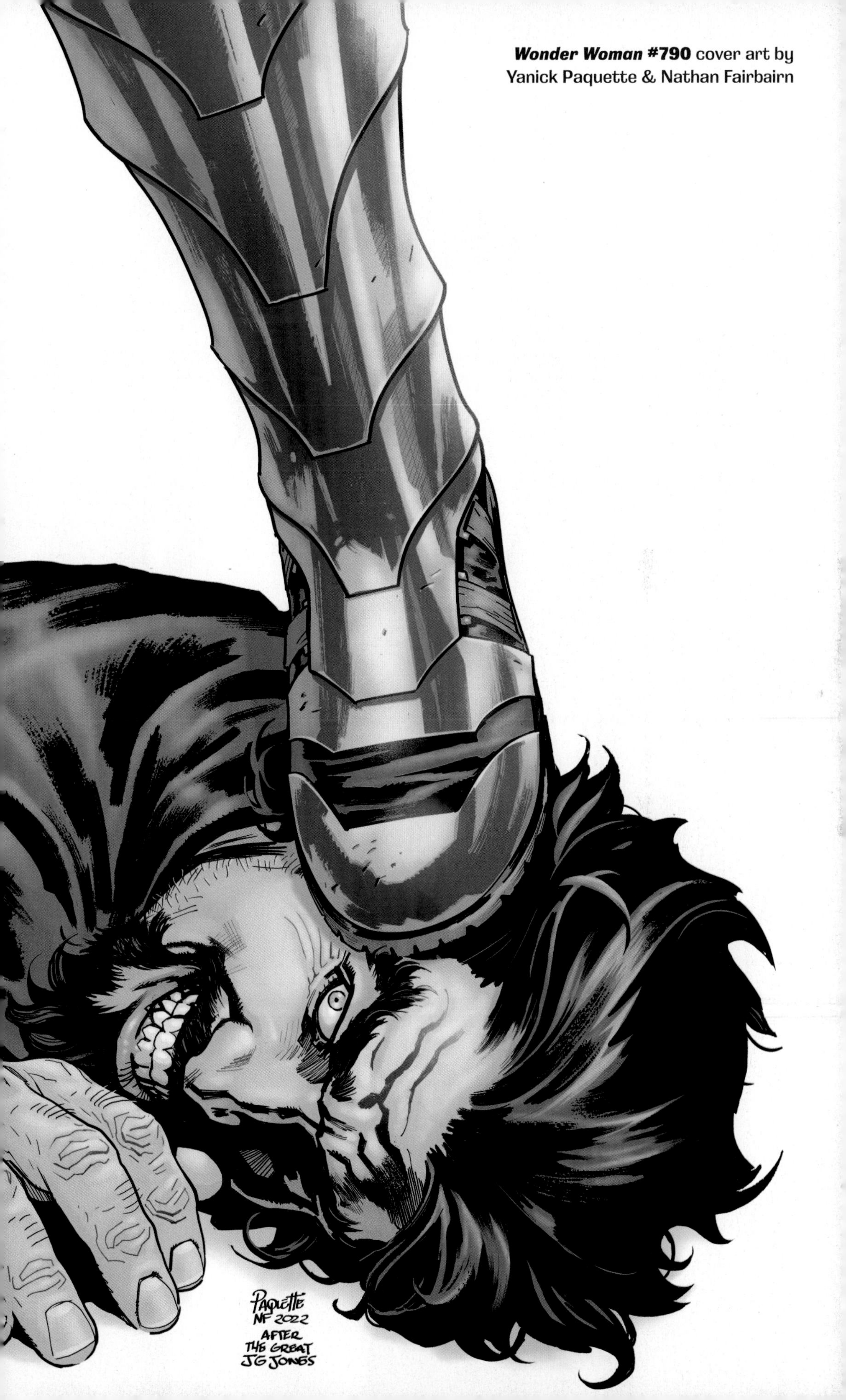
PAQUETTE
NF 2022
AFTER
THE GREAT
JG JONES

***Wonder Woman* #790** cover art by
Yanick Paquette & Nathan Fairbairn

***Wonder Woman* #790** variant cover
art by Paul Pope & José Villarrubia

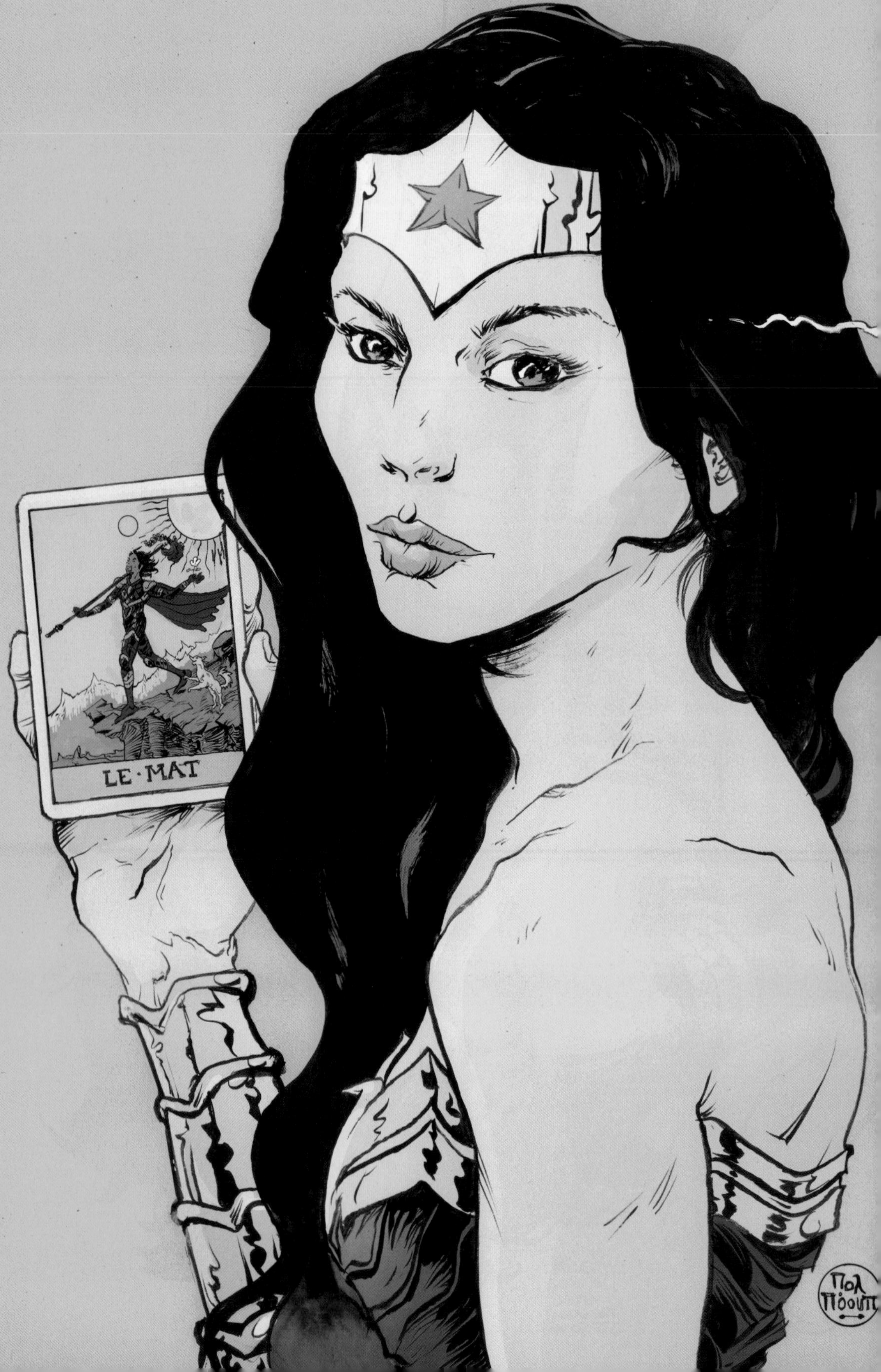
LE·MAT

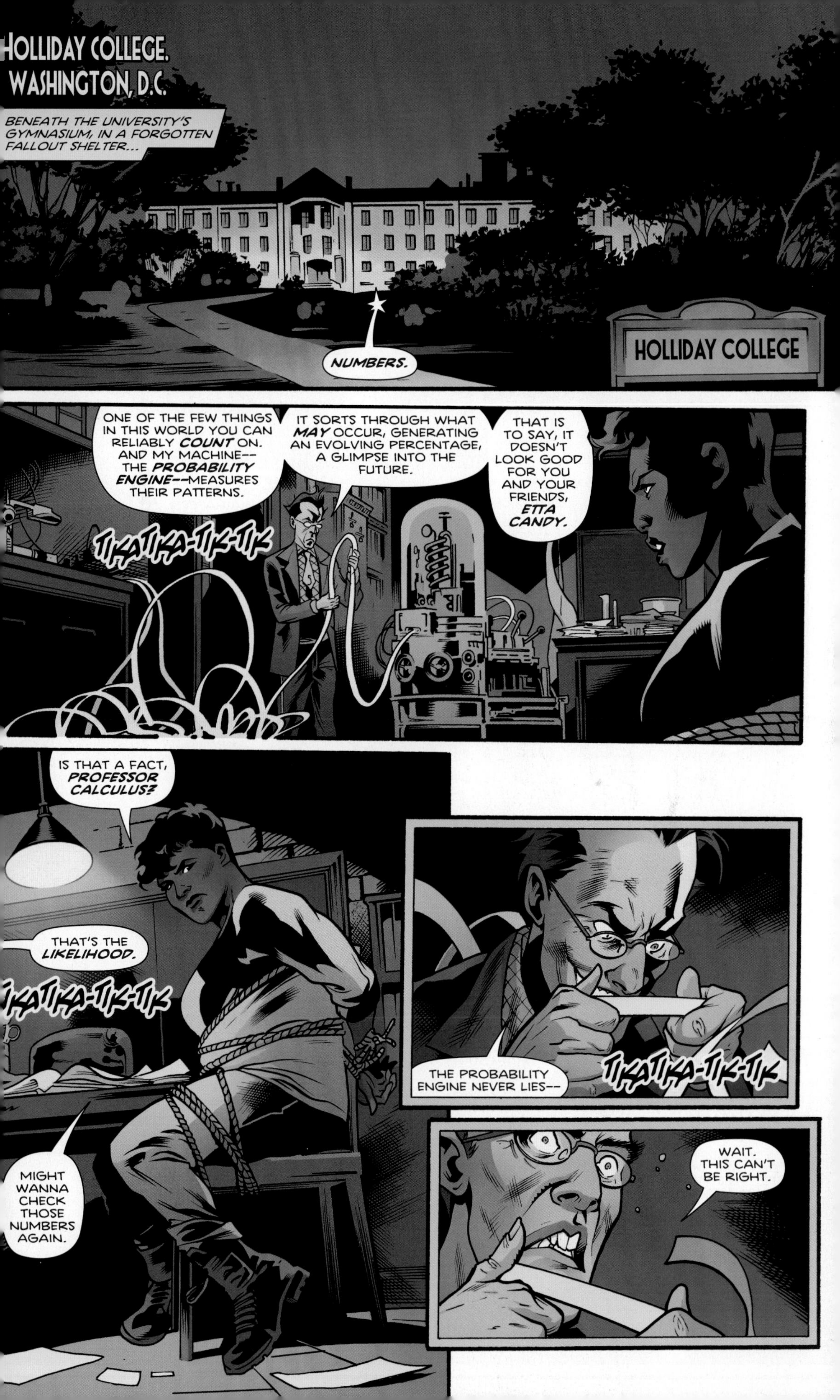
HOLLIDAY COLLEGE. WASHINGTON, D.C.
BENEATH THE UNIVERSITY'S GYMNASIUM, IN A FORGOTTEN FALLOUT SHELTER...
NUMBERS.
HOLLIDAY COLLEGE
ONE OF THE FEW THINGS IN THIS WORLD YOU CAN RELIABLY COUNT ON. AND MY MACHINE-- THE PROBABILITY ENGINE--MEASURES THEIR PATTERNS.
IT SORTS THROUGH WHAT MAY OCCUR, GENERATING AN EVOLVING PERCENTAGE, A GLIMPSE INTO THE FUTURE.
THAT IS TO SAY, IT DOESN'T LOOK GOOD FOR YOU AND YOUR FRIENDS, ETTA CANDY.
TIKATIKA-TIK-TIK
IS THAT A FACT, PROFESSOR CALCULUS?
THAT'S THE LIKELIHOOD.
TIKATIKA-TIK-TIK
THE PROBABILITY ENGINE NEVER LIES--
TIKATIKA-TIK-TIK
MIGHT WANNA CHECK THOSE NUMBERS AGAIN.
WAIT. THIS CAN'T BE RIGHT.

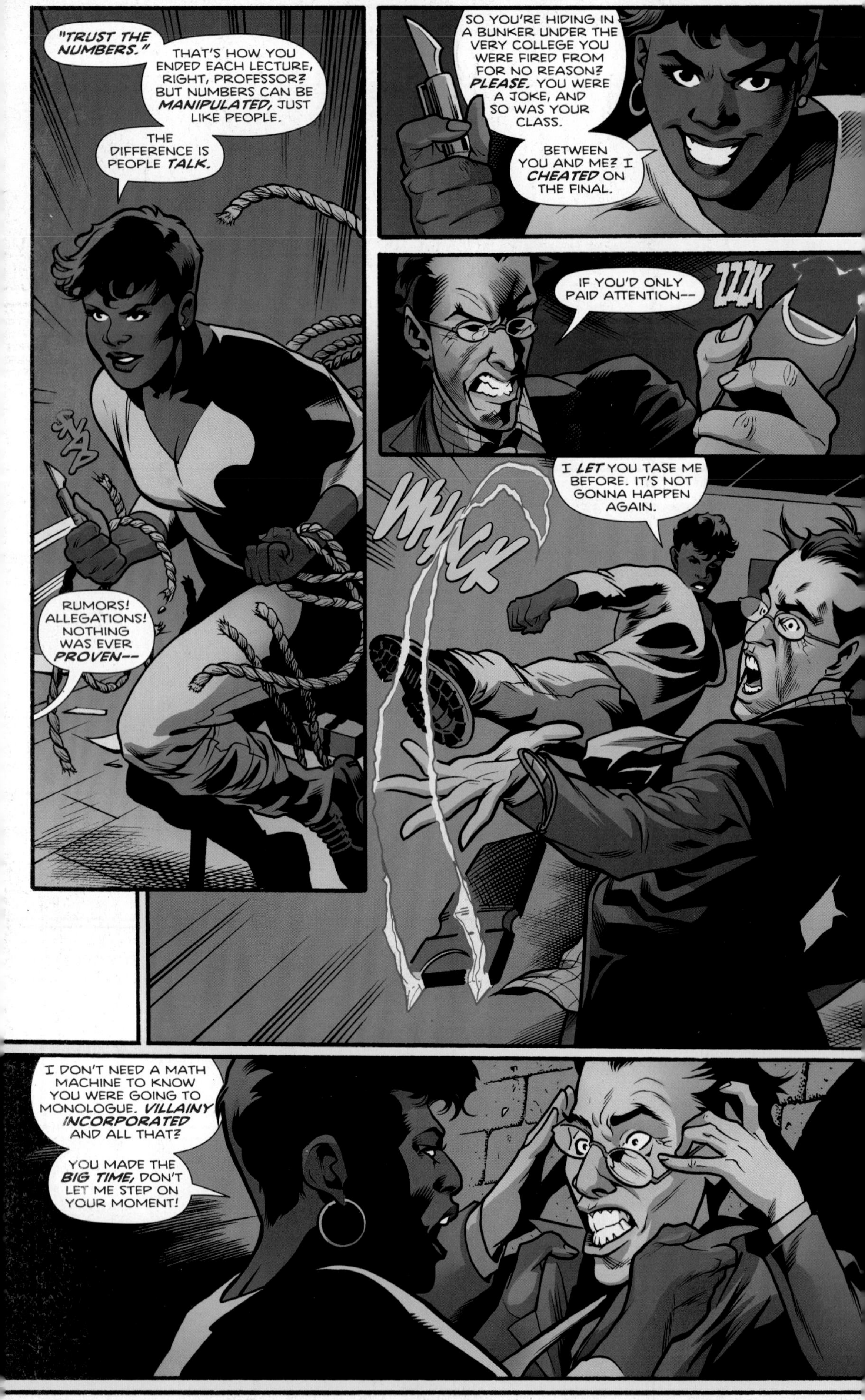
"TRUST THE NUMBERS."
THAT'S HOW YOU ENDED EACH LECTURE, RIGHT, PROFESSOR? BUT NUMBERS CAN BE MANIPULATED, JUST LIKE PEOPLE.
THE DIFFERENCE IS PEOPLE TALK.
RUMORS! ALLEGATIONS! NOTHING WAS EVER PROVEN--
SO YOU'RE HIDING IN A BUNKER UNDER THE VERY COLLEGE YOU WERE FIRED FROM FOR NO REASON? PLEASE. YOU WERE A JOKE, AND SO WAS YOUR CLASS.
BETWEEN YOU AND ME? I CHEATED ON THE FINAL.
IF YOU'D ONLY PAID ATTENTION--
ZZZK
I LET YOU TASE ME BEFORE. IT'S NOT GONNA HAPPEN AGAIN.
WHACK
I DON'T NEED A MATH MACHINE TO KNOW YOU WERE GOING TO MONOLOGUE. VILLAINY INCORPORATED AND ALL THAT?
YOU MADE THE BIG TIME, DON'T LET ME STEP ON YOUR MOMENT!

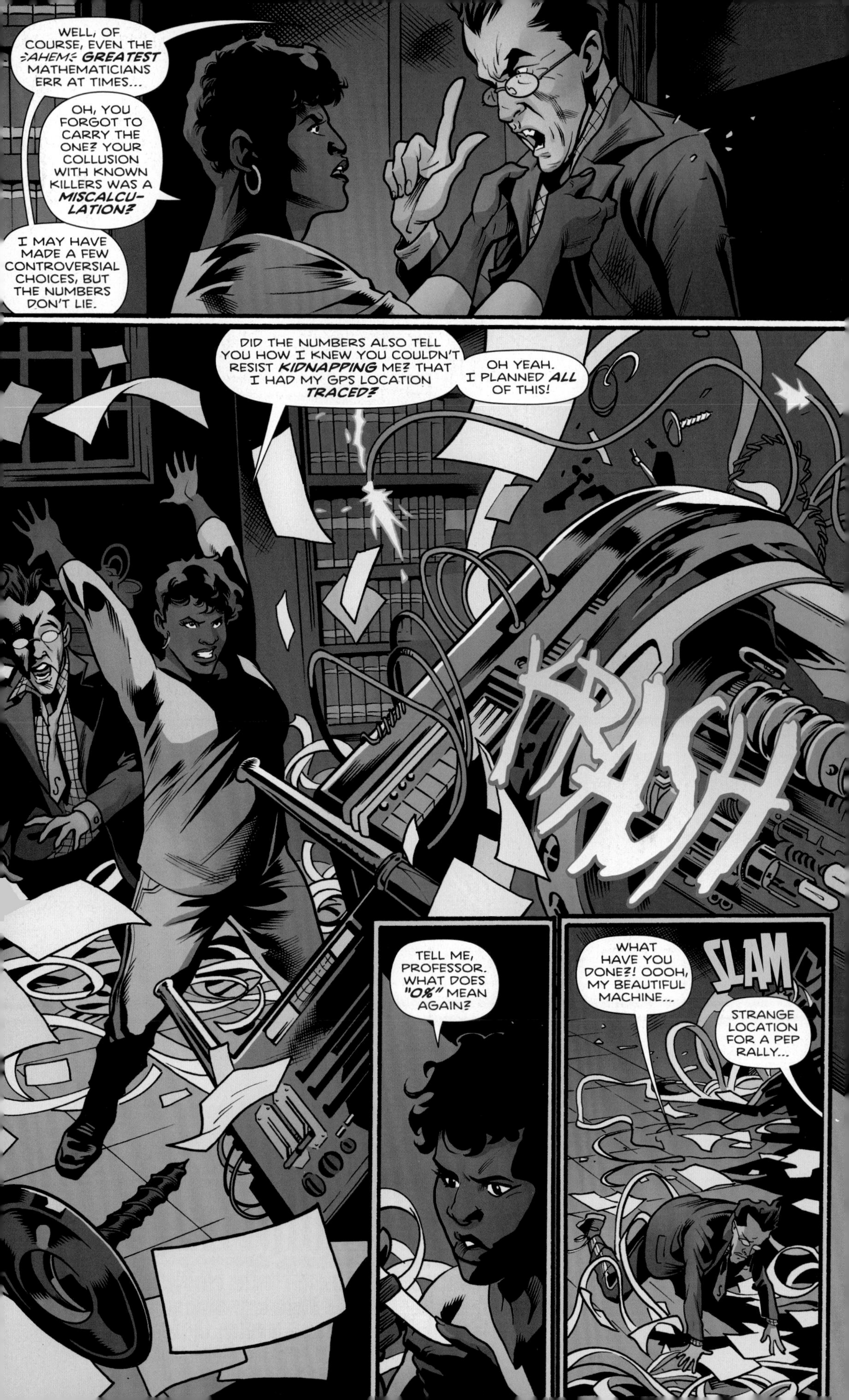
WELL, OF COURSE, EVEN THE ≈AHEM≈ GREATEST MATHEMATICIANS ERR AT TIMES...
OH, YOU FORGOT TO CARRY THE ONE? YOUR COLLUSION WITH KNOWN KILLERS WAS A MISCALCU-LATION?
I MAY HAVE MADE A FEW CONTROVERSIAL CHOICES, BUT THE NUMBERS DON'T LIE.
DID THE NUMBERS ALSO TELL YOU HOW I KNEW YOU COULDN'T RESIST KIDNAPPING ME? THAT I HAD MY GPS LOCATION TRACED?
OH YEAH. I PLANNED ALL OF THIS!
KRASH
TELL ME, PROFESSOR. WHAT DOES "0%" MEAN AGAIN?
SLAM
WHAT HAVE YOU DONE?! OOOH, MY BEAUTIFUL MACHINE...
STRANGE LOCATION FOR A PEP RALLY...

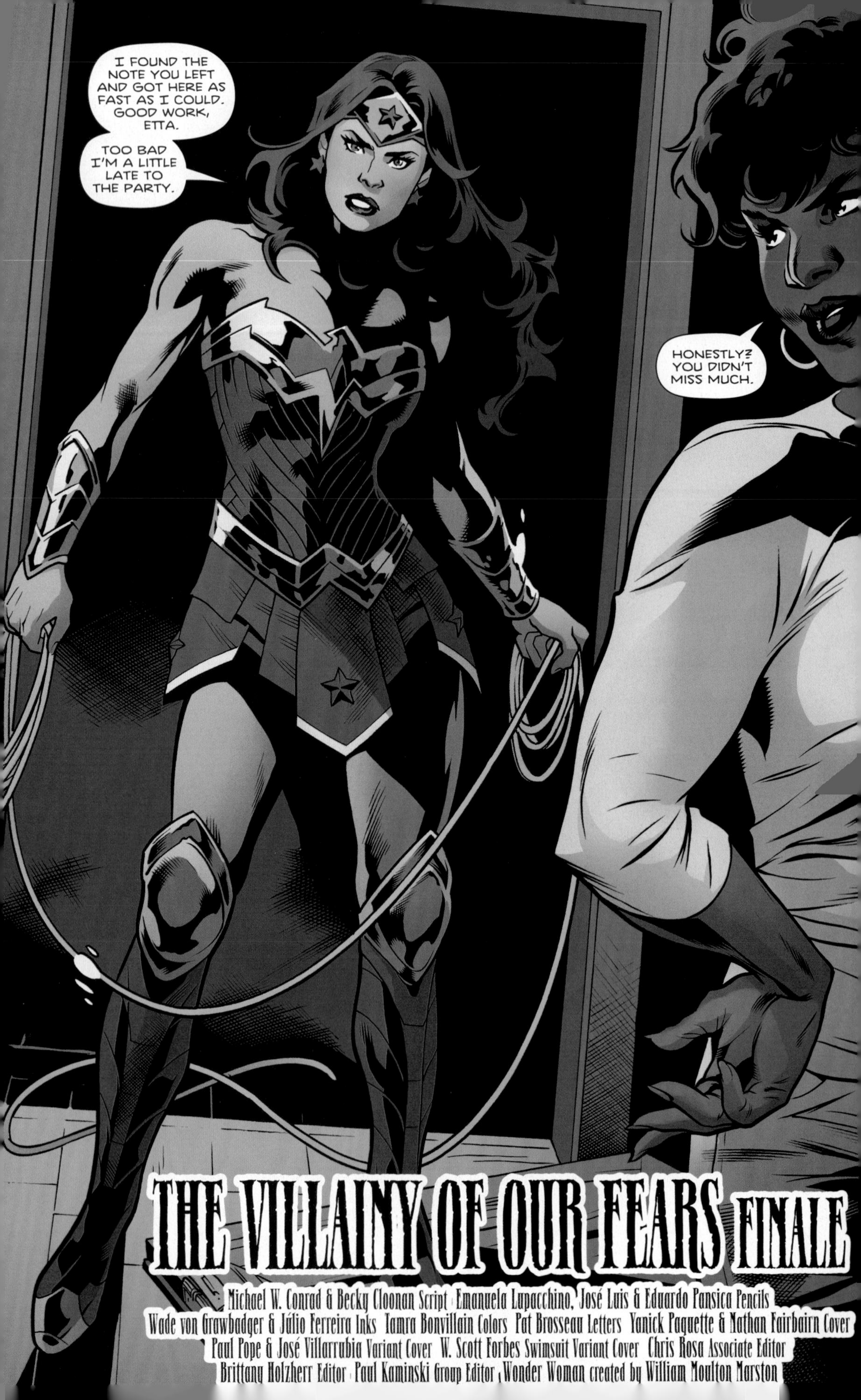
I FOUND THE NOTE YOU LEFT AND GOT HERE AS FAST AS I COULD. GOOD WORK, ETTA.
TOO BAD I'M A LITTLE LATE TO THE PARTY.
HONESTLY? YOU DIDN'T MISS MUCH.
THE VILLAINY OF OUR FEARS FINALE
Michael W. Conrad & Becky Cloonan Script Emanuela Lupacchino, José Luis & Eduardo Pansica Pencils
Wade von Grawbadger & Júlio Ferreira Inks Tamra Bonvillain Colors Pat Brosseau Letters Yanick Paquette & Nathan Fairbairn Cover
Paul Pope & José Villarrubia Variant Cover W. Scott Forbes Swimsuit Variant Cover Chris Rosa Associate Editor
Brittany Holzherr Editor Paul Kaminski Group Editor Wonder Woman created by William Moulton Marston

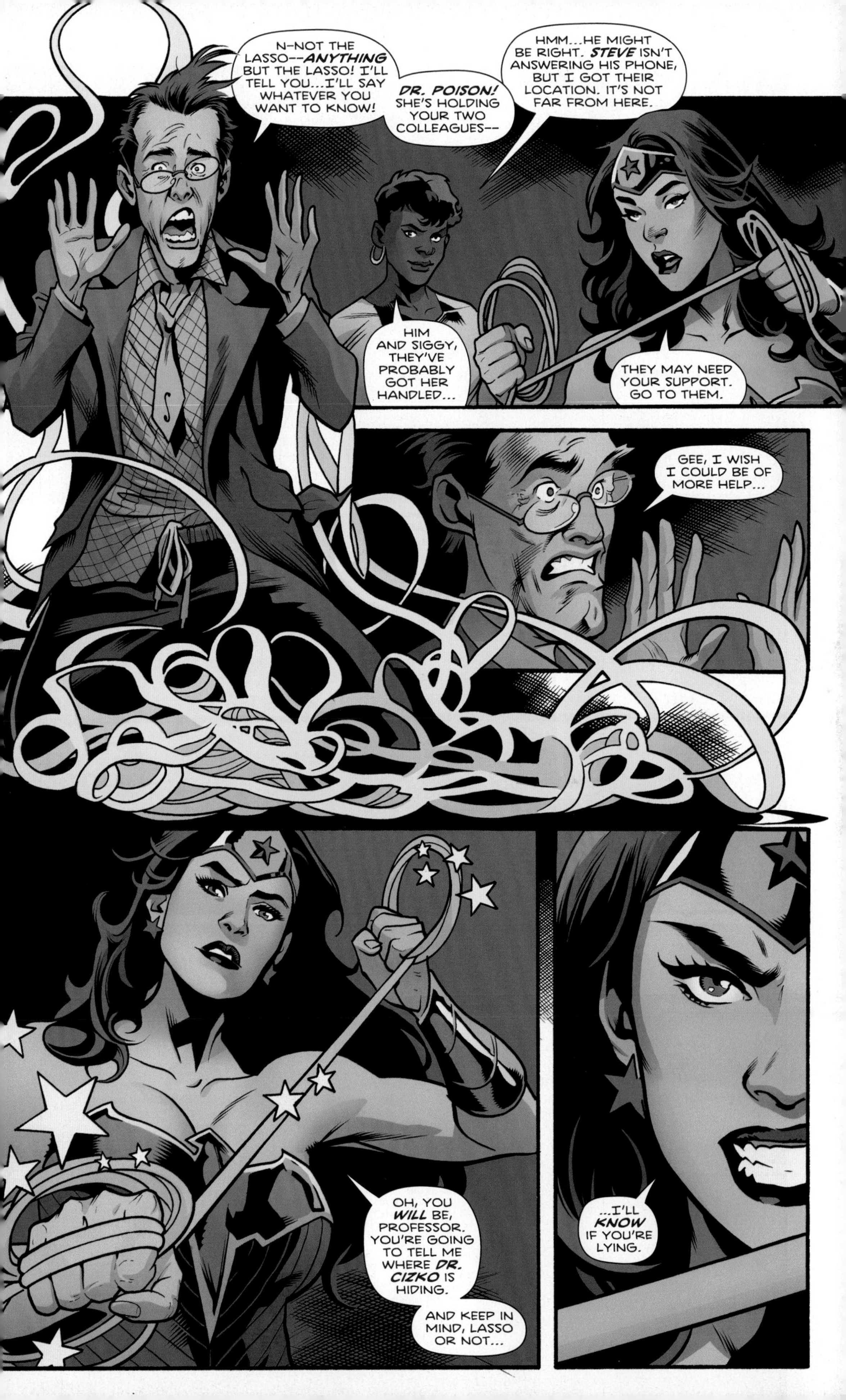
N-NOT THE LASSO--ANYTHING BUT THE LASSO! I'LL TELL YOU...I'LL SAY WHATEVER YOU WANT TO KNOW!
DR. POISON! SHE'S HOLDING YOUR TWO COLLEAGUES--
HMM...HE MIGHT BE RIGHT. STEVE ISN'T ANSWERING HIS PHONE, BUT I GOT THEIR LOCATION. IT'S NOT FAR FROM HERE.
HIM AND SIGGY, THEY'VE PROBABLY GOT HER HANDLED...
THEY MAY NEED YOUR SUPPORT. GO TO THEM.
GEE, I WISH I COULD BE OF MORE HELP...
OH, YOU WILL BE, PROFESSOR. YOU'RE GOING TO TELL ME WHERE DR. CIZKO IS HIDING.
AND KEEP IN MIND, LASSO OR NOT...
...I'LL KNOW IF YOU'RE LYING.

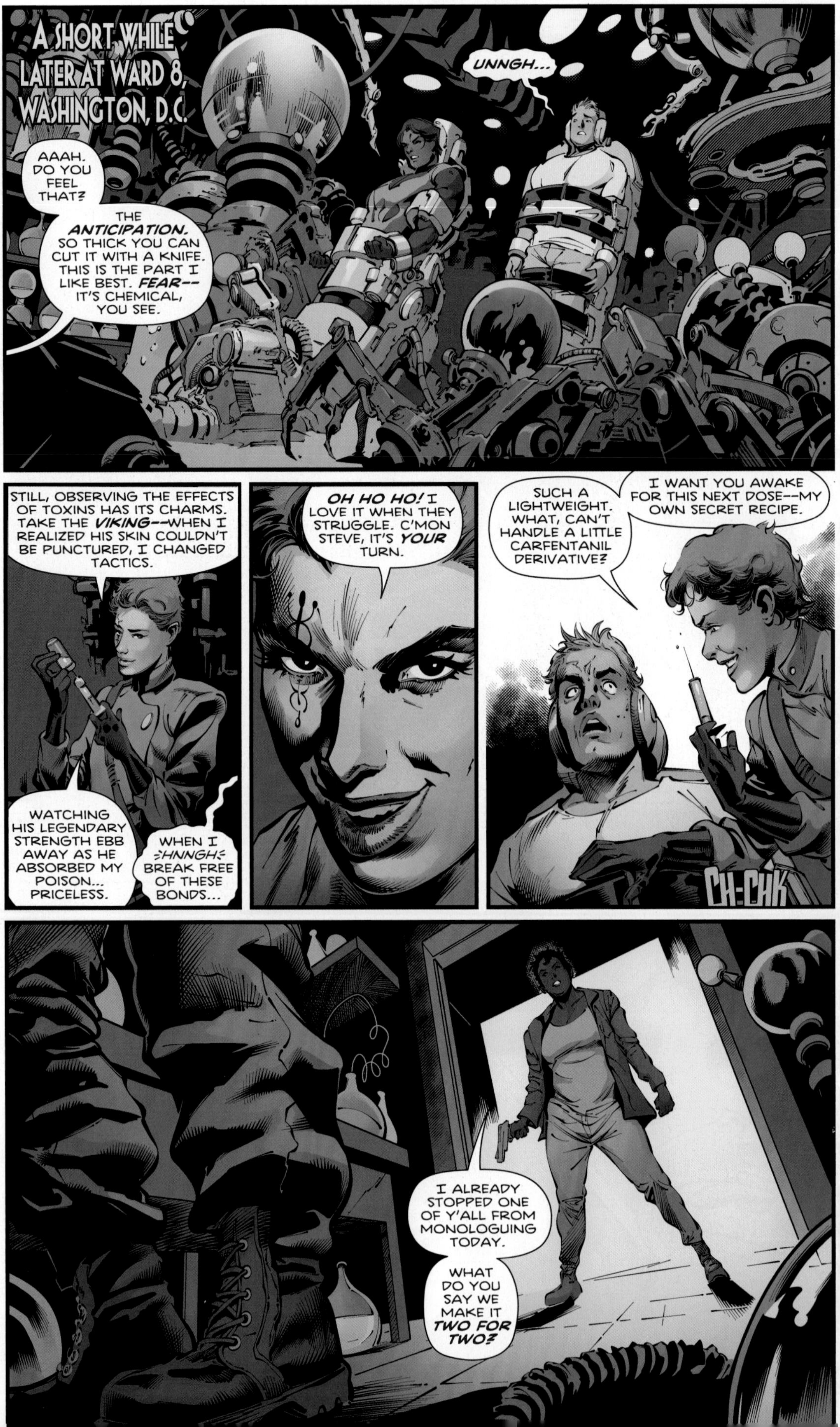

A SHORT WHILE LATER AT WARD 8, WASHINGTON, D.C.
UNNGH...
AAAH. DO YOU FEEL THAT?
THE *ANTICIPATION.* SO THICK YOU CAN CUT IT WITH A KNIFE. THIS IS THE PART I LIKE BEST. *FEAR--* IT'S CHEMICAL, YOU SEE.
STILL, OBSERVING THE EFFECTS OF TOXINS HAS ITS CHARMS. TAKE THE *VIKING*--WHEN I REALIZED HIS SKIN COULDN'T BE PUNCTURED, I CHANGED TACTICS.
WATCHING HIS LEGENDARY STRENGTH EBB AWAY AS HE ABSORBED MY POISON... PRICELESS.
WHEN I *HNNGH* BREAK FREE OF THESE BONDS...
OH HO HO! I LOVE IT WHEN THEY STRUGGLE. C'MON STEVE, IT'S *YOUR* TURN.
SUCH A LIGHTWEIGHT. WHAT, CAN'T HANDLE A LITTLE CARFENTANIL DERIVATIVE?
I WANT YOU AWAKE FOR THIS NEXT DOSE--MY OWN SECRET RECIPE.
CH-CHK
I ALREADY STOPPED ONE OF Y'ALL FROM MONOLOGUING TODAY.
WHAT DO YOU SAY WE MAKE IT *TWO FOR TWO?*

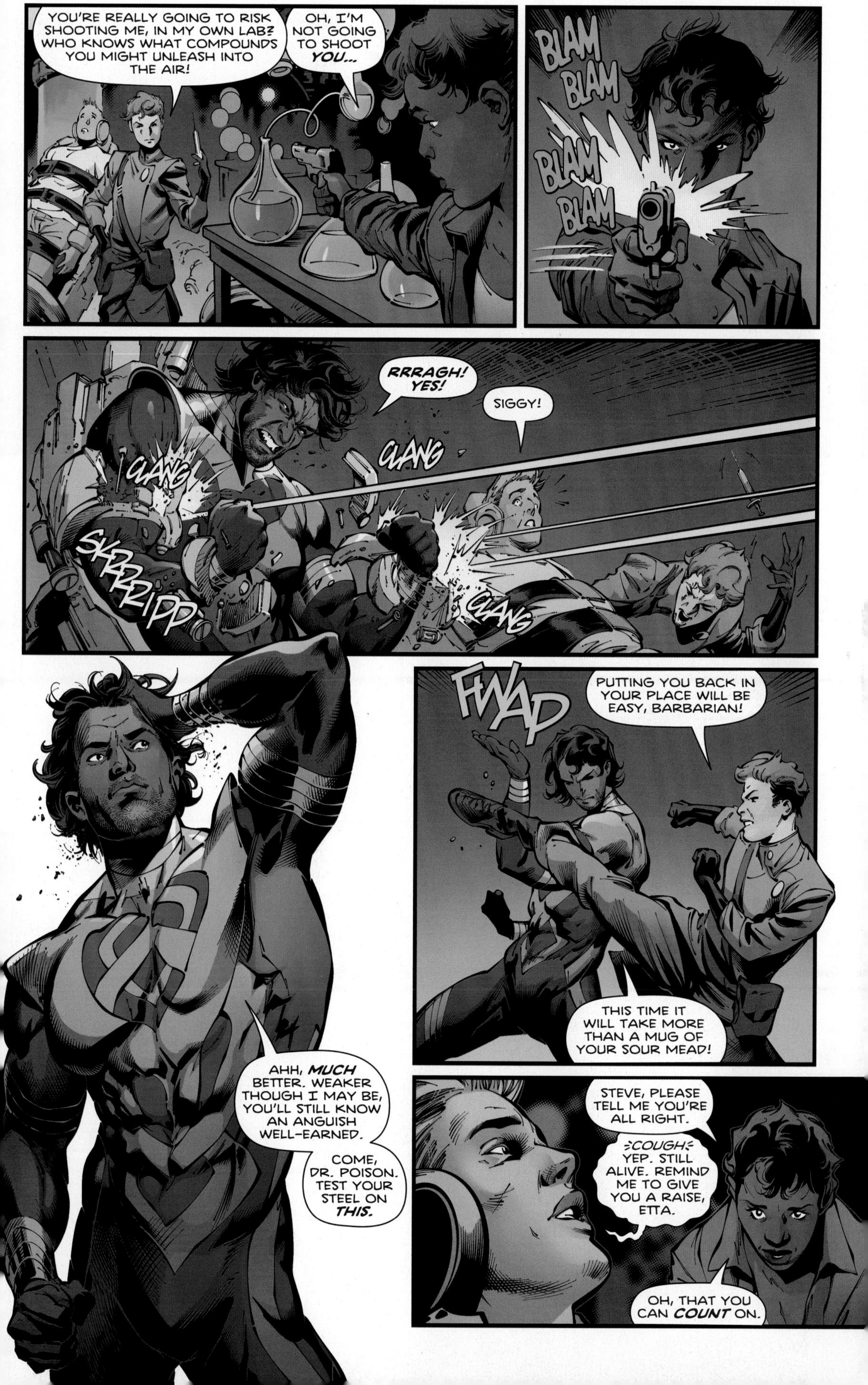

YOU'RE REALLY GOING TO RISK SHOOTING ME, IN MY OWN LAB? WHO KNOWS WHAT COMPOUNDS YOU MIGHT UNLEASH INTO THE AIR!
OH, I'M NOT GOING TO SHOOT *YOU...*
BLAM BLAM
BLAM BLAM
RRRAGH! YES!
SIGGY!
CLANG
CLANG
SKRRRIPP
CLANG
AHH, *MUCH* BETTER. WEAKER THOUGH I MAY BE, YOU'LL STILL KNOW AN ANGUISH WELL-EARNED.
COME, DR. POISON. TEST YOUR STEEL ON *THIS.*
FWAP
PUTTING YOU BACK IN YOUR PLACE WILL BE EASY, BARBARIAN!
THIS TIME IT WILL TAKE MORE THAN A MUG OF YOUR SOUR MEAD!
STEVE, PLEASE TELL ME YOU'RE ALL RIGHT.
COUGH YEP. STILL ALIVE. REMIND ME TO GIVE YOU A RAISE, ETTA.
OH, THAT YOU CAN *COUNT* ON.

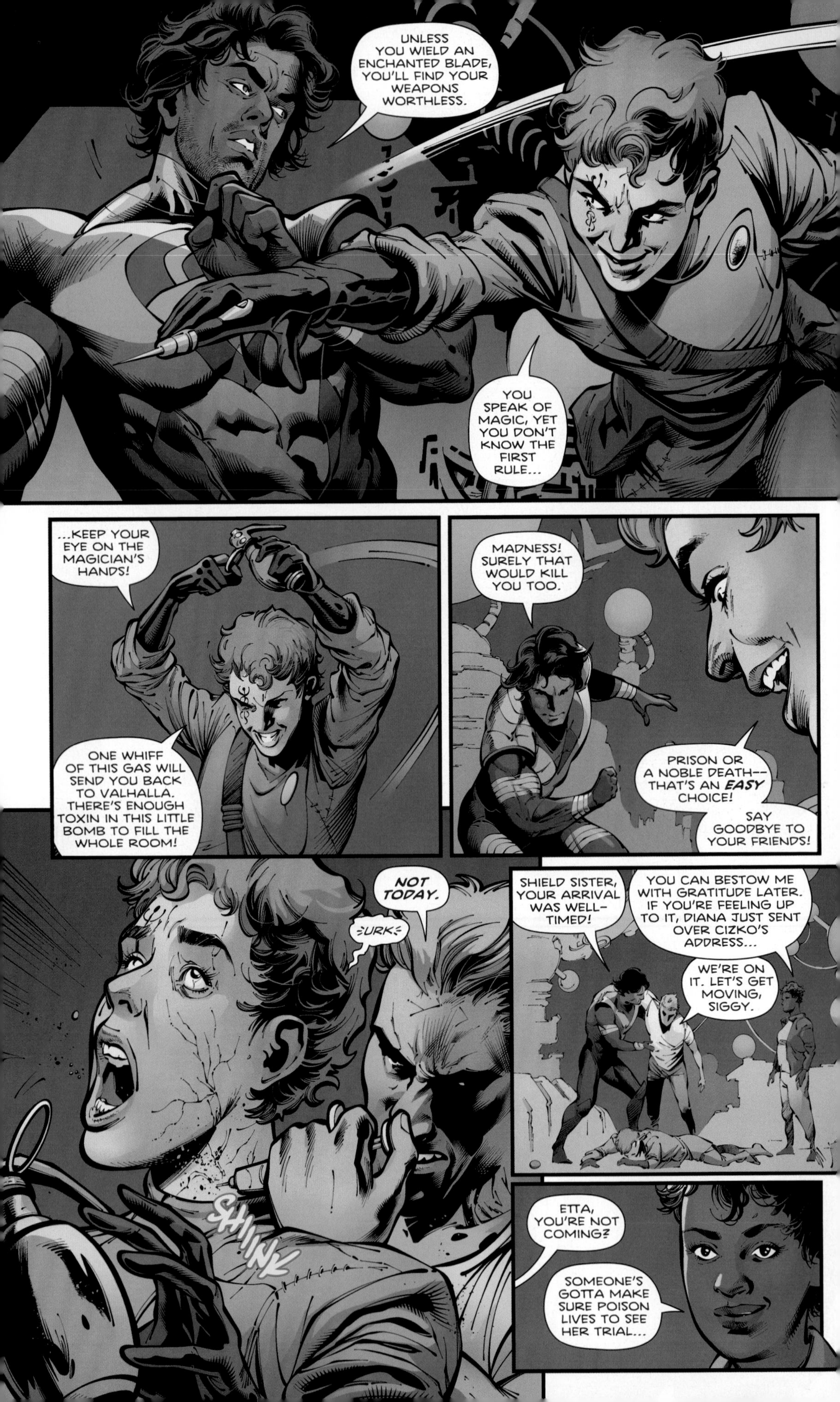
UNLESS YOU WIELD AN ENCHANTED BLADE, YOU'LL FIND YOUR WEAPONS WORTHLESS.
YOU SPEAK OF MAGIC, YET YOU DON'T KNOW THE FIRST RULE...
...KEEP YOUR EYE ON THE MAGICIAN'S HANDS!
ONE WHIFF OF THIS GAS WILL SEND YOU BACK TO VALHALLA. THERE'S ENOUGH TOXIN IN THIS LITTLE BOMB TO FILL THE WHOLE ROOM!
MADNESS! SURELY THAT WOULD KILL YOU TOO.
PRISON OR A NOBLE DEATH--THAT'S AN *EASY* CHOICE!
SAY GOODBYE TO YOUR FRIENDS!
NOT TODAY.
URK
SHIIINK
SHIELD SISTER, YOUR ARRIVAL WAS WELL-TIMED!
YOU CAN BESTOW ME WITH GRATITUDE LATER. IF YOU'RE FEELING UP TO IT, DIANA JUST SENT OVER CIZKO'S ADDRESS...
WE'RE ON IT. LET'S GET MOVING, SIGGY.
ETTA, YOU'RE NOT COMING?
SOMEONE'S GOTTA MAKE SURE POISON LIVES TO SEE HER TRIAL...

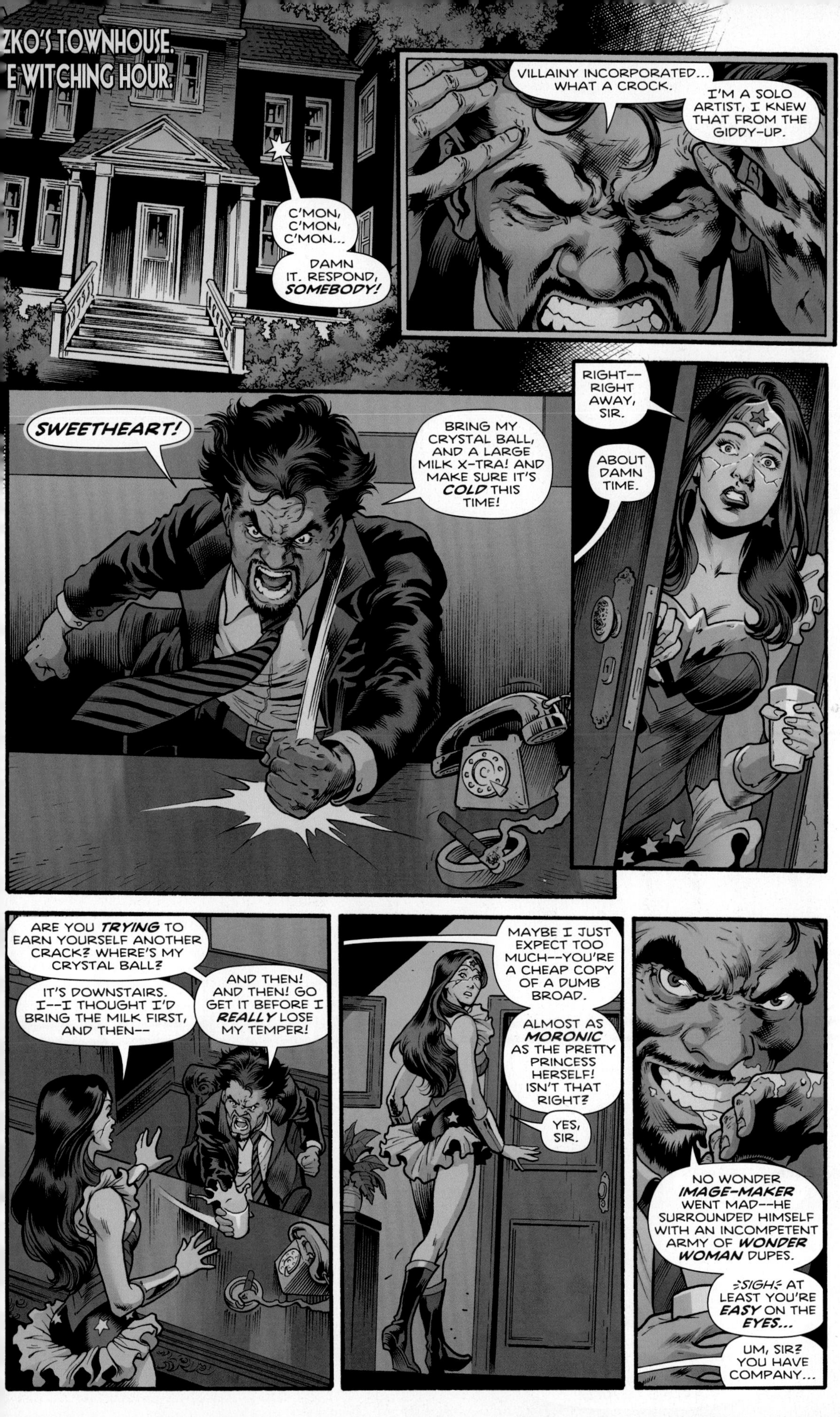
ZKO'S TOWNHOUSE.
E WITCHING HOUR.
C'MON, C'MON, C'MON...
DAMN IT. RESPOND, SOMEBODY!
VILLAINY INCORPORATED... WHAT A CROCK.
I'M A SOLO ARTIST, I KNEW THAT FROM THE GIDDY-UP.
SWEETHEART!
BRING MY CRYSTAL BALL, AND A LARGE MILK X-TRA! AND MAKE SURE IT'S COLD THIS TIME!
RIGHT-- RIGHT AWAY, SIR.
ABOUT DAMN TIME.
ARE YOU TRYING TO EARN YOURSELF ANOTHER CRACK? WHERE'S MY CRYSTAL BALL?
IT'S DOWNSTAIRS. I--I THOUGHT I'D BRING THE MILK FIRST, AND THEN--
AND THEN! AND THEN! GO GET IT BEFORE I REALLY LOSE MY TEMPER!
MAYBE I JUST EXPECT TOO MUCH--YOU'RE A CHEAP COPY OF A DUMB BROAD.
ALMOST AS MORONIC AS THE PRETTY PRINCESS HERSELF! ISN'T THAT RIGHT?
YES, SIR.
NO WONDER IMAGE-MAKER WENT MAD--HE SURROUNDED HIMSELF WITH AN INCOMPETENT ARMY OF WONDER WOMAN DUPES.
SIGH AT LEAST YOU'RE EASY ON THE EYES...
UM, SIR? YOU HAVE COMPANY...

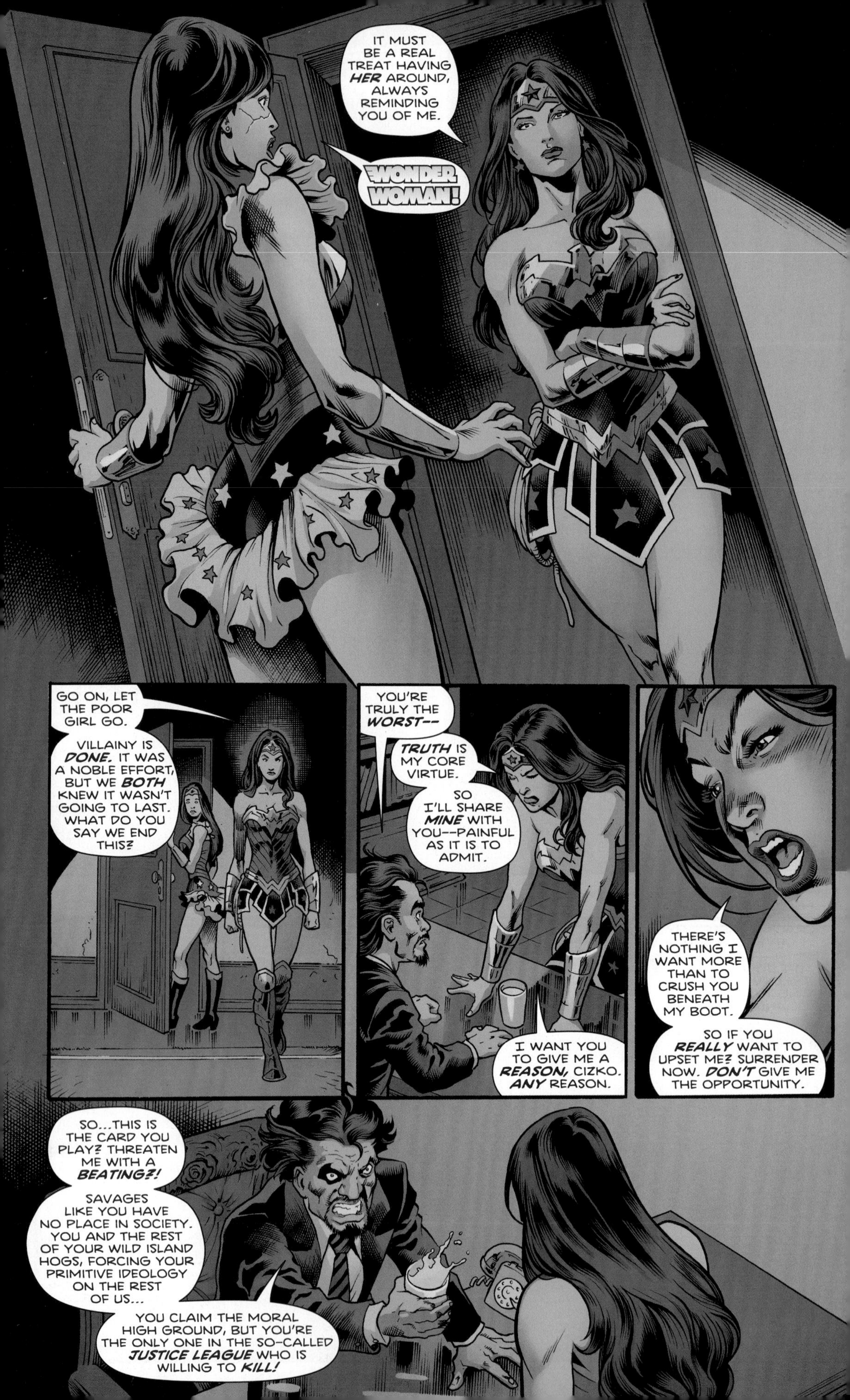
IT MUST BE A REAL TREAT HAVING HER AROUND, ALWAYS REMINDING YOU OF ME.
WONDER WOMAN!
GO ON, LET THE POOR GIRL GO.
VILLAINY IS DONE. IT WAS A NOBLE EFFORT, BUT WE BOTH KNEW IT WASN'T GOING TO LAST. WHAT DO YOU SAY WE END THIS?
YOU'RE TRULY THE WORST--
TRUTH IS MY CORE VIRTUE.
SO I'LL SHARE MINE WITH YOU--PAINFUL AS IT IS TO ADMIT.
I WANT YOU TO GIVE ME A REASON, CIZKO. ANY REASON.
THERE'S NOTHING I WANT MORE THAN TO CRUSH YOU BENEATH MY BOOT.
SO IF YOU REALLY WANT TO UPSET ME? SURRENDER NOW. DON'T GIVE ME THE OPPORTUNITY.
SO...THIS IS THE CARD YOU PLAY? THREATEN ME WITH A BEATING?!
SAVAGES LIKE YOU HAVE NO PLACE IN SOCIETY. YOU AND THE REST OF YOUR WILD ISLAND HOGS, FORCING YOUR PRIMITIVE IDEOLOGY ON THE REST OF US...
YOU CLAIM THE MORAL HIGH GROUND, BUT YOU'RE THE ONLY ONE IN THE SO-CALLED JUSTICE LEAGUE WHO IS WILLING TO KILL!

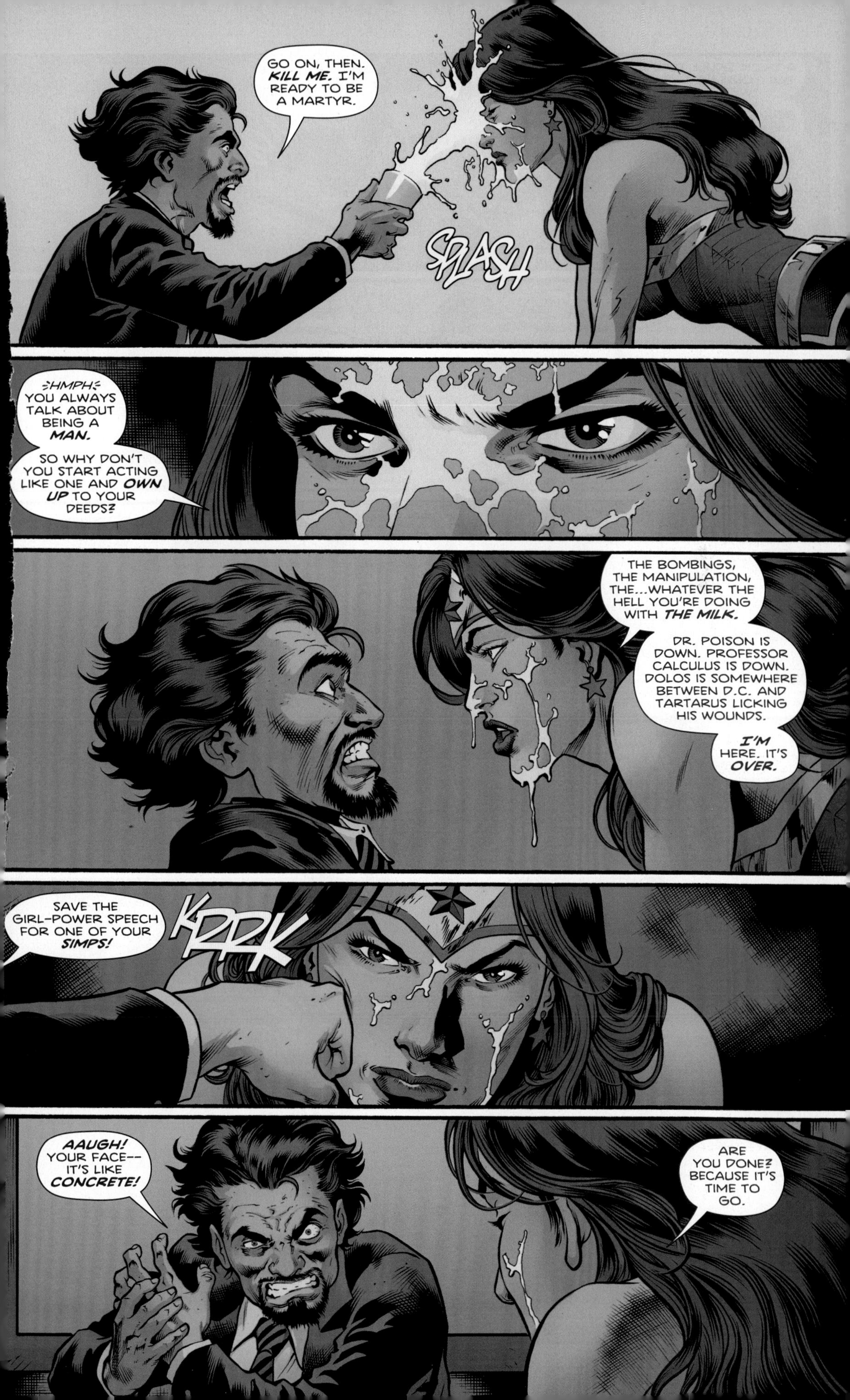
GO ON, THEN. KILL ME. I'M READY TO BE A MARTYR.
SPLASH
:HMPH: YOU ALWAYS TALK ABOUT BEING A MAN.
SO WHY DON'T YOU START ACTING LIKE ONE AND OWN UP TO YOUR DEEDS?
THE BOMBINGS, THE MANIPULATION, THE...WHATEVER THE HELL YOU'RE DOING WITH THE MILK.
DR. POISON IS DOWN. PROFESSOR CALCULUS IS DOWN. DOLOS IS SOMEWHERE BETWEEN D.C. AND TARTARUS LICKING HIS WOUNDS.
I'M HERE. IT'S OVER.
SAVE THE GIRL-POWER SPEECH FOR ONE OF YOUR SIMPS!
KRRK
AAUGH! YOUR FACE-- IT'S LIKE CONCRETE!
ARE YOU DONE? BECAUSE IT'S TIME TO GO.

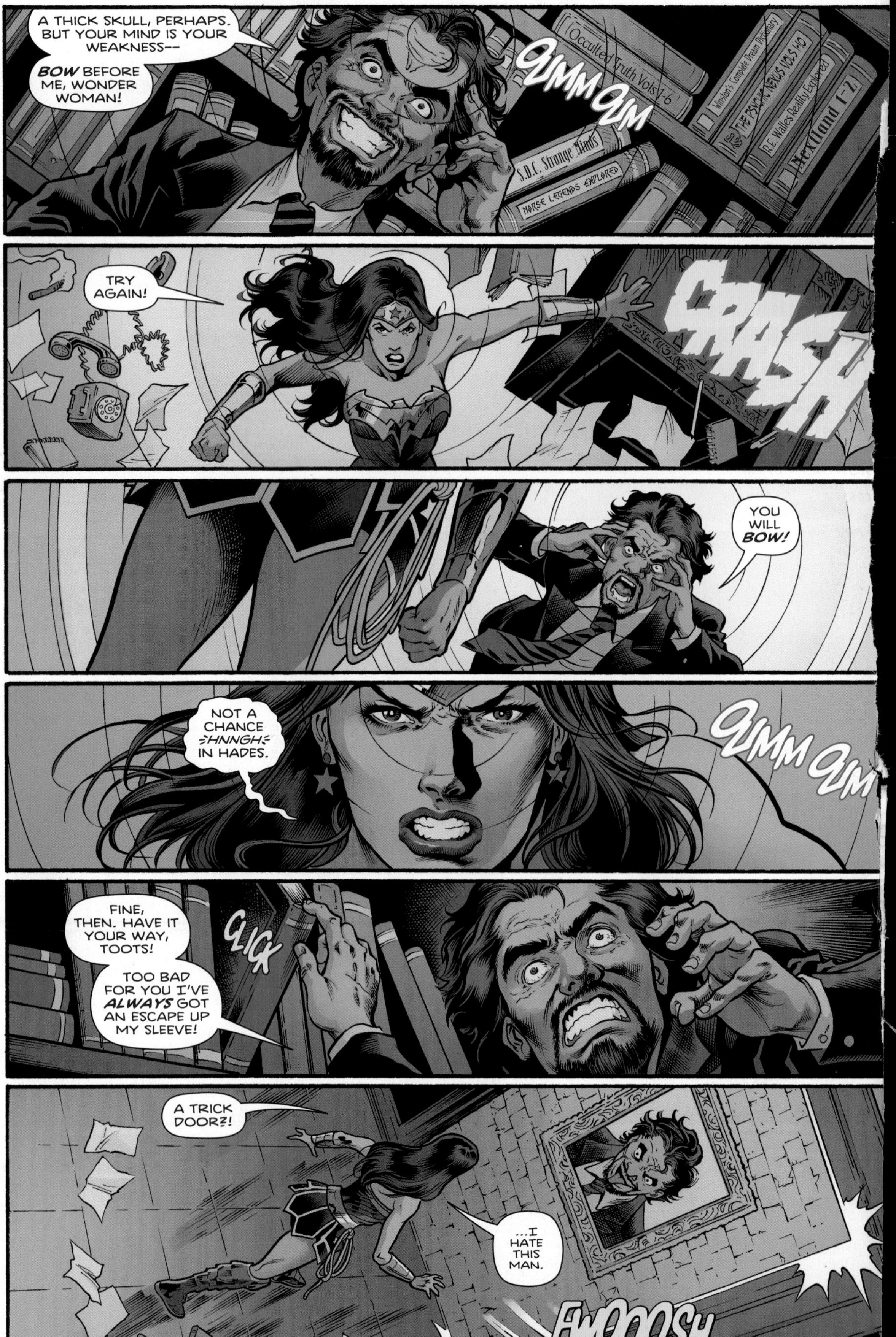
A THICK SKULL, PERHAPS. BUT YOUR MIND IS YOUR WEAKNESS--
BOW BEFORE ME, WONDER WOMAN!
QUMM QUM
Occulted Truth Vols 1-6
Winston's Complete Dream Dictionary
THE PSYCHIC NEWS VOLS 1-10
R.E. Walles Reality Explored
Nextland 1-2
S.D.C. Strange Minds
NORSE LEGENDS EXPLORED
TRY AGAIN!
CRASH
YOU WILL BOW!
NOT A CHANCE HNNGH IN HADES.
QUMM QUM
FINE, THEN. HAVE IT YOUR WAY, TOOTS!
TOO BAD FOR YOU I'VE ALWAYS GOT AN ESCAPE UP MY SLEEVE!
CLICK
A TRICK DOOR?!
...I HATE THIS MAN.
FWOOOSH

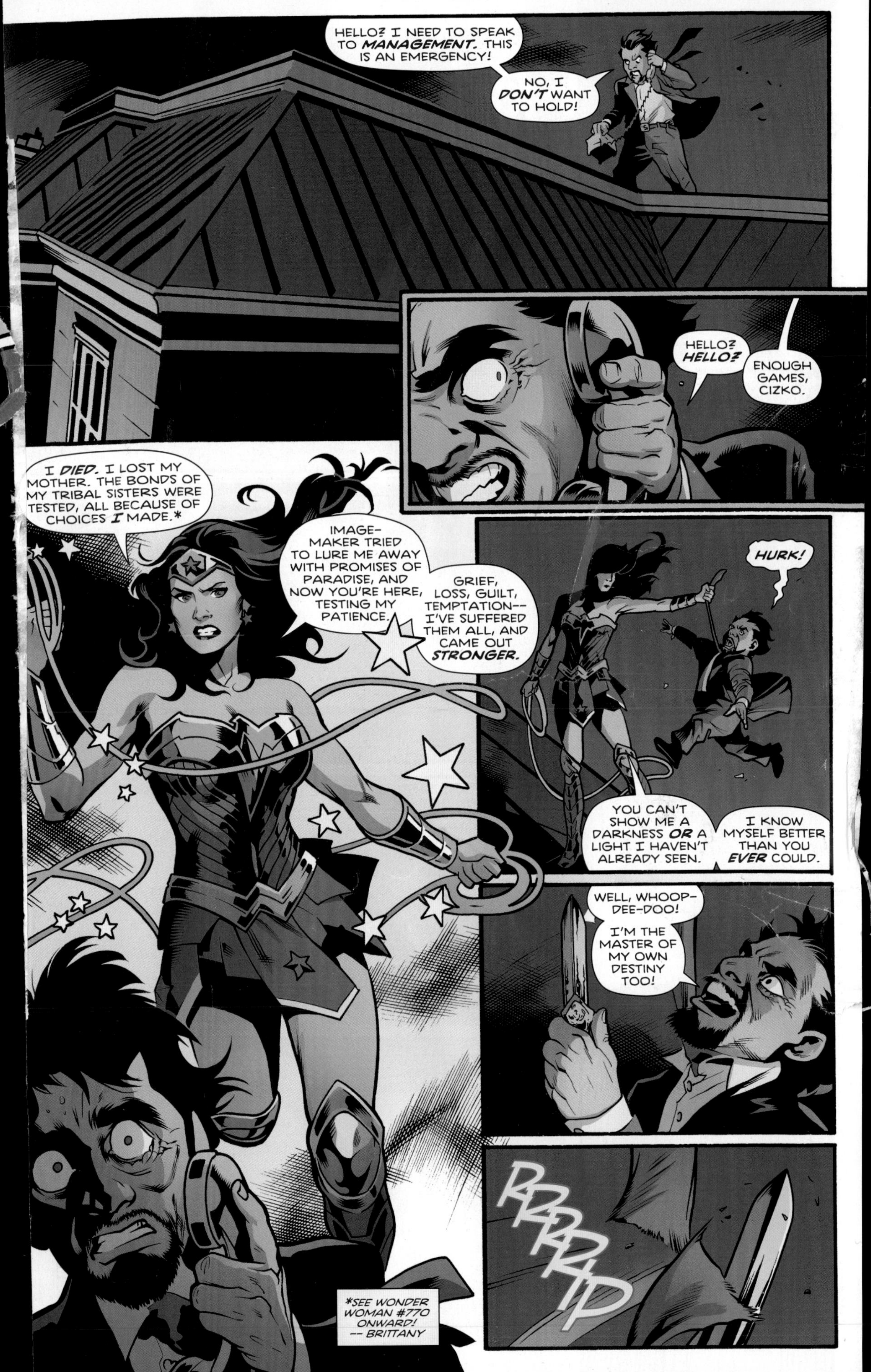
HELLO? I NEED TO SPEAK TO MANAGEMENT. THIS IS AN EMERGENCY!
NO, I DON'T WANT TO HOLD!
HELLO? HELLO?
ENOUGH GAMES, CIZKO.
I DIED. I LOST MY MOTHER. THE BONDS OF MY TRIBAL SISTERS WERE TESTED, ALL BECAUSE OF CHOICES I MADE.*
IMAGE-MAKER TRIED TO LURE ME AWAY WITH PROMISES OF PARADISE, AND NOW YOU'RE HERE, TESTING MY PATIENCE.
GRIEF, LOSS, GUILT, TEMPTATION-- I'VE SUFFERED THEM ALL, AND CAME OUT STRONGER.
HURK!
YOU CAN'T SHOW ME A DARKNESS OR A LIGHT I HAVEN'T ALREADY SEEN.
I KNOW MYSELF BETTER THAN YOU EVER COULD.
WELL, WHOOP-DEE-DOO!
I'M THE MASTER OF MY OWN DESTINY TOO!
*SEE WONDER WOMAN #770 ONWARD! -- BRITTANY
RRRRIP

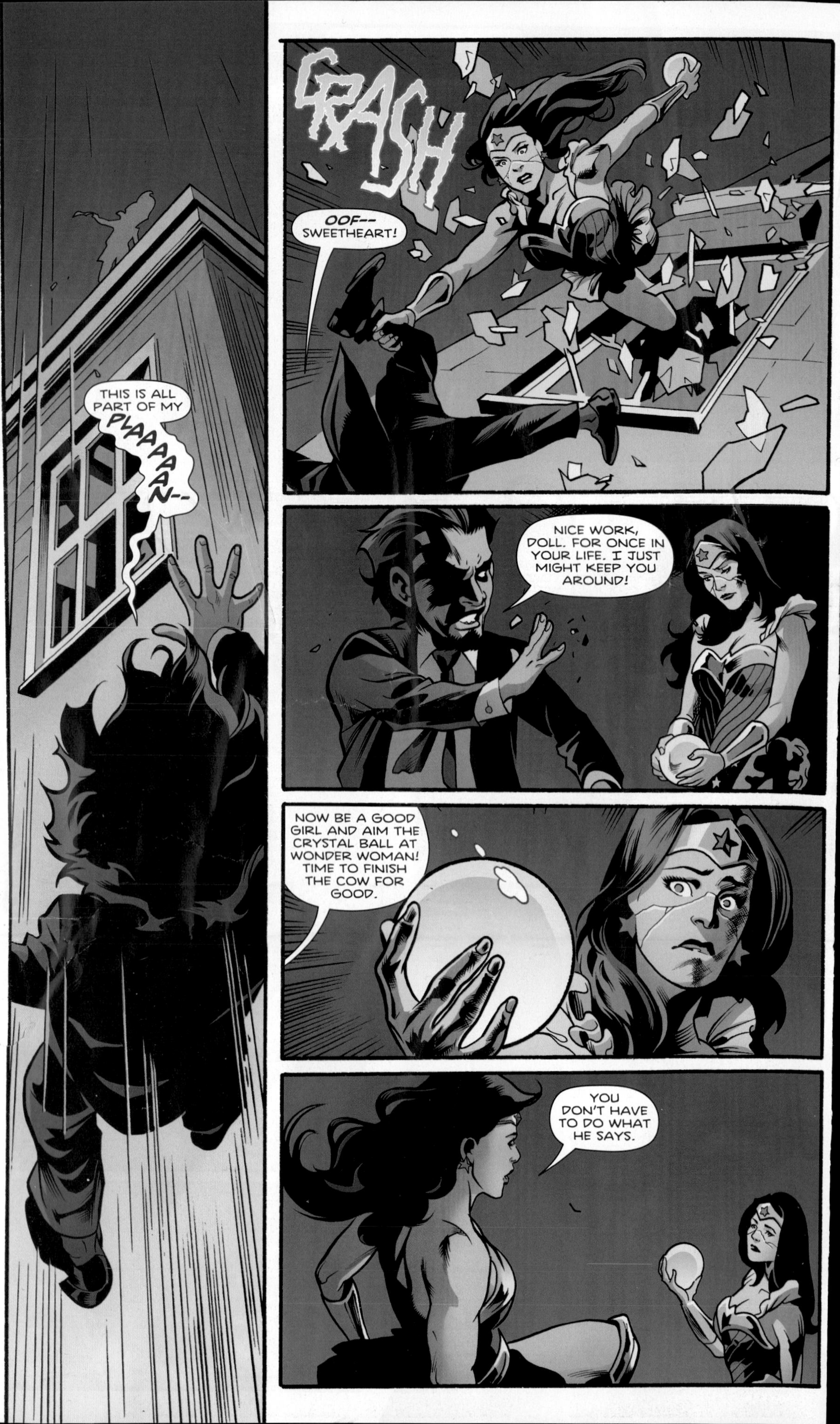
THIS IS ALL PART OF MY PLAAAAAN--
CRASH
OOF-- SWEETHEART!
NICE WORK, DOLL. FOR ONCE IN YOUR LIFE. I JUST MIGHT KEEP YOU AROUND!
NOW BE A GOOD GIRL AND AIM THE CRYSTAL BALL AT WONDER WOMAN! TIME TO FINISH THE COW FOR GOOD.
YOU DON'T HAVE TO DO WHAT HE SAYS.

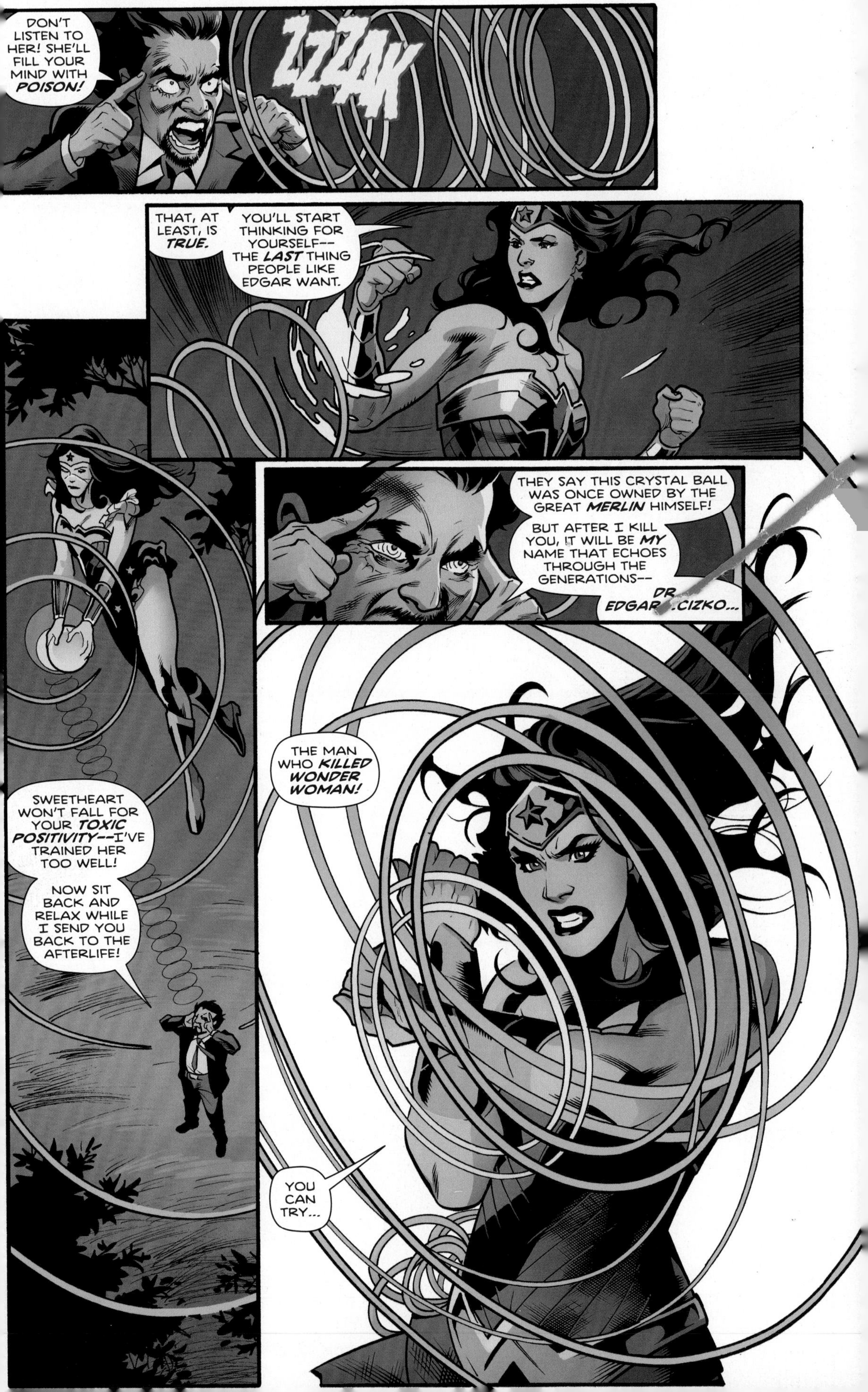
DON'T LISTEN TO HER! SHE'LL FILL YOUR MIND WITH *POISON!*
ZZZAK
THAT, AT LEAST, IS *TRUE.*
YOU'LL START THINKING FOR YOURSELF-- THE *LAST* THING PEOPLE LIKE EDGAR WANT.
THEY SAY THIS CRYSTAL BALL WAS ONCE OWNED BY THE GREAT *MERLIN* HIMSELF!
BUT AFTER I KILL YOU, IT WILL BE *MY* NAME THAT ECHOES THROUGH THE GENERATIONS--
DR EDGAR CIZKO...
THE MAN WHO *KILLED WONDER WOMAN!*
SWEETHEART WON'T FALL FOR YOUR *TOXIC POSITIVITY*--I'VE TRAINED HER TOO WELL!
NOW SIT BACK AND RELAX WHILE I SEND YOU BACK TO THE AFTERLIFE!
YOU CAN TRY...

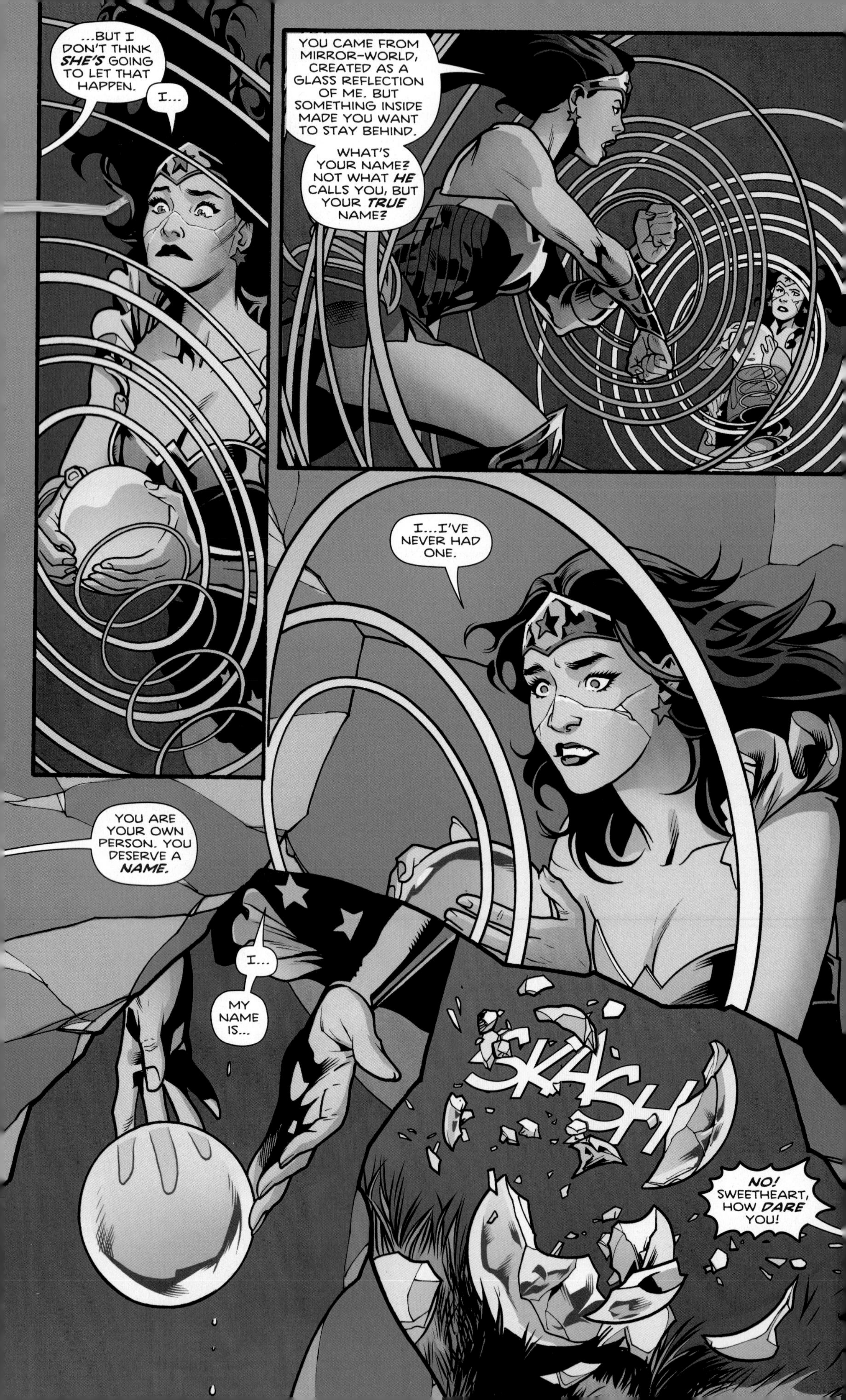
...BUT I DON'T THINK SHE'S GOING TO LET THAT HAPPEN.
I...
YOU CAME FROM MIRROR-WORLD, CREATED AS A GLASS REFLECTION OF ME. BUT SOMETHING INSIDE MADE YOU WANT TO STAY BEHIND.
WHAT'S YOUR NAME? NOT WHAT HE CALLS YOU, BUT YOUR TRUE NAME?
I...I'VE NEVER HAD ONE.
YOU ARE YOUR OWN PERSON. YOU DESERVE A NAME.
I...
MY NAME IS...
SKASH
NO! SWEETHEART, HOW DARE YOU!

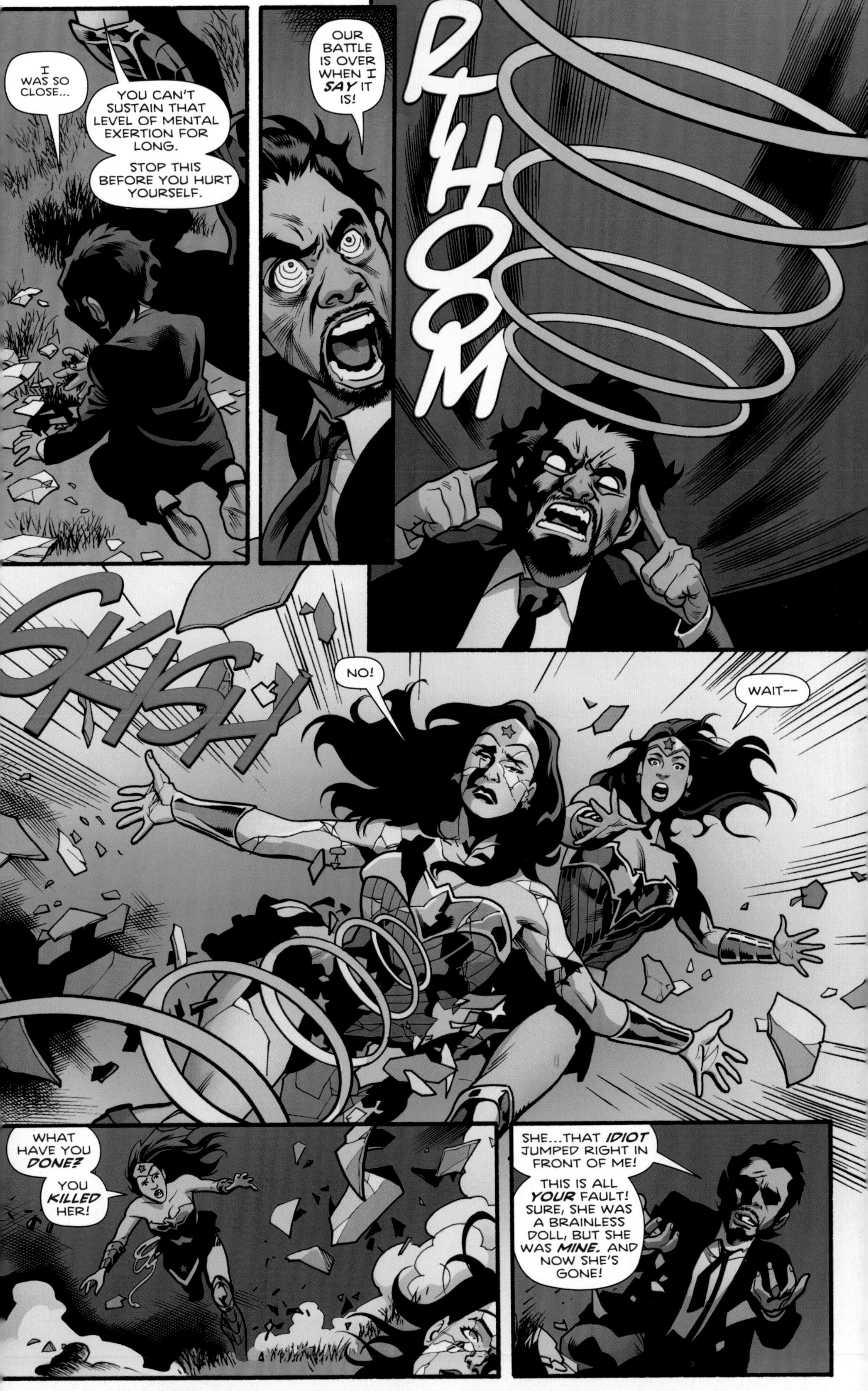
I WAS SO CLOSE...
YOU CAN'T SUSTAIN THAT LEVEL OF MENTAL EXERTION FOR LONG.
STOP THIS BEFORE YOU HURT YOURSELF.
OUR BATTLE IS OVER WHEN I SAY IT IS!
RTHOOM
SKISH
NO!
WAIT--
WHAT HAVE YOU DONE?
YOU KILLED HER!
SHE...THAT IDIOT JUMPED RIGHT IN FRONT OF ME!
THIS IS ALL YOUR FAULT! SURE, SHE WAS A BRAINLESS DOLL, BUT SHE WAS MINE. AND NOW SHE'S GONE!

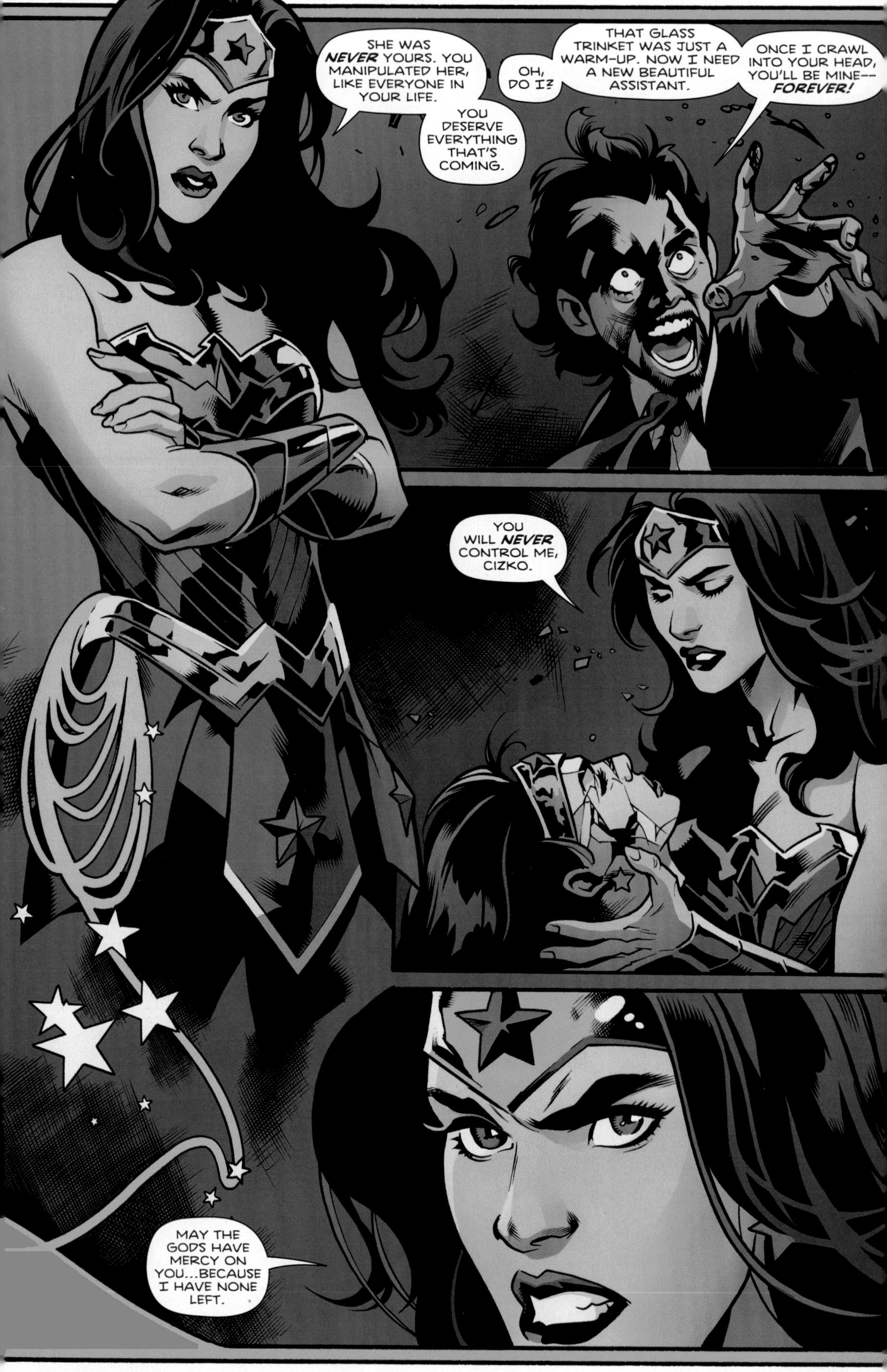
SHE WAS NEVER YOURS. YOU MANIPULATED HER, LIKE EVERYONE IN YOUR LIFE.
YOU DESERVE EVERYTHING THAT'S COMING.
OH, DO I?
THAT GLASS TRINKET WAS JUST A WARM-UP. NOW I NEED A NEW BEAUTIFUL ASSISTANT.
ONCE I CRAWL INTO YOUR HEAD, YOU'LL BE MINE-- FOREVER!
YOU WILL NEVER CONTROL ME, CIZKO.
MAY THE GODS HAVE MERCY ON YOU...BECAUSE I HAVE NONE LEFT.

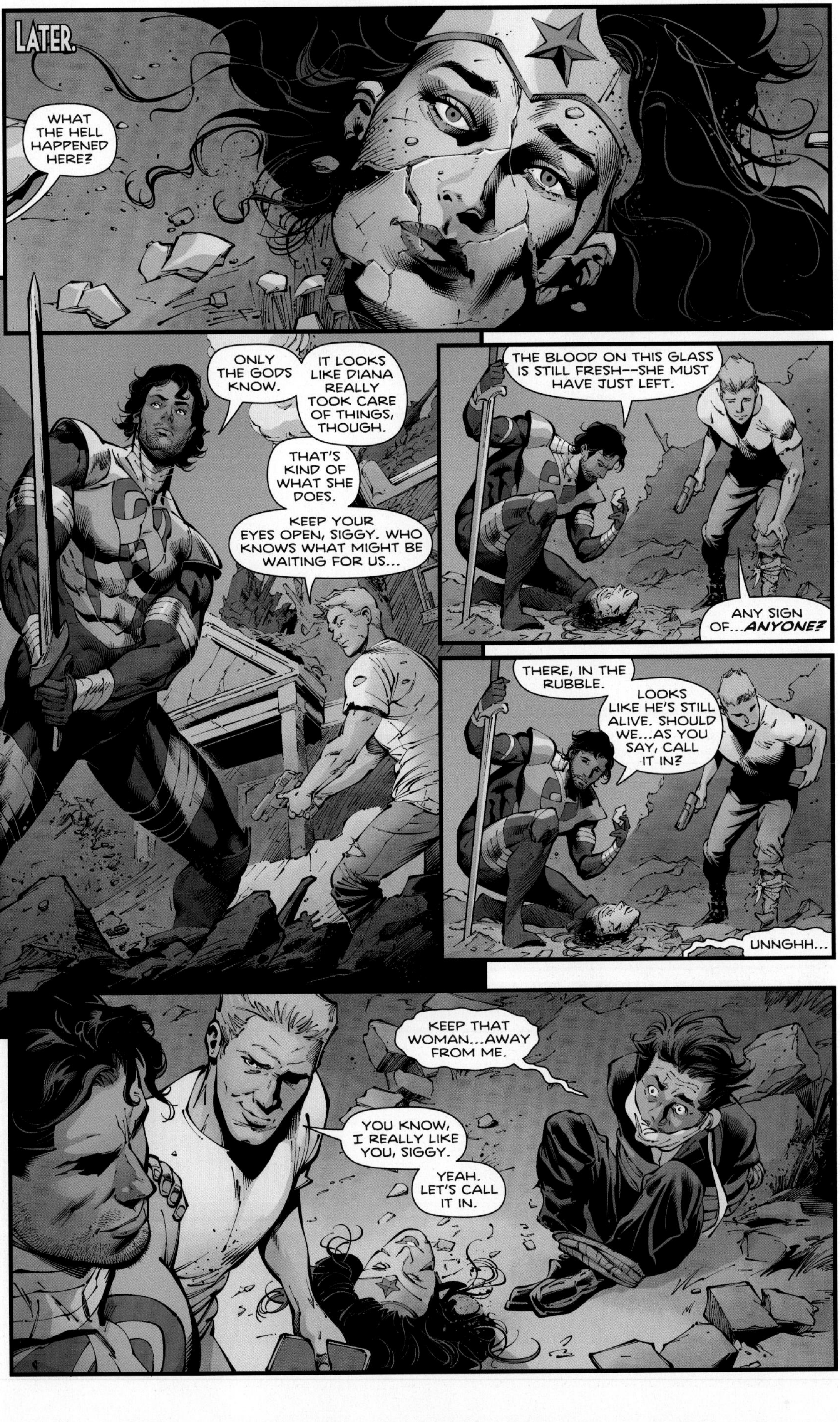
LATER.
WHAT THE HELL HAPPENED HERE?
ONLY THE GODS KNOW.
IT LOOKS LIKE DIANA REALLY TOOK CARE OF THINGS, THOUGH.
THAT'S KIND OF WHAT SHE DOES.
KEEP YOUR EYES OPEN, SIGGY. WHO KNOWS WHAT MIGHT BE WAITING FOR US...
THE BLOOD ON THIS GLASS IS STILL FRESH--SHE MUST HAVE JUST LEFT.
ANY SIGN OF...*ANYONE?*
THERE, IN THE RUBBLE.
LOOKS LIKE HE'S STILL ALIVE. SHOULD WE...AS YOU SAY, CALL IT IN?
UNNGHH...
KEEP THAT WOMAN...AWAY FROM ME.
YOU KNOW, I REALLY LIKE YOU, SIGGY.
YEAH. LET'S CALL IT IN.

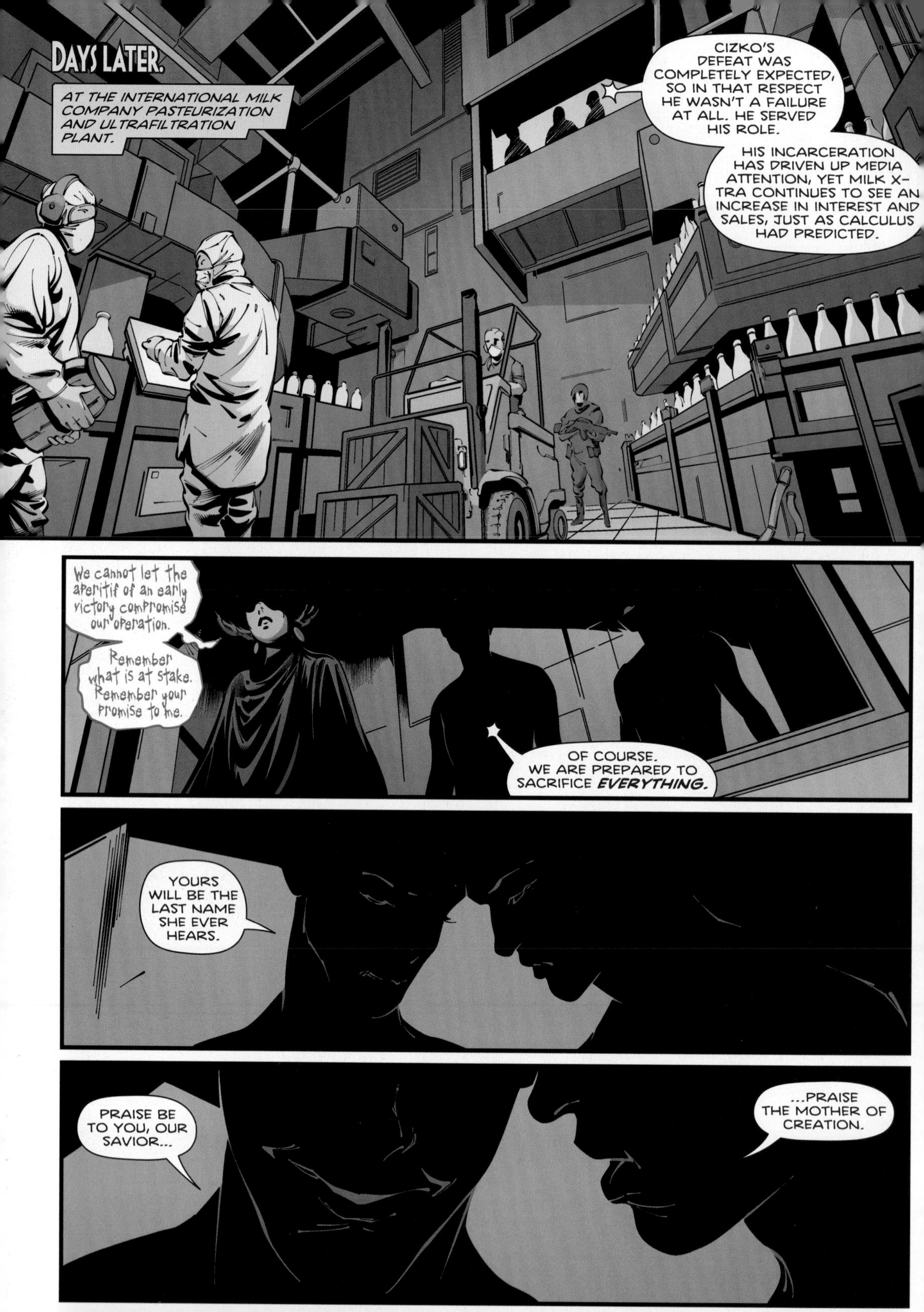
DAYS LATER.
AT THE INTERNATIONAL MILK COMPANY PASTEURIZATION AND ULTRAFILTRATION PLANT.
CIZKO'S DEFEAT WAS COMPLETELY EXPECTED, SO IN THAT RESPECT HE WASN'T A FAILURE AT ALL. HE SERVED HIS ROLE.
HIS INCARCERATION HAS DRIVEN UP MEDIA ATTENTION, YET MILK X-TRA CONTINUES TO SEE AN INCREASE IN INTEREST AND SALES, JUST AS CALCULUS HAD PREDICTED.
We cannot let the aperitif of an early victory compromise our operation.
Remember what is at stake. Remember your promise to me.
OF COURSE. WE ARE PREPARED TO SACRIFICE EVERYTHING.
YOURS WILL BE THE LAST NAME SHE EVER HEARS.
PRAISE BE TO YOU, OUR SAVIOR...
...PRAISE THE MOTHER OF CREATION.

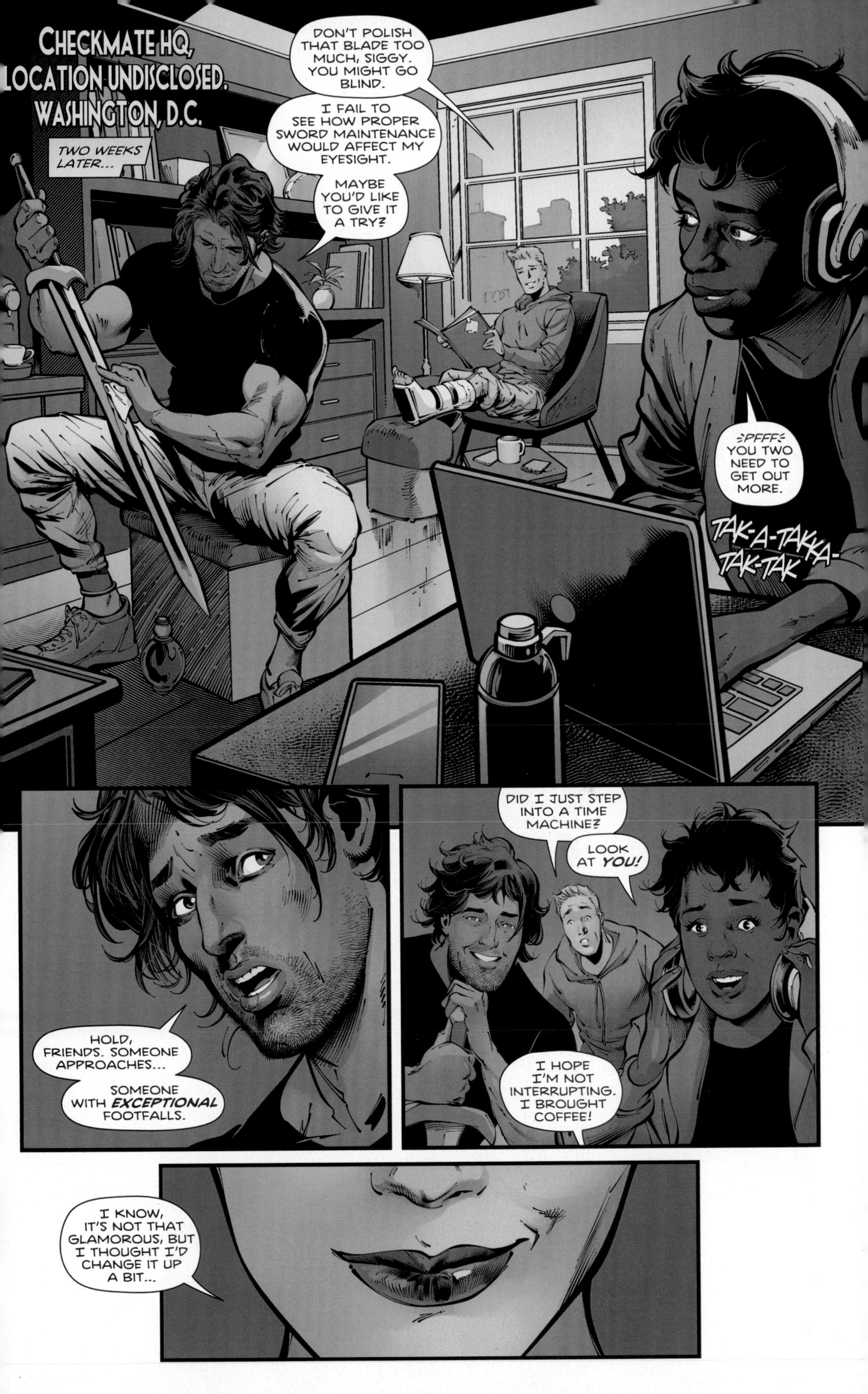
CHECKMATE HQ, LOCATION UNDISCLOSED. WASHINGTON, D.C.
TWO WEEKS LATER...
DON'T POLISH THAT BLADE TOO MUCH, SIGGY. YOU MIGHT GO BLIND.
I FAIL TO SEE HOW PROPER SWORD MAINTENANCE WOULD AFFECT MY EYESIGHT.
MAYBE YOU'D LIKE TO GIVE IT A TRY?
PFFF
YOU TWO NEED TO GET OUT MORE.
TAK-A-TAKKA-TAK-TAK
HOLD, FRIENDS. SOMEONE APPROACHES...
SOMEONE WITH *EXCEPTIONAL* FOOTFALLS.
DID I JUST STEP INTO A TIME MACHINE?
LOOK AT *YOU!*
I HOPE I'M NOT INTERRUPTING. I BROUGHT COFFEE!
I KNOW, IT'S NOT THAT GLAMOROUS, BUT I THOUGHT I'D CHANGE IT UP A BIT...

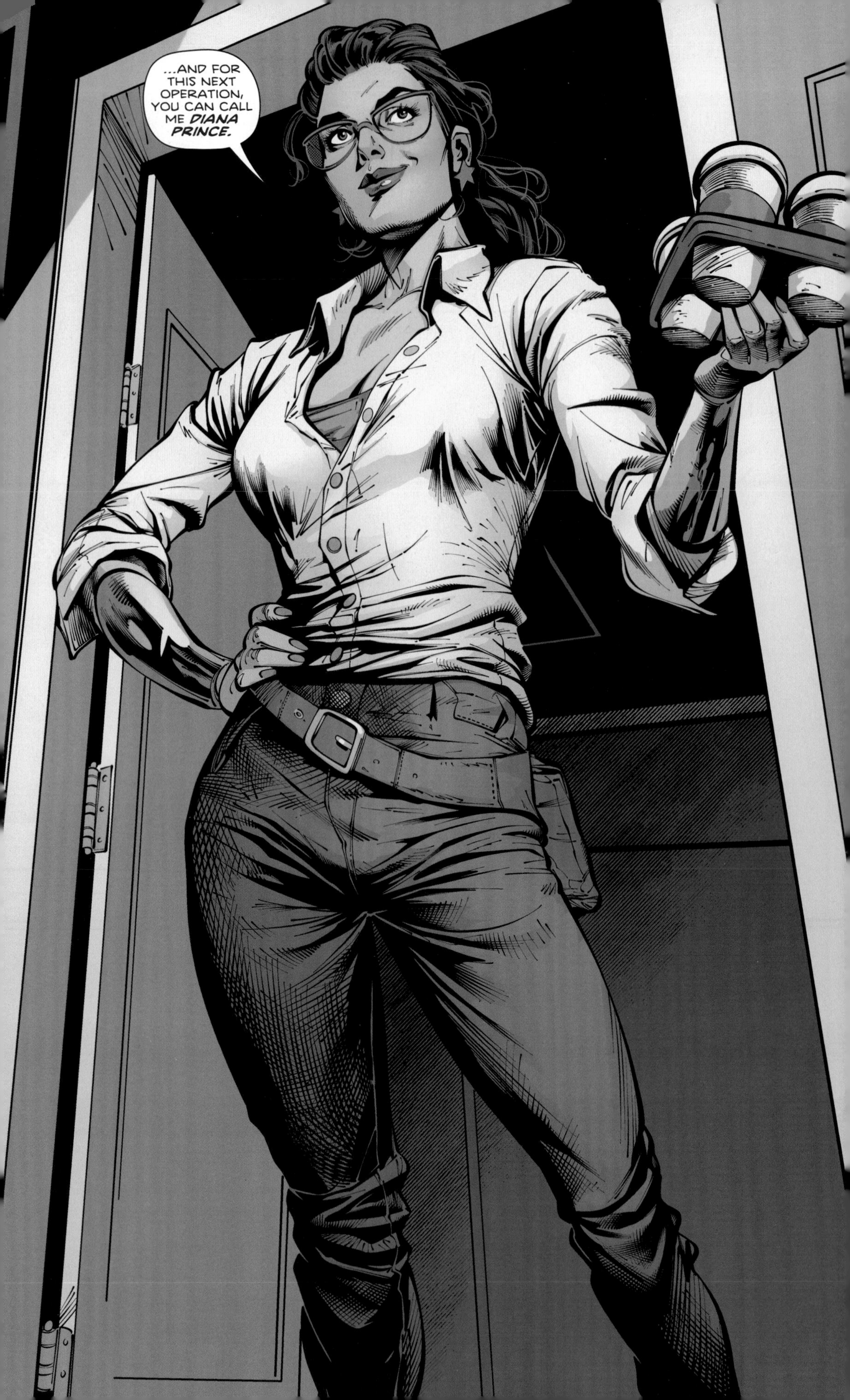
...AND FOR THIS NEXT OPERATION, YOU CAN CALL ME *DIANA PRINCE.*

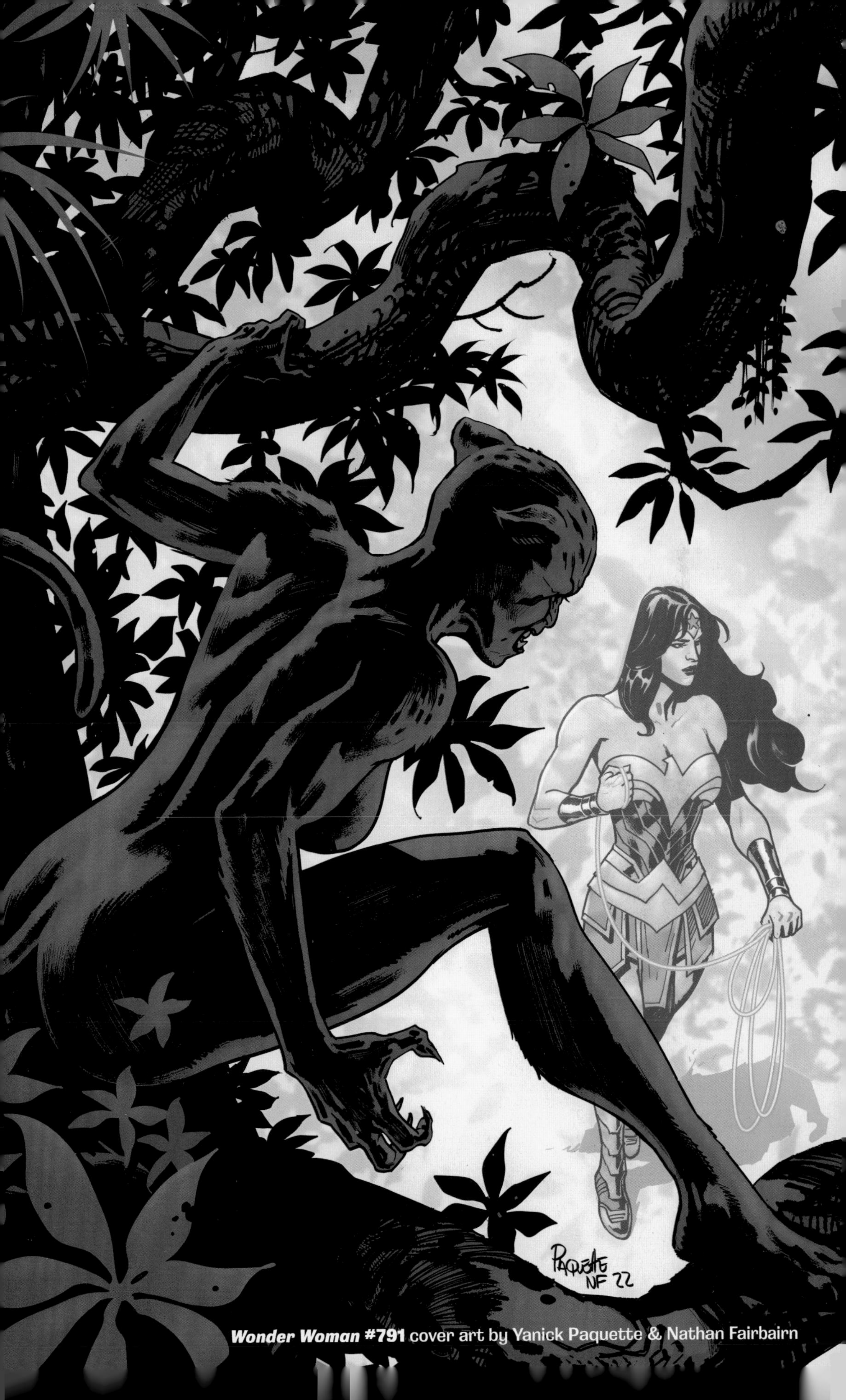

***Wonder Woman* #791** cover art by Yanick Paquette & Nathan Fairbairn

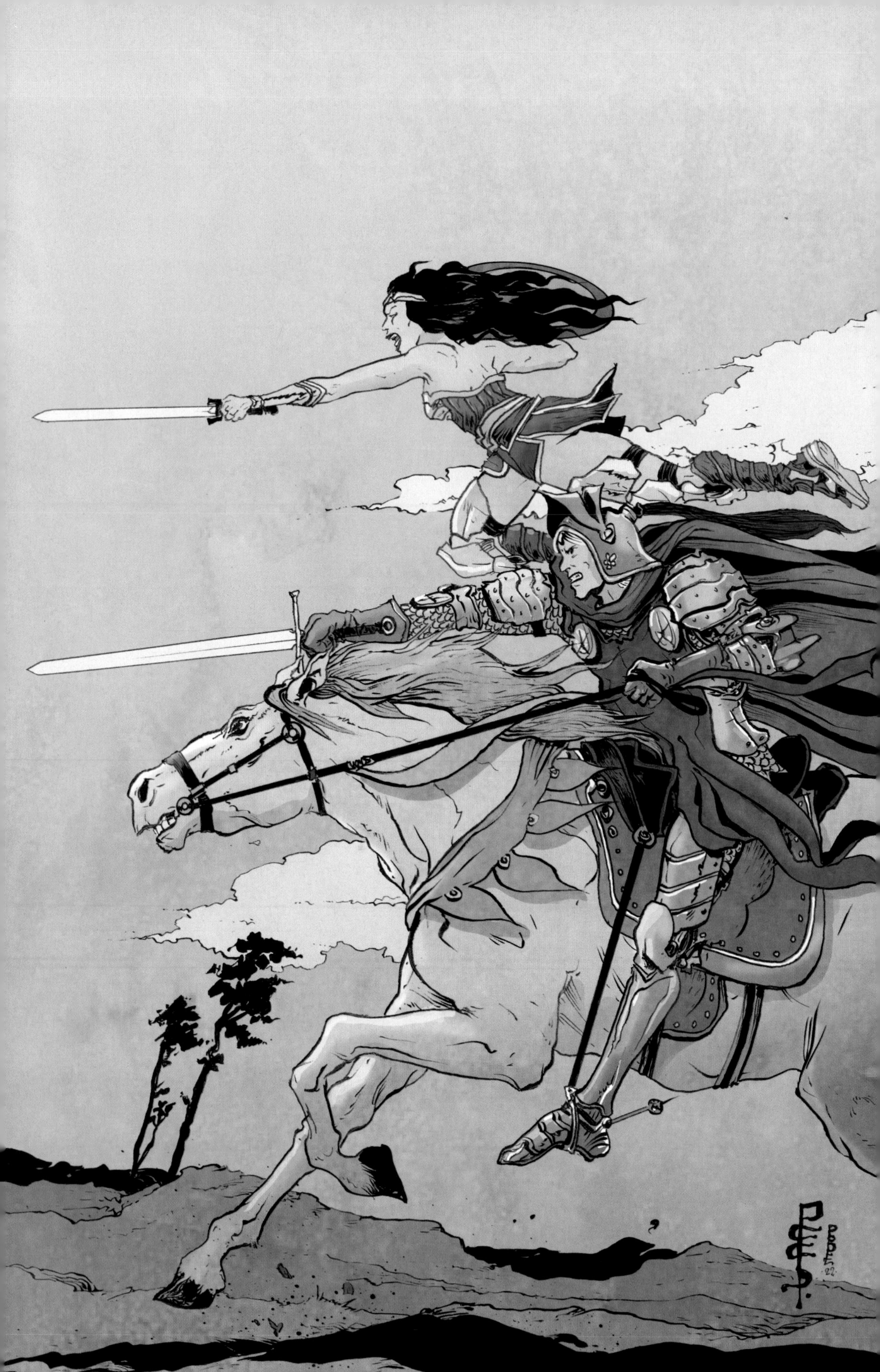

***Wonder Woman* #791** variant cover art by Paul Pope

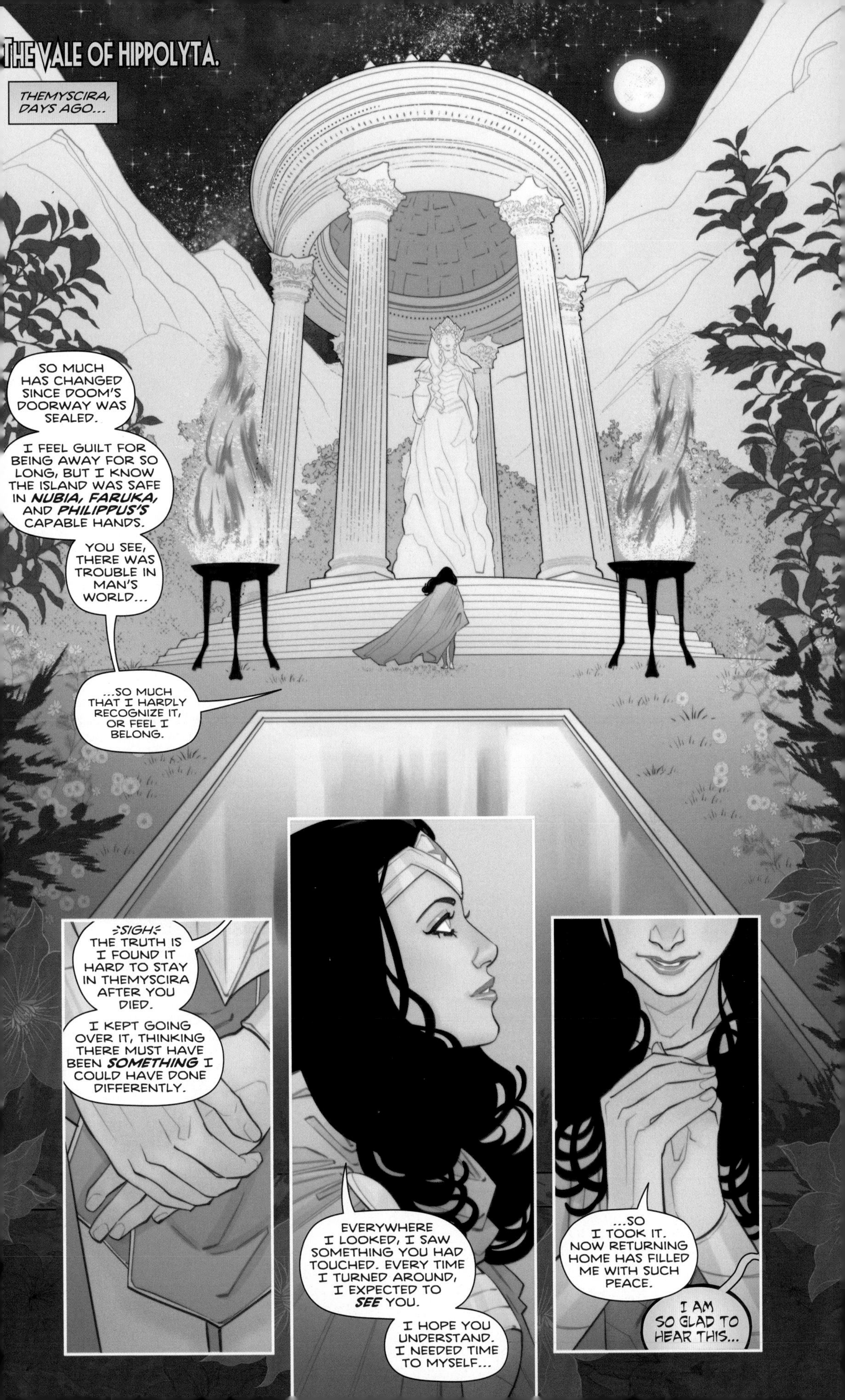
THE VALE OF HIPPOLYTA.
THEMYSCIRA, DAYS AGO...
SO MUCH HAS CHANGED SINCE DOOM'S DOORWAY WAS SEALED.
I FEEL GUILT FOR BEING AWAY FOR SO LONG, BUT I KNOW THE ISLAND WAS SAFE IN NUBIA, FARUKA, AND PHILIPPUS'S CAPABLE HANDS.
YOU SEE, THERE WAS TROUBLE IN MAN'S WORLD...
...SO MUCH THAT I HARDLY RECOGNIZE IT, OR FEEL I BELONG.
SIGH
THE TRUTH IS I FOUND IT HARD TO STAY IN THEMYSCIRA AFTER YOU DIED.
I KEPT GOING OVER IT, THINKING THERE MUST HAVE BEEN SOMETHING I COULD HAVE DONE DIFFERENTLY.
EVERYWHERE I LOOKED, I SAW SOMETHING YOU HAD TOUCHED. EVERY TIME I TURNED AROUND, I EXPECTED TO SEE YOU.
I HOPE YOU UNDERSTAND. I NEEDED TIME TO MYSELF...
...SO I TOOK IT. NOW RETURNING HOME HAS FILLED ME WITH SUCH PEACE.
I AM SO GLAD TO HEAR THIS...

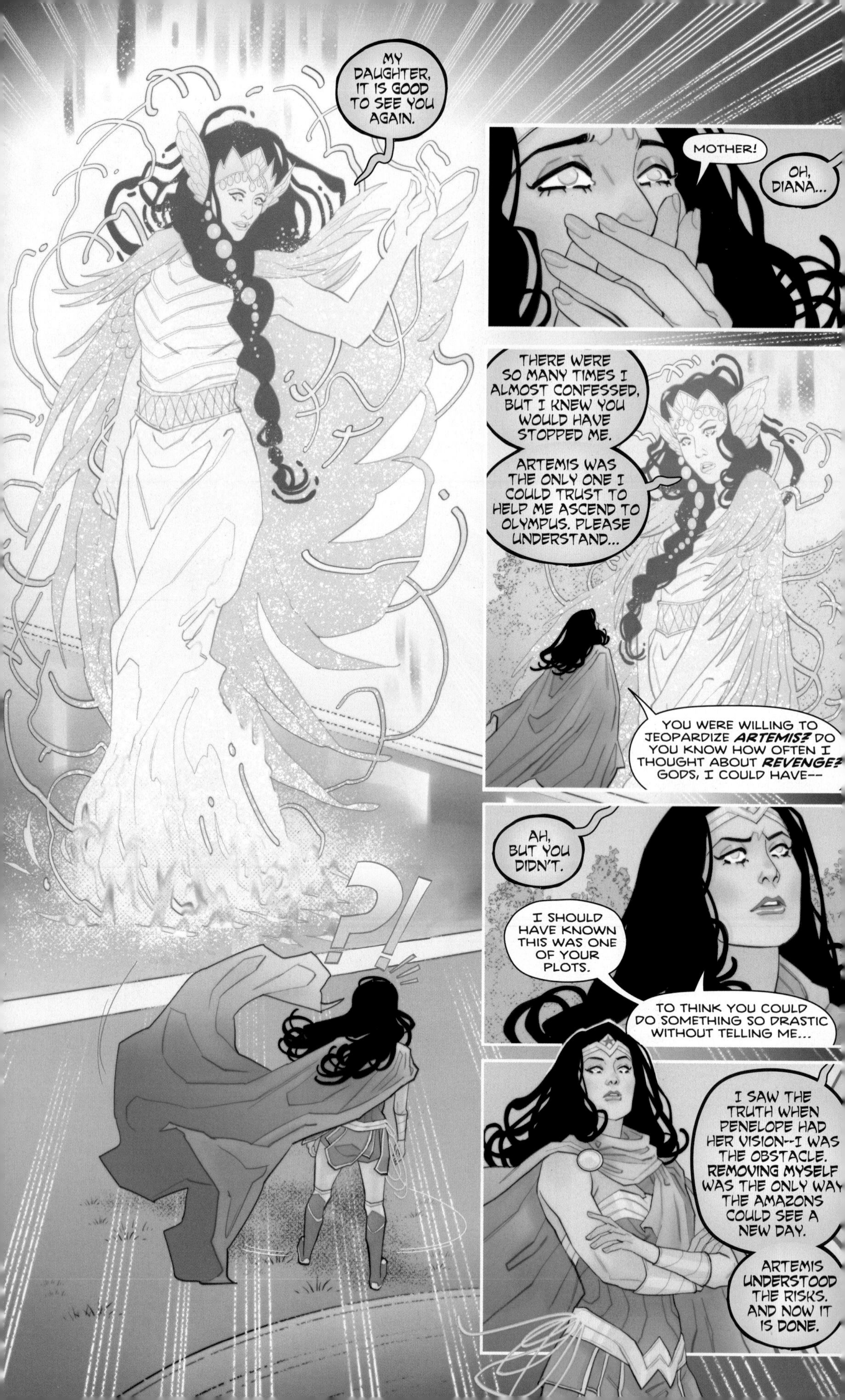
MY DAUGHTER, IT IS GOOD TO SEE YOU AGAIN.
?!
MOTHER!
OH, DIANA...
THERE WERE SO MANY TIMES I ALMOST CONFESSED, BUT I KNEW YOU WOULD HAVE STOPPED ME.
ARTEMIS WAS THE ONLY ONE I COULD TRUST TO HELP ME ASCEND TO OLYMPUS. PLEASE UNDERSTAND...
YOU WERE WILLING TO JEOPARDIZE ARTEMIS? DO YOU KNOW HOW OFTEN I THOUGHT ABOUT REVENGE? GODS, I COULD HAVE--
AH, BUT YOU DIDN'T.
I SHOULD HAVE KNOWN THIS WAS ONE OF YOUR PLOTS.
TO THINK YOU COULD DO SOMETHING SO DRASTIC WITHOUT TELLING ME...
I SAW THE TRUTH WHEN PENELOPE HAD HER VISION--I WAS THE OBSTACLE. REMOVING MYSELF WAS THE ONLY WAY THE AMAZONS COULD SEE A NEW DAY.
ARTEMIS UNDERSTOOD THE RISKS. AND NOW IT IS DONE.

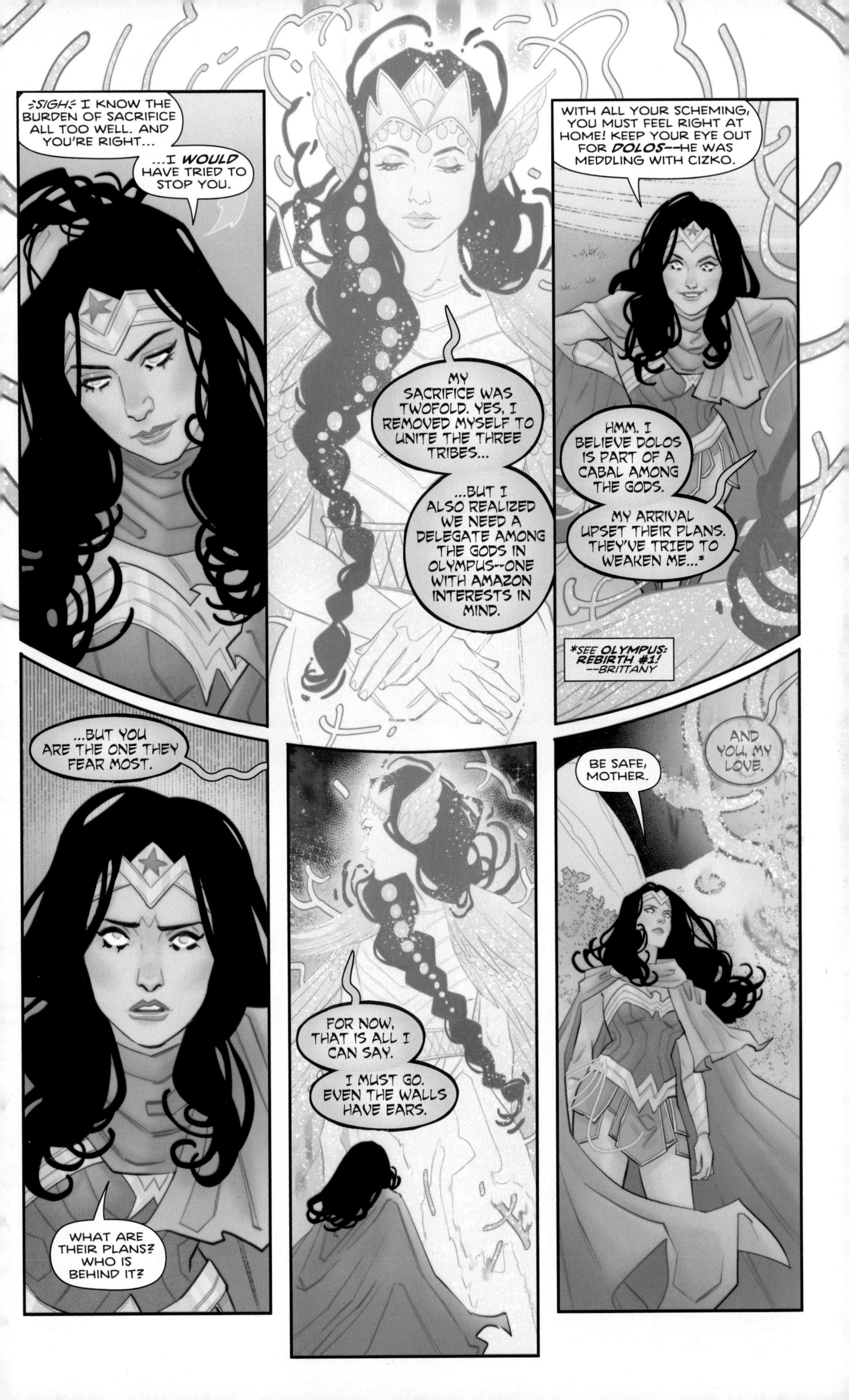

:SIGH: I KNOW THE BURDEN OF SACRIFICE ALL TOO WELL. AND YOU'RE RIGHT...
...I WOULD HAVE TRIED TO STOP YOU.
MY SACRIFICE WAS TWOFOLD. YES, I REMOVED MYSELF TO UNITE THE THREE TRIBES...
...BUT I ALSO REALIZED WE NEED A DELEGATE AMONG THE GODS IN OLYMPUS--ONE WITH AMAZON INTERESTS IN MIND.
WITH ALL YOUR SCHEMING, YOU MUST FEEL RIGHT AT HOME! KEEP YOUR EYE OUT FOR DOLOS--HE WAS MEDDLING WITH CIZKO.
HMM. I BELIEVE DOLOS IS PART OF A CABAL AMONG THE GODS.
MY ARRIVAL UPSET THEIR PLANS. THEY'VE TRIED TO WEAKEN ME...*
*SEE OLYMPUS: REBIRTH #1! --BRITTANY
...BUT YOU ARE THE ONE THEY FEAR MOST.
WHAT ARE THEIR PLANS? WHO IS BEHIND IT?
FOR NOW, THAT IS ALL I CAN SAY.
I MUST GO. EVEN THE WALLS HAVE EARS.
BE SAFE, MOTHER.
AND YOU, MY LOVE.

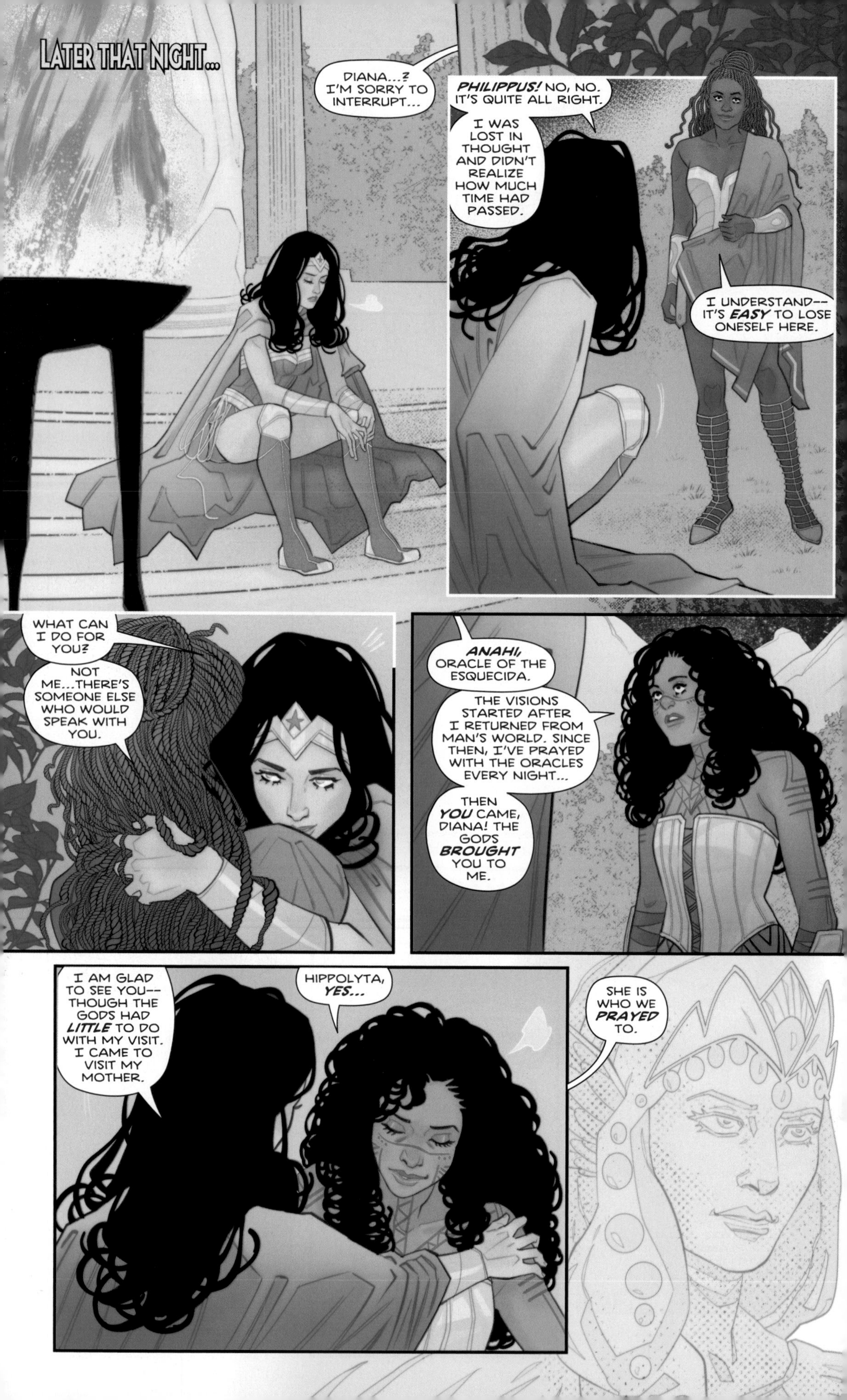
LATER THAT NIGHT...
DIANA...? I'M SORRY TO INTERRUPT...
PHILIPPUS! NO, NO. IT'S QUITE ALL RIGHT.
I WAS LOST IN THOUGHT AND DIDN'T REALIZE HOW MUCH TIME HAD PASSED.
I UNDERSTAND-- IT'S EASY TO LOSE ONESELF HERE.
WHAT CAN I DO FOR YOU?
NOT ME...THERE'S SOMEONE ELSE WHO WOULD SPEAK WITH YOU.
ANAHI, ORACLE OF THE ESQUECIDA.
THE VISIONS STARTED AFTER I RETURNED FROM MAN'S WORLD. SINCE THEN, I'VE PRAYED WITH THE ORACLES EVERY NIGHT...
THEN YOU CAME, DIANA! THE GODS BROUGHT YOU TO ME.
I AM GLAD TO SEE YOU-- THOUGH THE GODS HAD LITTLE TO DO WITH MY VISIT. I CAME TO VISIT MY MOTHER.
HIPPOLYTA, YES...
SHE IS WHO WE PRAYED TO.

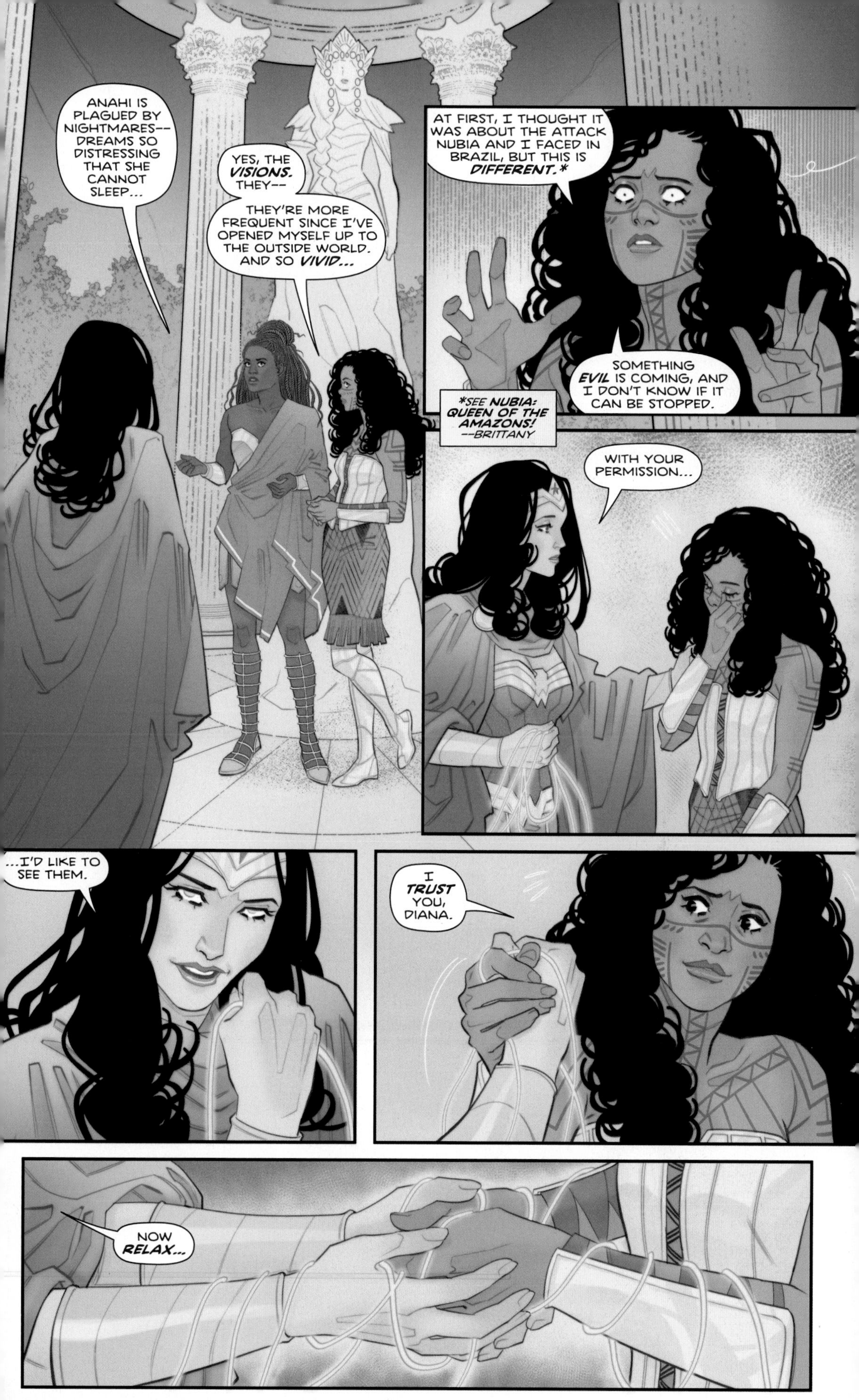
ANAHI IS PLAGUED BY NIGHTMARES-- DREAMS SO DISTRESSING THAT SHE CANNOT SLEEP...
YES, THE VISIONS. THEY--
THEY'RE MORE FREQUENT SINCE I'VE OPENED MYSELF UP TO THE OUTSIDE WORLD. AND SO VIVID...
AT FIRST, I THOUGHT IT WAS ABOUT THE ATTACK NUBIA AND I FACED IN BRAZIL, BUT THIS IS DIFFERENT.*
SOMETHING EVIL IS COMING, AND I DON'T KNOW IF IT CAN BE STOPPED.
*SEE NUBIA: QUEEN OF THE AMAZONS! --BRITTANY
WITH YOUR PERMISSION...
...I'D LIKE TO SEE THEM.
I TRUST YOU, DIANA.
NOW RELAX...

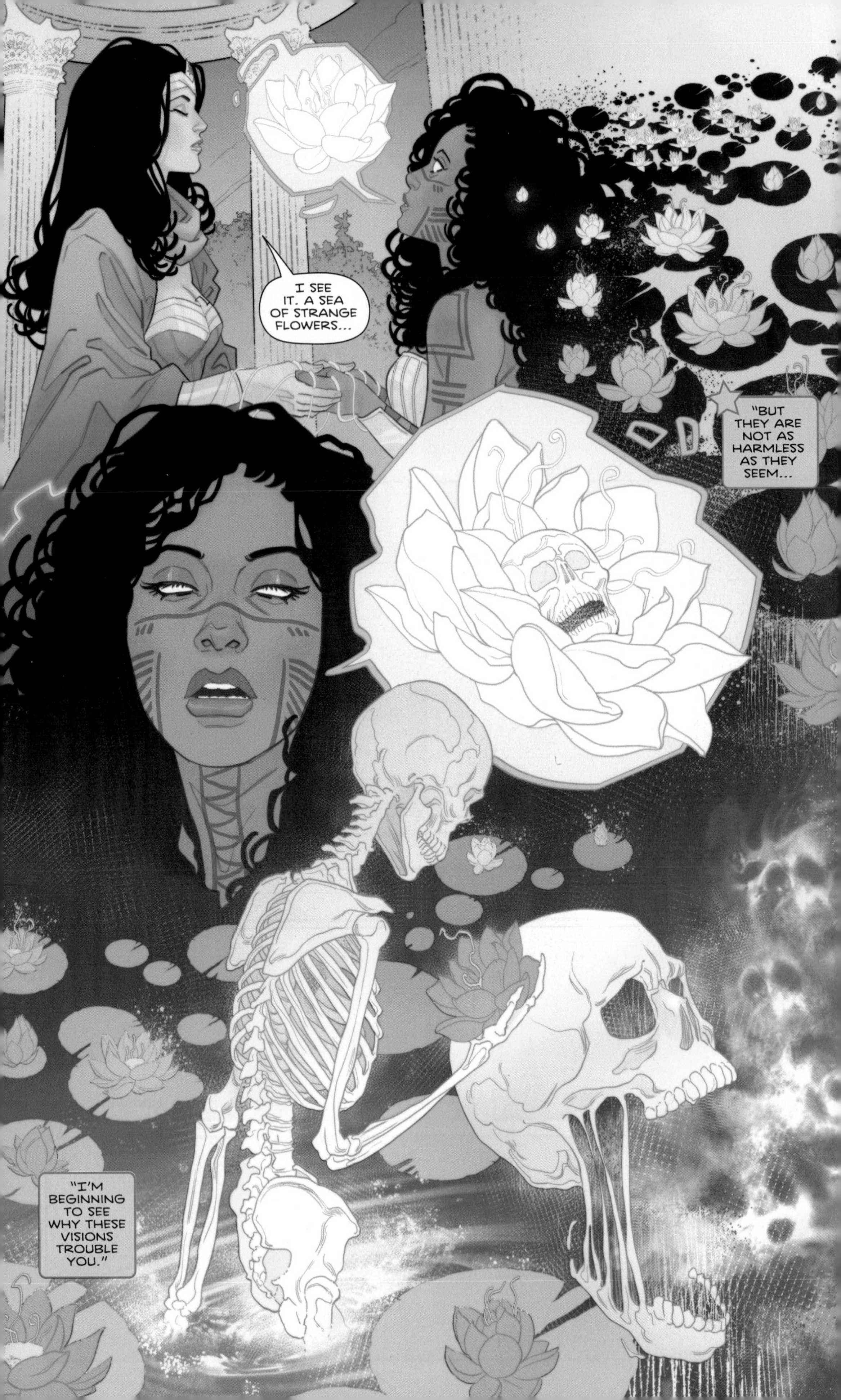
I SEE IT. A SEA OF STRANGE FLOWERS...
"BUT THEY ARE NOT AS HARMLESS AS THEY SEEM...
"I'M BEGINNING TO SEE WHY THESE VISIONS TROUBLE YOU."

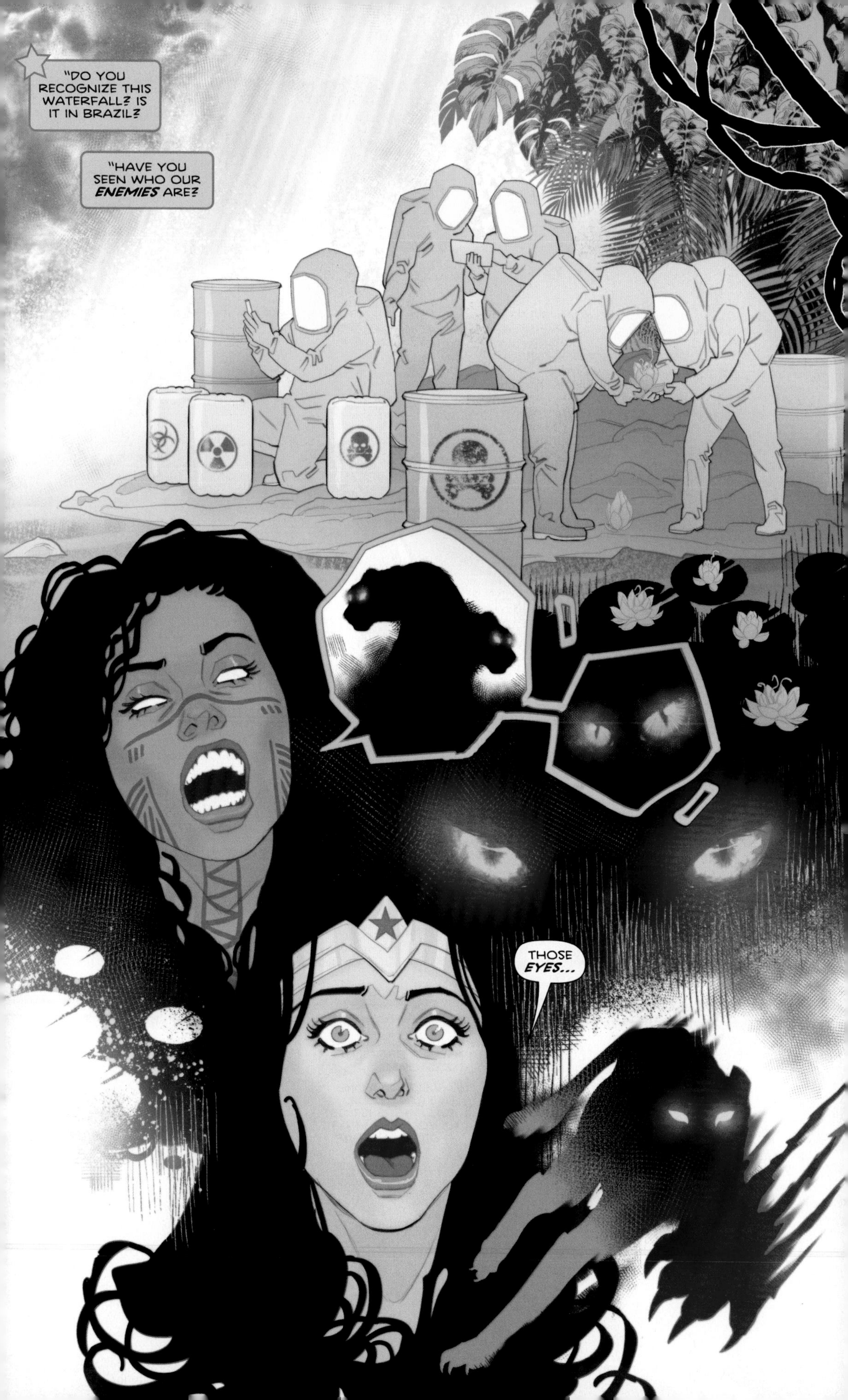
"DO YOU RECOGNIZE THIS WATERFALL? IS IT IN BRAZIL?
"HAVE YOU SEEN WHO OUR *ENEMIES* ARE?
THOSE *EYES...*

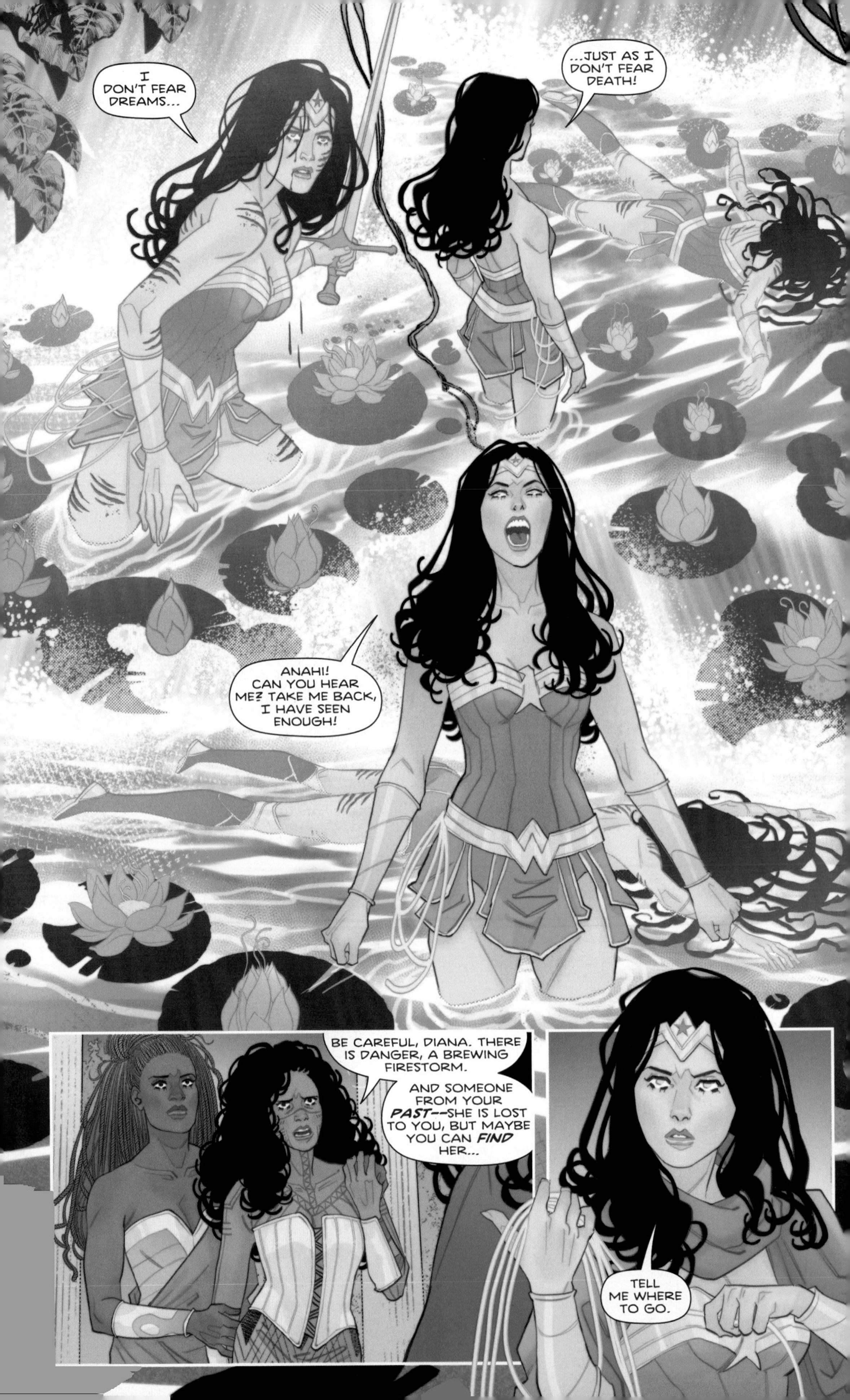
I DON'T FEAR DREAMS...
...JUST AS I DON'T FEAR DEATH!
ANAHI! CAN YOU HEAR ME? TAKE ME BACK, I HAVE SEEN ENOUGH!
BE CAREFUL, DIANA. THERE IS DANGER, A BREWING FIRESTORM.
AND SOMEONE FROM YOUR PAST--SHE IS LOST TO YOU, BUT MAYBE YOU CAN FIND HER...
TELL ME WHERE TO GO.

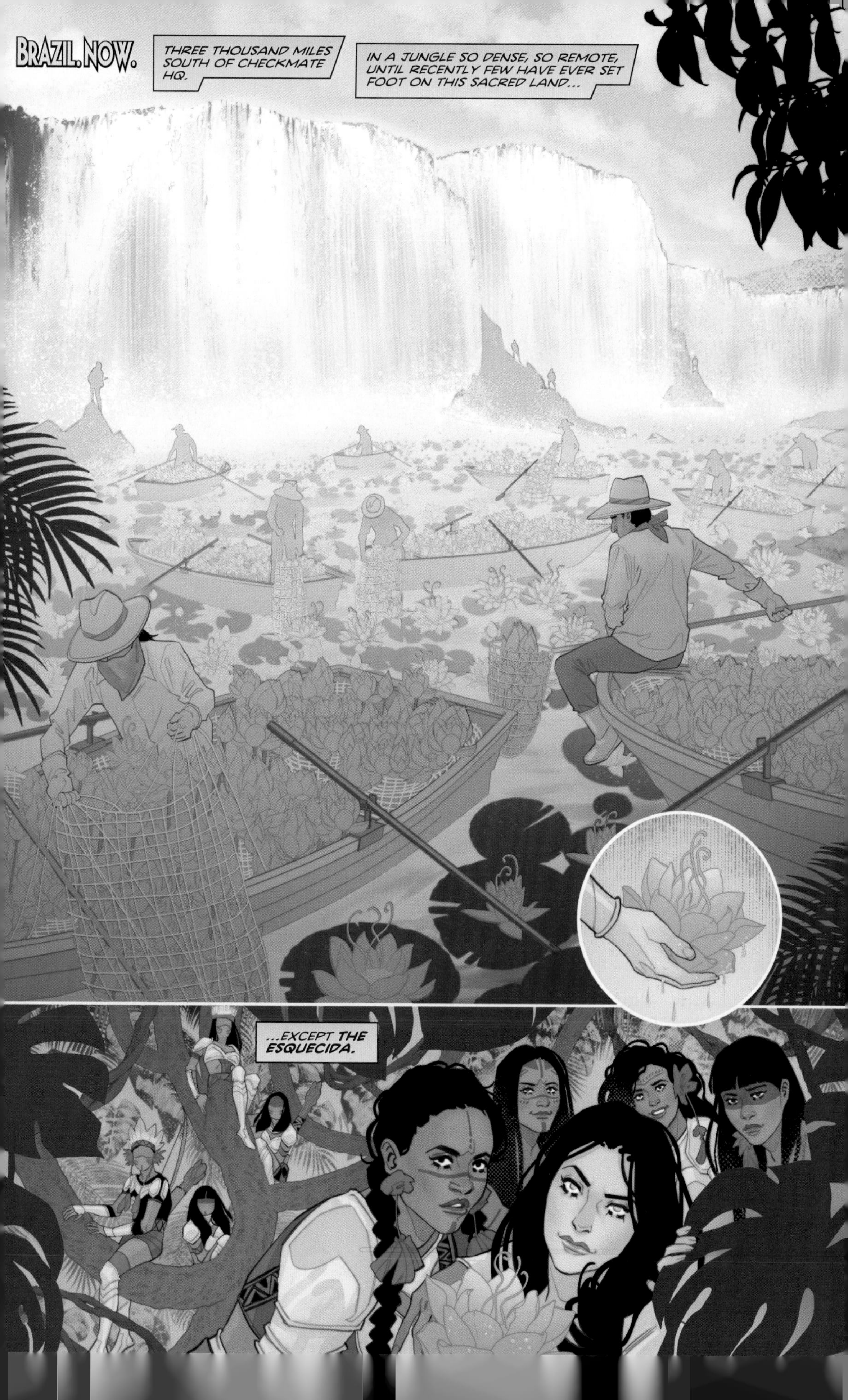
BRAZIL. NOW.
THREE THOUSAND MILES SOUTH OF CHECKMATE HQ.
IN A JUNGLE SO DENSE, SO REMOTE, UNTIL RECENTLY FEW HAVE EVER SET FOOT ON THIS SACRED LAND...
...EXCEPT THE ESQUECIDA.

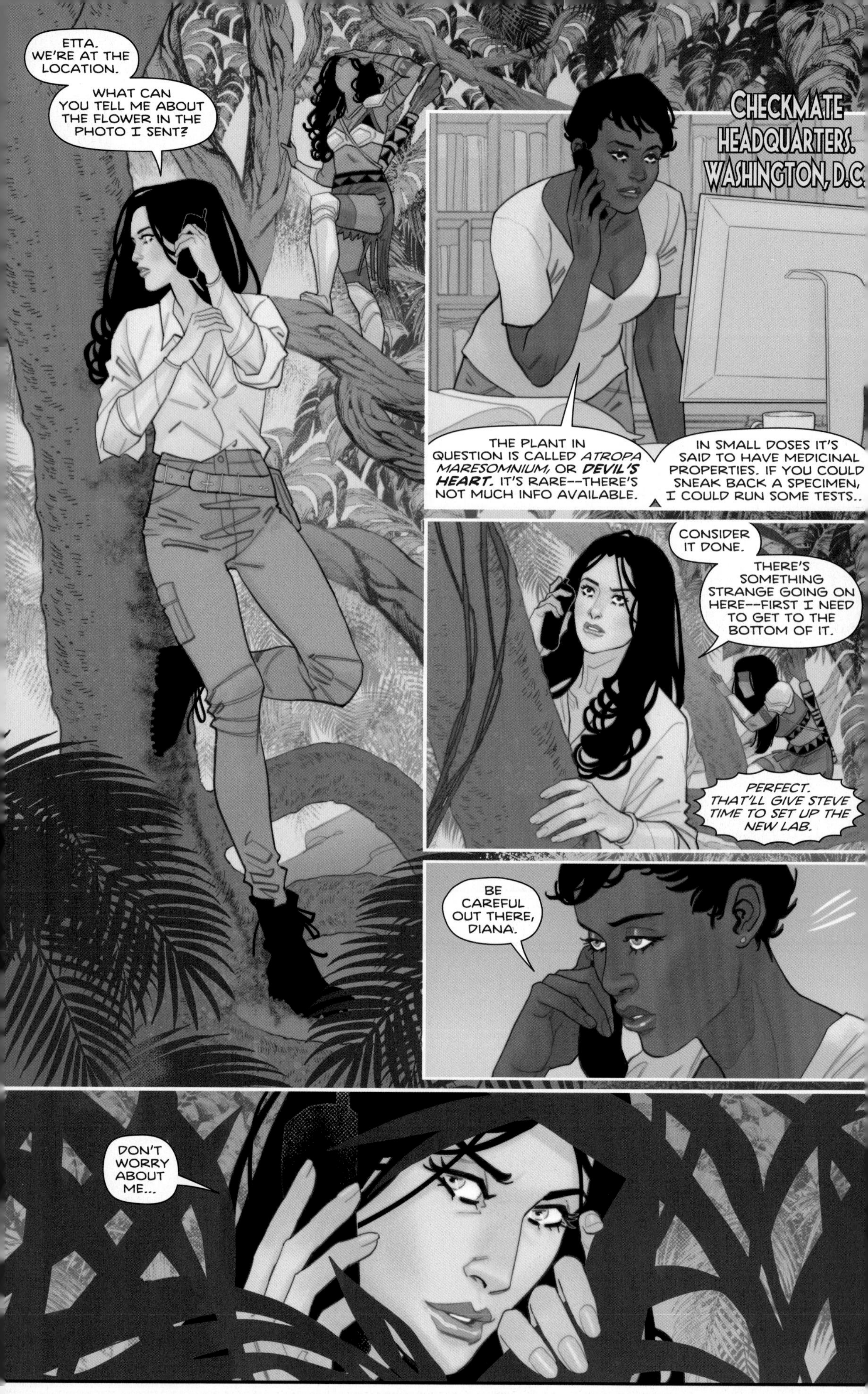
ETTA. WE'RE AT THE LOCATION.
WHAT CAN YOU TELL ME ABOUT THE FLOWER IN THE PHOTO I SENT?
CHECKMATE HEADQUARTERS. WASHINGTON, D.C.
THE PLANT IN QUESTION IS CALLED ATROPA MARESOMNIUM, OR DEVIL'S HEART. IT'S RARE--THERE'S NOT MUCH INFO AVAILABLE.
IN SMALL DOSES IT'S SAID TO HAVE MEDICINAL PROPERTIES. IF YOU COULD SNEAK BACK A SPECIMEN, I COULD RUN SOME TESTS..
CONSIDER IT DONE.
THERE'S SOMETHING STRANGE GOING ON HERE--FIRST I NEED TO GET TO THE BOTTOM OF IT.
PERFECT. THAT'LL GIVE STEVE TIME TO SET UP THE NEW LAB.
BE CAREFUL OUT THERE, DIANA.
DON'T WORRY ABOUT ME...

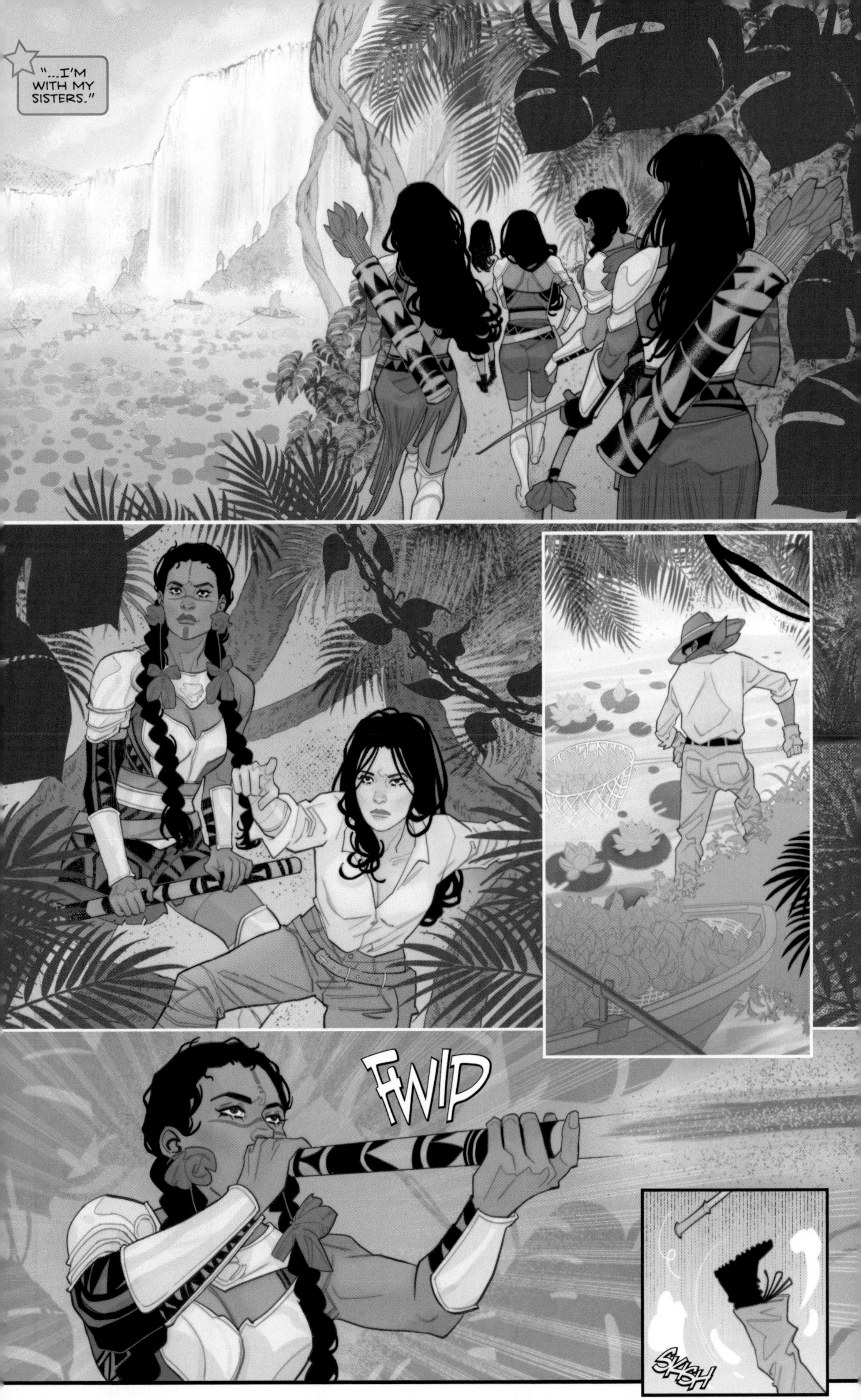
"...I'M WITH MY SISTERS."
FWIP
SHASH

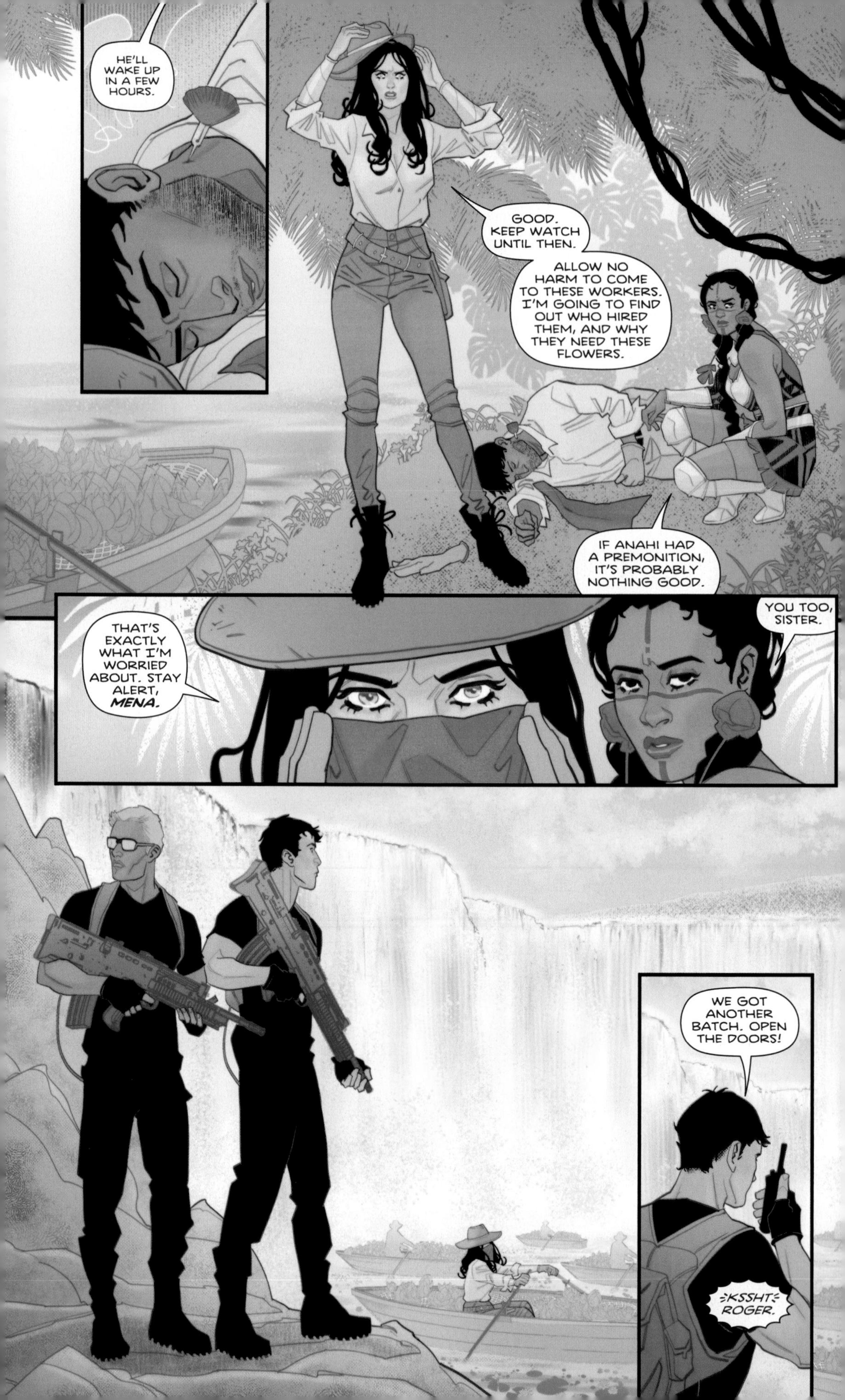
HE'LL WAKE UP IN A FEW HOURS.
GOOD. KEEP WATCH UNTIL THEN.
ALLOW NO HARM TO COME TO THESE WORKERS. I'M GOING TO FIND OUT WHO HIRED THEM, AND WHY THEY NEED THESE FLOWERS.
IF ANAHI HAD A PREMONITION, IT'S PROBABLY NOTHING GOOD.
THAT'S EXACTLY WHAT I'M WORRIED ABOUT. STAY ALERT, *MENA.*
YOU TOO, SISTER.
WE GOT ANOTHER BATCH. OPEN THE DOORS!
KSSHT ROGER.

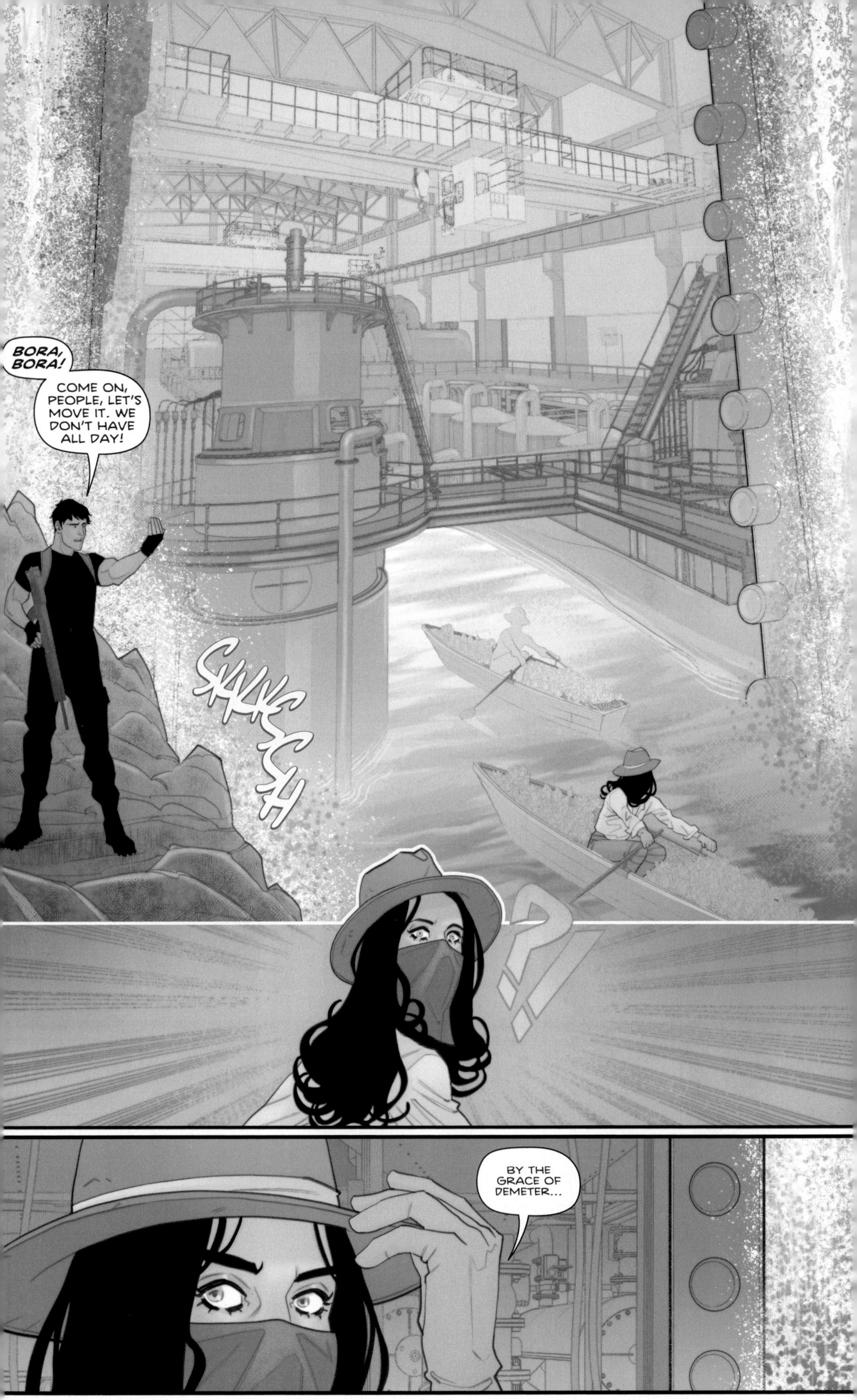
BORA, BORA!
COME ON, PEOPLE, LET'S MOVE IT. WE DON'T HAVE ALL DAY!
SKKKCCHH
?!
BY THE GRACE OF DEMETER...

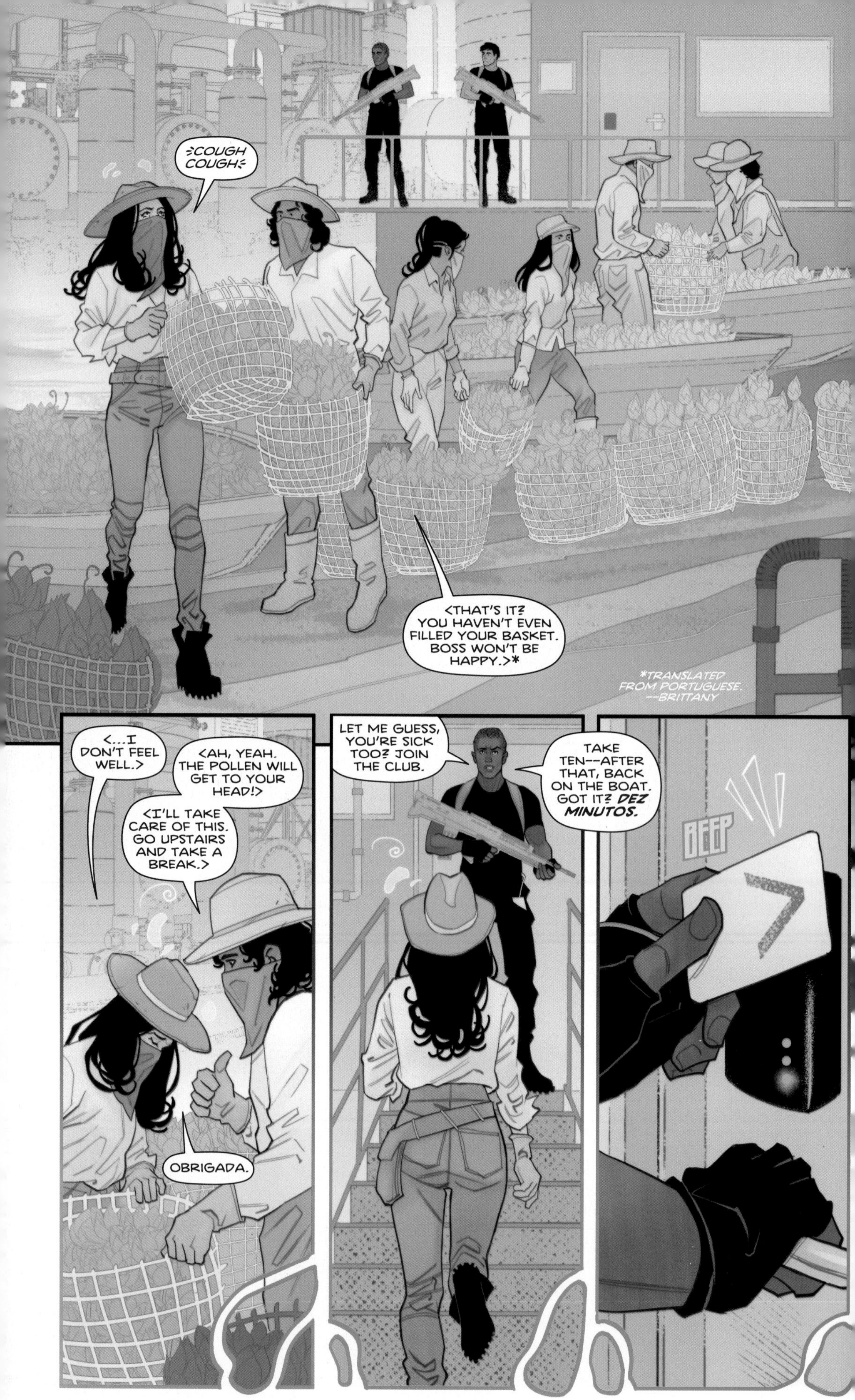

:COUGH COUGH:
<THAT'S IT? YOU HAVEN'T EVEN FILLED YOUR BASKET. BOSS WON'T BE HAPPY.>*
*TRANSLATED FROM PORTUGUESE. --BRITTANY
<...I DON'T FEEL WELL.>
<AH, YEAH. THE POLLEN WILL GET TO YOUR HEAD!>
<I'LL TAKE CARE OF THIS. GO UPSTAIRS AND TAKE A BREAK.>
OBRIGADA.
LET ME GUESS, YOU'RE SICK TOO? JOIN THE CLUB.
TAKE TEN--AFTER THAT, BACK ON THE BOAT. GOT IT? DEZ MINUTOS.
BEEP

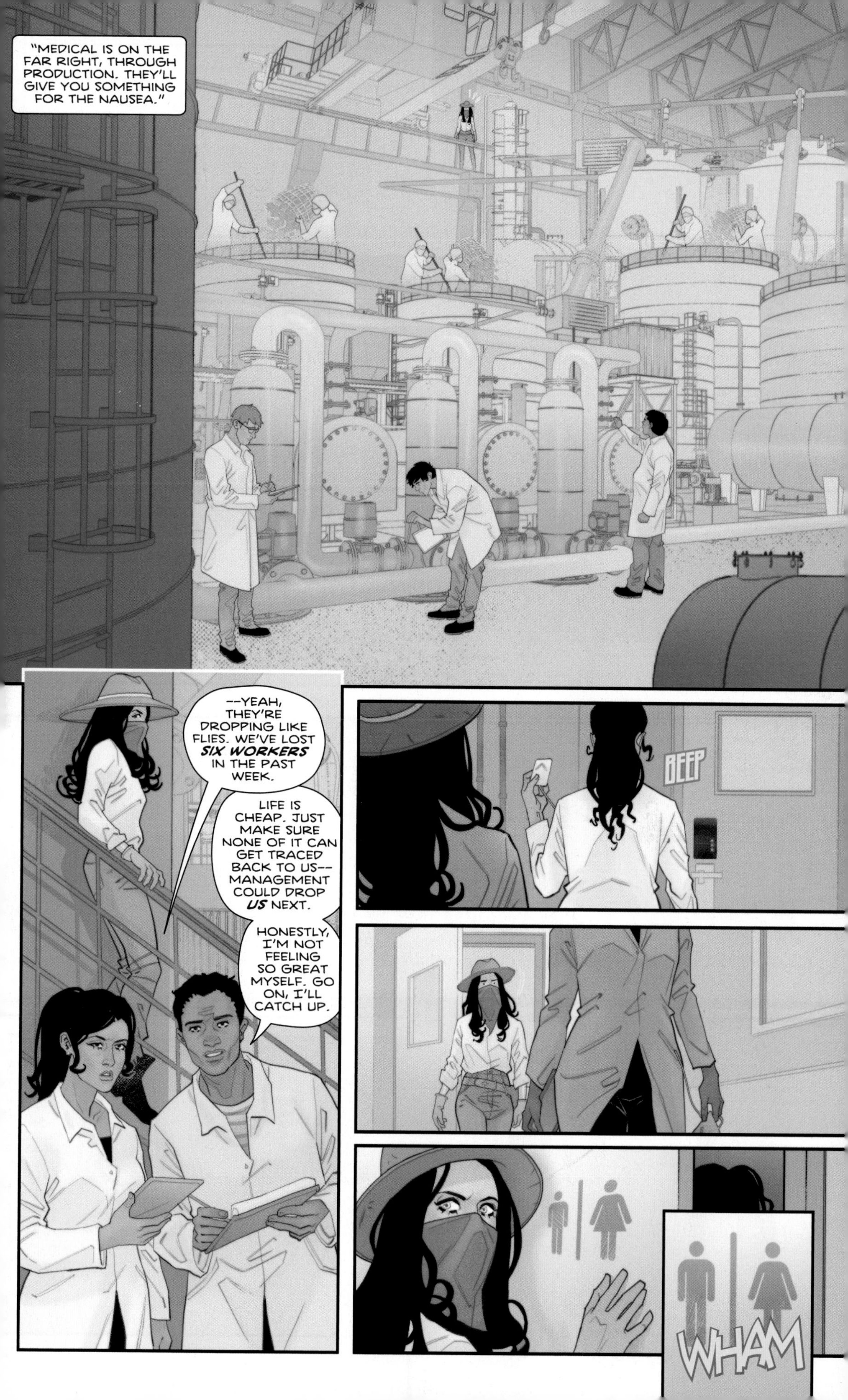
"MEDICAL IS ON THE FAR RIGHT, THROUGH PRODUCTION. THEY'LL GIVE YOU SOMETHING FOR THE NAUSEA."
--YEAH, THEY'RE DROPPING LIKE FLIES. WE'VE LOST SIX WORKERS IN THE PAST WEEK.
LIFE IS CHEAP. JUST MAKE SURE NONE OF IT CAN GET TRACED BACK TO US-- MANAGEMENT COULD DROP US NEXT.
HONESTLY, I'M NOT FEELING SO GREAT MYSELF. GO ON, I'LL CATCH UP.
BEEP
WHAM

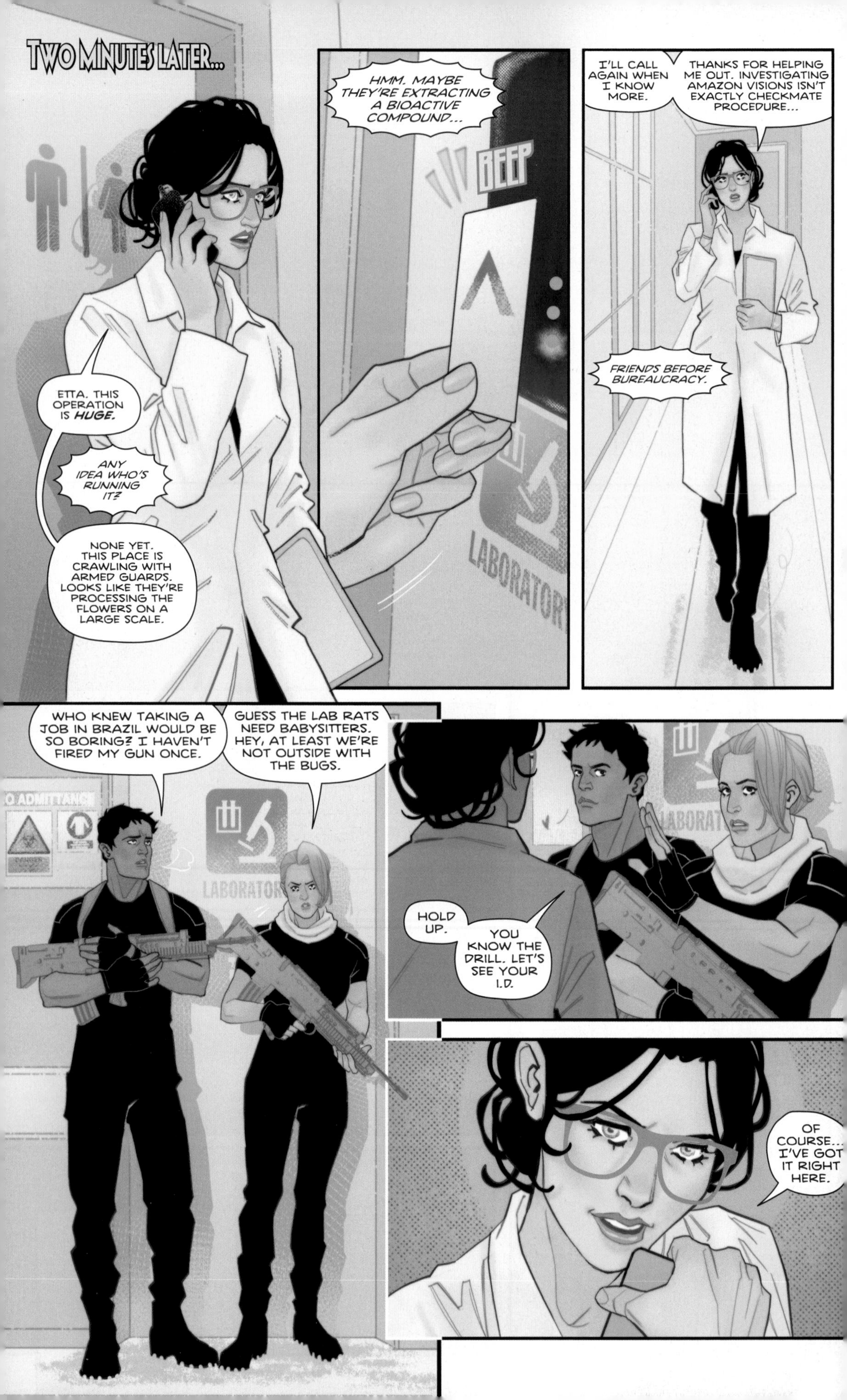
TWO MINUTES LATER...
ETTA. THIS OPERATION IS *HUGE.*
ANY IDEA WHO'S RUNNING IT?
NONE YET. THIS PLACE IS CRAWLING WITH ARMED GUARDS. LOOKS LIKE THEY'RE PROCESSING THE FLOWERS ON A LARGE SCALE.
HMM. MAYBE THEY'RE EXTRACTING A BIOACTIVE COMPOUND...
BEEP
LABORATORY
I'LL CALL AGAIN WHEN I KNOW MORE.
THANKS FOR HELPING ME OUT. INVESTIGATING AMAZON VISIONS ISN'T EXACTLY CHECKMATE PROCEDURE...
FRIENDS BEFORE BUREAUCRACY.
WHO KNEW TAKING A JOB IN BRAZIL WOULD BE SO BORING? I HAVEN'T FIRED MY GUN ONCE.
GUESS THE LAB RATS NEED BABYSITTERS. HEY, AT LEAST WE'RE NOT OUTSIDE WITH THE BUGS.
LABORATORY
HOLD UP.
YOU KNOW THE DRILL. LET'S SEE YOUR I.D.
OF COURSE... I'VE GOT IT RIGHT HERE.

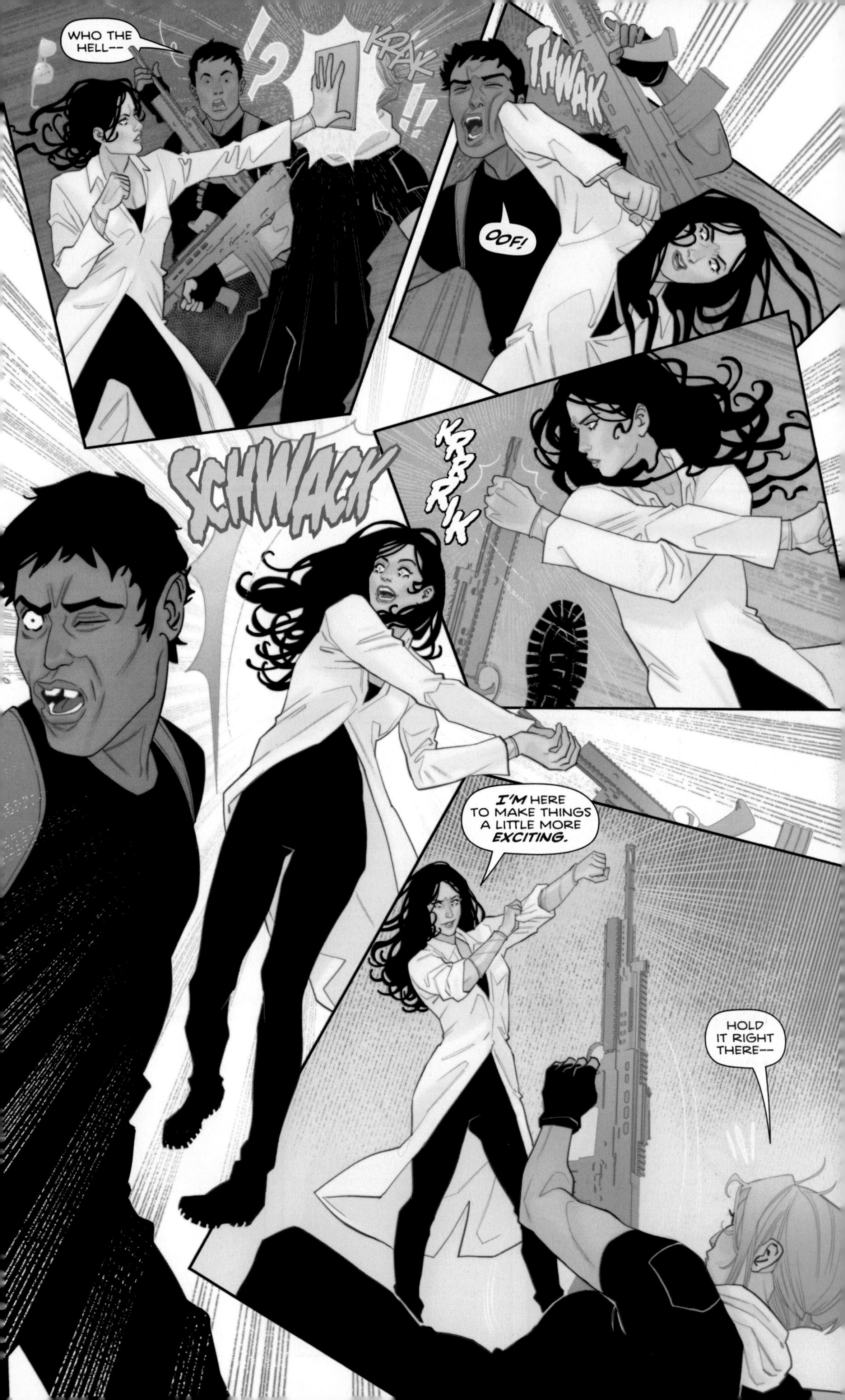
WHO THE HELL--
!?
KRAK
!!
THWAK
OOF!
SCHWACK
KRRRK
I'M HERE TO MAKE THINGS A LITTLE MORE EXCITING.
HOLD IT RIGHT THERE--

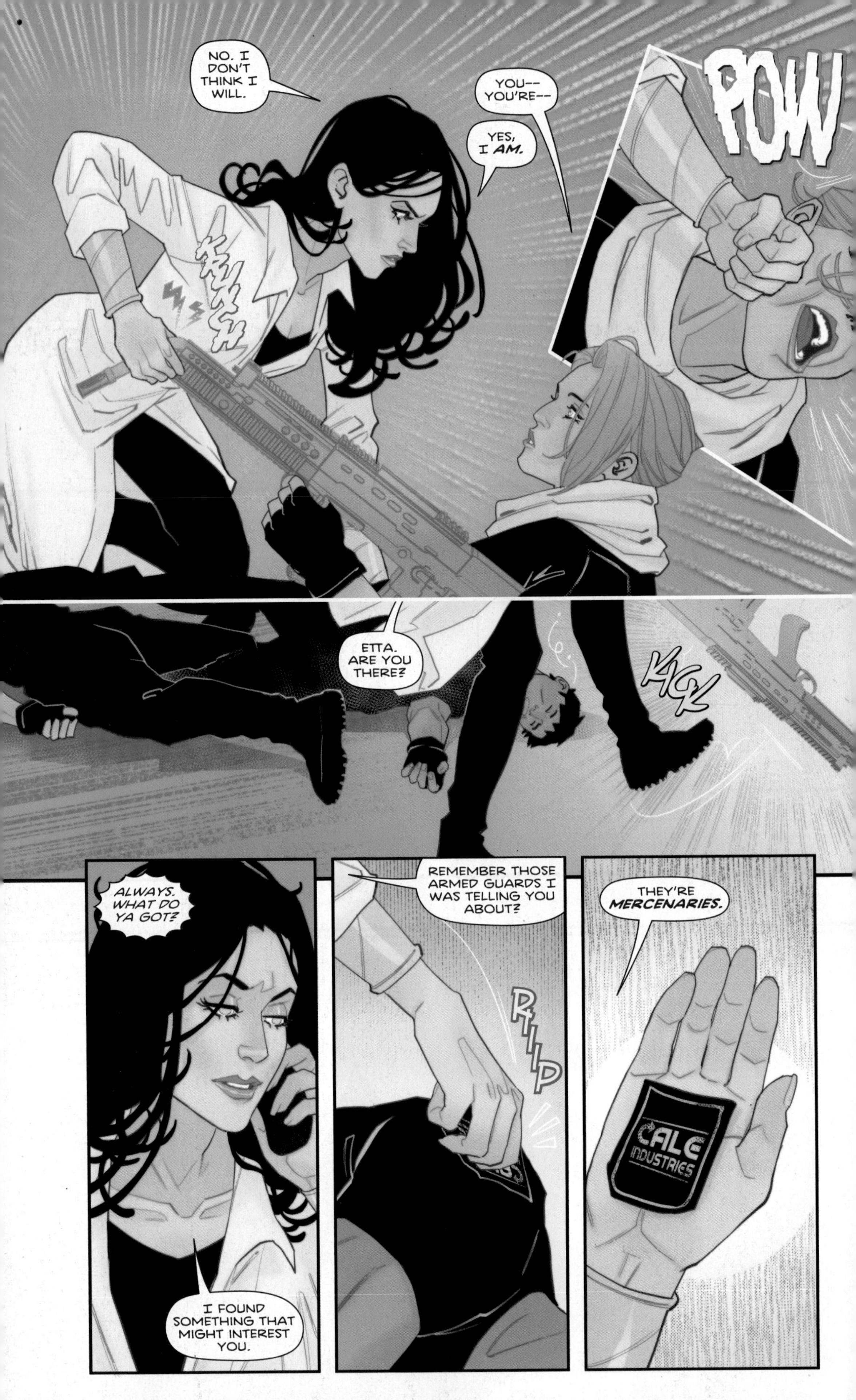
NO. I DON'T THINK I WILL.
YOU-- YOU'RE--
YES, I *AM.*
KRUNCH
WHSH
POW
ETTA. ARE YOU THERE?
KICK
ALWAYS. WHAT DO YA GOT?
I FOUND SOMETHING THAT MIGHT INTEREST YOU.
REMEMBER THOSE ARMED GUARDS I WAS TELLING YOU ABOUT?
RIIP
THEY'RE *MERCENARIES.*
CALE INDUSTRIES

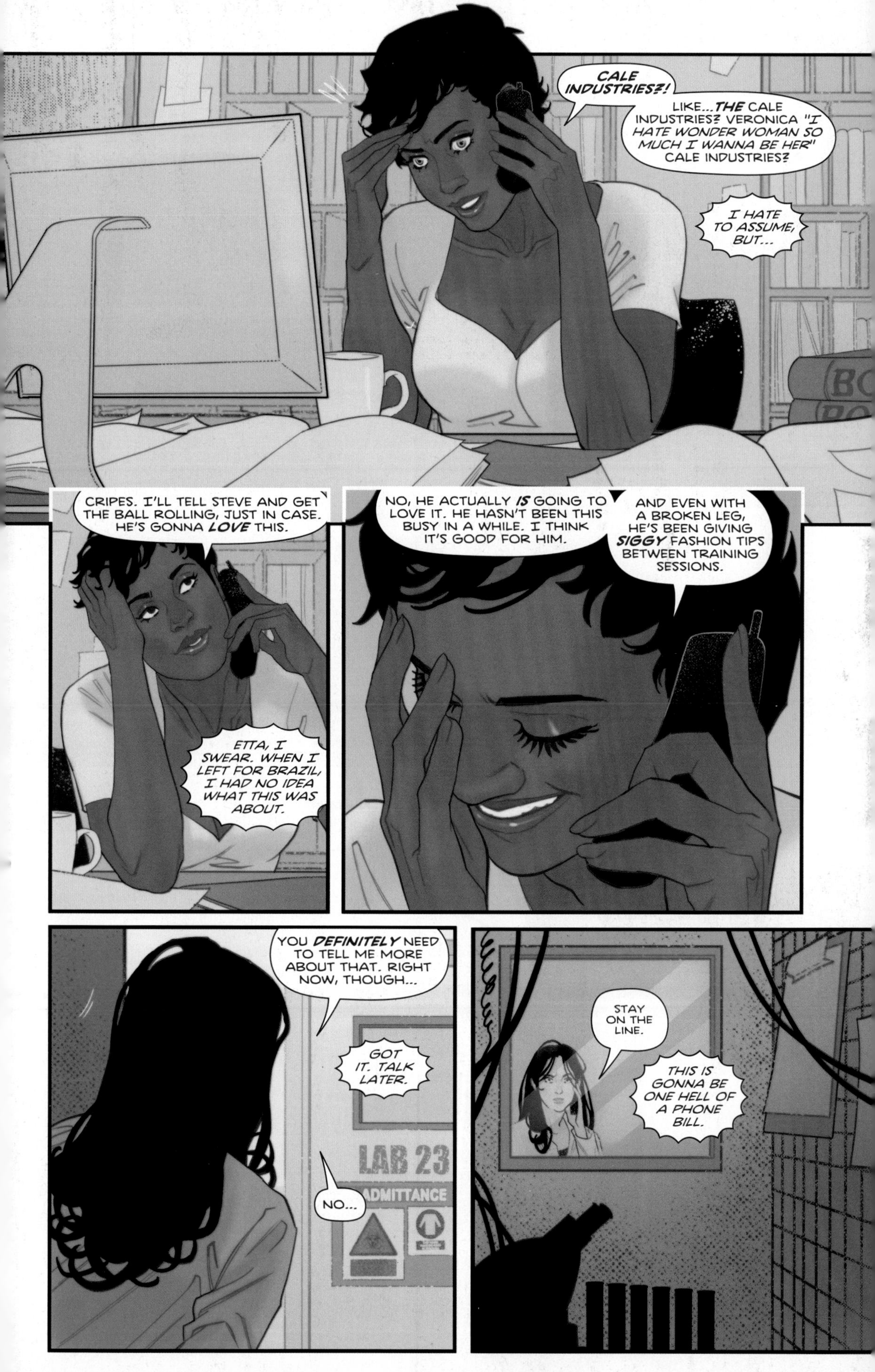
CALE INDUSTRIES?!
LIKE... THE CALE INDUSTRIES? VERONICA "I HATE WONDER WOMAN SO MUCH I WANNA BE HER" CALE INDUSTRIES?
I HATE TO ASSUME, BUT...
CRIPES. I'LL TELL STEVE AND GET THE BALL ROLLING, JUST IN CASE. HE'S GONNA LOVE THIS.
ETTA, I SWEAR. WHEN I LEFT FOR BRAZIL, I HAD NO IDEA WHAT THIS WAS ABOUT.
NO, HE ACTUALLY IS GOING TO LOVE IT. HE HASN'T BEEN THIS BUSY IN A WHILE. I THINK IT'S GOOD FOR HIM.
AND EVEN WITH A BROKEN LEG, HE'S BEEN GIVING SIGGY FASHION TIPS BETWEEN TRAINING SESSIONS.
YOU DEFINITELY NEED TO TELL ME MORE ABOUT THAT. RIGHT NOW, THOUGH...
GOT IT. TALK LATER.
LAB 23
ADMITTANCE
NO...
STAY ON THE LINE.
THIS IS GONNA BE ONE HELL OF A PHONE BILL.

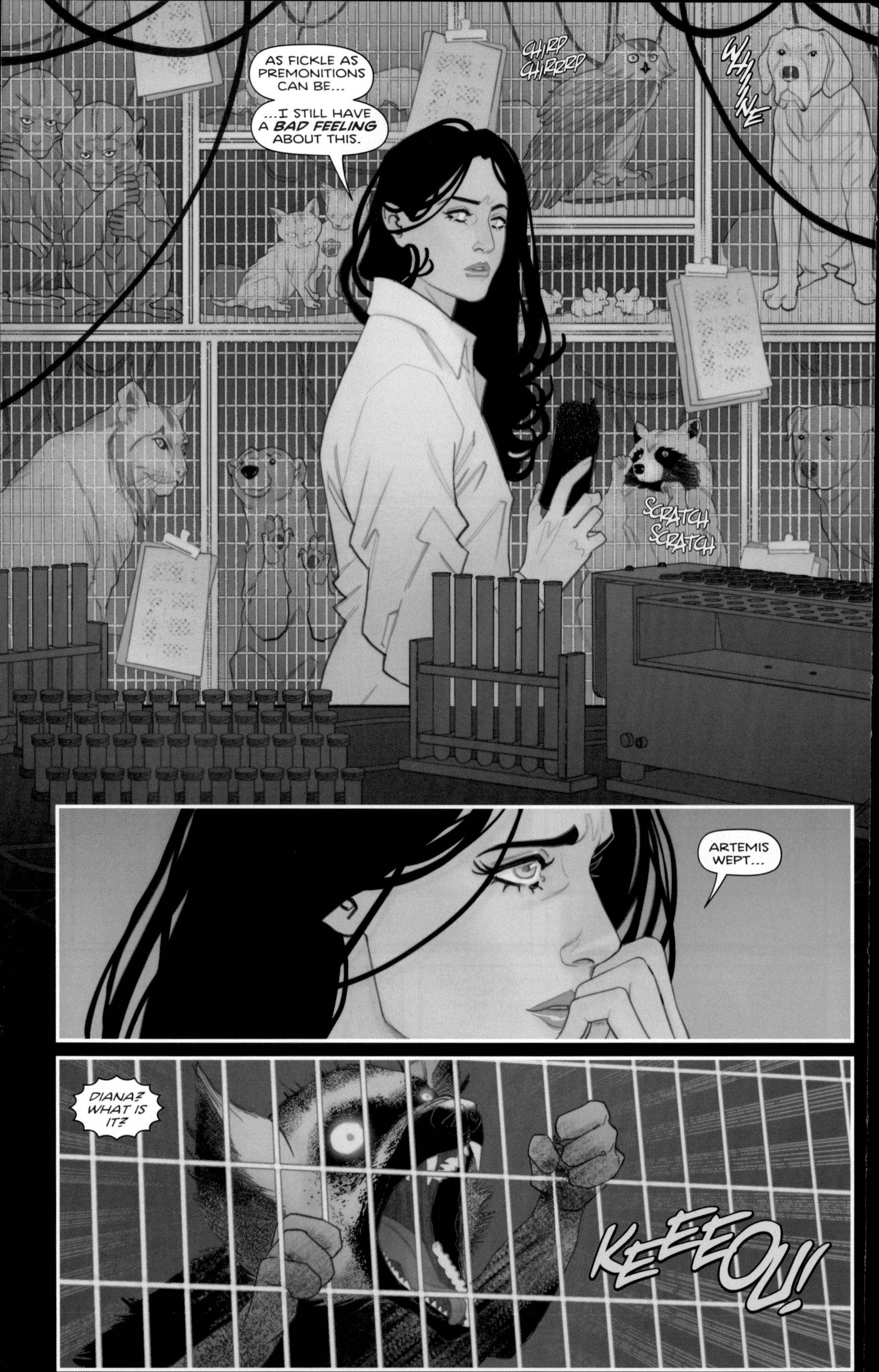
AS FICKLE AS PREMONITIONS CAN BE...
...I STILL HAVE A BAD FEELING ABOUT THIS.
CHIRP CHIRRRP
WHINE
SCRATCH SCRATCH
ARTEMIS WEPT...
DIANA? WHAT IS IT?
KEEEOU!!

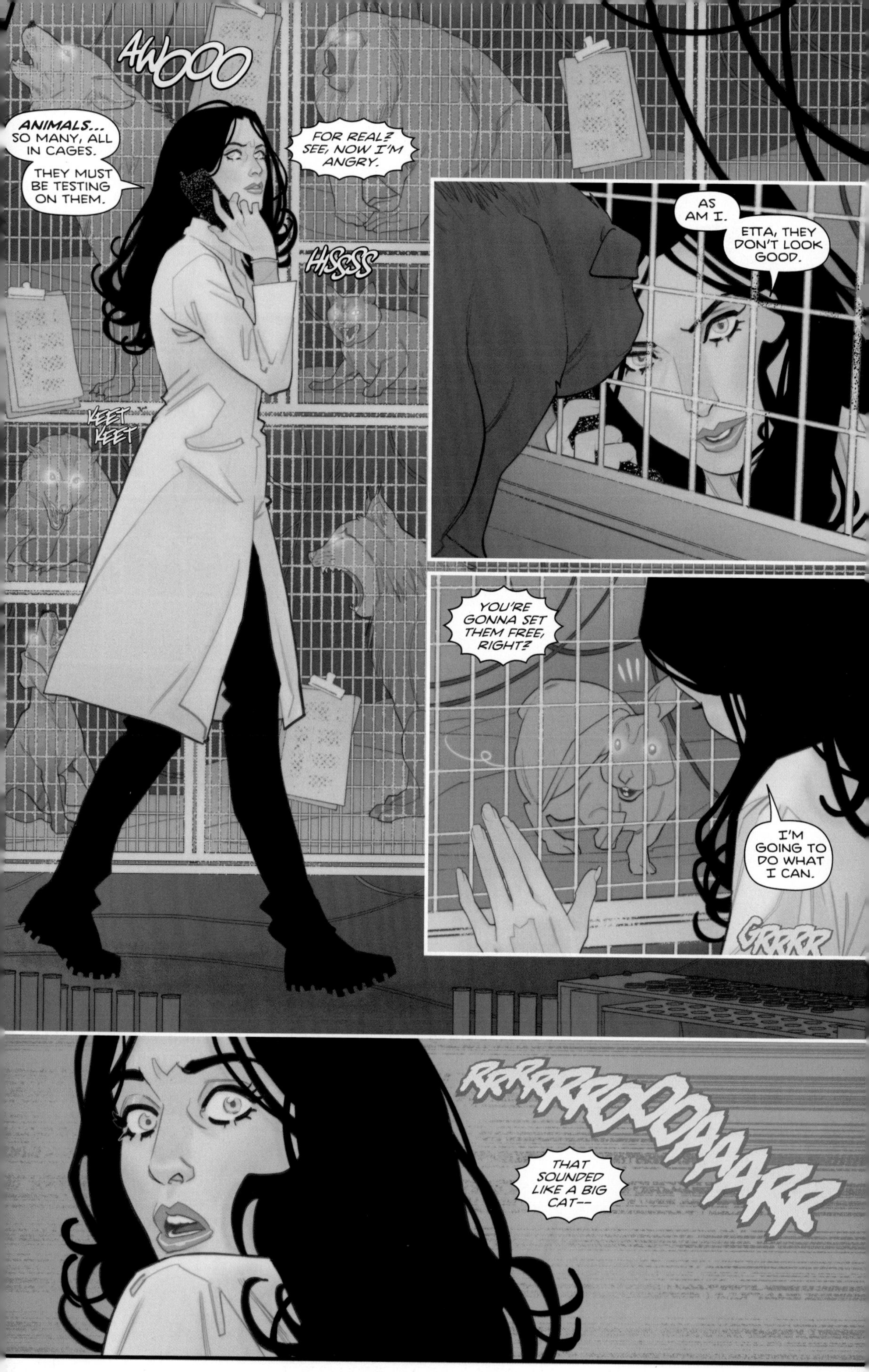
AWOOO
ANIMALS... SO MANY, ALL IN CAGES.
THEY MUST BE TESTING ON THEM.
FOR REAL? SEE, NOW I'M ANGRY.
HISSSS
KEET KEET
AS AM I.
ETTA, THEY DON'T LOOK GOOD.
YOU'RE GONNA SET THEM FREE, RIGHT?
I'M GOING TO DO WHAT I CAN.
GRRRR
RRRRRROOOOAAAARR
THAT SOUNDED LIKE A BIG CAT--

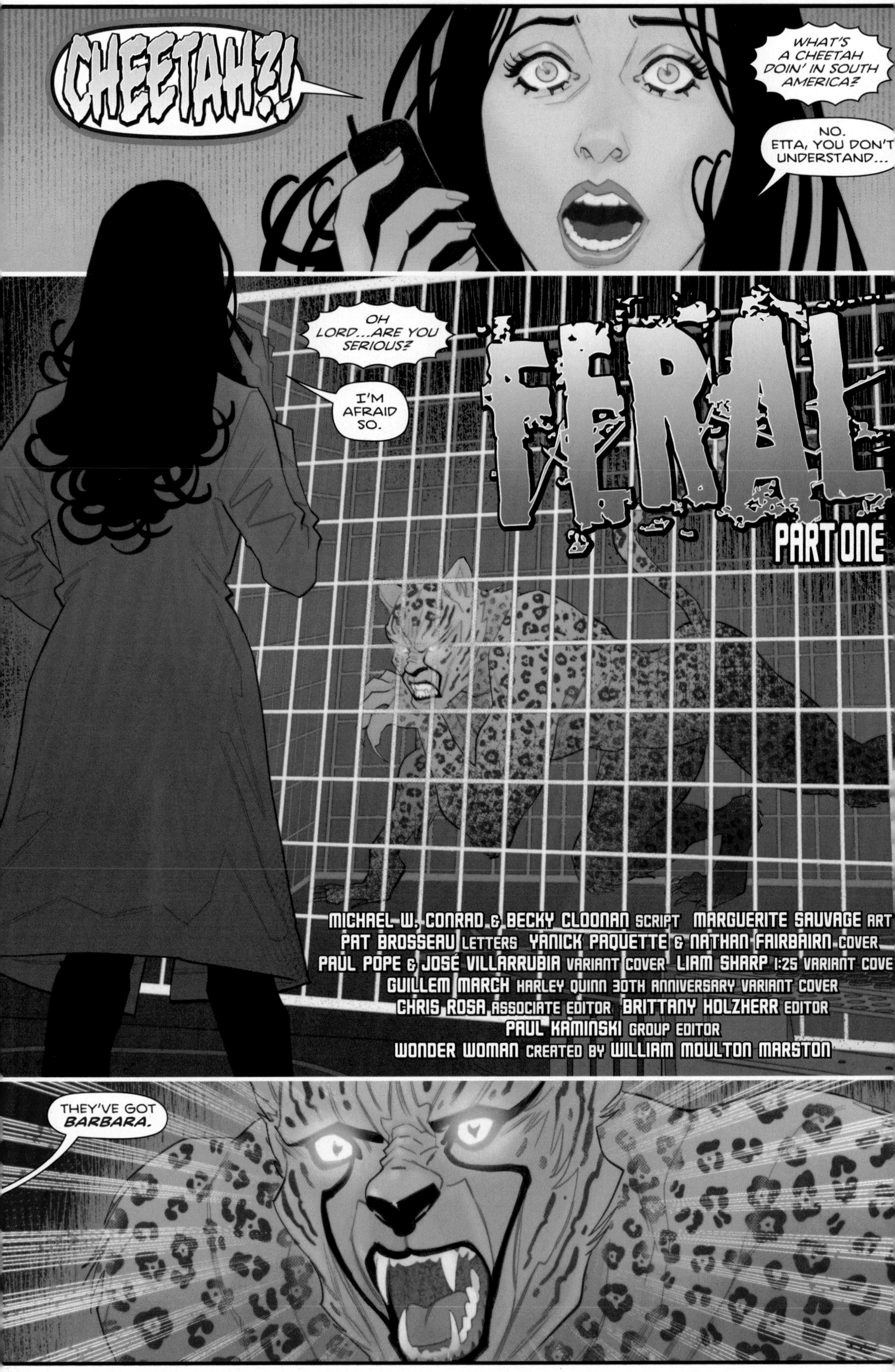
CHEETAH?!
WHAT'S A CHEETAH DOIN' IN SOUTH AMERICA?
NO. ETTA, YOU DON'T UNDERSTAND...
OH LORD...ARE YOU SERIOUS?
I'M AFRAID SO.
FERAL
PART ONE
MICHAEL W. CONRAD & BECKY CLOONAN SCRIPT MARGUERITE SAUVAGE ART
PAT BROSSEAU LETTERS YANICK PAQUETTE & NATHAN FAIRBAIRN COVER
PAUL POPE & JOSÉ VILLARRUBIA VARIANT COVER LIAM SHARP 1:25 VARIANT COVE
GUILLEM MARCH HARLEY QUINN 30TH ANNIVERSARY VARIANT COVER
CHRIS ROSA ASSOCIATE EDITOR BRITTANY HOLZHERR EDITOR
PAUL KAMINSKI GROUP EDITOR
WONDER WOMAN CREATED BY WILLIAM MOULTON MARSTON
THEY'VE GOT *BARBARA.*

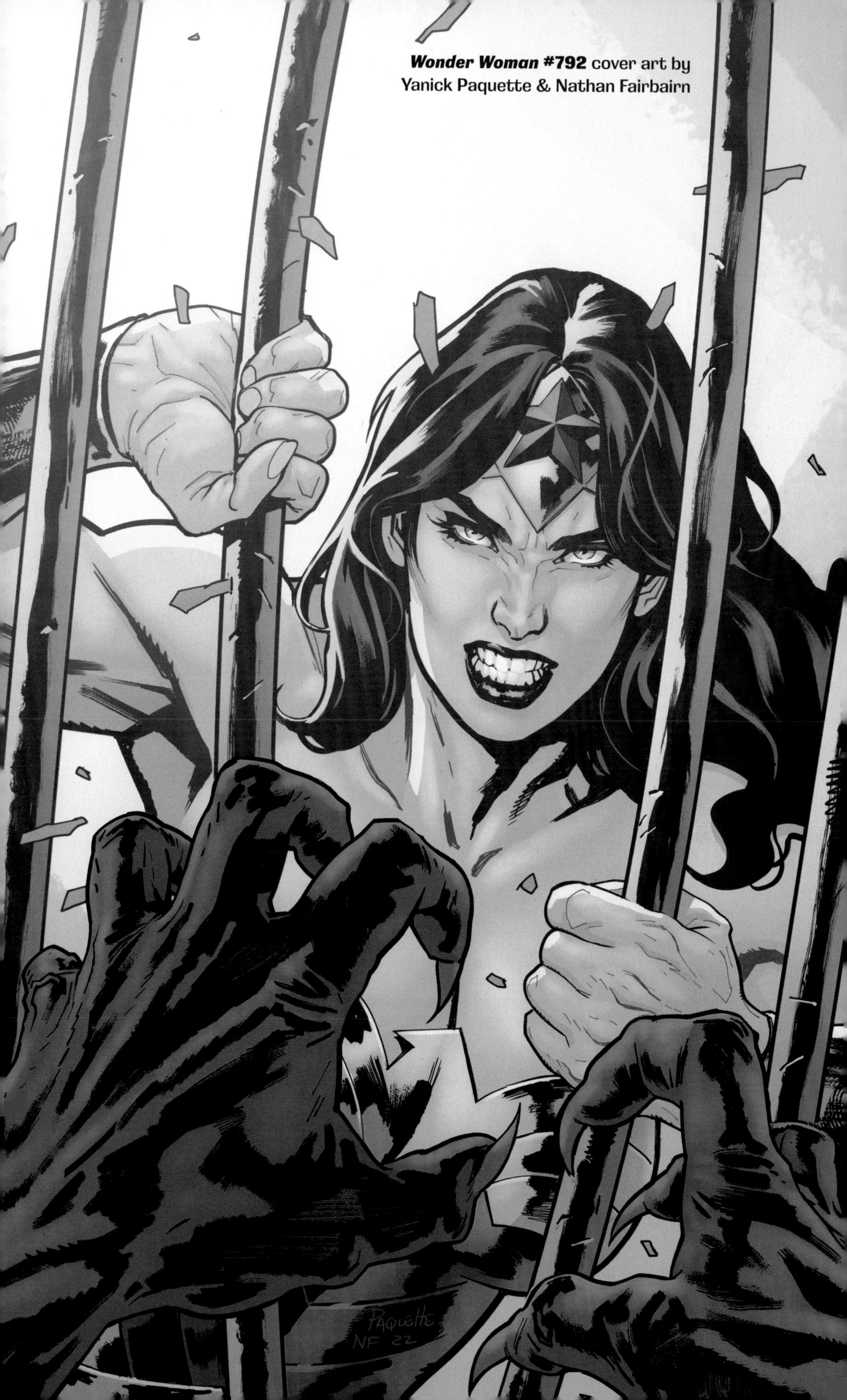
PAQUETTE
NF 22

***Wonder Woman* #792** cover art by
Yanick Paquette & Nathan Fairbairn

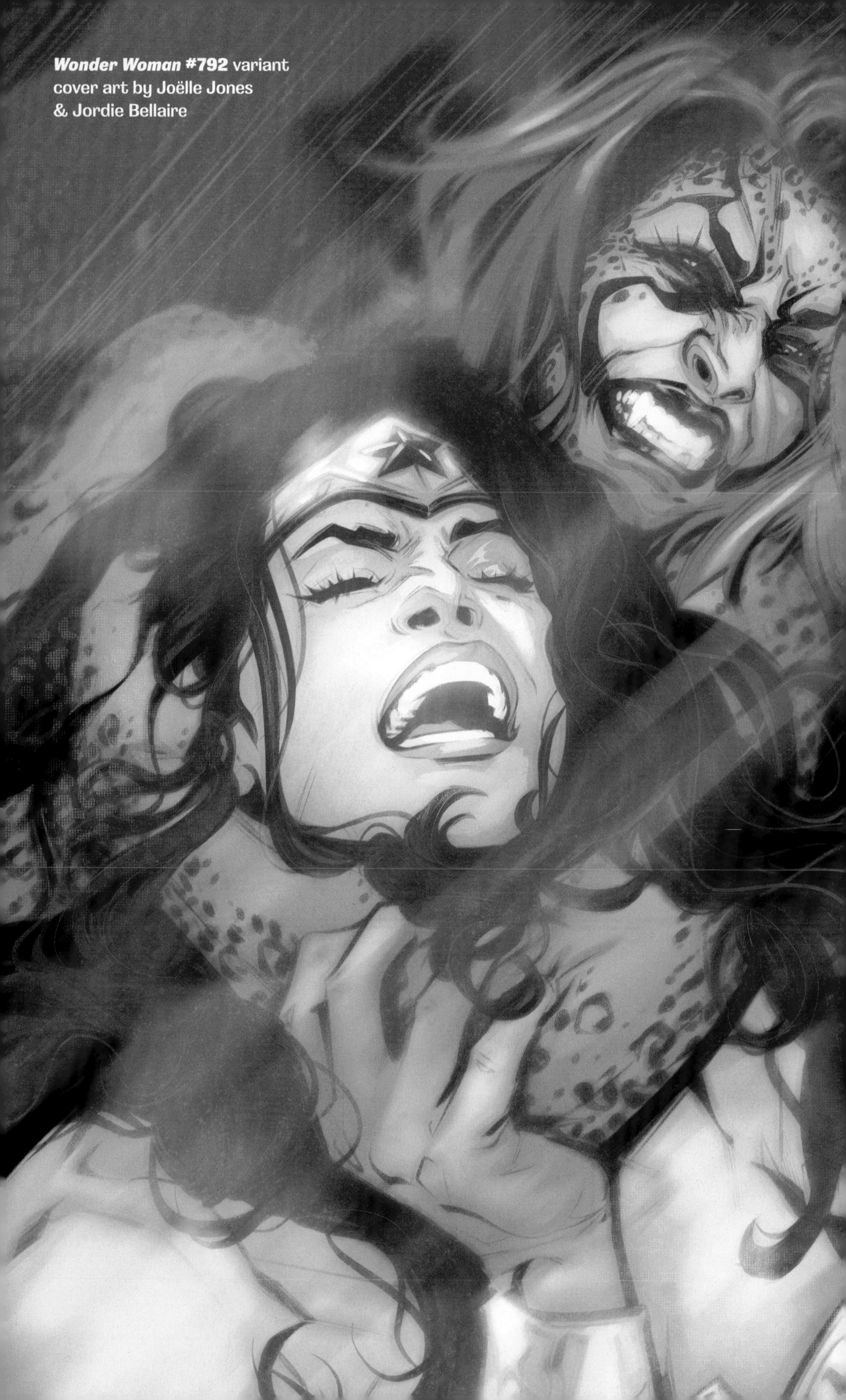

***Wonder Woman* #792** variant cover art by Joëlle Jones & Jordie Bellaire

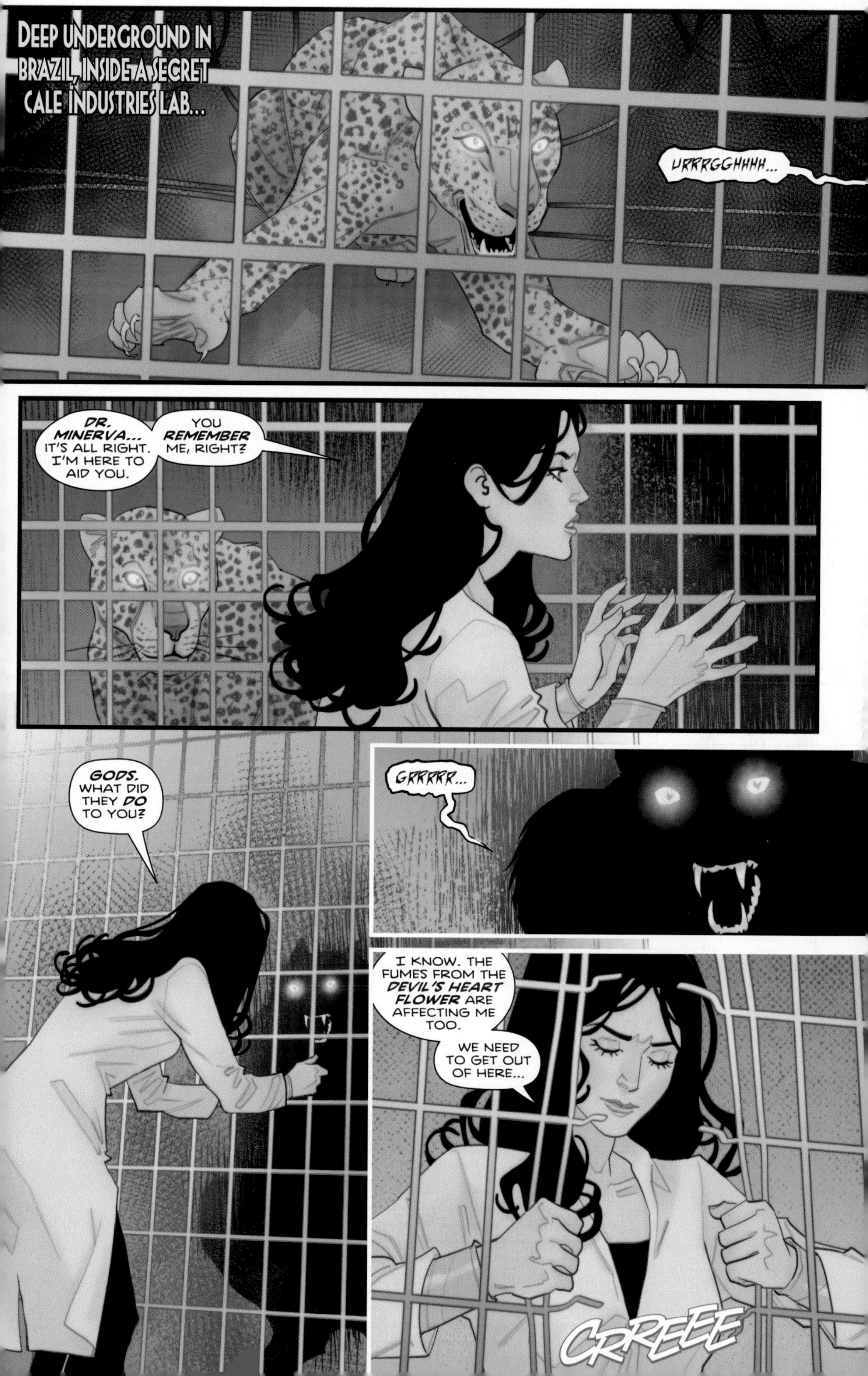
DEEP UNDERGROUND IN BRAZIL, INSIDE A SECRET CALE INDUSTRIES LAB...
URRRGGHHHH...
DR. MINERVA... IT'S ALL RIGHT. I'M HERE TO AID YOU.
YOU REMEMBER ME, RIGHT?
GODS. WHAT DID THEY DO TO YOU?
GRRRRR...
I KNOW. THE FUMES FROM THE DEVIL'S HEART FLOWER ARE AFFECTING ME TOO.
WE NEED TO GET OUT OF HERE...
CRREEE

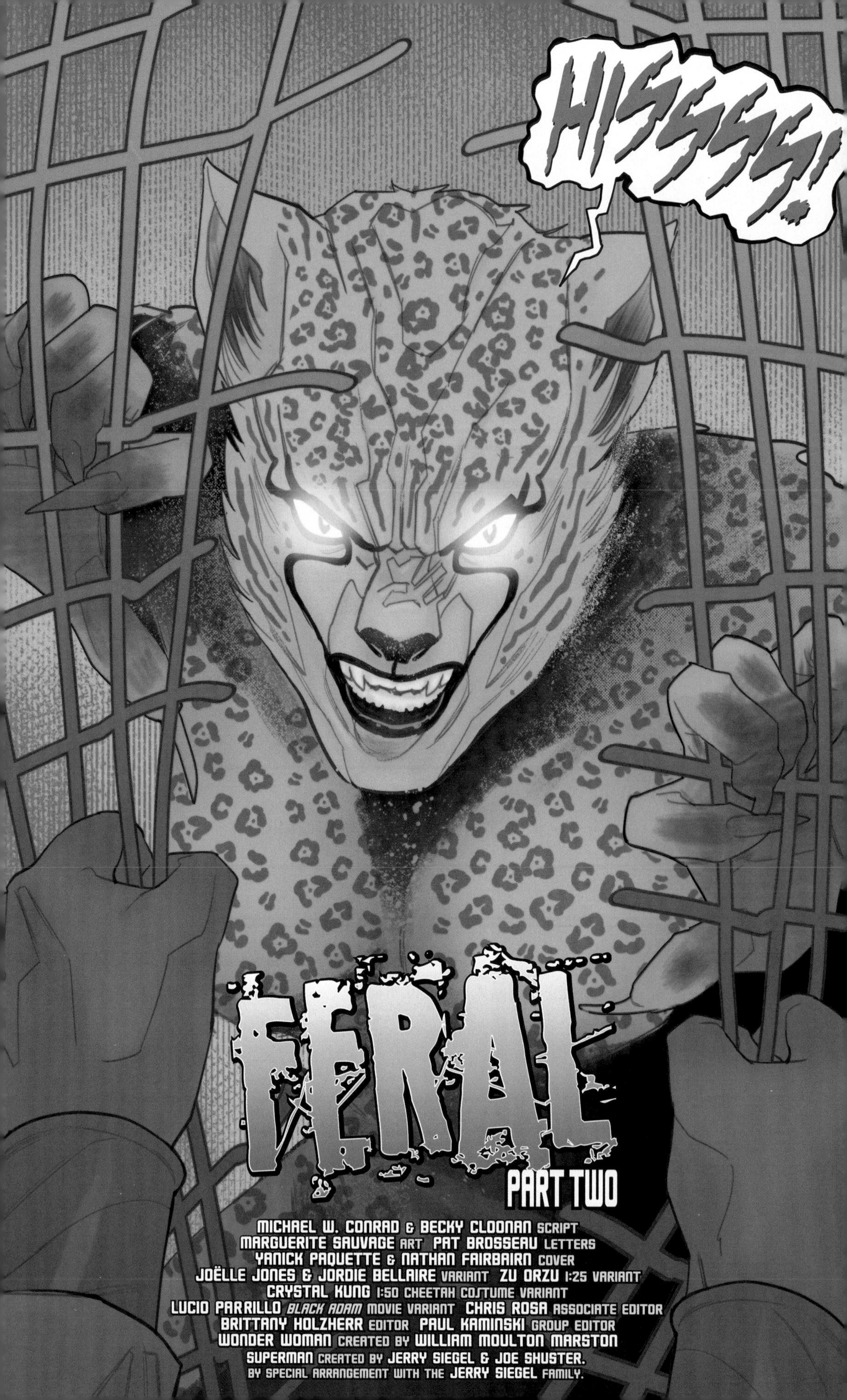

HISSSS!
FERAL
PART TWO
MICHAEL W. CONRAD & BECKY CLOONAN SCRIPT
MARGUERITE SAUVAGE ART PAT BROSSEAU LETTERS
YANICK PAQUETTE & NATHAN FAIRBAIRN COVER
JOËLLE JONES & JORDIE BELLAIRE VARIANT ZU ORZU 1:25 VARIANT
CRYSTAL KUNG 1:50 CHEETAH COSTUME VARIANT
LUCIO PARRILLO BLACK ADAM MOVIE VARIANT CHRIS ROSA ASSOCIATE EDITOR
BRITTANY HOLZHERR EDITOR PAUL KAMINSKI GROUP EDITOR
WONDER WOMAN CREATED BY WILLIAM MOULTON MARSTON
SUPERMAN CREATED BY JERRY SIEGEL & JOE SHUSTER.
BY SPECIAL ARRANGEMENT WITH THE JERRY SIEGEL FAMILY.

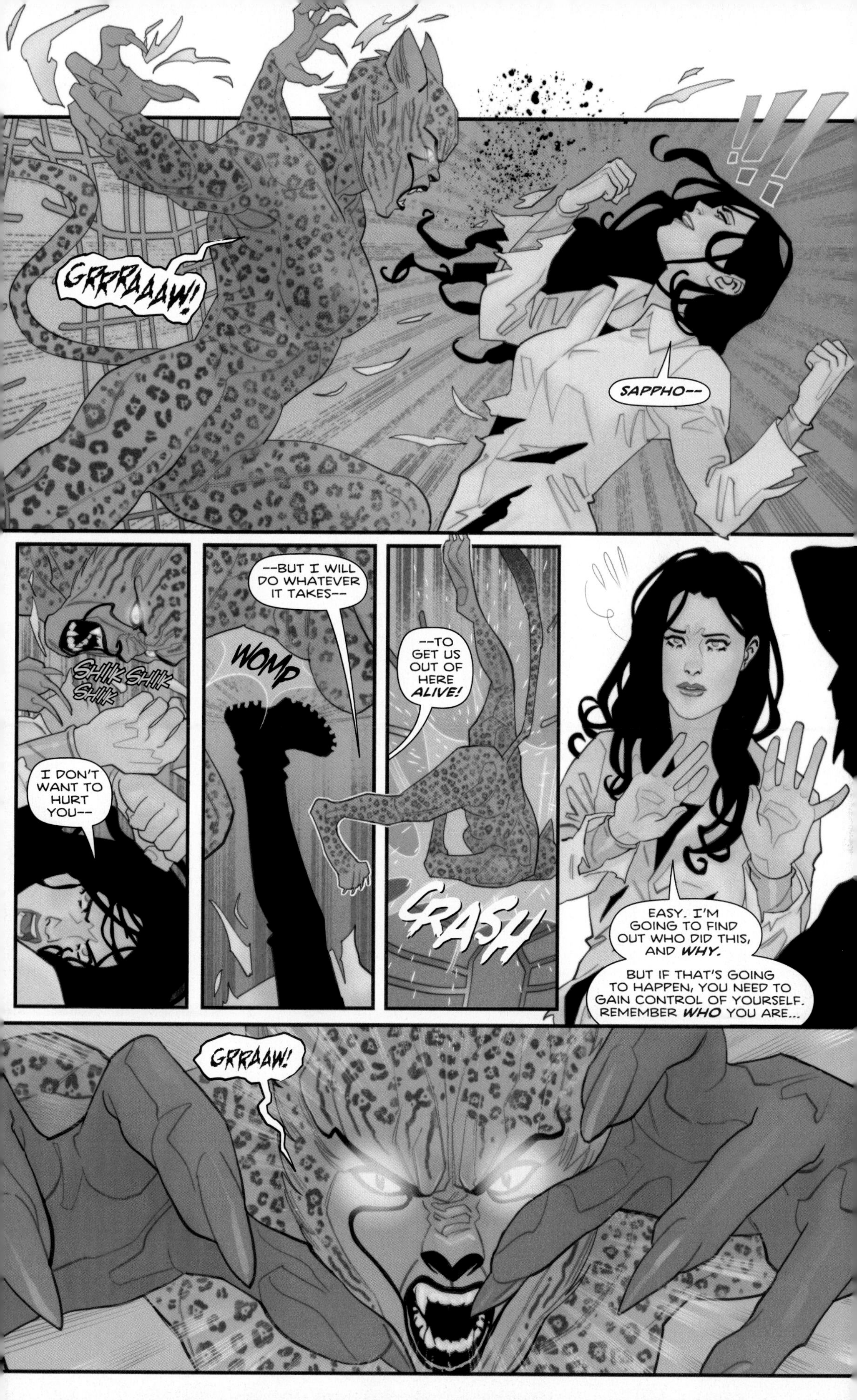
GRRRAAAW!
SAPPHO--
SHIK SHIK SHIK
I DON'T WANT TO HURT YOU--
--BUT I WILL DO WHATEVER IT TAKES--
WOMP
--TO GET US OUT OF HERE ALIVE!
CRASH
EASY. I'M GOING TO FIND OUT WHO DID THIS, AND WHY.
BUT IF THAT'S GOING TO HAPPEN, YOU NEED TO GAIN CONTROL OF YOURSELF. REMEMBER WHO YOU ARE...
GRRAAW!

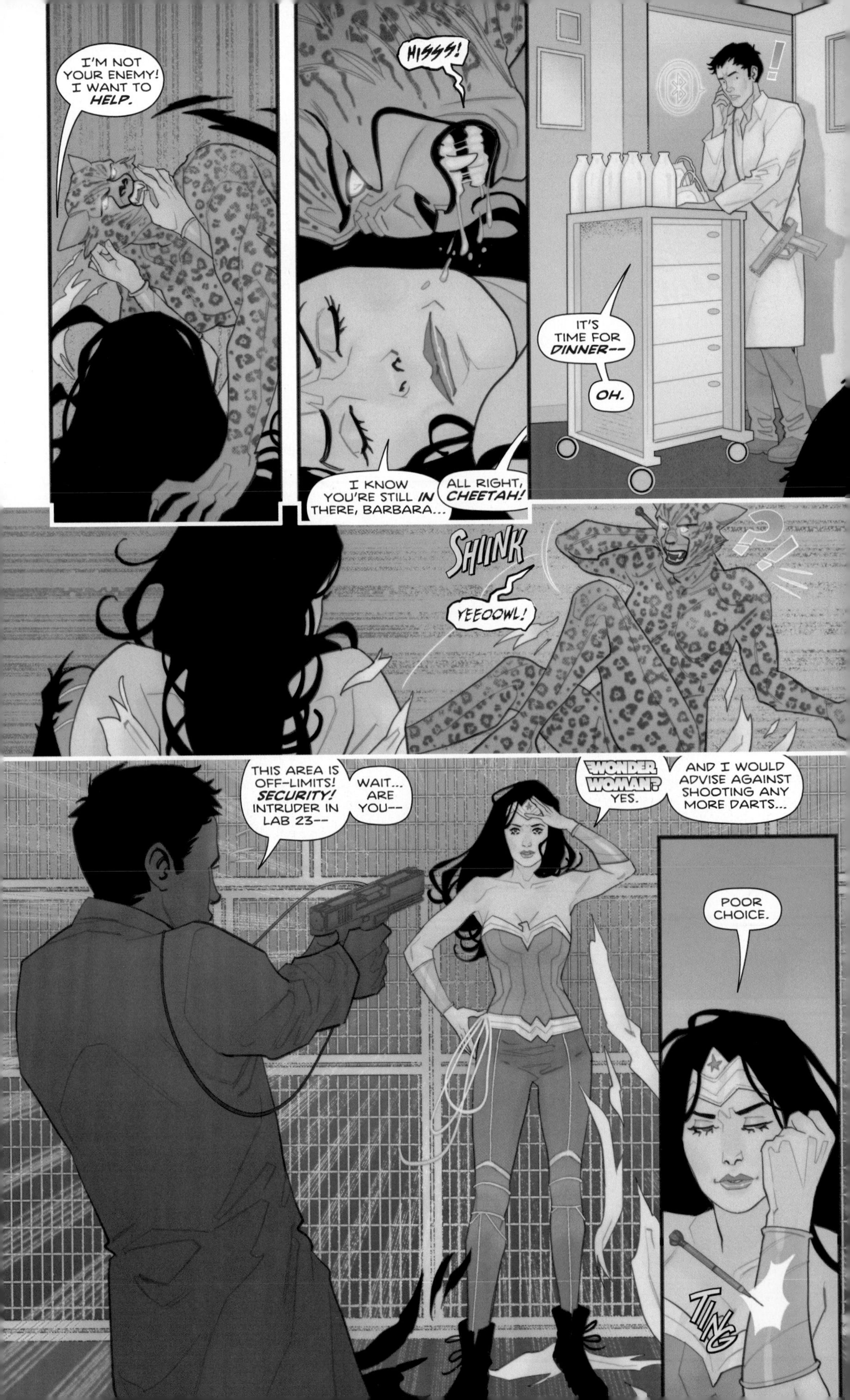
I'M NOT YOUR ENEMY! I WANT TO HELP.
HISSS!
I KNOW YOU'RE STILL IN THERE, BARBARA...
ALL RIGHT, CHEETAH!
IT'S TIME FOR DINNER--
OH.
SHUNK
YEEOOWL!
THIS AREA IS OFF-LIMITS! SECURITY! INTRUDER IN LAB 23--
WAIT... ARE YOU--
WONDER WOMAN? YES.
AND I WOULD ADVISE AGAINST SHOOTING ANY MORE DARTS...
POOR CHOICE.
TING

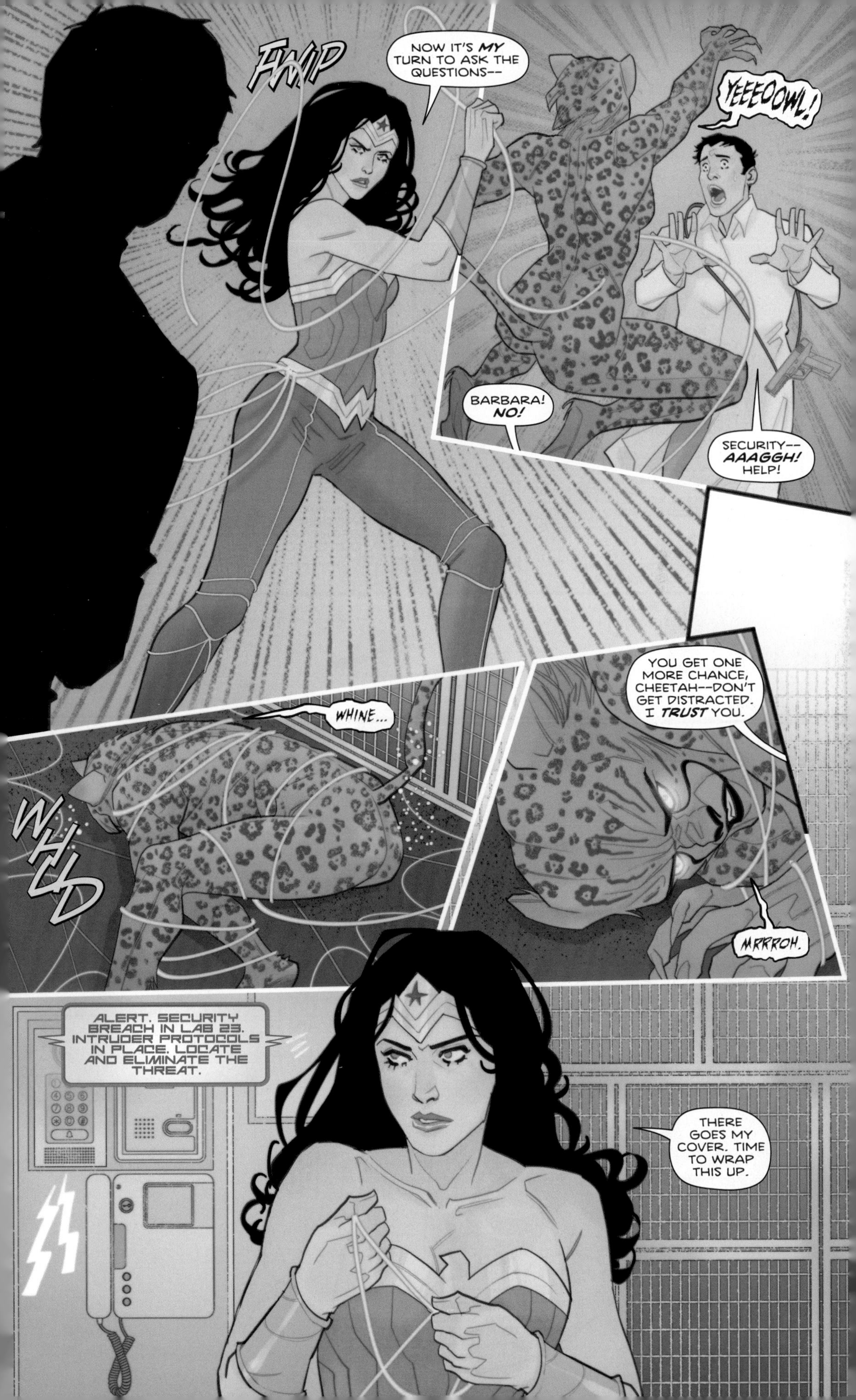

FWIP
NOW IT'S MY TURN TO ASK THE QUESTIONS--
YEEEOOWL!
BARBARA! NO!
SECURITY-- AAAGGH! HELP!
WHINE...
WHUD
YOU GET ONE MORE CHANCE, CHEETAH--DON'T GET DISTRACTED. I TRUST YOU.
MRRROH.
ALERT. SECURITY BREACH IN LAB 23. INTRUDER PROTOCOLS IN PLACE. LOCATE AND ELIMINATE THE THREAT.
THERE GOES MY COVER. TIME TO WRAP THIS UP.

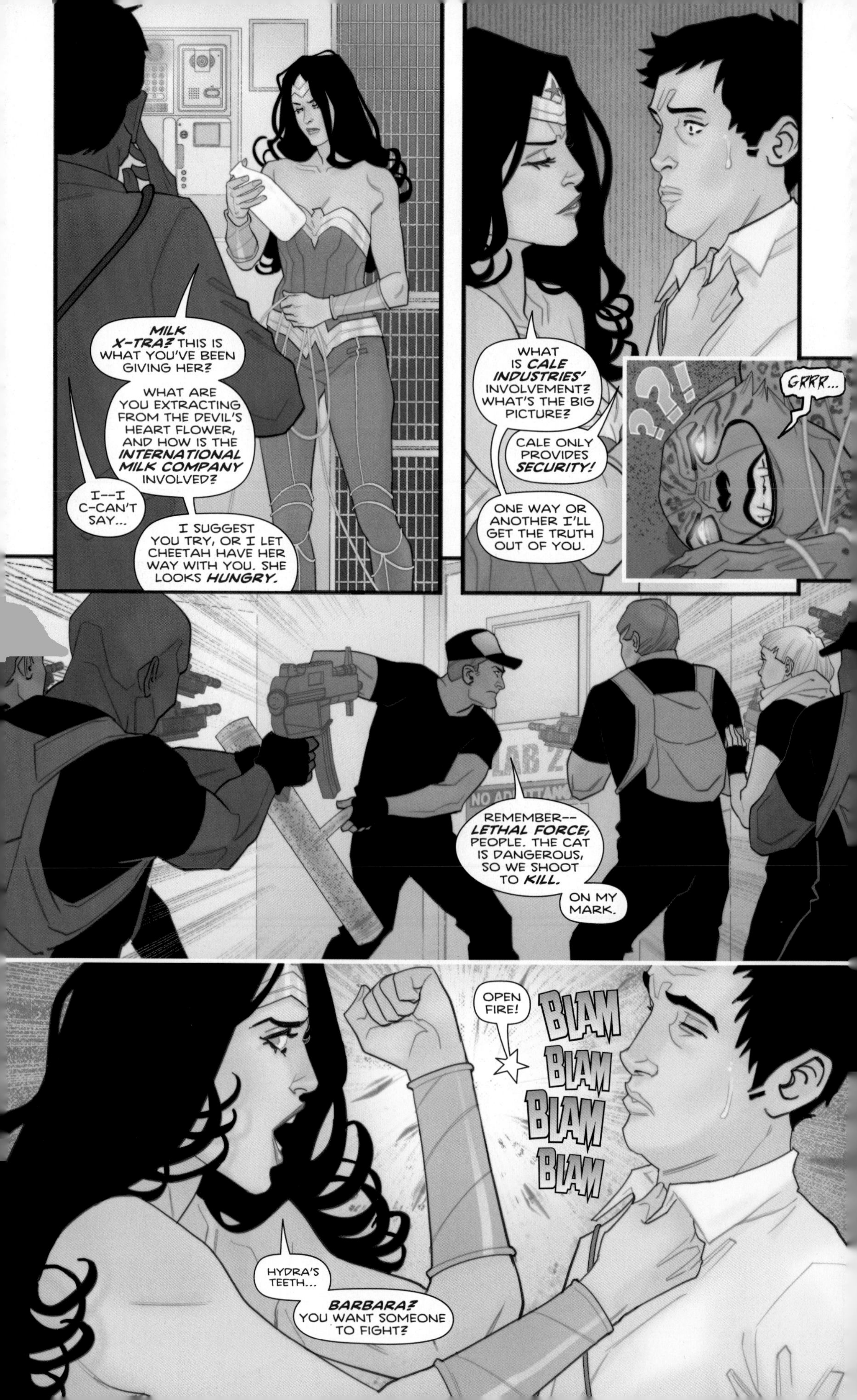
MILK X-TRA? THIS IS WHAT YOU'VE BEEN GIVING HER?
WHAT ARE YOU EXTRACTING FROM THE DEVIL'S HEART FLOWER, AND HOW IS THE INTERNATIONAL MILK COMPANY INVOLVED?
I--I C-CAN'T SAY...
I SUGGEST YOU TRY, OR I LET CHEETAH HAVE HER WAY WITH YOU. SHE LOOKS HUNGRY.
WHAT IS CALE INDUSTRIES' INVOLVEMENT? WHAT'S THE BIG PICTURE?
CALE ONLY PROVIDES SECURITY!
ONE WAY OR ANOTHER I'LL GET THE TRUTH OUT OF YOU.
?!
GRRR...
LAB 2
NO ADMITTANCE
REMEMBER-- LETHAL FORCE, PEOPLE. THE CAT IS DANGEROUS, SO WE SHOOT TO KILL.
ON MY MARK.
OPEN FIRE!
BLAM
BLAM
BLAM
BLAM
HYDRA'S TEETH...
BARBARA? YOU WANT SOMEONE TO FIGHT?

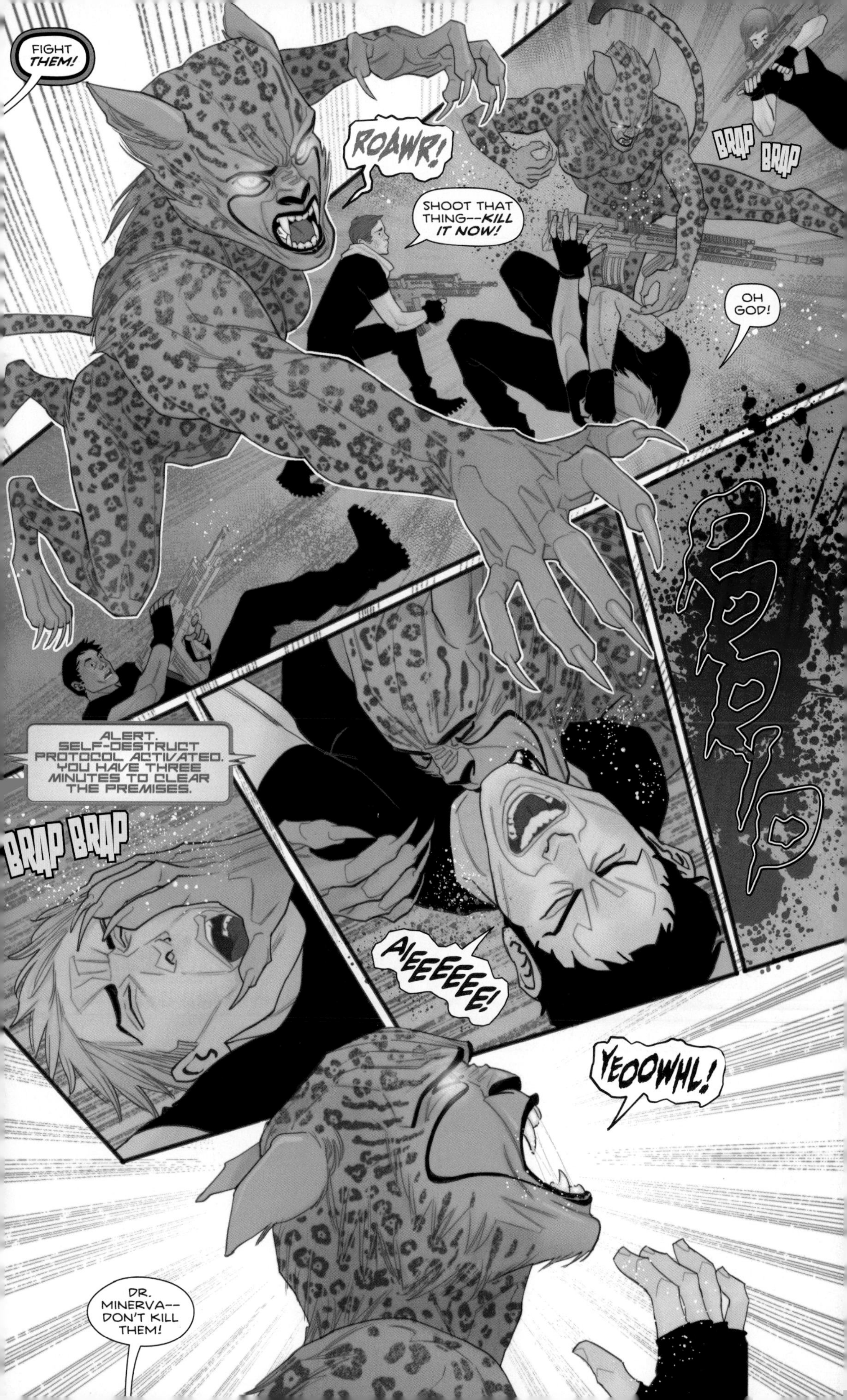
FIGHT THEM!
ROAWR!
SHOOT THAT THING--KILL IT NOW!
BRAP BRAP
OH GOD!
ALERT. SELF-DESTRUCT PROTOCOL ACTIVATED. YOU HAVE THREE MINUTES TO CLEAR THE PREMISES.
BRAP BRAP
AIEEEEEE!
YEOOWHL!
DR. MINERVA-- DON'T KILL THEM!

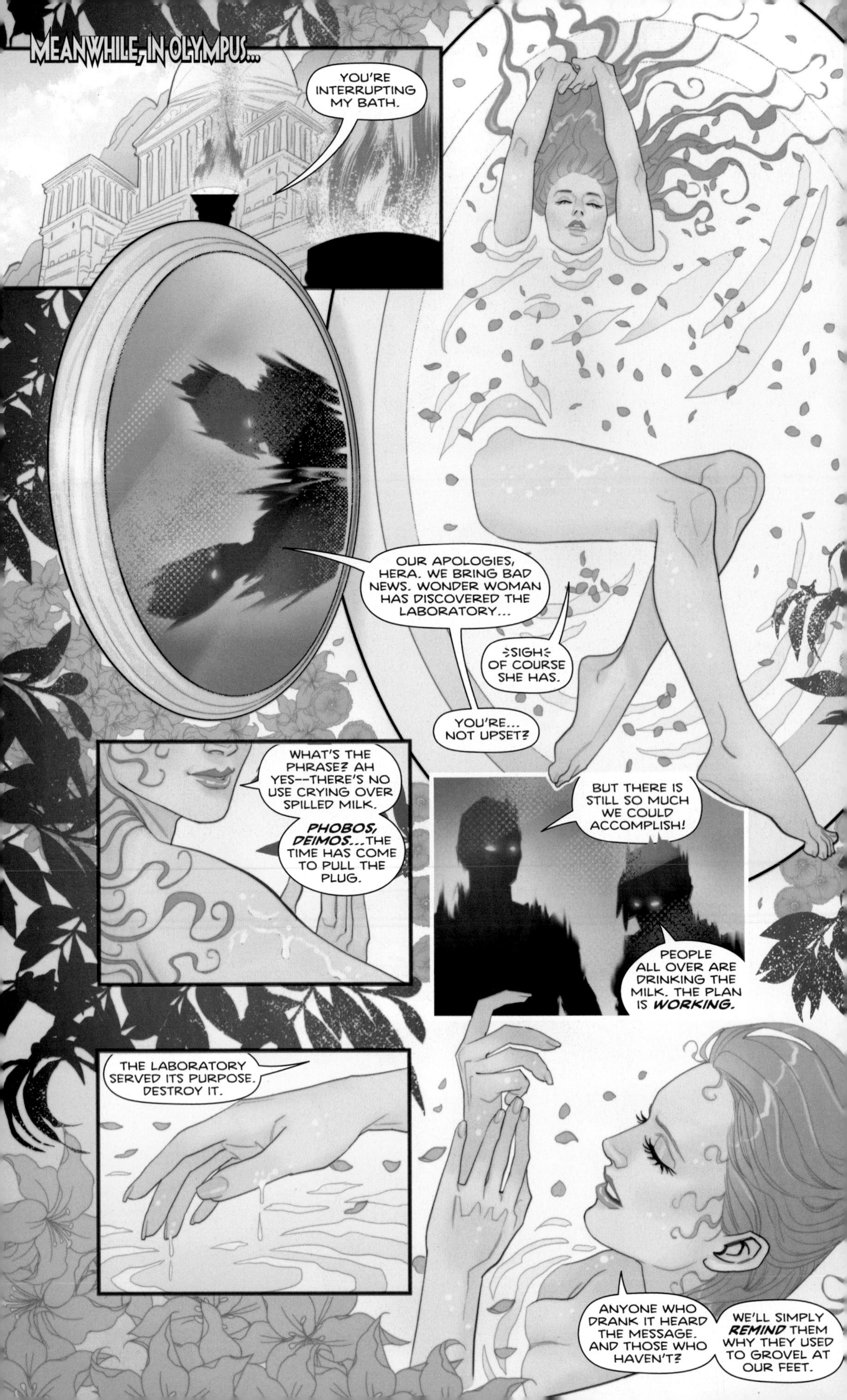
MEANWHILE, IN OLYMPUS...
YOU'RE INTERRUPTING MY BATH.
OUR APOLOGIES, HERA. WE BRING BAD NEWS. WONDER WOMAN HAS DISCOVERED THE LABORATORY...
SIGH OF COURSE SHE HAS.
YOU'RE... NOT UPSET?
WHAT'S THE PHRASE? AH YES--THERE'S NO USE CRYING OVER SPILLED MILK.
PHOBOS, DEIMOS... THE TIME HAS COME TO PULL THE PLUG.
BUT THERE IS STILL SO MUCH WE COULD ACCOMPLISH!
PEOPLE ALL OVER ARE DRINKING THE MILK. THE PLAN IS WORKING.
THE LABORATORY SERVED ITS PURPOSE. DESTROY IT.
ANYONE WHO DRANK IT HEARD THE MESSAGE. AND THOSE WHO HAVEN'T?
WE'LL SIMPLY REMIND THEM WHY THEY USED TO GROVEL AT OUR FEET.

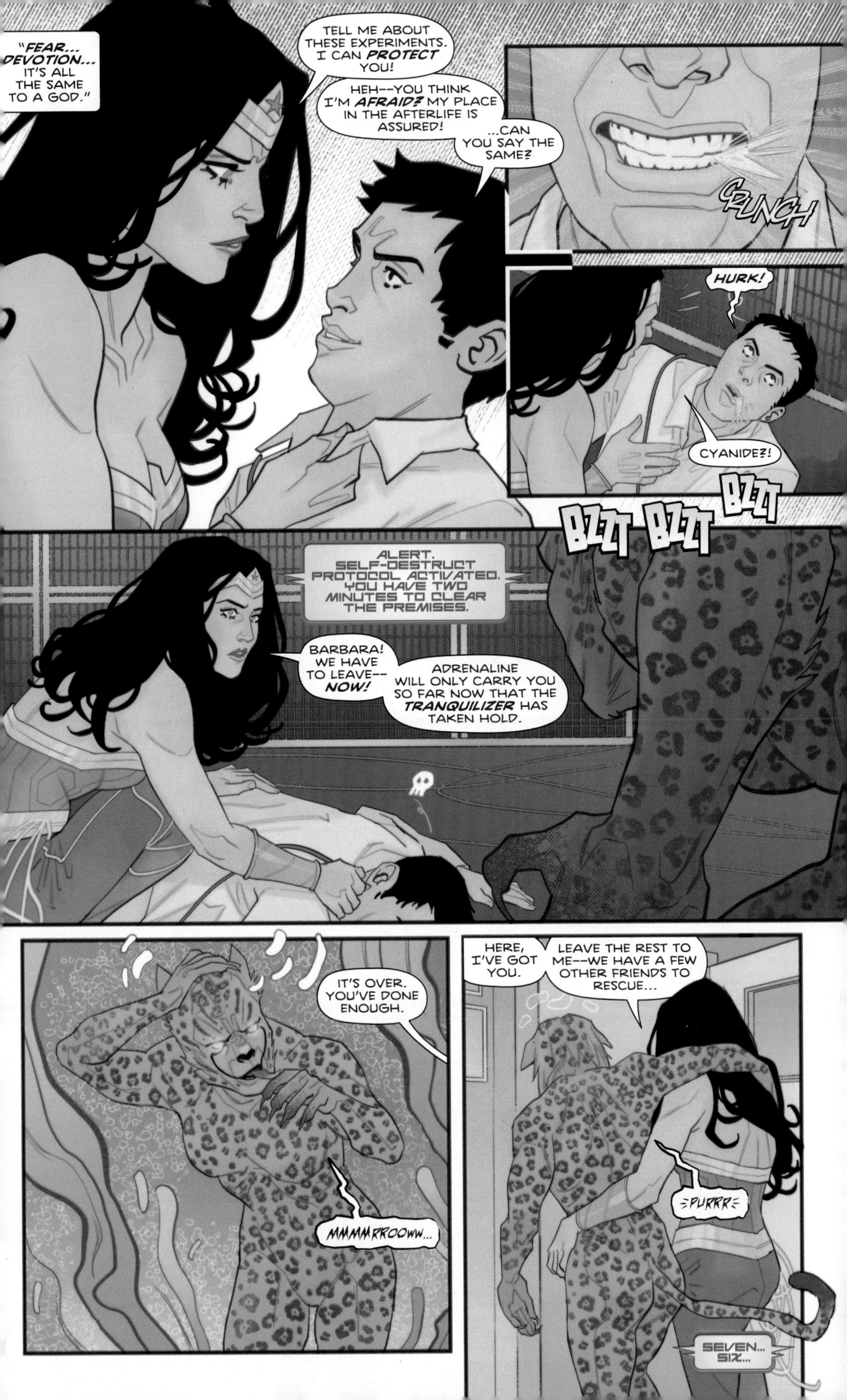
"FEAR... DEVOTION... IT'S ALL THE SAME TO A GOD."
TELL ME ABOUT THESE EXPERIMENTS. I CAN PROTECT YOU!
HEH--YOU THINK I'M AFRAID?! MY PLACE IN THE AFTERLIFE IS ASSURED!
...CAN YOU SAY THE SAME?
CRUNCH
HURK!
CYANIDE?!
BZZT BZZT BZZT
ALERT. SELF-DESTRUCT PROTOCOL ACTIVATED. YOU HAVE TWO MINUTES TO CLEAR THE PREMISES.
BARBARA! WE HAVE TO LEAVE--NOW!
ADRENALINE WILL ONLY CARRY YOU SO FAR NOW THAT THE TRANQUILIZER HAS TAKEN HOLD.
IT'S OVER. YOU'VE DONE ENOUGH.
MMMMRROOWW...
HERE, I'VE GOT YOU.
LEAVE THE REST TO ME--WE HAVE A FEW OTHER FRIENDS TO RESCUE...
PURRR
SEVEN... SIX...

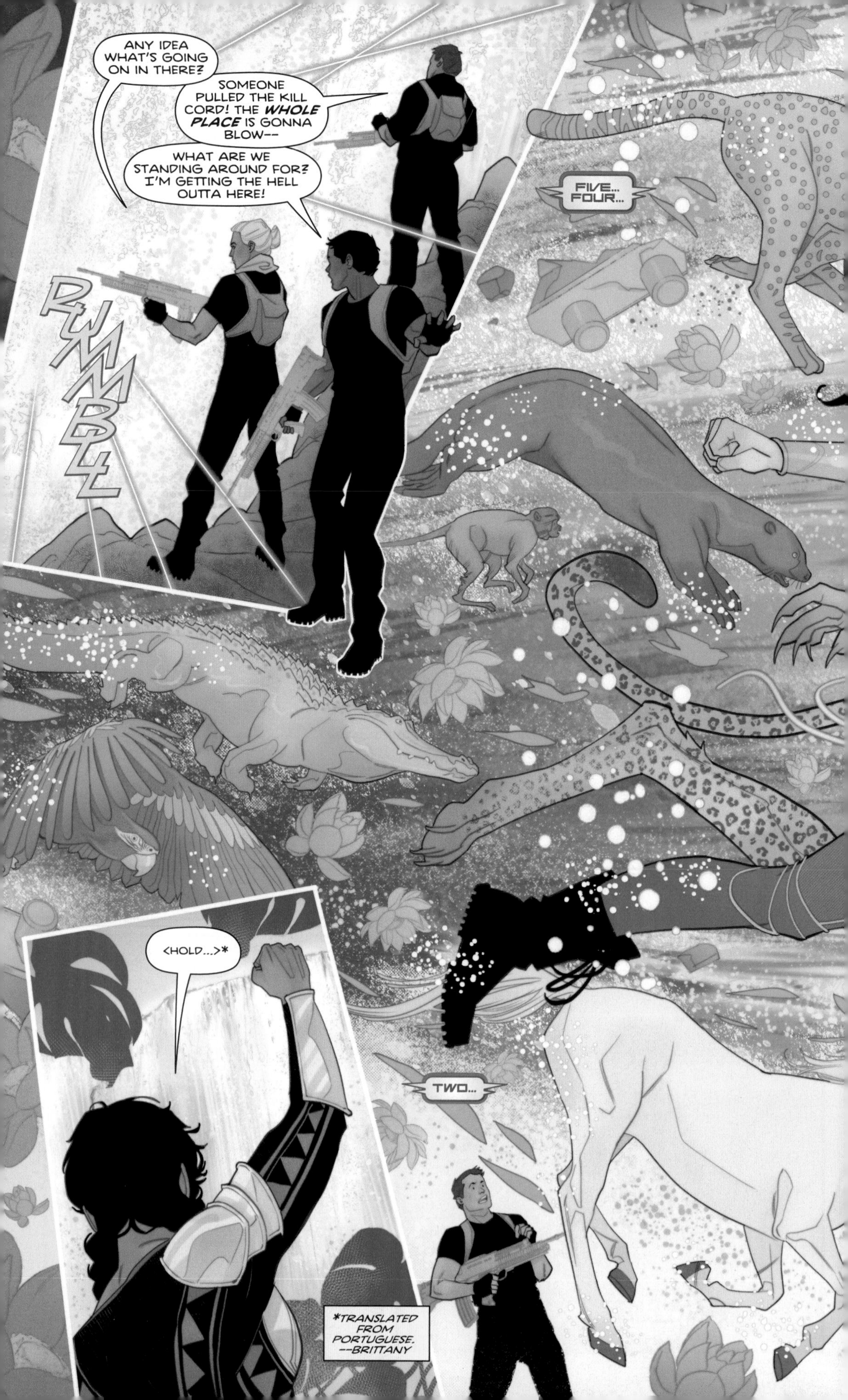

ANY IDEA WHAT'S GOING ON IN THERE?
SOMEONE PULLED THE KILL CORD! THE ***WHOLE PLACE*** IS GONNA BLOW--
WHAT ARE WE STANDING AROUND FOR? I'M GETTING THE HELL OUTTA HERE!
RUMMBLL
FIVE... FOUR...
<HOLD...>*
TWO...
*TRANSLATED FROM PORTUGUESE. --BRITTANY

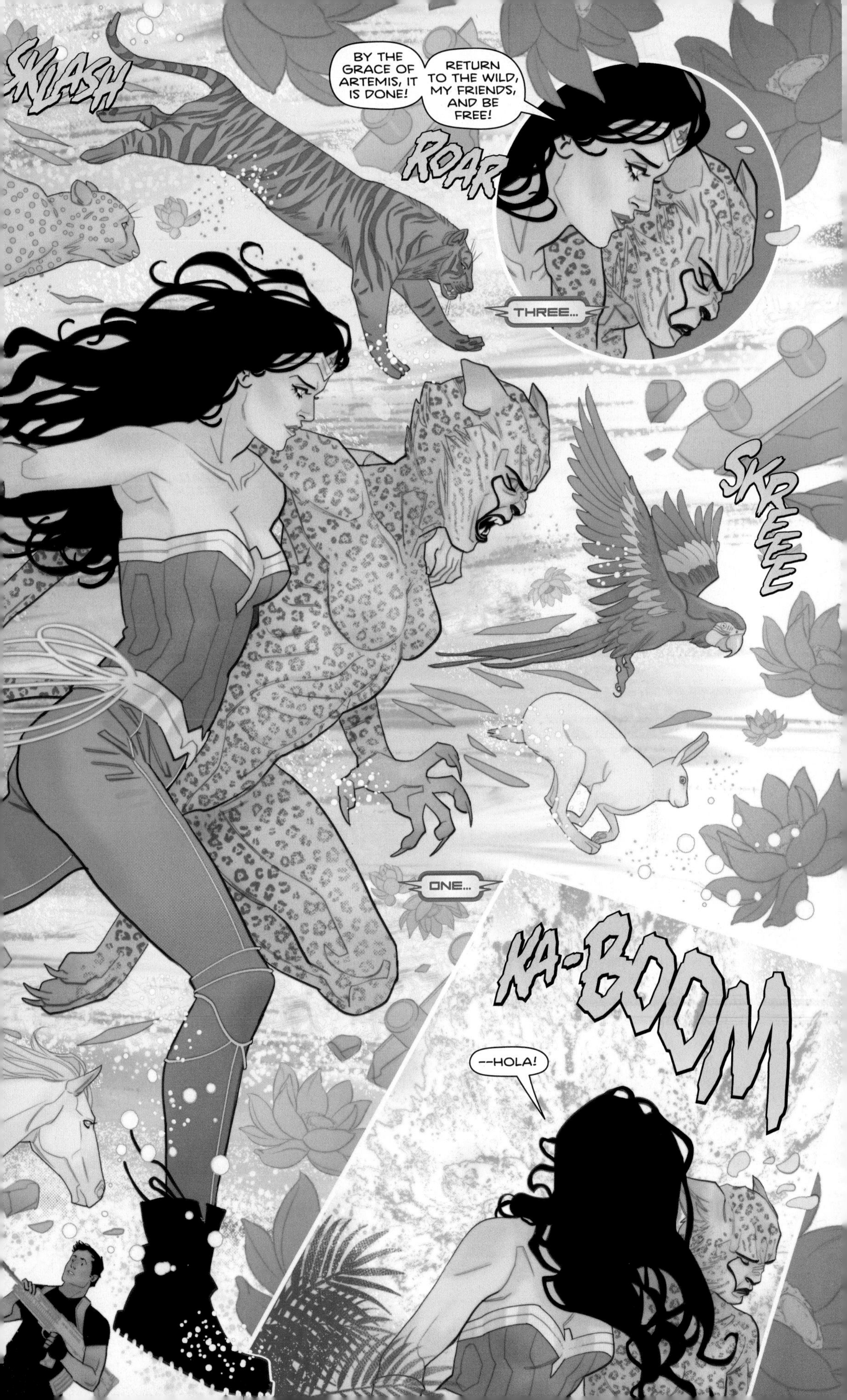
SKLASH
BY THE GRACE OF ARTEMIS, IT IS DONE!
RETURN TO THE WILD, MY FRIENDS, AND BE FREE!
ROAR
THREE...
SKREEE
ONE...
KA-BOOM
--HOLA!

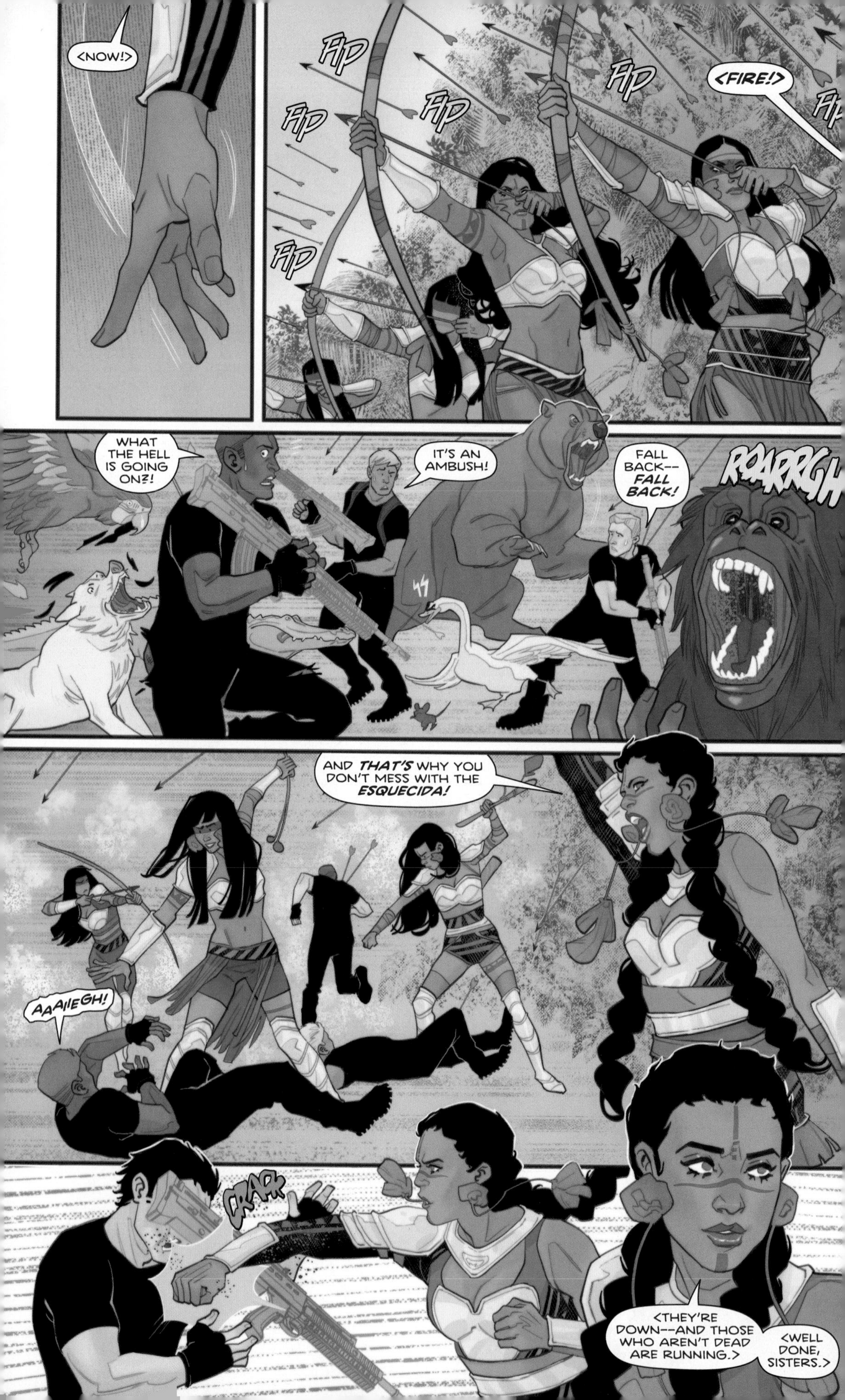

<NOW!>
FIP
FIP
FIP
FIP
FIP
<FIRE!>
FIP
WHAT THE HELL IS GOING ON?!
IT'S AN AMBUSH!
FALL BACK-- FALL BACK!
ROARRGH
AND THAT'S WHY YOU DON'T MESS WITH THE ESQUECIDA!
AAAIIEGH!
CRACK
<THEY'RE DOWN--AND THOSE WHO AREN'T DEAD ARE RUNNING.>
<WELL DONE, SISTERS.>

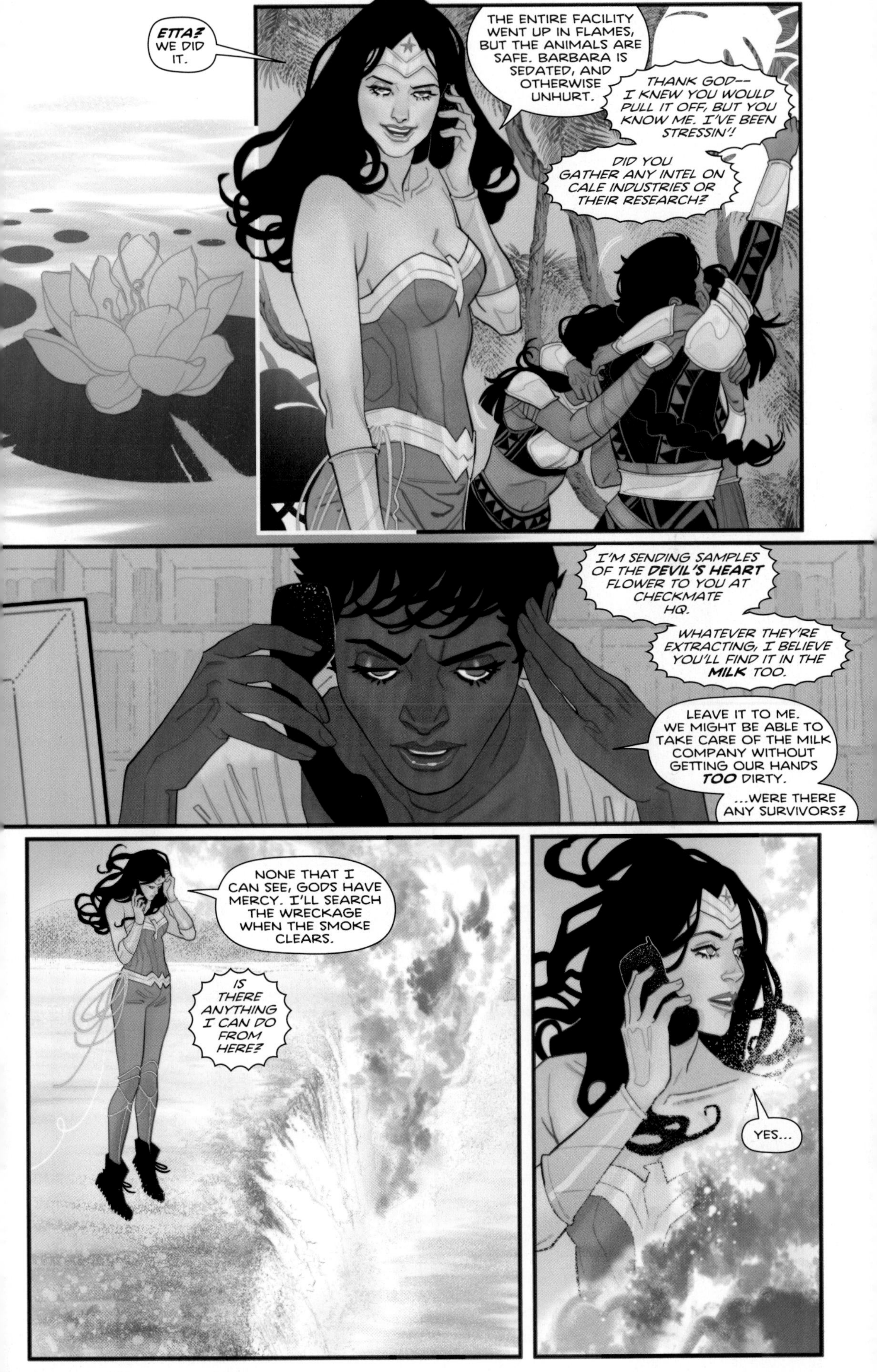

ETTA? WE DID IT.
THE ENTIRE FACILITY WENT UP IN FLAMES, BUT THE ANIMALS ARE SAFE. BARBARA IS SEDATED, AND OTHERWISE UNHURT.
THANK GOD-- I KNEW YOU WOULD PULL IT OFF, BUT YOU KNOW ME. I'VE BEEN STRESSIN'!
DID YOU GATHER ANY INTEL ON CALE INDUSTRIES OR THEIR RESEARCH?
I'M SENDING SAMPLES OF THE DEVIL'S HEART FLOWER TO YOU AT CHECKMATE HQ.
WHATEVER THEY'RE EXTRACTING, I BELIEVE YOU'LL FIND IT IN THE MILK TOO.
LEAVE IT TO ME. WE MIGHT BE ABLE TO TAKE CARE OF THE MILK COMPANY WITHOUT GETTING OUR HANDS TOO DIRTY.
...WERE THERE ANY SURVIVORS?
NONE THAT I CAN SEE, GODS HAVE MERCY. I'LL SEARCH THE WRECKAGE WHEN THE SMOKE CLEARS.
IS THERE ANYTHING I CAN DO FROM HERE?
YES...

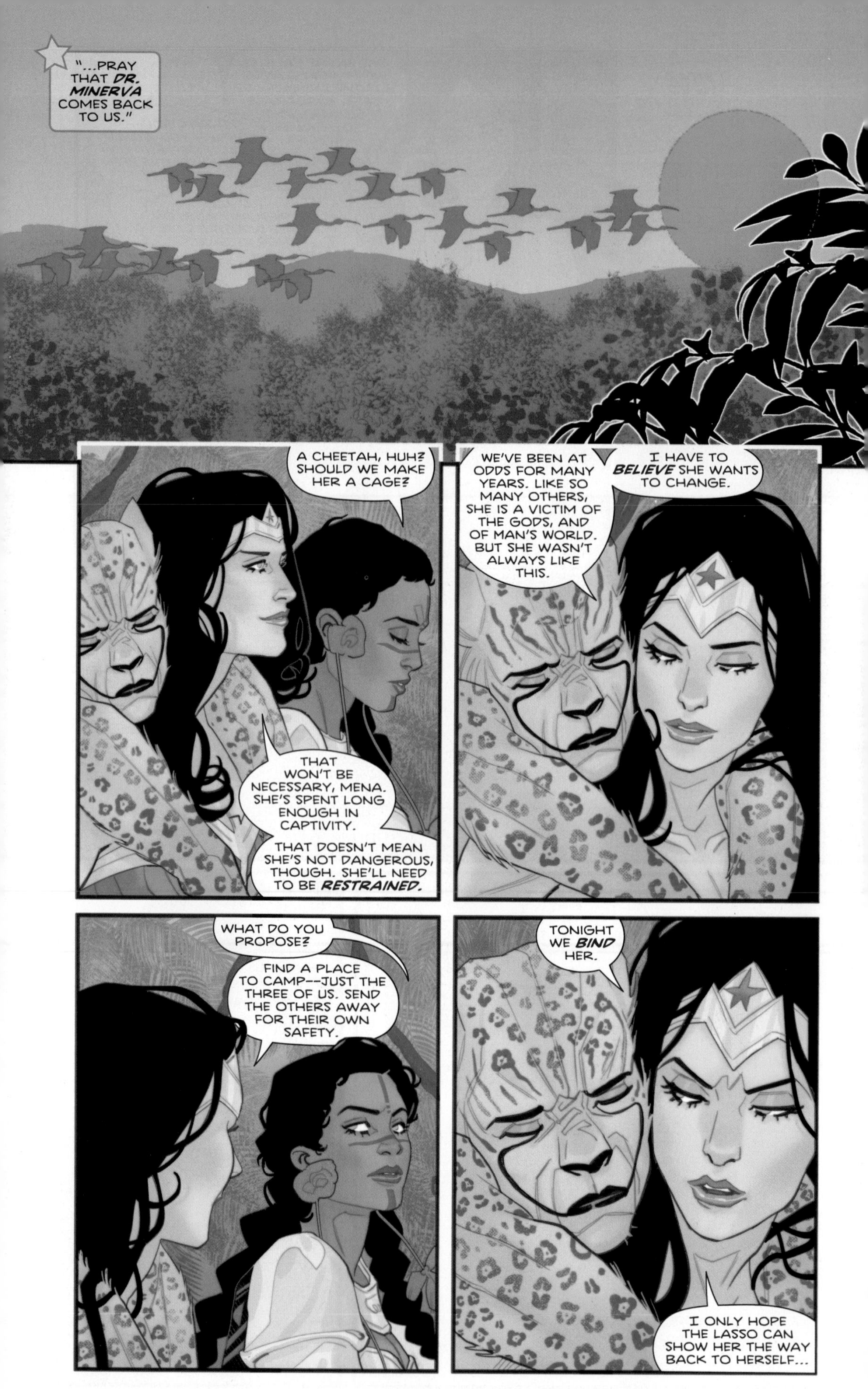
"...PRAY THAT DR. MINERVA COMES BACK TO US."
A CHEETAH, HUH? SHOULD WE MAKE HER A CAGE?
THAT WON'T BE NECESSARY, MENA. SHE'S SPENT LONG ENOUGH IN CAPTIVITY.
THAT DOESN'T MEAN SHE'S NOT DANGEROUS, THOUGH. SHE'LL NEED TO BE RESTRAINED.
WE'VE BEEN AT ODDS FOR MANY YEARS. LIKE SO MANY OTHERS, SHE IS A VICTIM OF THE GODS, AND OF MAN'S WORLD. BUT SHE WASN'T ALWAYS LIKE THIS.
I HAVE TO BELIEVE SHE WANTS TO CHANGE.
WHAT DO YOU PROPOSE?
FIND A PLACE TO CAMP--JUST THE THREE OF US. SEND THE OTHERS AWAY FOR THEIR OWN SAFETY.
TONIGHT WE BIND HER.
I ONLY HOPE THE LASSO CAN SHOW HER THE WAY BACK TO HERSELF...

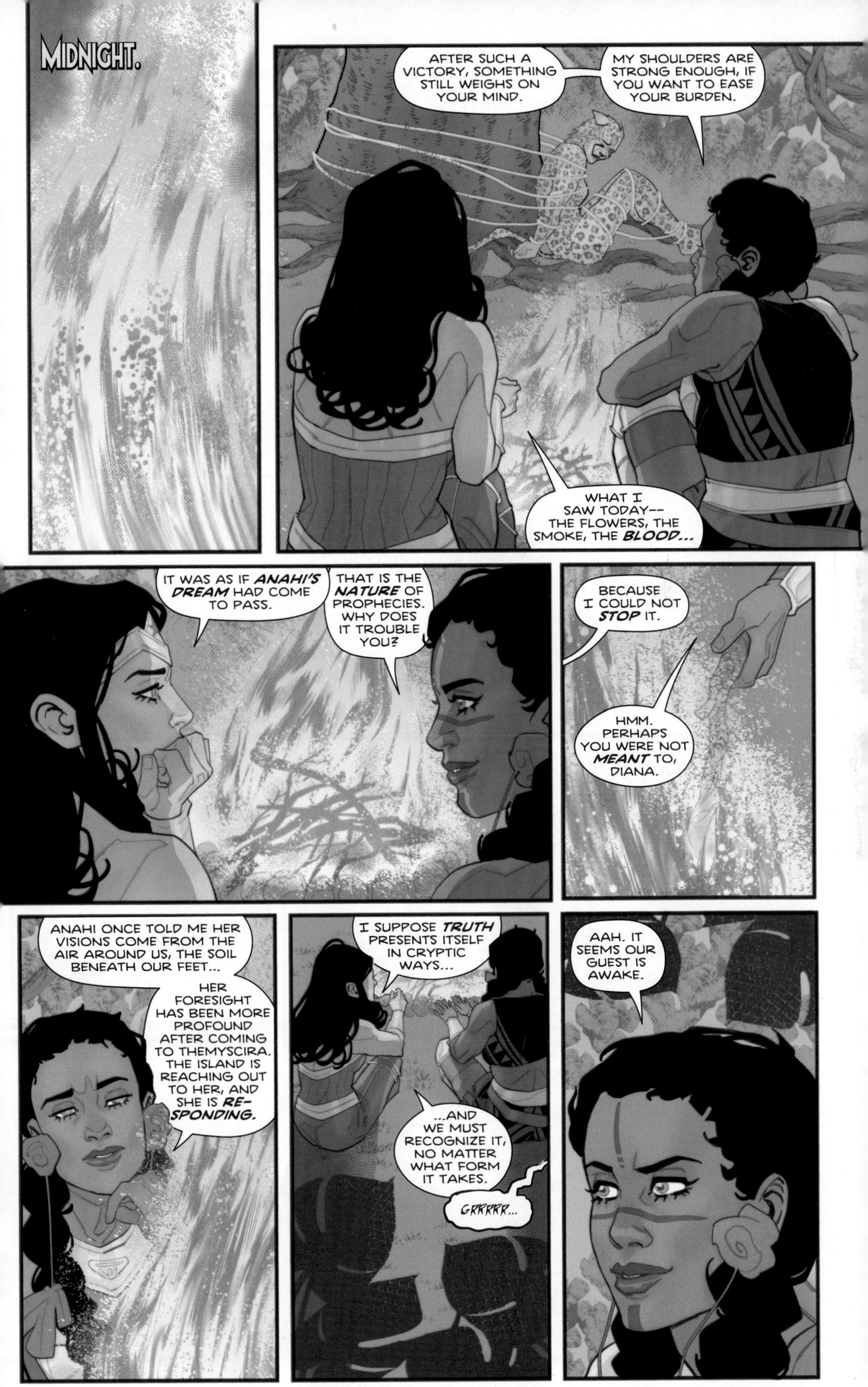
MIDNIGHT.
AFTER SUCH A VICTORY, SOMETHING STILL WEIGHS ON YOUR MIND.
MY SHOULDERS ARE STRONG ENOUGH, IF YOU WANT TO EASE YOUR BURDEN.
WHAT I SAW TODAY-- THE FLOWERS, THE SMOKE, THE BLOOD...
IT WAS AS IF ANAHI'S DREAM HAD COME TO PASS.
THAT IS THE NATURE OF PROPHECIES. WHY DOES IT TROUBLE YOU?
BECAUSE I COULD NOT STOP IT.
HMM. PERHAPS YOU WERE NOT MEANT TO, DIANA.
ANAHI ONCE TOLD ME HER VISIONS COME FROM THE AIR AROUND US, THE SOIL BENEATH OUR FEET...
HER FORESIGHT HAS BEEN MORE PROFOUND AFTER COMING TO THEMYSCIRA. THE ISLAND IS REACHING OUT TO HER, AND SHE IS RE-SPONDING.
I SUPPOSE TRUTH PRESENTS ITSELF IN CRYPTIC WAYS...
...AND WE MUST RECOGNIZE IT, NO MATTER WHAT FORM IT TAKES.
GRRRRR...
AAH. IT SEEMS OUR GUEST IS AWAKE.

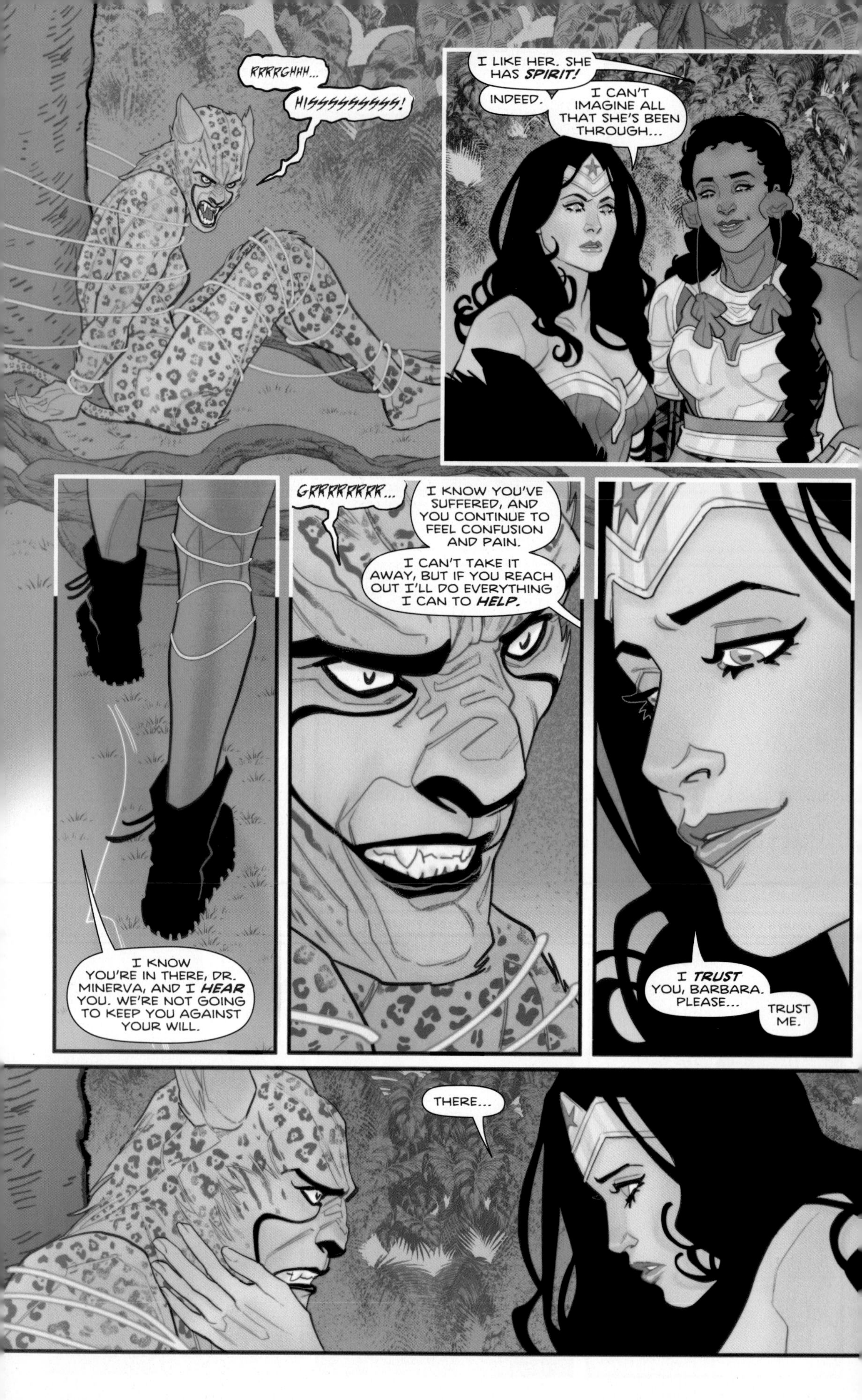
RRRRGHHH...
HISSSSSSSSSS!
I LIKE HER. SHE HAS SPIRIT!
INDEED.
I CAN'T IMAGINE ALL THAT SHE'S BEEN THROUGH...
I KNOW YOU'RE IN THERE, DR. MINERVA, AND I HEAR YOU. WE'RE NOT GOING TO KEEP YOU AGAINST YOUR WILL.
GRRRRRRRR...
I KNOW YOU'VE SUFFERED, AND YOU CONTINUE TO FEEL CONFUSION AND PAIN.
I CAN'T TAKE IT AWAY, BUT IF YOU REACH OUT I'LL DO EVERYTHING I CAN TO HELP.
I TRUST YOU, BARBARA. PLEASE...
TRUST ME.
THERE...

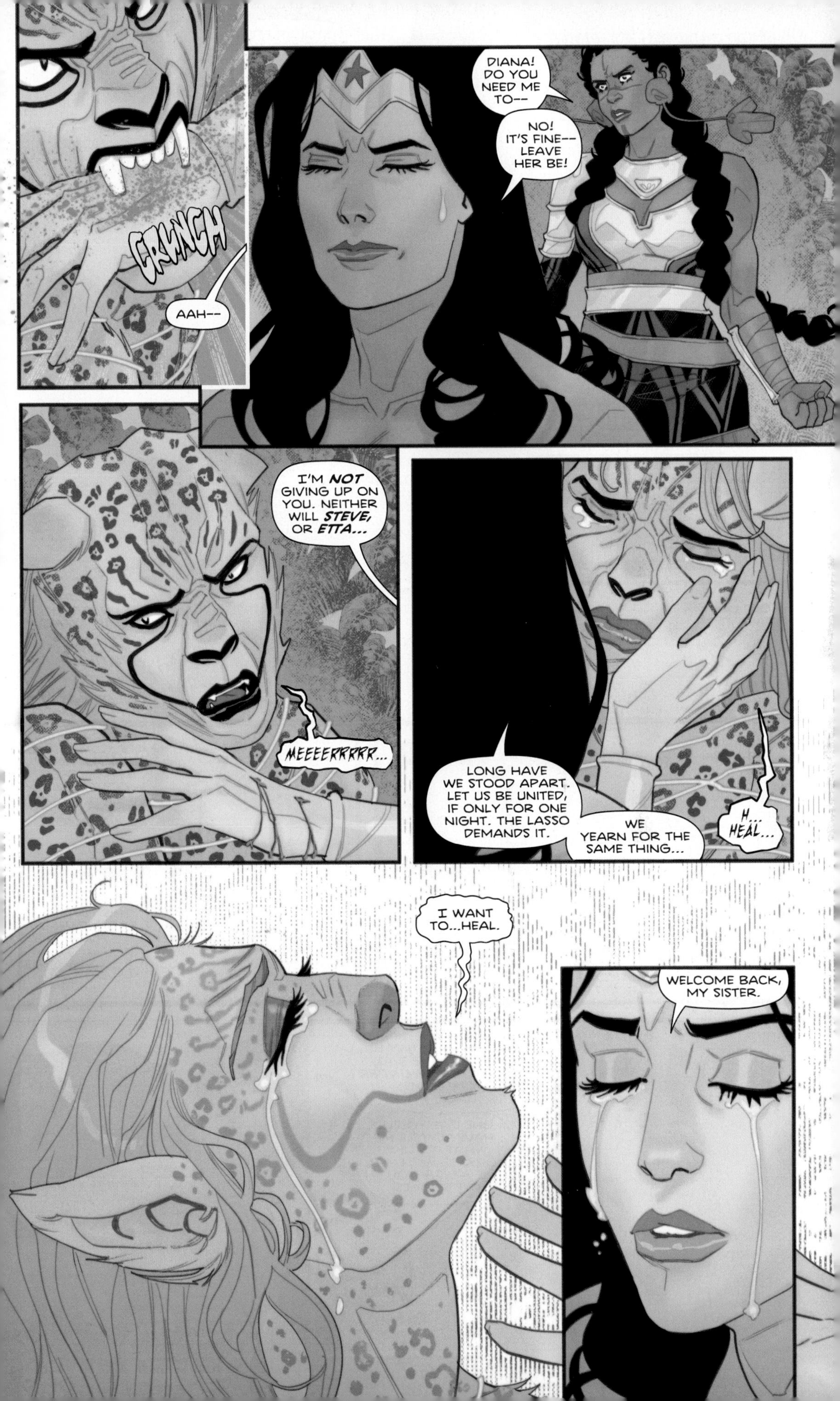
CRUNCH
AAH--
DIANA! DO YOU NEED ME TO--
NO! IT'S FINE-- LEAVE HER BE!
I'M NOT GIVING UP ON YOU. NEITHER WILL STEVE, OR ETTA...
MEEEERRRRR...
LONG HAVE WE STOOD APART. LET US BE UNITED, IF ONLY FOR ONE NIGHT. THE LASSO DEMANDS IT.
WE YEARN FOR THE SAME THING...
H... HEAL...
I WANT TO...HEAL.
WELCOME BACK, MY SISTER.

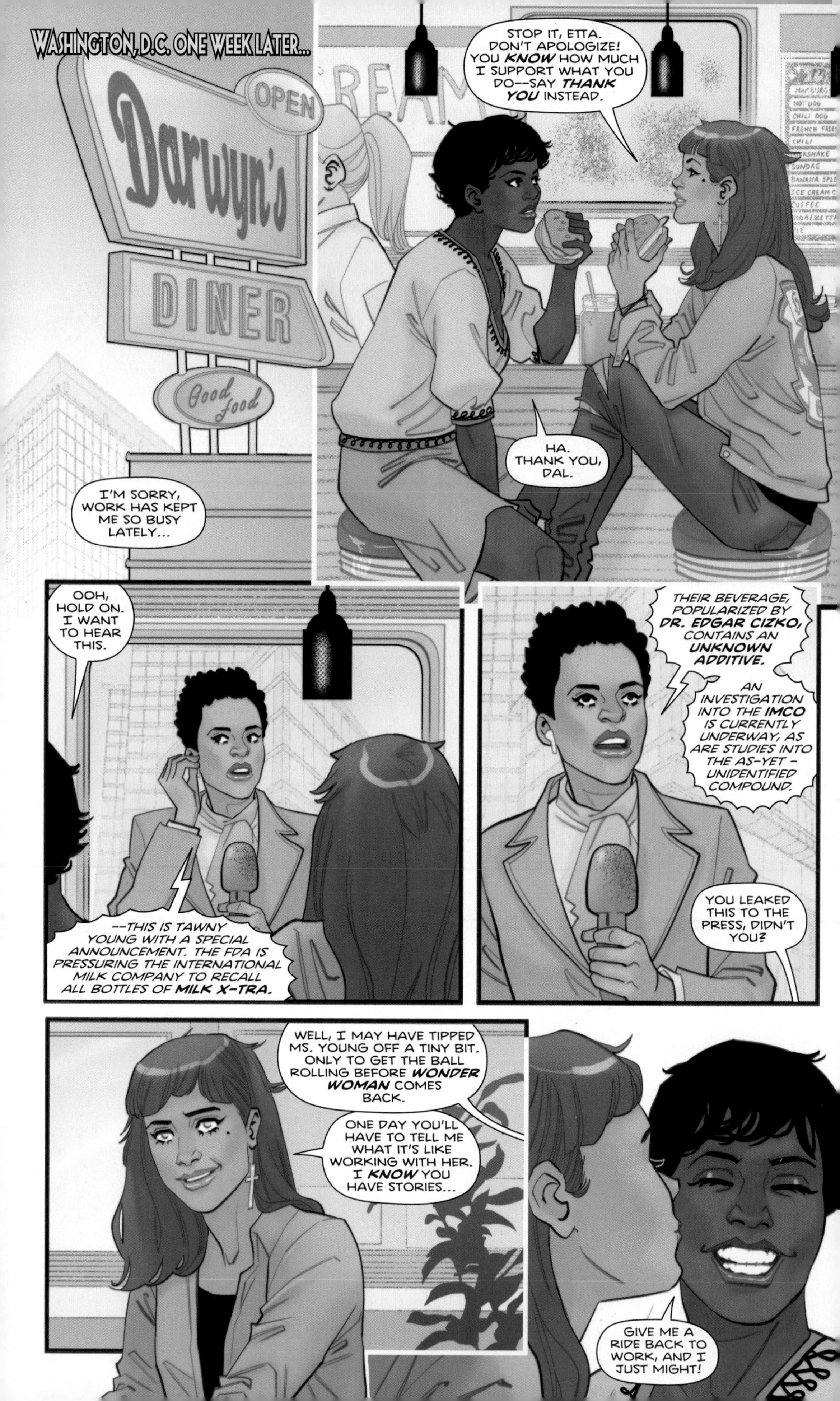
WASHINGTON, D.C. ONE WEEK LATER...
Darwyn's
OPEN
DINER
Good food
I'M SORRY, WORK HAS KEPT ME SO BUSY LATELY...
STOP IT, ETTA. DON'T APOLOGIZE! YOU KNOW HOW MUCH I SUPPORT WHAT YOU DO--SAY THANK YOU INSTEAD.
HA. THANK YOU, DAL.
OOH, HOLD ON. I WANT TO HEAR THIS.
--THIS IS TAWNY YOUNG WITH A SPECIAL ANNOUNCEMENT. THE FDA IS PRESSURING THE INTERNATIONAL MILK COMPANY TO RECALL ALL BOTTLES OF MILK X-TRA.
THEIR BEVERAGE, POPULARIZED BY DR. EDGAR CIZKO, CONTAINS AN UNKNOWN ADDITIVE.
AN INVESTIGATION INTO THE IMCO IS CURRENTLY UNDERWAY, AS ARE STUDIES INTO THE AS-YET-UNIDENTIFIED COMPOUND.
YOU LEAKED THIS TO THE PRESS, DIDN'T YOU?
WELL, I MAY HAVE TIPPED MS. YOUNG OFF A TINY BIT. ONLY TO GET THE BALL ROLLING BEFORE WONDER WOMAN COMES BACK.
ONE DAY YOU'LL HAVE TO TELL ME WHAT IT'S LIKE WORKING WITH HER. I KNOW YOU HAVE STORIES...
GIVE ME A RIDE BACK TO WORK, AND I JUST MIGHT!

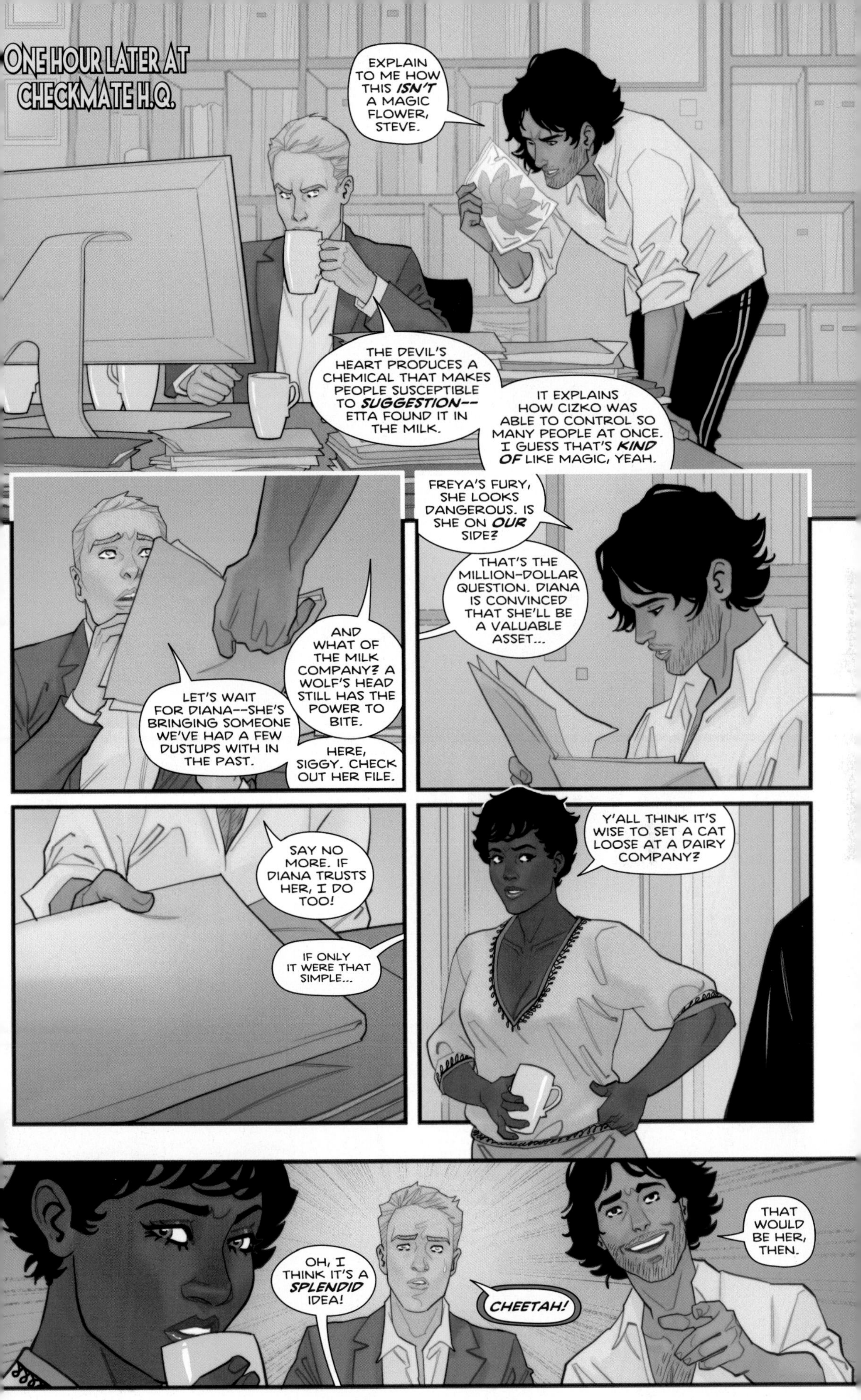
ONE HOUR LATER AT CHECKMATE H.Q.
EXPLAIN TO ME HOW THIS ISN'T A MAGIC FLOWER, STEVE.
THE DEVIL'S HEART PRODUCES A CHEMICAL THAT MAKES PEOPLE SUSCEPTIBLE TO SUGGESTION-- ETTA FOUND IT IN THE MILK.
IT EXPLAINS HOW CIZKO WAS ABLE TO CONTROL SO MANY PEOPLE AT ONCE. I GUESS THAT'S KIND OF LIKE MAGIC, YEAH.
LET'S WAIT FOR DIANA--SHE'S BRINGING SOMEONE WE'VE HAD A FEW DUSTUPS WITH IN THE PAST.
AND WHAT OF THE MILK COMPANY? A WOLF'S HEAD STILL HAS THE POWER TO BITE.
HERE, SIGGY. CHECK OUT HER FILE.
FREYA'S FURY, SHE LOOKS DANGEROUS. IS SHE ON OUR SIDE?
THAT'S THE MILLION-DOLLAR QUESTION. DIANA IS CONVINCED THAT SHE'LL BE A VALUABLE ASSET...
SAY NO MORE. IF DIANA TRUSTS HER, I DO TOO!
IF ONLY IT WERE THAT SIMPLE...
Y'ALL THINK IT'S WISE TO SET A CAT LOOSE AT A DAIRY COMPANY?
OH, I THINK IT'S A SPLENDID IDEA!
CHEETAH!
THAT WOULD BE HER, THEN.

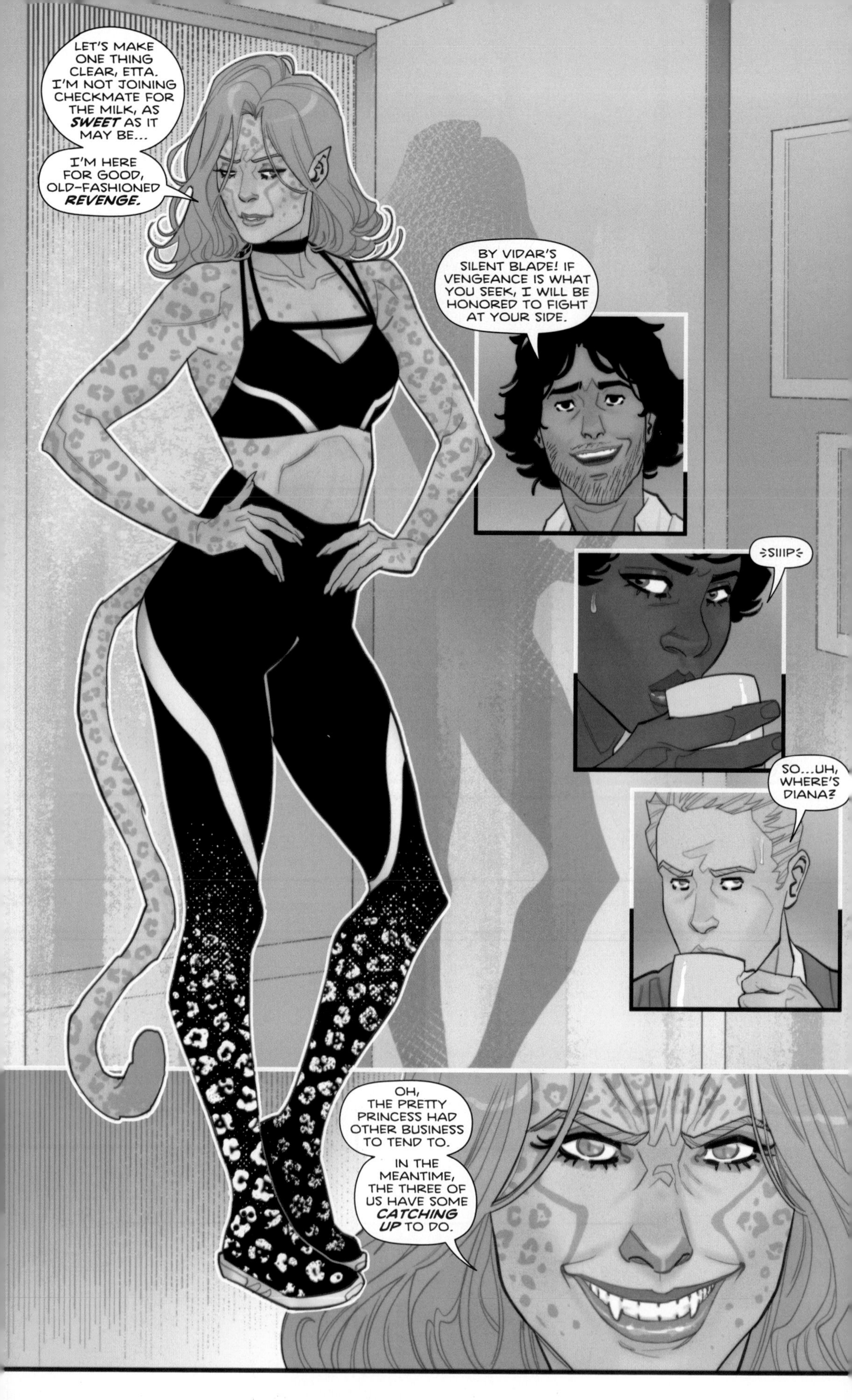
LET'S MAKE ONE THING CLEAR, ETTA. I'M NOT JOINING CHECKMATE FOR THE MILK, AS SWEET AS IT MAY BE...
I'M HERE FOR GOOD, OLD-FASHIONED REVENGE.
BY VIDAR'S SILENT BLADE! IF VENGEANCE IS WHAT YOU SEEK, I WILL BE HONORED TO FIGHT AT YOUR SIDE.
SIIIP
SO...UH, WHERE'S DIANA?
OH, THE PRETTY PRINCESS HAD OTHER BUSINESS TO TEND TO.
IN THE MEANTIME, THE THREE OF US HAVE SOME CATCHING UP TO DO.

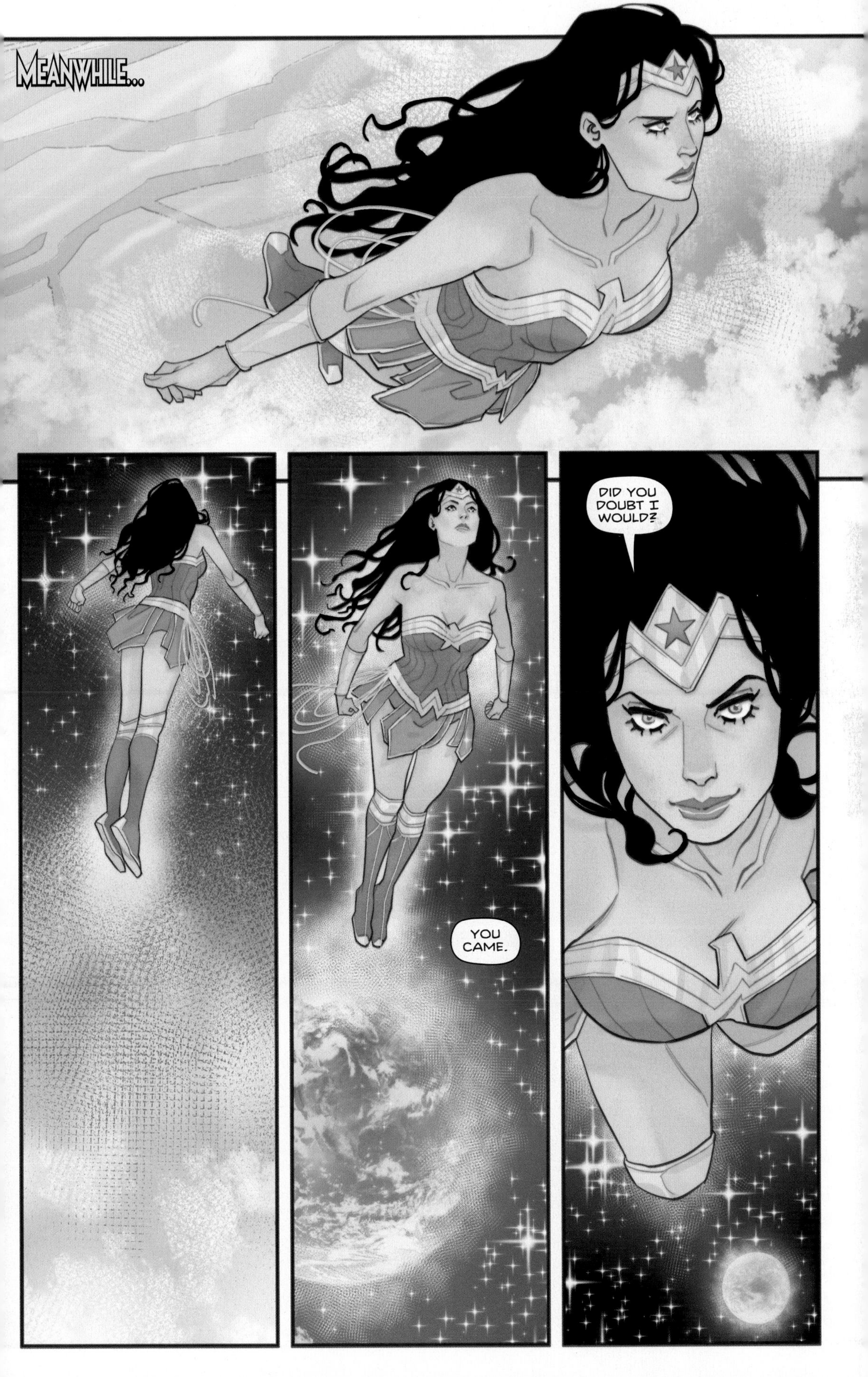
MEANWHILE...
YOU CAME.
DID YOU DOUBT I WOULD?

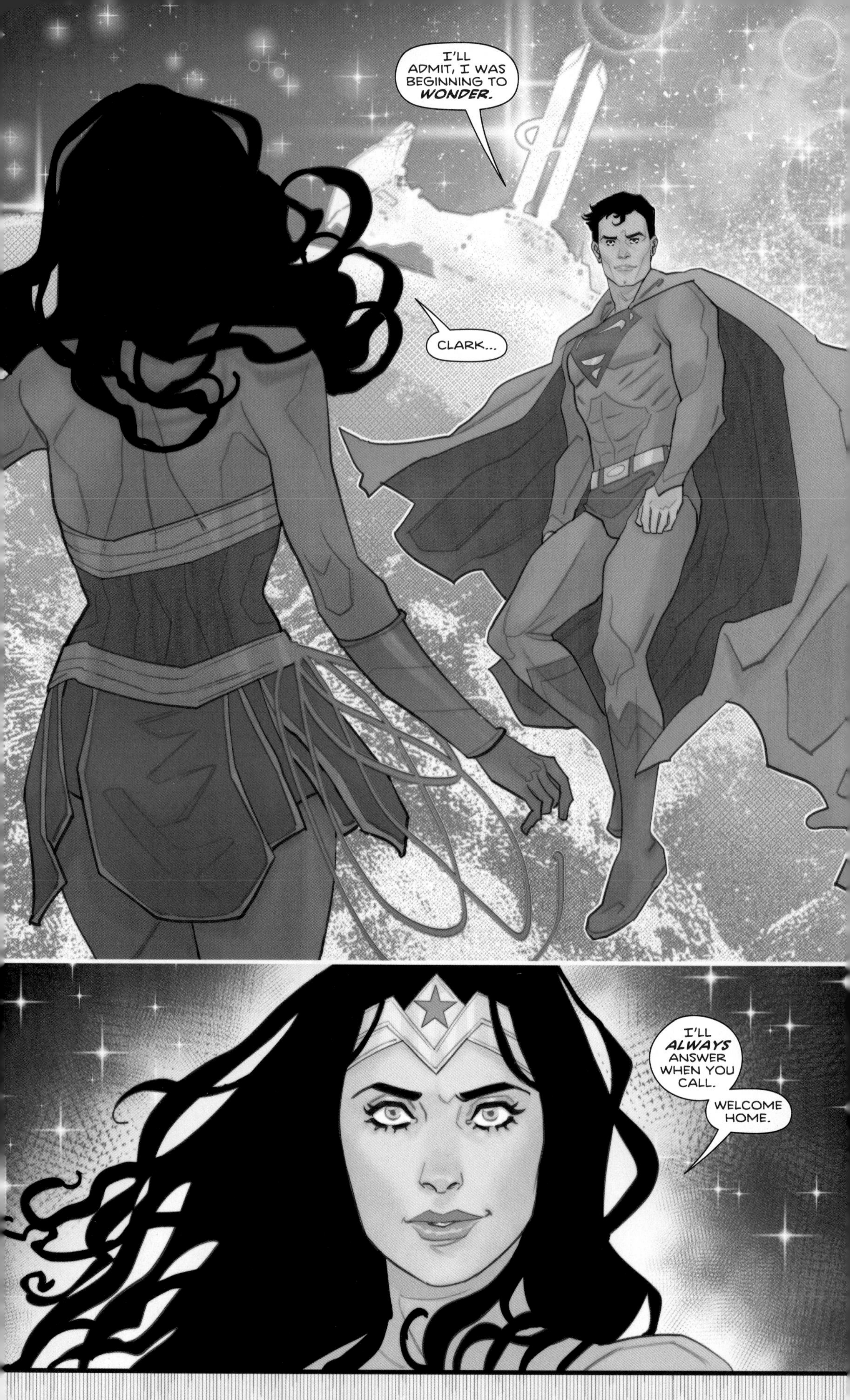
I'LL ADMIT, I WAS BEGINNING TO WONDER.
CLARK...
I'LL ALWAYS ANSWER WHEN YOU CALL.
WELCOME HOME.

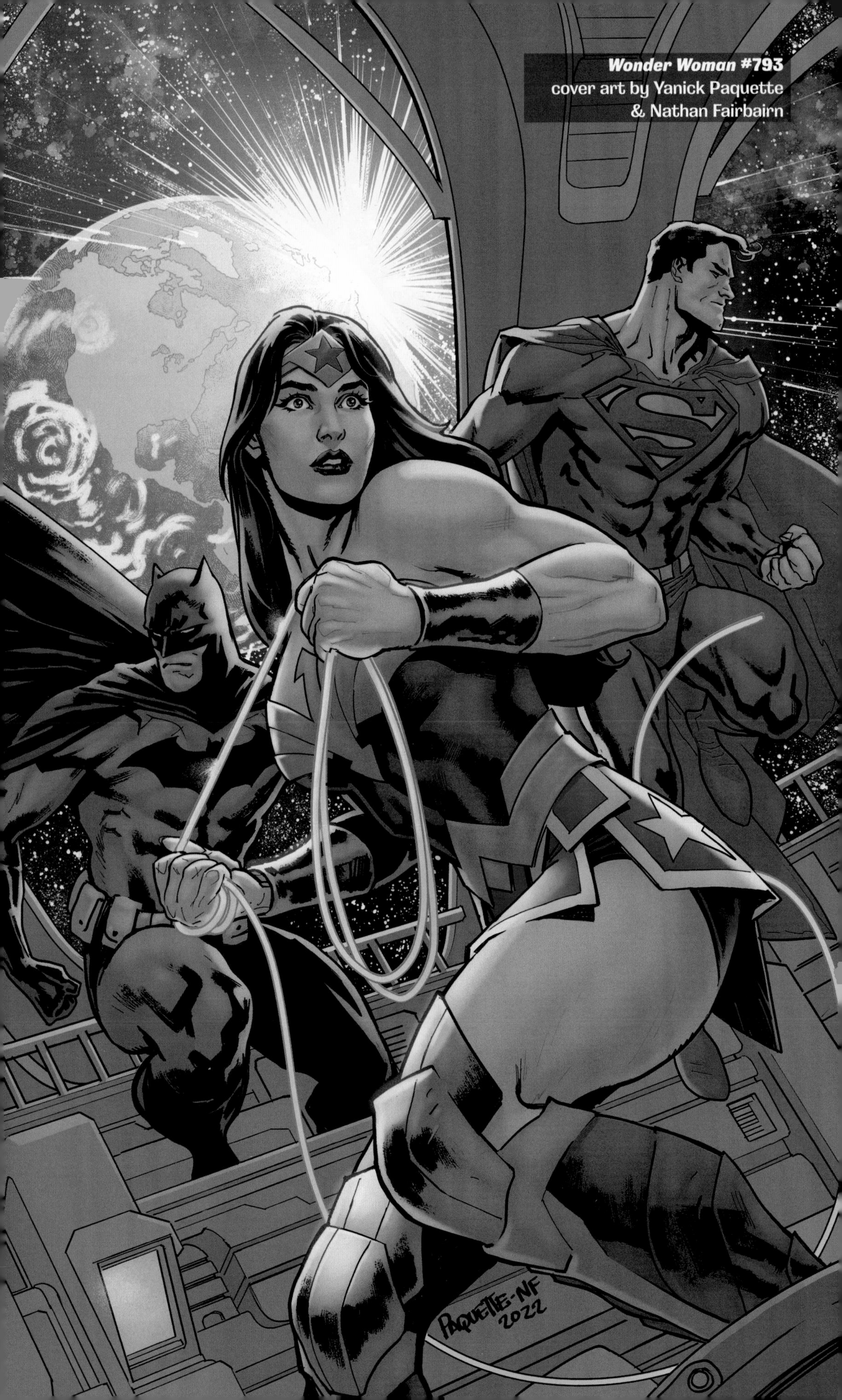
PAQUETTE-NF
2022

***Wonder Woman* #793**
cover art by Yanick Paquette
& Nathan Fairbairn

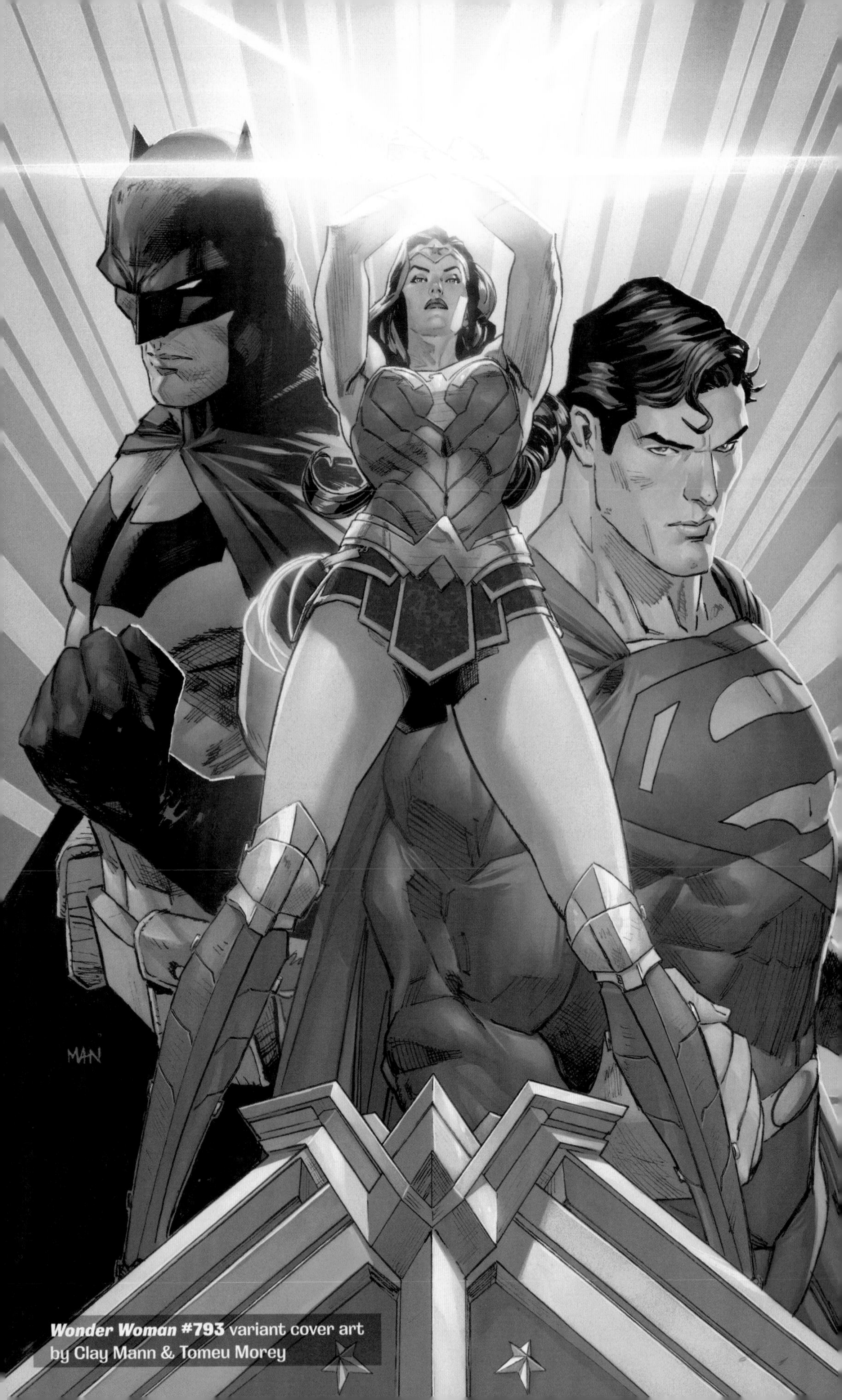
MAN

***Wonder Woman* #793** variant cover art
by Clay Mann & Tomeu Morey

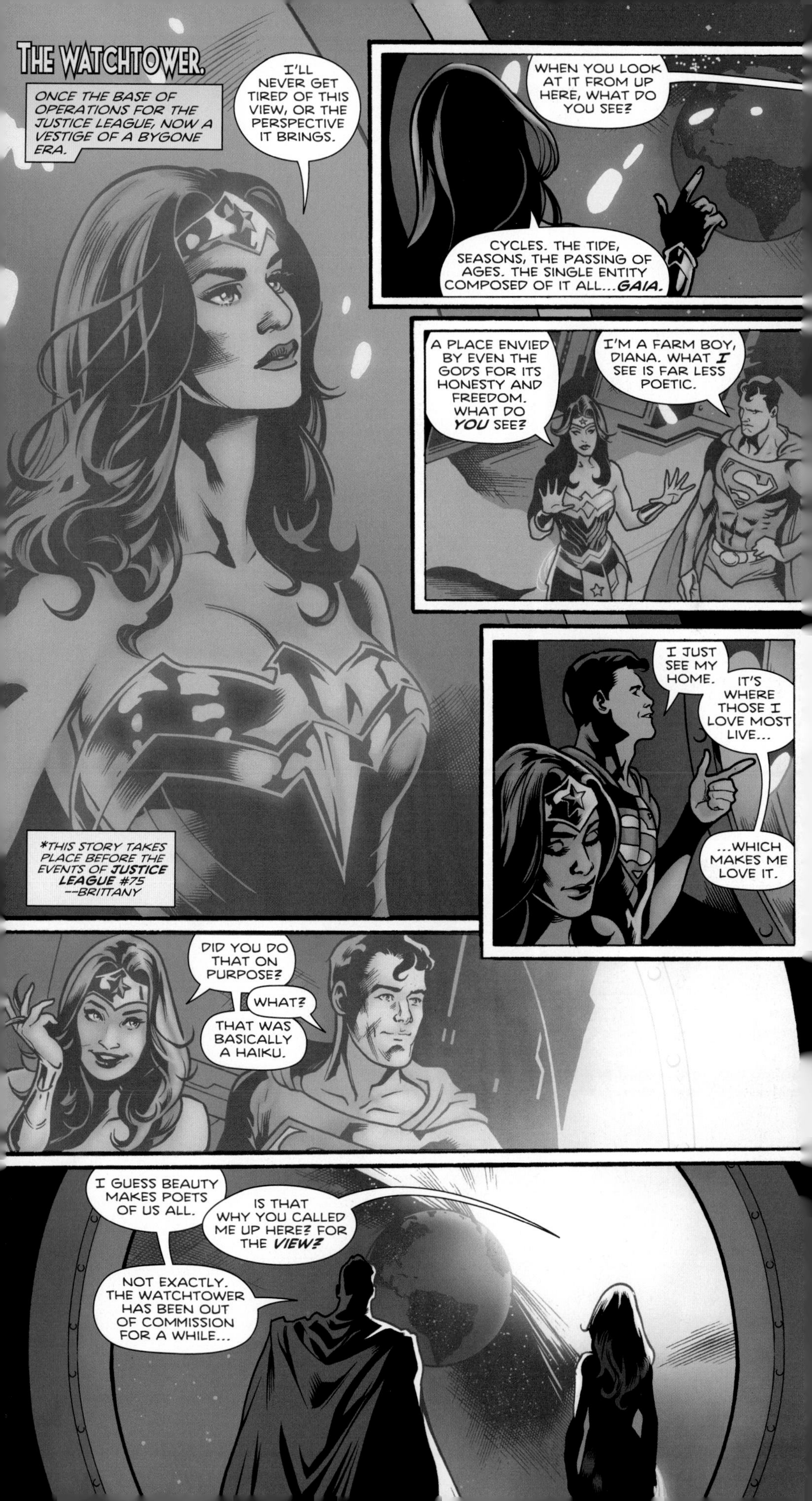
THE WATCHTOWER.
ONCE THE BASE OF OPERATIONS FOR THE JUSTICE LEAGUE, NOW A VESTIGE OF A BYGONE ERA.
I'LL NEVER GET TIRED OF THIS VIEW, OR THE PERSPECTIVE IT BRINGS.
*THIS STORY TAKES PLACE BEFORE THE EVENTS OF JUSTICE LEAGUE #75 --BRITTANY
WHEN YOU LOOK AT IT FROM UP HERE, WHAT DO YOU SEE?
CYCLES. THE TIDE, SEASONS, THE PASSING OF AGES. THE SINGLE ENTITY COMPOSED OF IT ALL...GAIA.
A PLACE ENVIED BY EVEN THE GODS FOR ITS HONESTY AND FREEDOM. WHAT DO YOU SEE?
I'M A FARM BOY, DIANA. WHAT I SEE IS FAR LESS POETIC.
I JUST SEE MY HOME.
IT'S WHERE THOSE I LOVE MOST LIVE...
...WHICH MAKES ME LOVE IT.
DID YOU DO THAT ON PURPOSE?
WHAT?
THAT WAS BASICALLY A HAIKU.
I GUESS BEAUTY MAKES POETS OF US ALL.
IS THAT WHY YOU CALLED ME UP HERE? FOR THE VIEW?
NOT EXACTLY. THE WATCHTOWER HAS BEEN OUT OF COMMISSION FOR A WHILE...

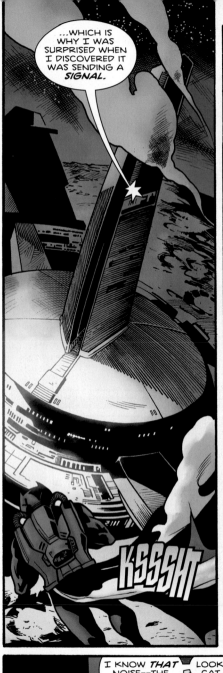

...WHICH IS WHY I WAS SURPRISED WHEN I DISCOVERED IT WAS SENDING A *SIGNAL.*

KSSSHT

WAIT. I THINK I JUST SAW...

THERE'S SOMETHING OUT THERE.

AN EXHAUST TRAIL. WATER MOLECULES.

FROM A MICRO-ROTATING DETONATION ENGINE, IF I'M NOT MISTAKEN. PRETTY HIGH TECH STUFF.

OH, YOU KNOW ABOUT ROCKETS NOW? JUST A SIMPLE COUNTRY BOY.

I HAVE TO PAY ATTENTION TO TECHNOLOGY.

CLICK-SHSSSHK

I KNOW *THAT* NOISE--THE *AIR LOCK.*

LOOK WHAT THE CAT DRAGGED IN...

PSSSSHHH

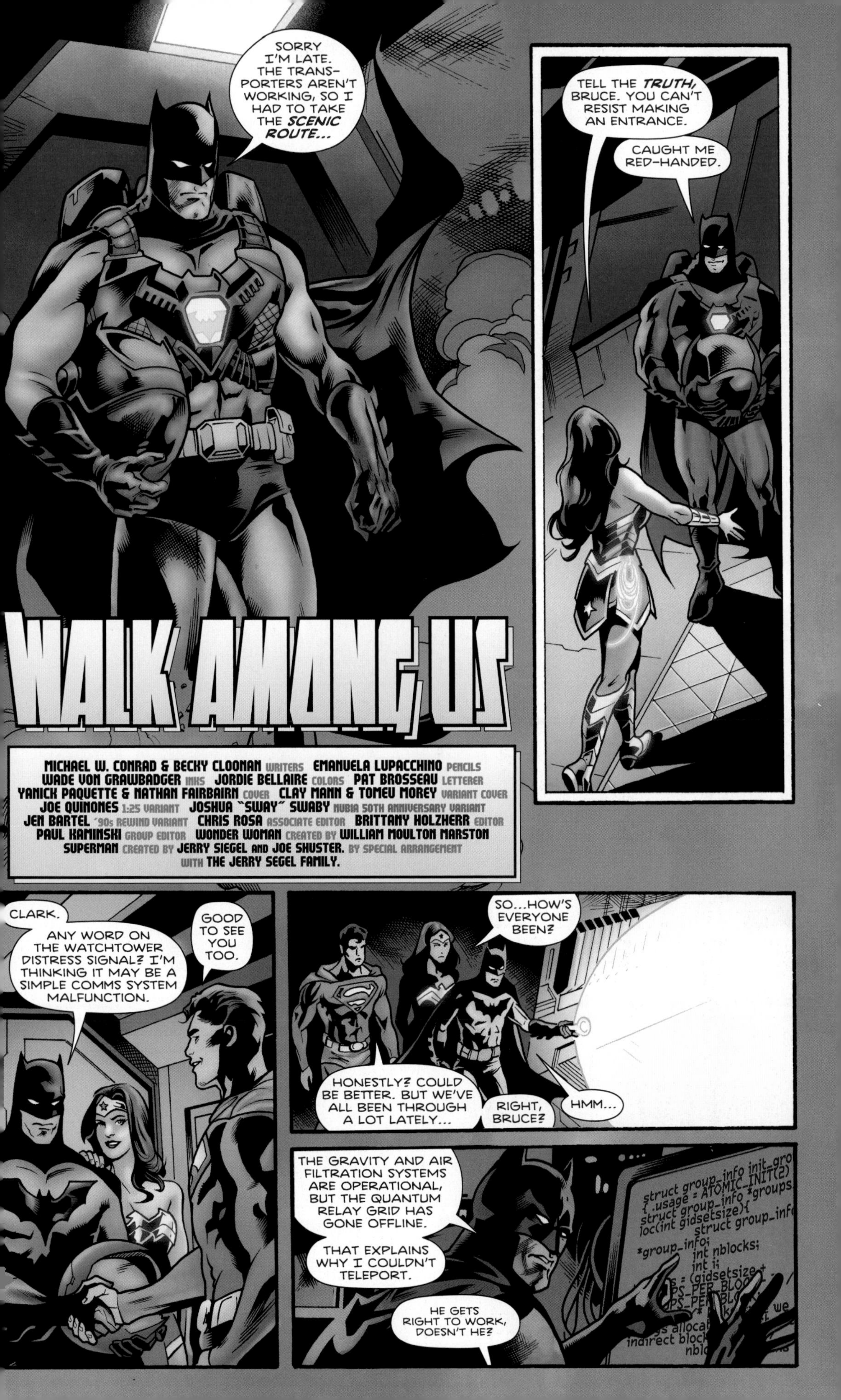

SORRY I'M LATE. THE TRANS-PORTERS AREN'T WORKING, SO I HAD TO TAKE THE *SCENIC ROUTE...*
TELL THE *TRUTH,* BRUCE. YOU CAN'T RESIST MAKING AN ENTRANCE.
CAUGHT ME RED-HANDED.
WALK AMONG US
MICHAEL W. CONRAD & BECKY CLOONAN WRITERS EMANUELA LUPACCHINO PENCILS
WADE VON GRAWBADGER INKS JORDIE BELLAIRE COLORS PAT BROSSEAU LETTERER
YANICK PAQUETTE & NATHAN FAIRBAIRN COVER CLAY MANN & TOMEU MOREY VARIANT COVER
JOE QUINONES 1:25 VARIANT JOSHUA "SWAY" SWABY NUBIA 50TH ANNIVERSARY VARIANT
JEN BARTEL '90s REWIND VARIANT CHRIS ROSA ASSOCIATE EDITOR BRITTANY HOLZHERR EDITOR
PAUL KAMINSKI GROUP EDITOR WONDER WOMAN CREATED BY WILLIAM MOULTON MARSTON
SUPERMAN CREATED BY JERRY SIEGEL AND JOE SHUSTER. BY SPECIAL ARRANGEMENT WITH THE JERRY SEGEL FAMILY.
CLARK.
ANY WORD ON THE WATCHTOWER DISTRESS SIGNAL? I'M THINKING IT MAY BE A SIMPLE COMMS SYSTEM MALFUNCTION.
GOOD TO SEE YOU TOO.
SO...HOW'S EVERYONE BEEN?
HONESTLY? COULD BE BETTER. BUT WE'VE ALL BEEN THROUGH A LOT LATELY...
RIGHT, BRUCE?
HMM...
THE GRAVITY AND AIR FILTRATION SYSTEMS ARE OPERATIONAL, BUT THE QUANTUM RELAY GRID HAS GONE OFFLINE.
THAT EXPLAINS WHY I COULDN'T TELEPORT.
HE GETS RIGHT TO WORK, DOESN'T HE?

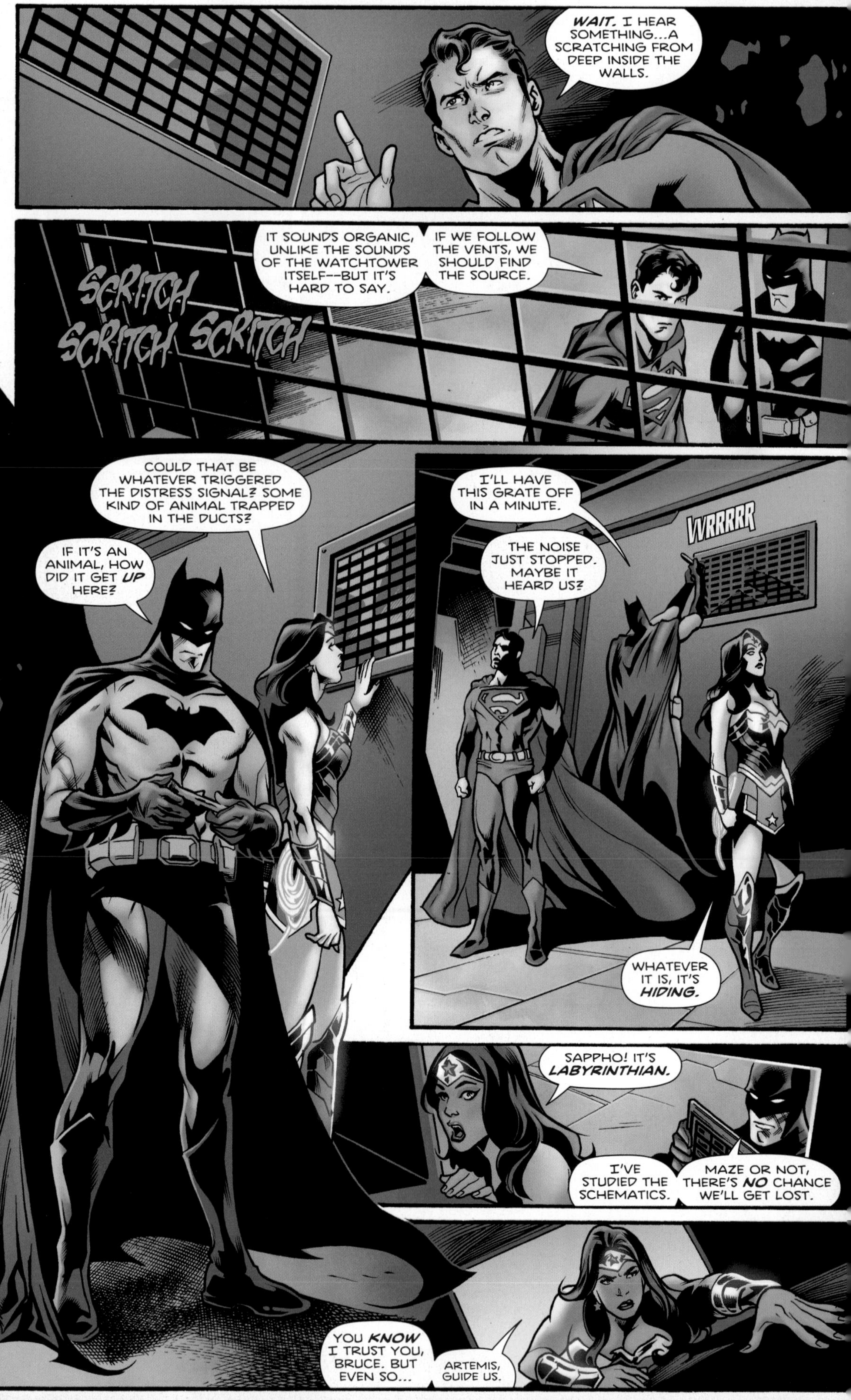
WAIT. I HEAR SOMETHING...A SCRATCHING FROM DEEP INSIDE THE WALLS.
SCRITCH SCRITCH SCRITCH
IT SOUNDS ORGANIC, UNLIKE THE SOUNDS OF THE WATCHTOWER ITSELF--BUT IT'S HARD TO SAY.
IF WE FOLLOW THE VENTS, WE SHOULD FIND THE SOURCE.
COULD THAT BE WHATEVER TRIGGERED THE DISTRESS SIGNAL? SOME KIND OF ANIMAL TRAPPED IN THE DUCTS?
IF IT'S AN ANIMAL, HOW DID IT GET UP HERE?
I'LL HAVE THIS GRATE OFF IN A MINUTE.
VVRRRRR
THE NOISE JUST STOPPED. MAYBE IT HEARD US?
WHATEVER IT IS, IT'S HIDING.
SAPPHO! IT'S LABYRINTHIAN.
I'VE STUDIED THE SCHEMATICS.
MAZE OR NOT, THERE'S NO CHANCE WE'LL GET LOST.
YOU KNOW I TRUST YOU, BRUCE. BUT EVEN SO...
ARTEMIS, GUIDE US.

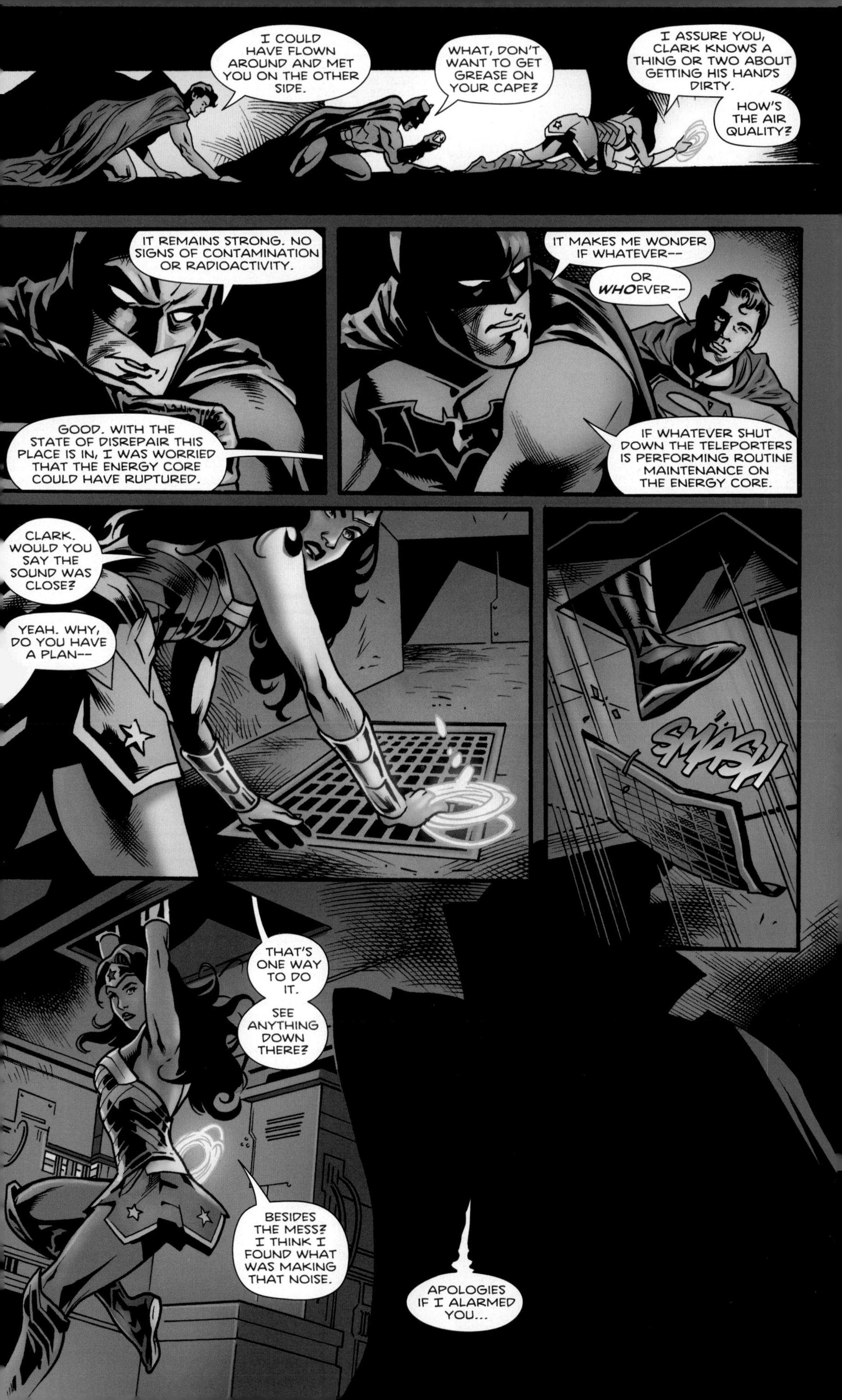
I COULD HAVE FLOWN AROUND AND MET YOU ON THE OTHER SIDE.
WHAT, DON'T WANT TO GET GREASE ON YOUR CAPE?
I ASSURE YOU, CLARK KNOWS A THING OR TWO ABOUT GETTING HIS HANDS DIRTY.
HOW'S THE AIR QUALITY?
IT REMAINS STRONG. NO SIGNS OF CONTAMINATION OR RADIOACTIVITY.
GOOD. WITH THE STATE OF DISREPAIR THIS PLACE IS IN, I WAS WORRIED THAT THE ENERGY CORE COULD HAVE RUPTURED.
IT MAKES ME WONDER IF WHATEVER--
OR WHOEVER--
IF WHATEVER SHUT DOWN THE TELEPORTERS IS PERFORMING ROUTINE MAINTENANCE ON THE ENERGY CORE.
CLARK. WOULD YOU SAY THE SOUND WAS CLOSE?
YEAH. WHY, DO YOU HAVE A PLAN--
SMASH
THAT'S ONE WAY TO DO IT.
SEE ANYTHING DOWN THERE?
BESIDES THE MESS? I THINK I FOUND WHAT WAS MAKING THAT NOISE.
APOLOGIES IF I ALARMED YOU...

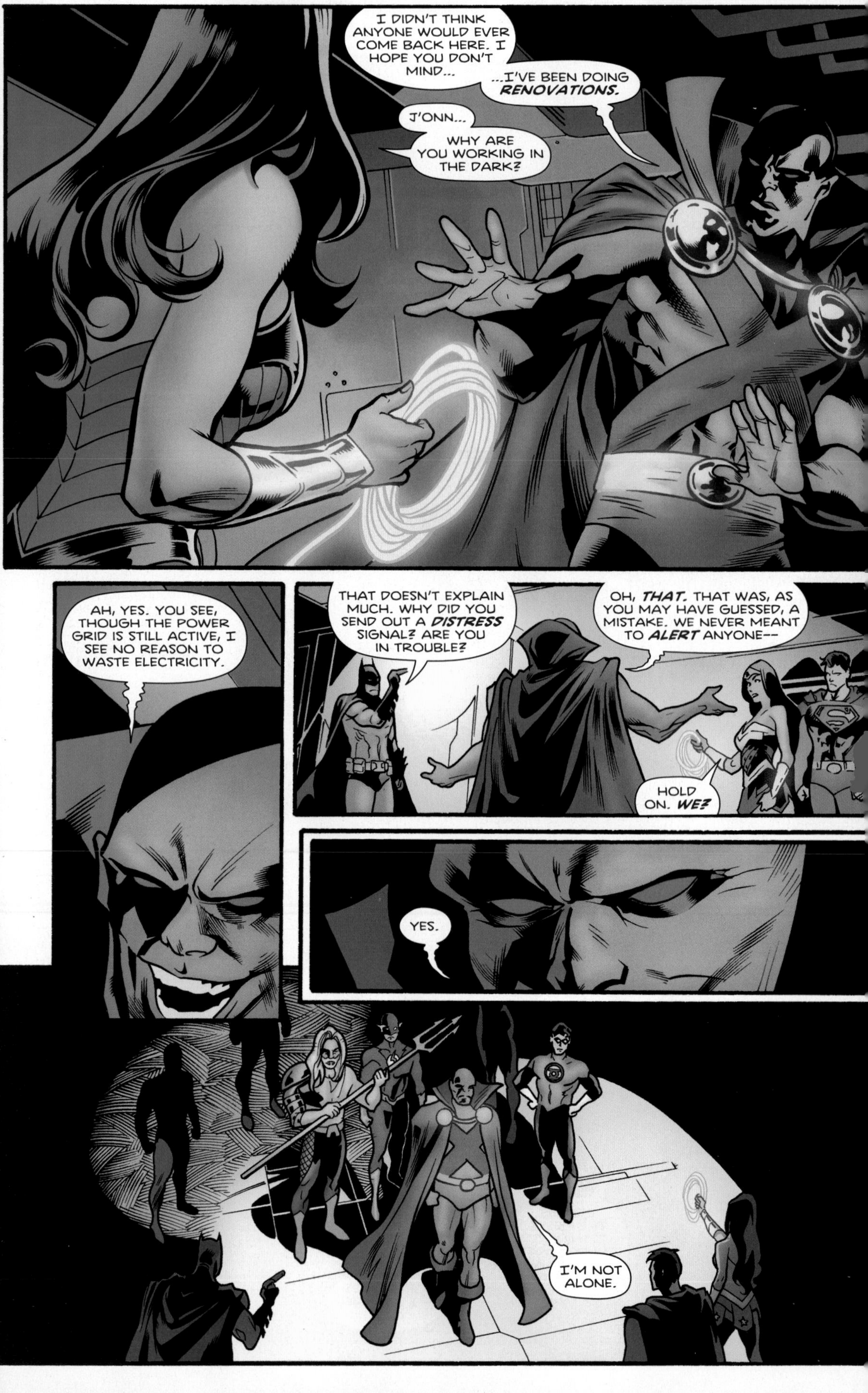
I DIDN'T THINK ANYONE WOULD EVER COME BACK HERE. I HOPE YOU DON'T MIND...
...I'VE BEEN DOING RENOVATIONS.
J'ONN...
WHY ARE YOU WORKING IN THE DARK?
AH, YES. YOU SEE, THOUGH THE POWER GRID IS STILL ACTIVE, I SEE NO REASON TO WASTE ELECTRICITY.
THAT DOESN'T EXPLAIN MUCH. WHY DID YOU SEND OUT A DISTRESS SIGNAL? ARE YOU IN TROUBLE?
OH, THAT. THAT WAS, AS YOU MAY HAVE GUESSED, A MISTAKE. WE NEVER MEANT TO ALERT ANYONE--
HOLD ON. WE?
YES.
I'M NOT ALONE.

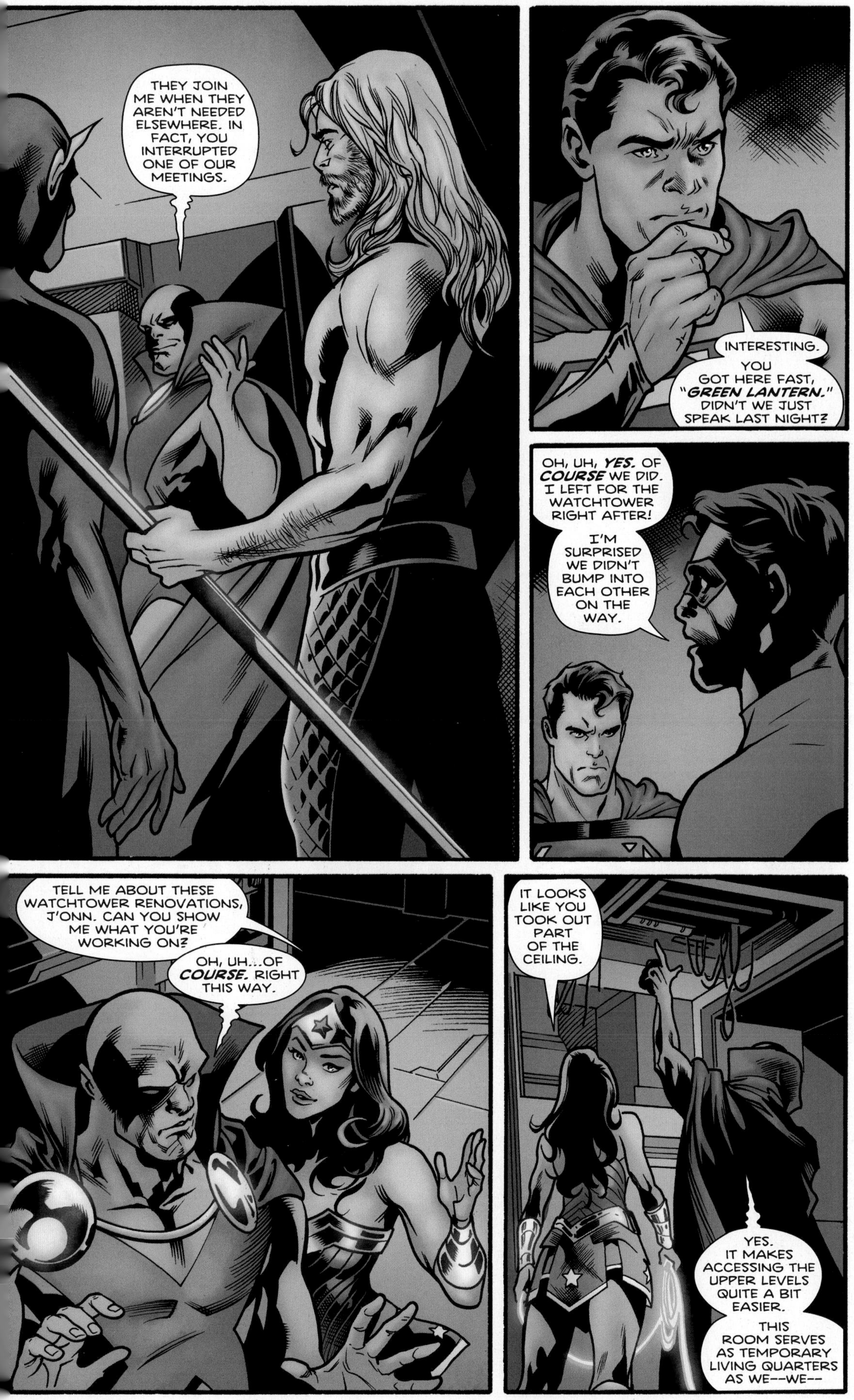
THEY JOIN ME WHEN THEY AREN'T NEEDED ELSEWHERE. IN FACT, YOU INTERRUPTED ONE OF OUR MEETINGS.
INTERESTING.
YOU GOT HERE FAST, "GREEN LANTERN." DIDN'T WE JUST SPEAK LAST NIGHT?
OH, UH, YES. OF COURSE WE DID. I LEFT FOR THE WATCHTOWER RIGHT AFTER!
I'M SURPRISED WE DIDN'T BUMP INTO EACH OTHER ON THE WAY.
TELL ME ABOUT THESE WATCHTOWER RENOVATIONS, J'ONN. CAN YOU SHOW ME WHAT YOU'RE WORKING ON?
OH, UH...OF COURSE. RIGHT THIS WAY.
IT LOOKS LIKE YOU TOOK OUT PART OF THE CEILING.
YES. IT MAKES ACCESSING THE UPPER LEVELS QUITE A BIT EASIER.
THIS ROOM SERVES AS TEMPORARY LIVING QUARTERS AS WE--WE--

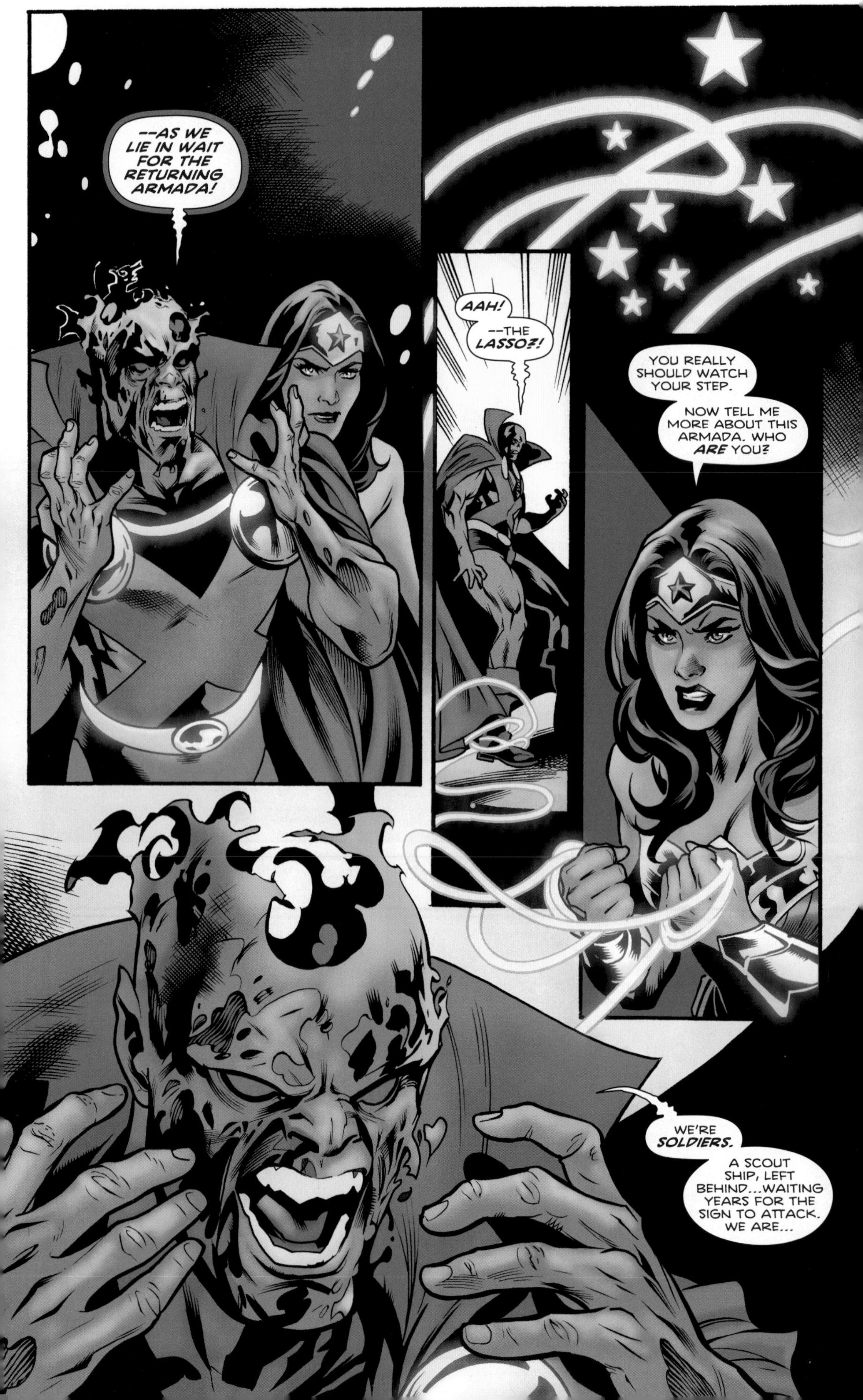
--AS WE LIE IN WAIT FOR THE RETURNING ARMADA!
AAH! --THE LASSO?!
YOU REALLY SHOULD WATCH YOUR STEP.
NOW TELL ME MORE ABOUT THIS ARMADA. WHO ARE YOU?
WE'RE SOLDIERS.
A SCOUT SHIP, LEFT BEHIND...WAITING YEARS FOR THE SIGN TO ATTACK. WE ARE...

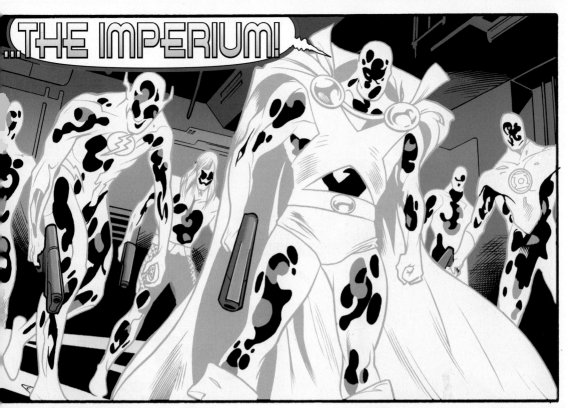

WOOOSH

HOLA!

AT LEAST THEIR RUSE WAS SHORT-LIVED!

WHUD

I'VE READ SO MUCH ABOUT YOU, WONDER WOMAN...

IT WILL BE AN *HONOR* TO TAKE YOUR PLACE.

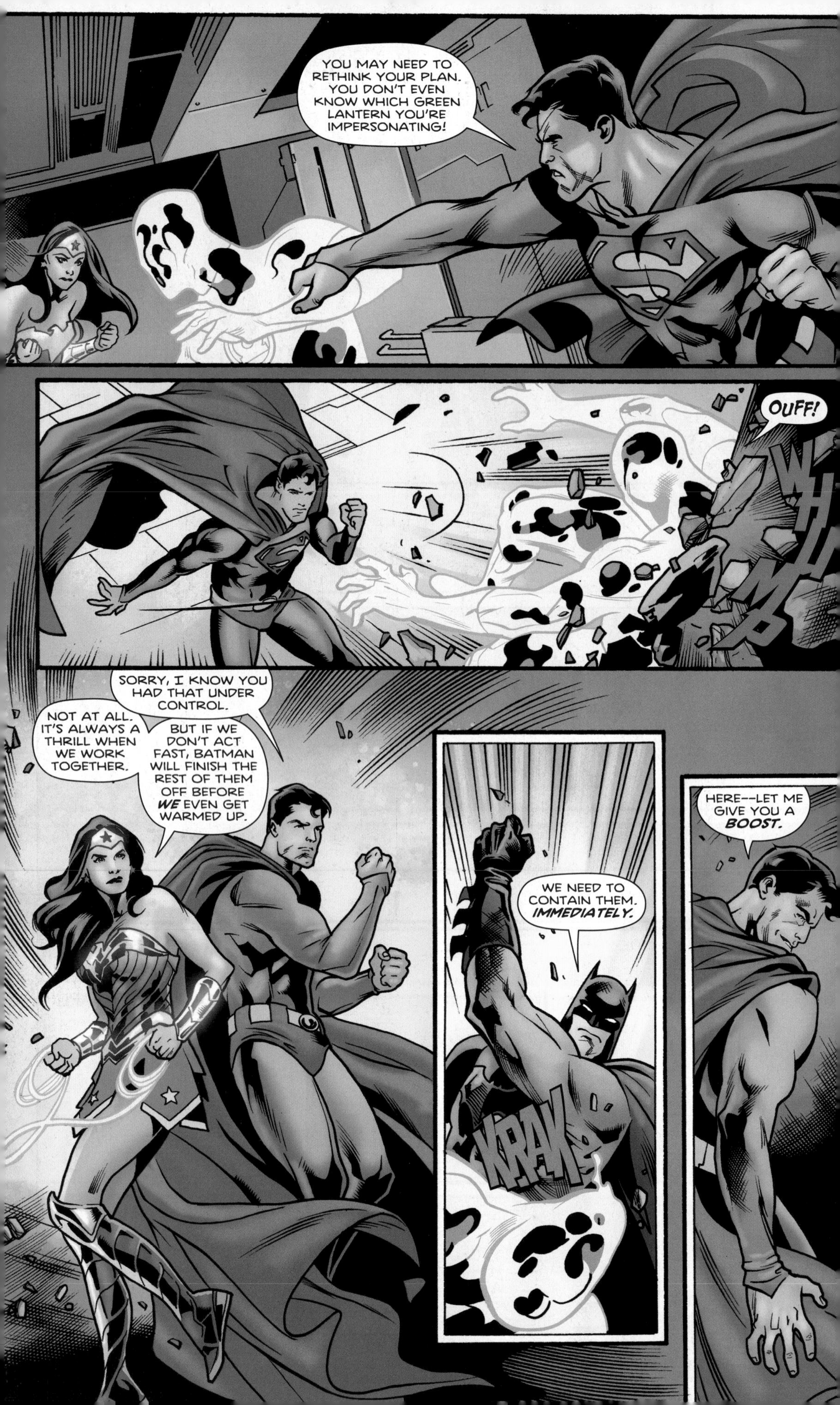
YOU MAY NEED TO RETHINK YOUR PLAN. YOU DON'T EVEN KNOW WHICH GREEN LANTERN YOU'RE IMPERSONATING!
OUFF!
WHUMP
SORRY, I KNOW YOU HAD THAT UNDER CONTROL.
NOT AT ALL. IT'S ALWAYS A THRILL WHEN WE WORK TOGETHER.
BUT IF WE DON'T ACT FAST, BATMAN WILL FINISH THE REST OF THEM OFF BEFORE WE EVEN GET WARMED UP.
WE NEED TO CONTAIN THEM. IMMEDIATELY.
KRAK
HERE--LET ME GIVE YOU A BOOST.

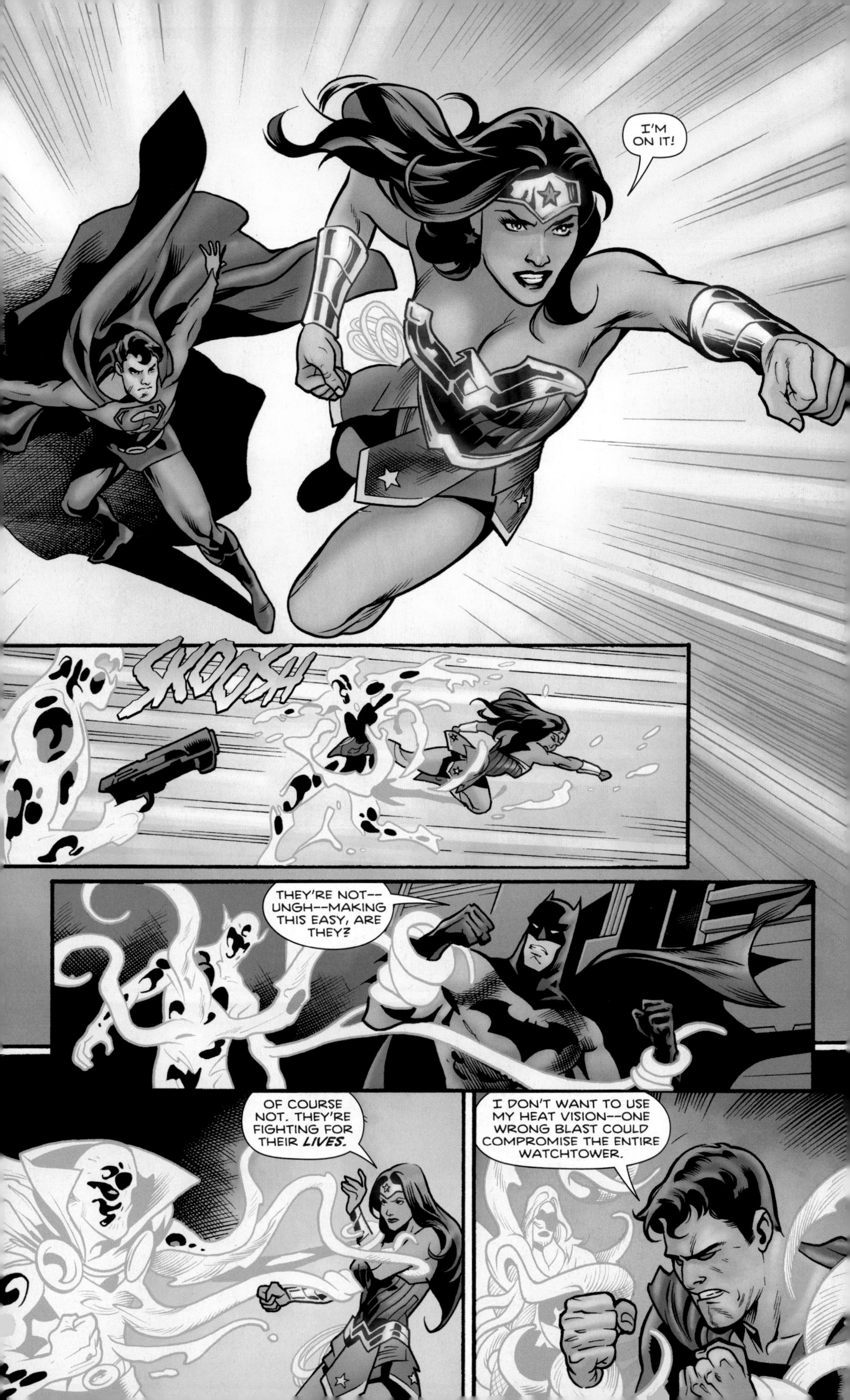
I'M ON IT!
SKOOSH
THEY'RE NOT--UNGH--MAKING THIS EASY, ARE THEY?
OF COURSE NOT. THEY'RE FIGHTING FOR THEIR *LIVES.*
I DON'T WANT TO USE MY HEAT VISION--ONE WRONG BLAST COULD COMPROMISE THE ENTIRE WATCHTOWER.

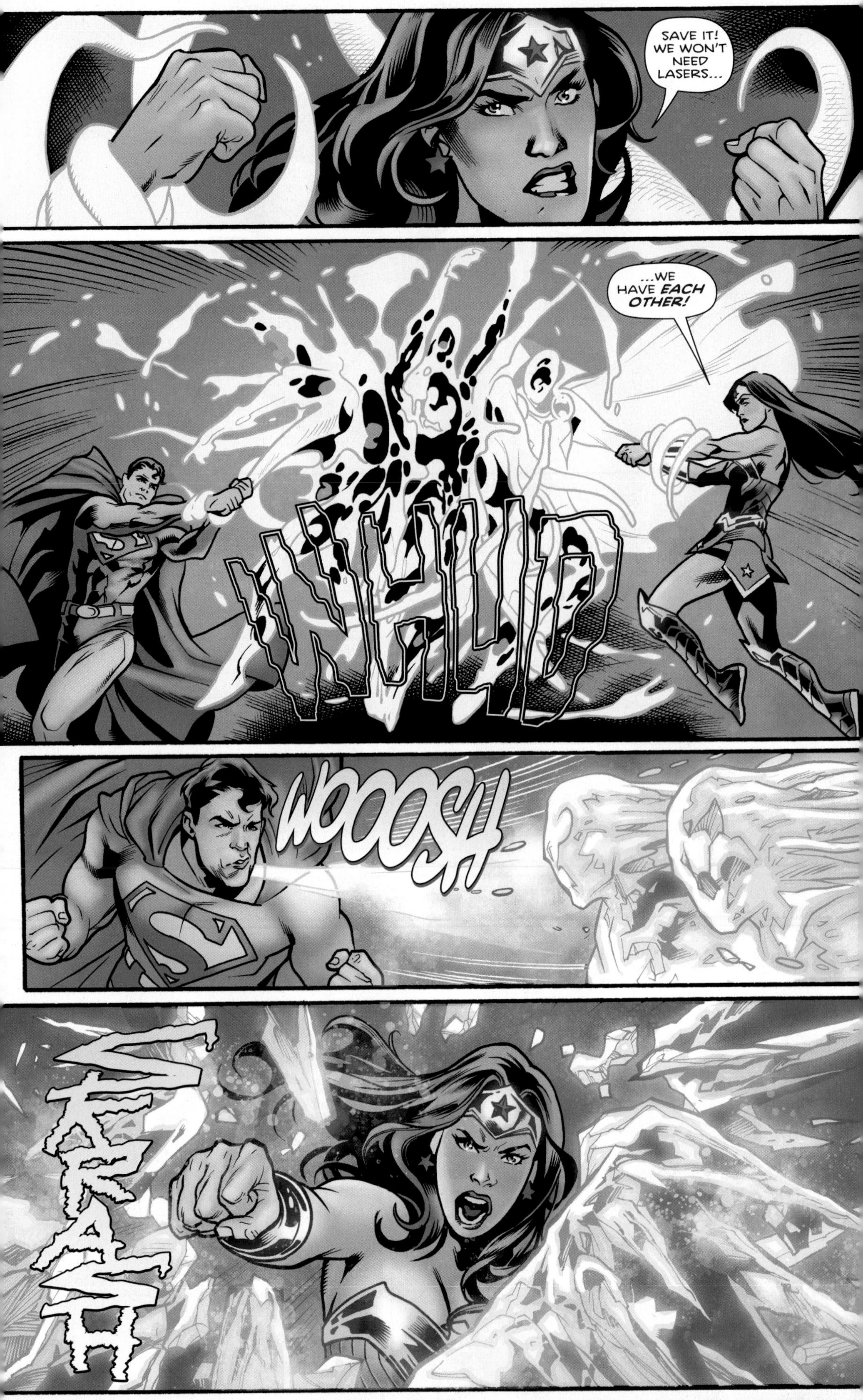
SAVE IT! WE WON'T NEED LASERS...
...WE HAVE *EACH OTHER!*
WHUD
WOOOSH
KRASH

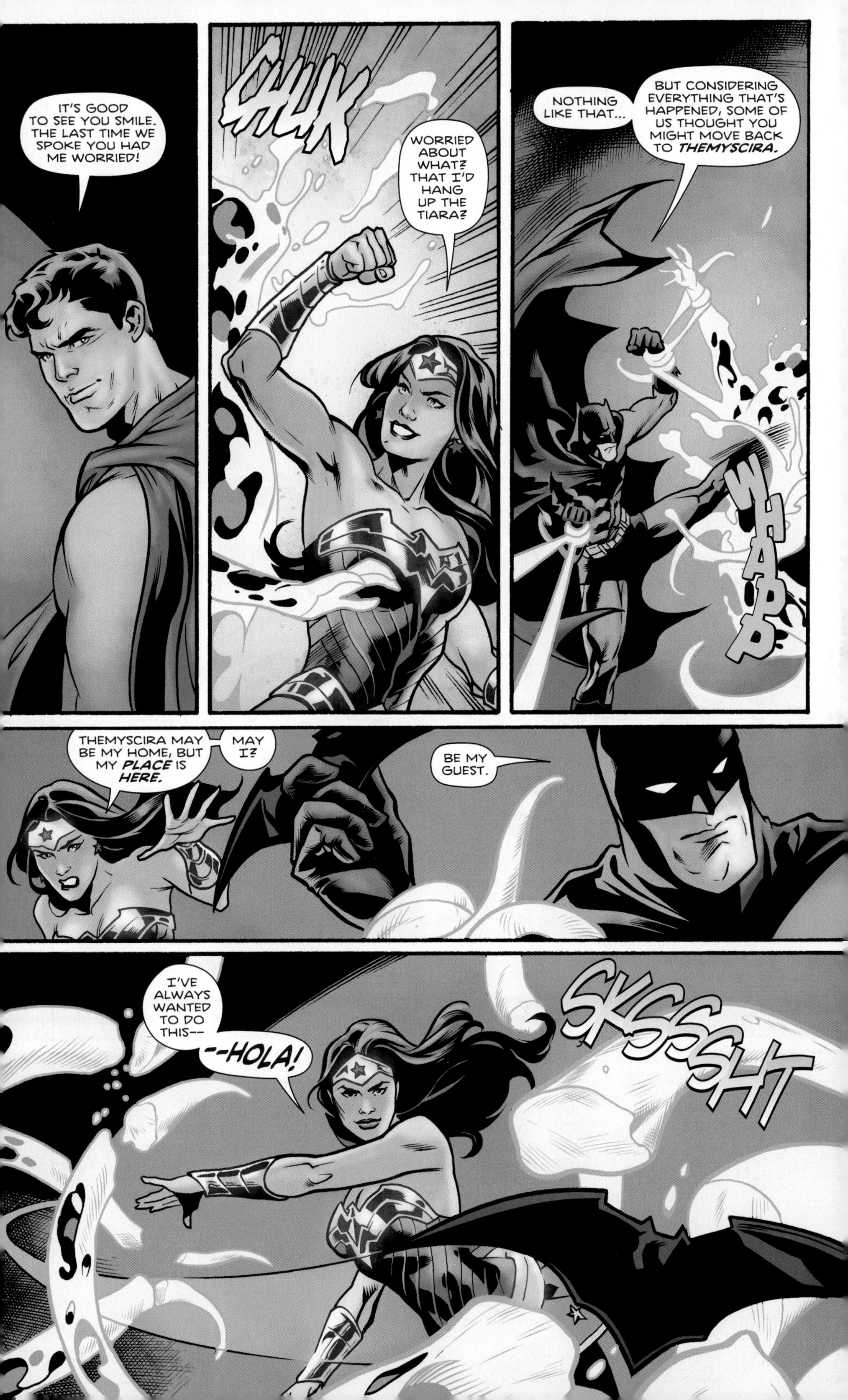
IT'S GOOD TO SEE YOU SMILE. THE LAST TIME WE SPOKE YOU HAD ME WORRIED!
CHUK
WORRIED ABOUT WHAT? THAT I'D HANG UP THE TIARA?
NOTHING LIKE THAT...
BUT CONSIDERING EVERYTHING THAT'S HAPPENED, SOME OF US THOUGHT YOU MIGHT MOVE BACK TO *THEMYSCIRA.*
WHAPP
THEMYSCIRA MAY BE MY HOME, BUT MY *PLACE* IS *HERE.*
MAY I?
BE MY GUEST.
I'VE ALWAYS WANTED TO DO THIS--
--HOLA!
SKSSSHT

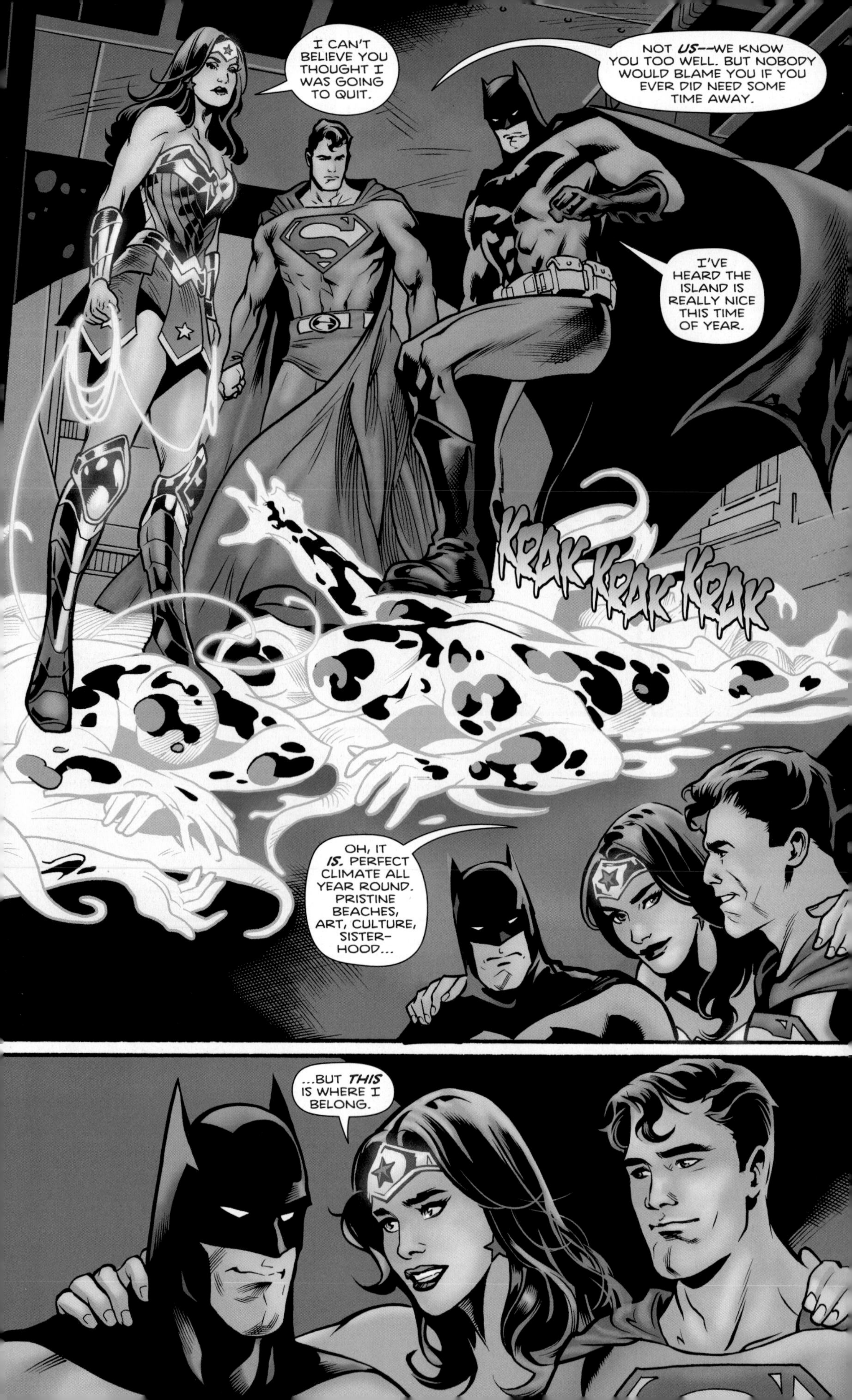
I CAN'T BELIEVE YOU THOUGHT I WAS GOING TO QUIT.
NOT *US*--WE KNOW YOU TOO WELL. BUT NOBODY WOULD BLAME YOU IF YOU EVER DID NEED SOME TIME AWAY.
I'VE HEARD THE ISLAND IS REALLY NICE THIS TIME OF YEAR.
KRAK KRAK KRAK
OH, IT *IS.* PERFECT CLIMATE ALL YEAR ROUND. PRISTINE BEACHES, ART, CULTURE, SISTER-HOOD...
...BUT *THIS* IS WHERE I BELONG.

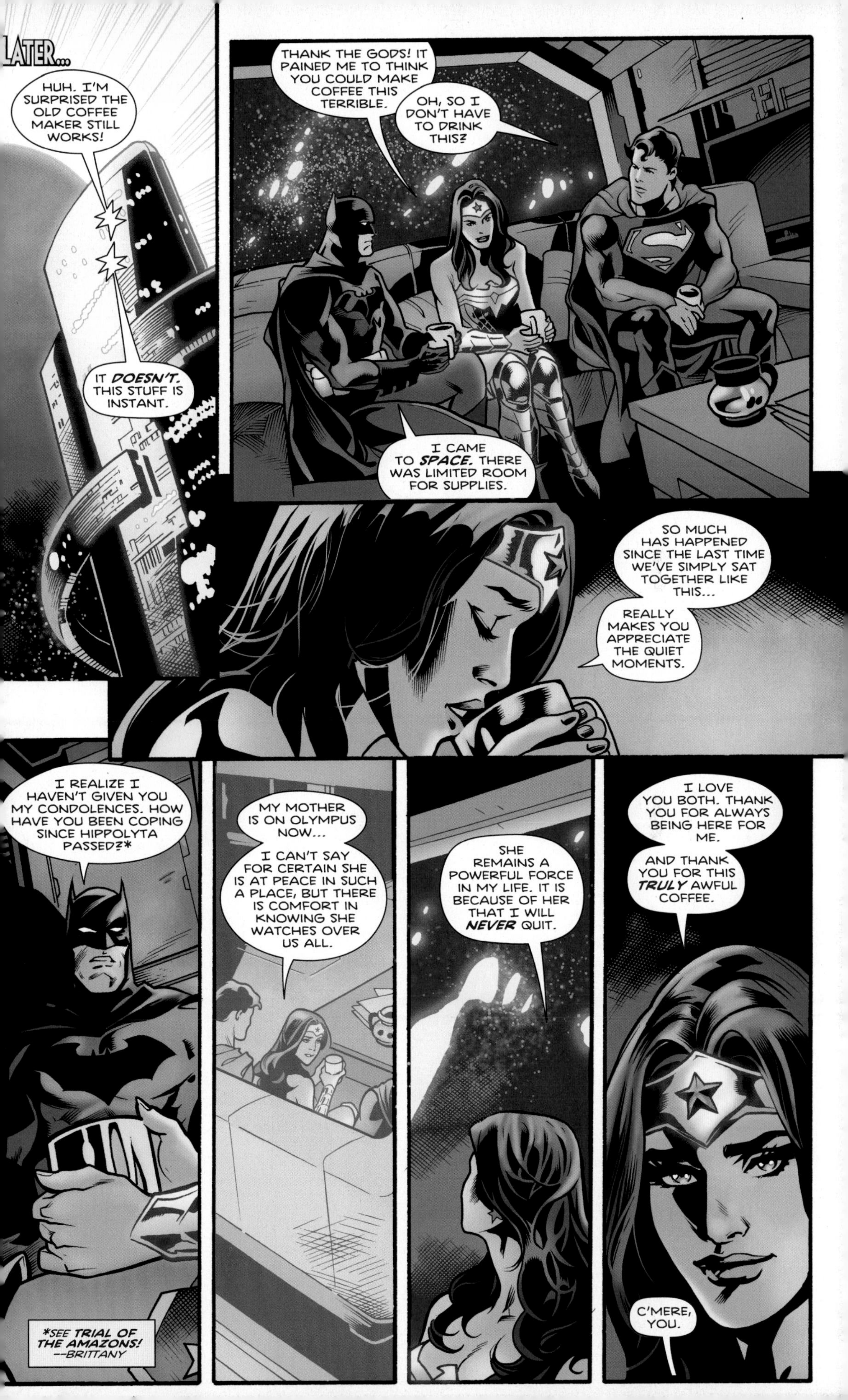
LATER...
HUH. I'M SURPRISED THE OLD COFFEE MAKER STILL WORKS!
IT DOESN'T. THIS STUFF IS INSTANT.
THANK THE GODS! IT PAINED ME TO THINK YOU COULD MAKE COFFEE THIS TERRIBLE.
OH, SO I DON'T HAVE TO DRINK THIS?
I CAME TO SPACE. THERE WAS LIMITED ROOM FOR SUPPLIES.
SO MUCH HAS HAPPENED SINCE THE LAST TIME WE'VE SIMPLY SAT TOGETHER LIKE THIS...
REALLY MAKES YOU APPRECIATE THE QUIET MOMENTS.
I REALIZE I HAVEN'T GIVEN YOU MY CONDOLENCES. HOW HAVE YOU BEEN COPING SINCE HIPPOLYTA PASSED?*
*SEE TRIAL OF THE AMAZONS! --BRITTANY
MY MOTHER IS ON OLYMPUS NOW...
I CAN'T SAY FOR CERTAIN SHE IS AT PEACE IN SUCH A PLACE, BUT THERE IS COMFORT IN KNOWING SHE WATCHES OVER US ALL.
SHE REMAINS A POWERFUL FORCE IN MY LIFE. IT IS BECAUSE OF HER THAT I WILL NEVER QUIT.
I LOVE YOU BOTH. THANK YOU FOR ALWAYS BEING HERE FOR ME.
AND THANK YOU FOR THIS TRULY AWFUL COFFEE.
C'MERE, YOU.

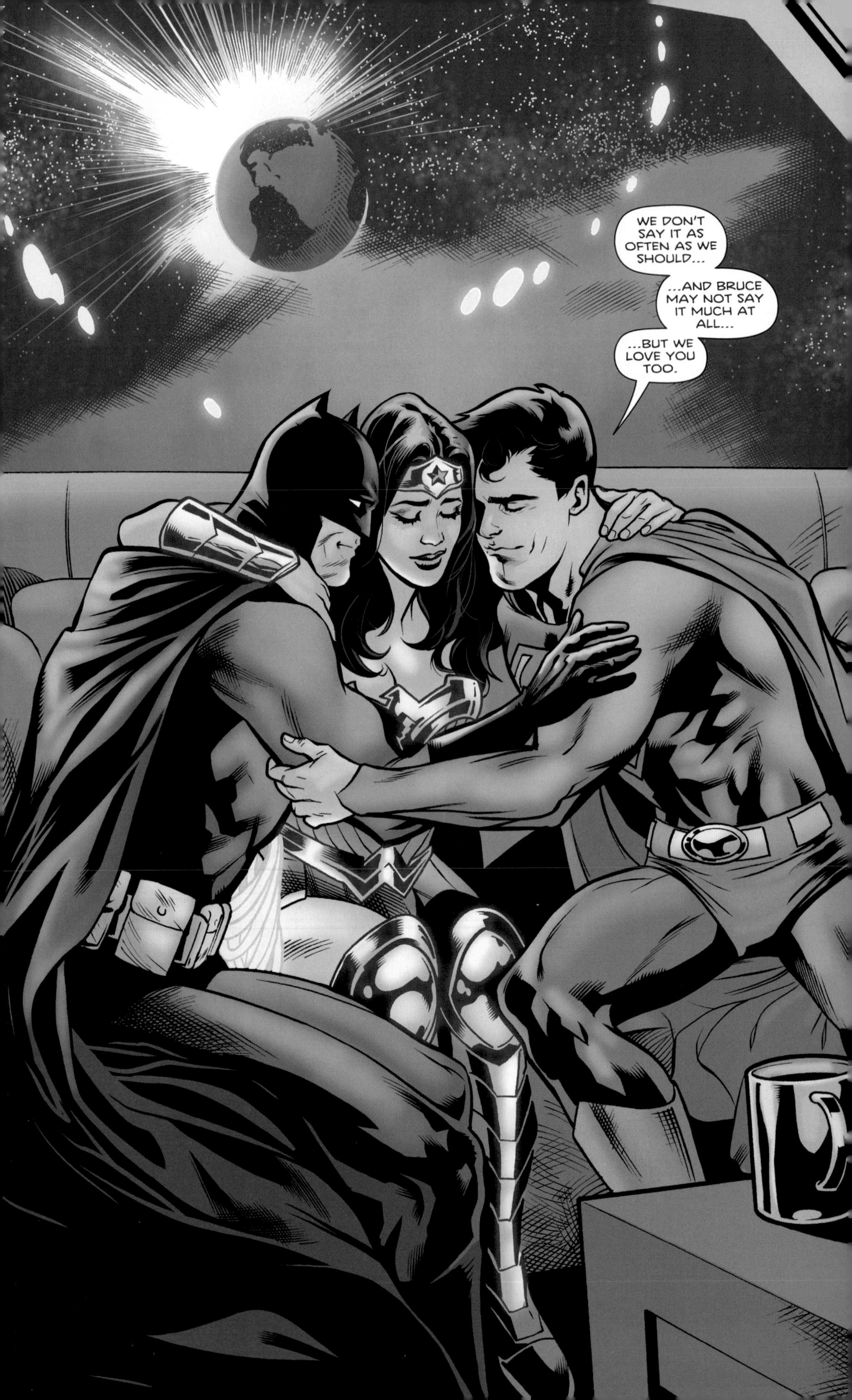
WE DON'T SAY IT AS OFTEN AS WE SHOULD...
...AND BRUCE MAY NOT SAY IT MUCH AT ALL...
...BUT WE LOVE YOU TOO.

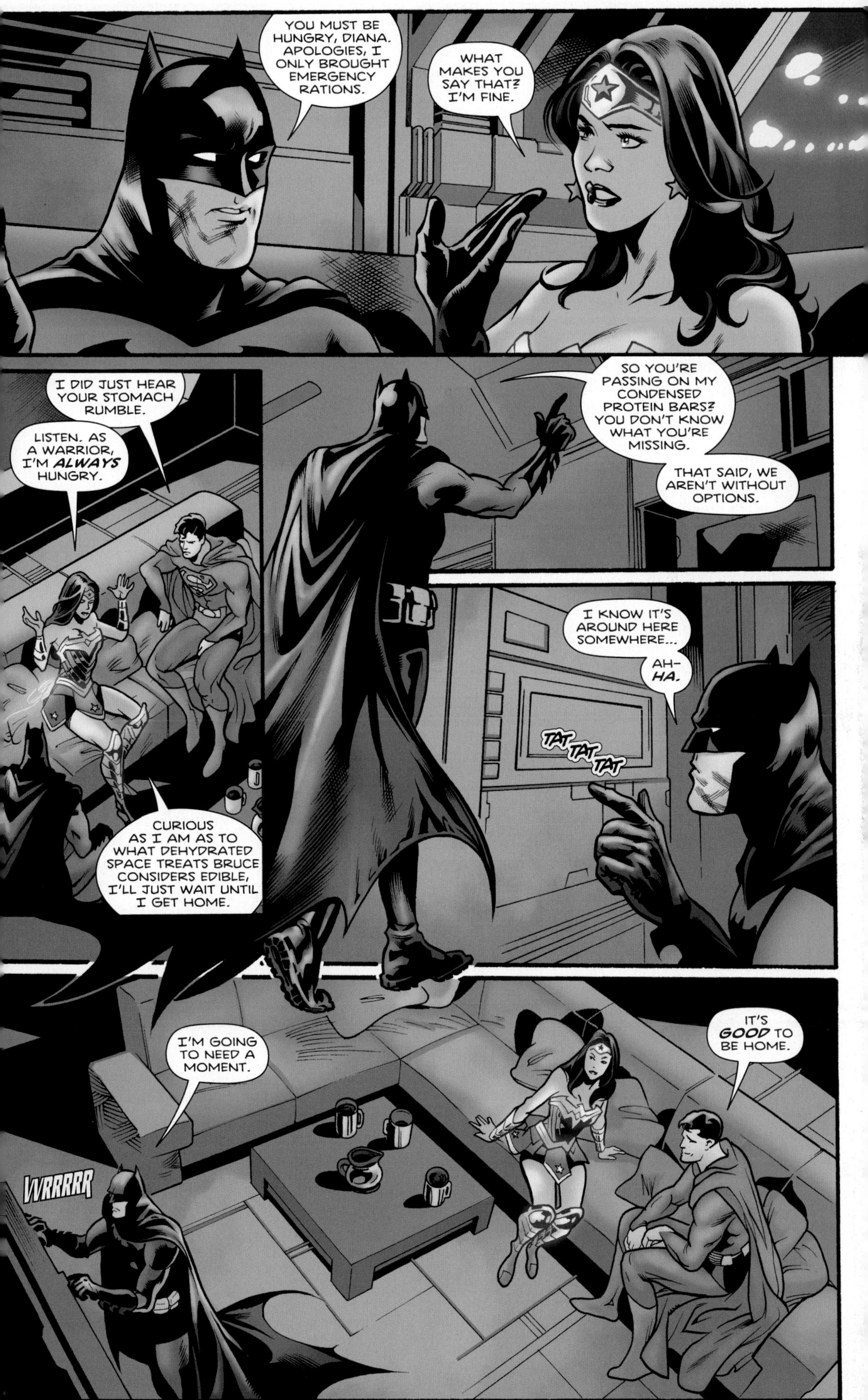
YOU MUST BE HUNGRY, DIANA. APOLOGIES, I ONLY BROUGHT EMERGENCY RATIONS.
WHAT MAKES YOU SAY THAT? I'M FINE.
I DID JUST HEAR YOUR STOMACH RUMBLE.
LISTEN. AS A WARRIOR, I'M *ALWAYS* HUNGRY.
SO YOU'RE PASSING ON MY CONDENSED PROTEIN BARS? YOU DON'T KNOW WHAT YOU'RE MISSING.
THAT SAID, WE AREN'T WITHOUT OPTIONS.
CURIOUS AS I AM AS TO WHAT DEHYDRATED SPACE TREATS BRUCE CONSIDERS EDIBLE, I'LL JUST WAIT UNTIL I GET HOME.
I KNOW IT'S AROUND HERE SOMEWHERE...
AH-*HA.*
TAT TAT TAT
I'M GOING TO NEED A MOMENT.
IT'S *GOOD* TO BE HOME.
VVRRRRR

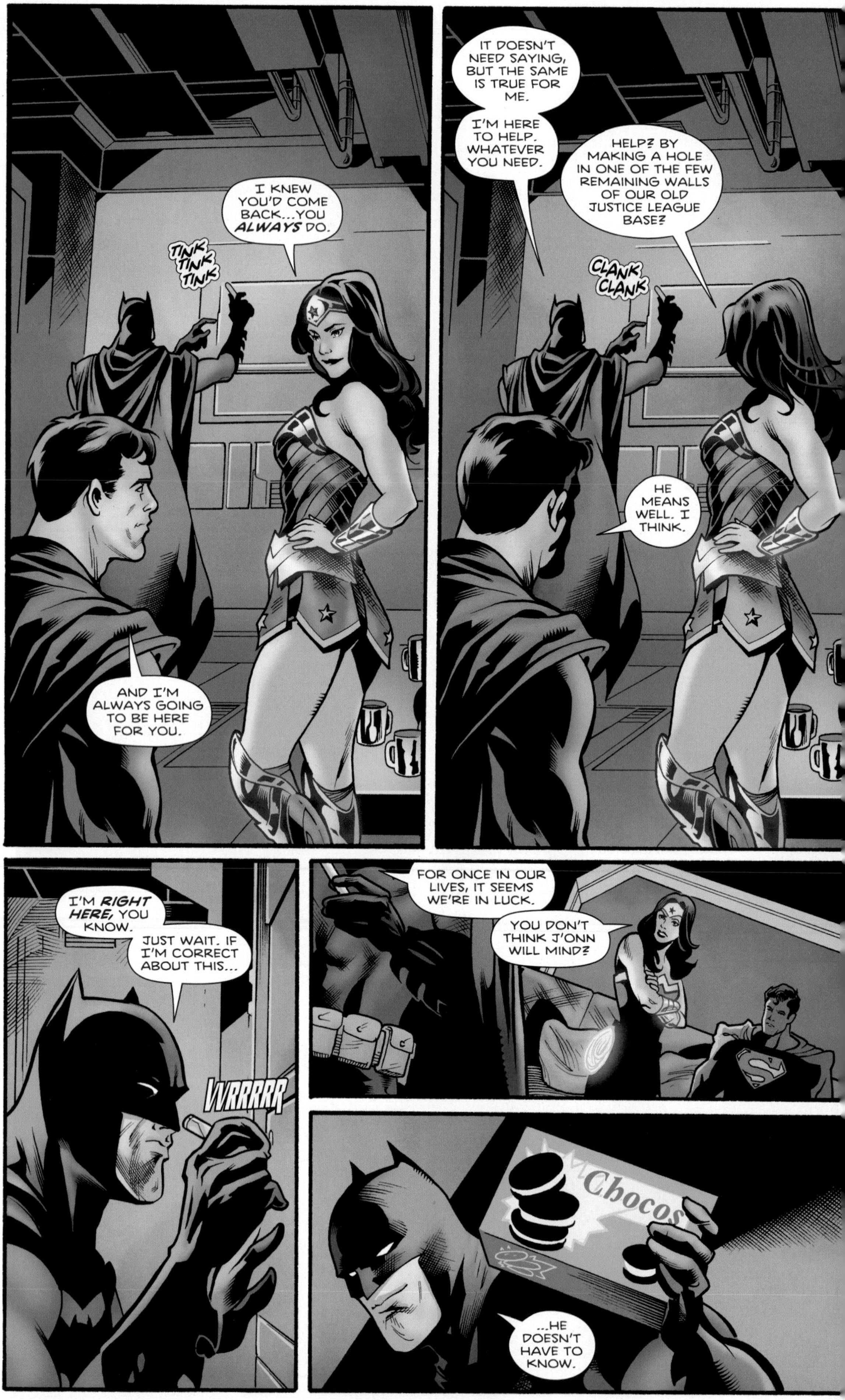

I KNEW YOU'D COME BACK...YOU ALWAYS DO.
TINK TINK TINK
AND I'M ALWAYS GOING TO BE HERE FOR YOU.
IT DOESN'T NEED SAYING, BUT THE SAME IS TRUE FOR ME.
I'M HERE TO HELP. WHATEVER YOU NEED.
HELP? BY MAKING A HOLE IN ONE OF THE FEW REMAINING WALLS OF OUR OLD JUSTICE LEAGUE BASE?
CLANK CLANK
HE MEANS WELL. I THINK.
I'M RIGHT HERE, YOU KNOW.
JUST WAIT. IF I'M CORRECT ABOUT THIS...
VVRRRRR
FOR ONCE IN OUR LIVES, IT SEEMS WE'RE IN LUCK.
YOU DON'T THINK J'ONN WILL MIND?
Chocos
...HE DOESN'T HAVE TO KNOW.

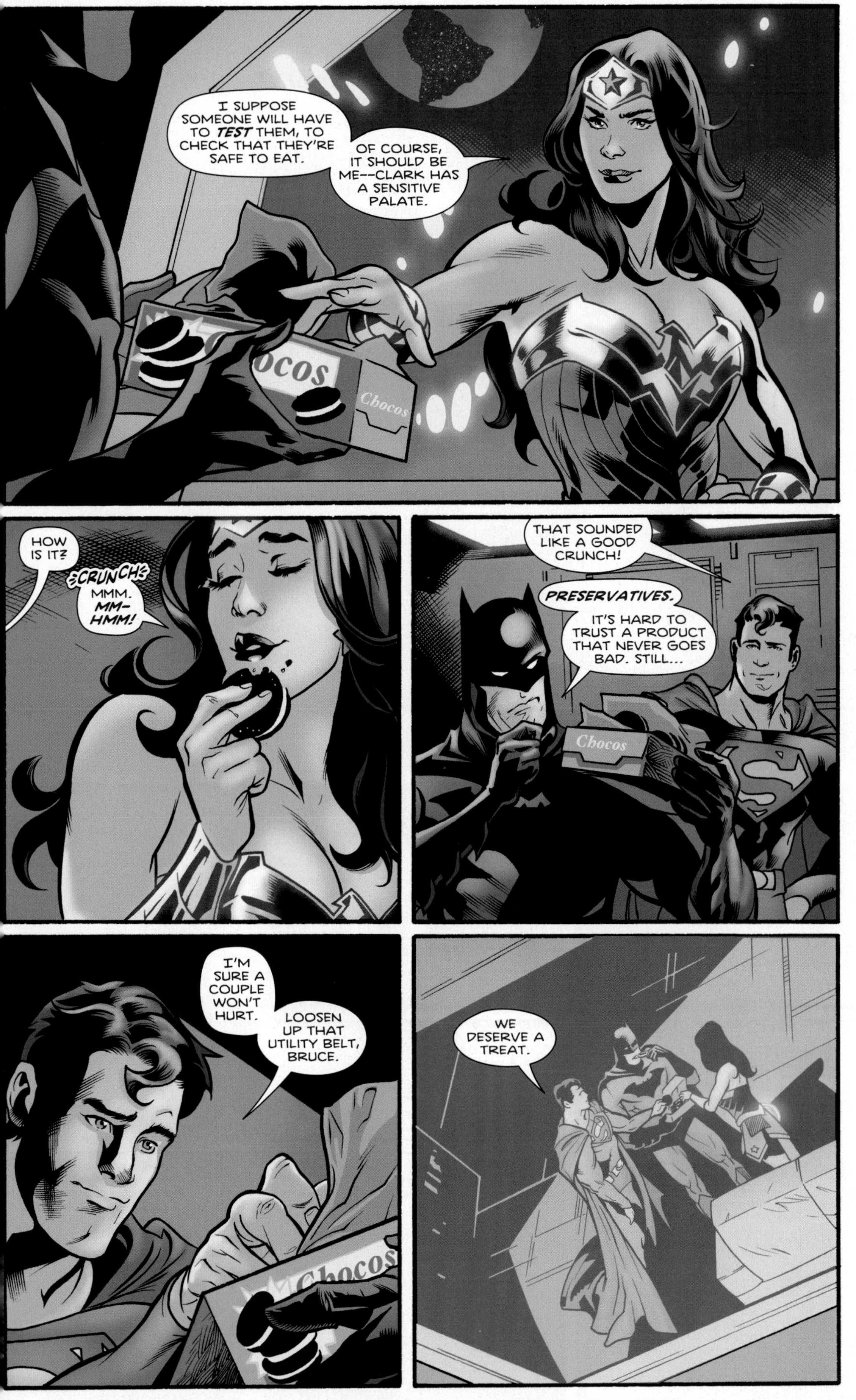

I SUPPOSE SOMEONE WILL HAVE TO TEST THEM, TO CHECK THAT THEY'RE SAFE TO EAT.
OF COURSE, IT SHOULD BE ME--CLARK HAS A SENSITIVE PALATE.
Chocos
HOW IS IT?
CRUNCH
MMM. MM-HMM!
THAT SOUNDED LIKE A GOOD CRUNCH!
PRESERVATIVES.
IT'S HARD TO TRUST A PRODUCT THAT NEVER GOES BAD. STILL...
Chocos
I'M SURE A COUPLE WON'T HURT.
LOOSEN UP THAT UTILITY BELT, BRUCE.
Chocos
WE DESERVE A TREAT.

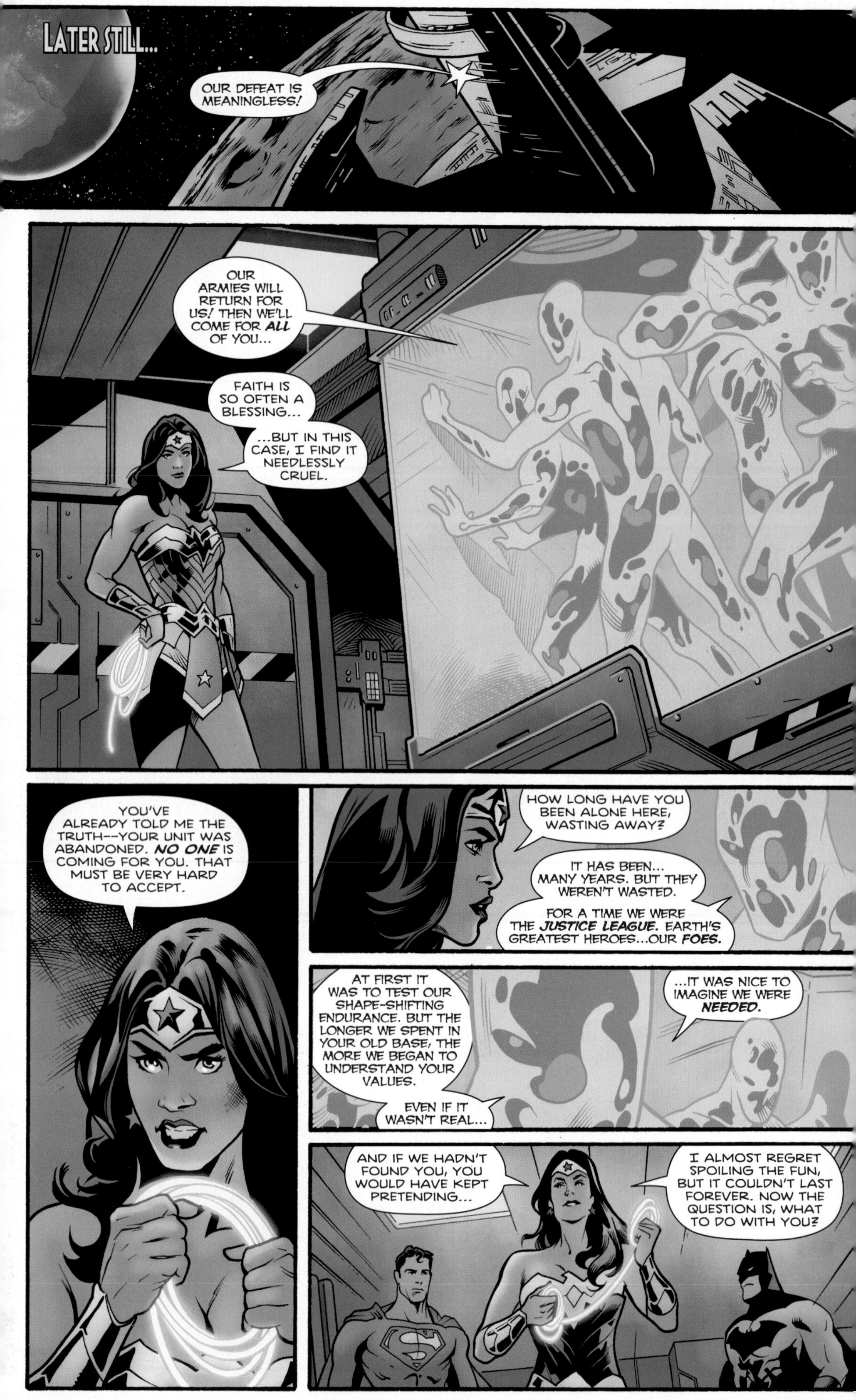
LATER STILL...
OUR DEFEAT IS MEANINGLESS!
OUR ARMIES WILL RETURN FOR US! THEN WE'LL COME FOR ALL OF YOU...
FAITH IS SO OFTEN A BLESSING...
...BUT IN THIS CASE, I FIND IT NEEDLESSLY CRUEL.
YOU'VE ALREADY TOLD ME THE TRUTH--YOUR UNIT WAS ABANDONED. NO ONE IS COMING FOR YOU. THAT MUST BE VERY HARD TO ACCEPT.
HOW LONG HAVE YOU BEEN ALONE HERE, WASTING AWAY?
IT HAS BEEN... MANY YEARS. BUT THEY WEREN'T WASTED.
FOR A TIME WE WERE THE JUSTICE LEAGUE. EARTH'S GREATEST HEROES...OUR FOES.
AT FIRST IT WAS TO TEST OUR SHAPE-SHIFTING ENDURANCE. BUT THE LONGER WE SPENT IN YOUR OLD BASE, THE MORE WE BEGAN TO UNDERSTAND YOUR VALUES.
EVEN IF IT WASN'T REAL...
...IT WAS NICE TO IMAGINE WE WERE NEEDED.
AND IF WE HADN'T FOUND YOU, YOU WOULD HAVE KEPT PRETENDING...
I ALMOST REGRET SPOILING THE FUN, BUT IT COULDN'T LAST FOREVER. NOW THE QUESTION IS, WHAT TO DO WITH YOU?

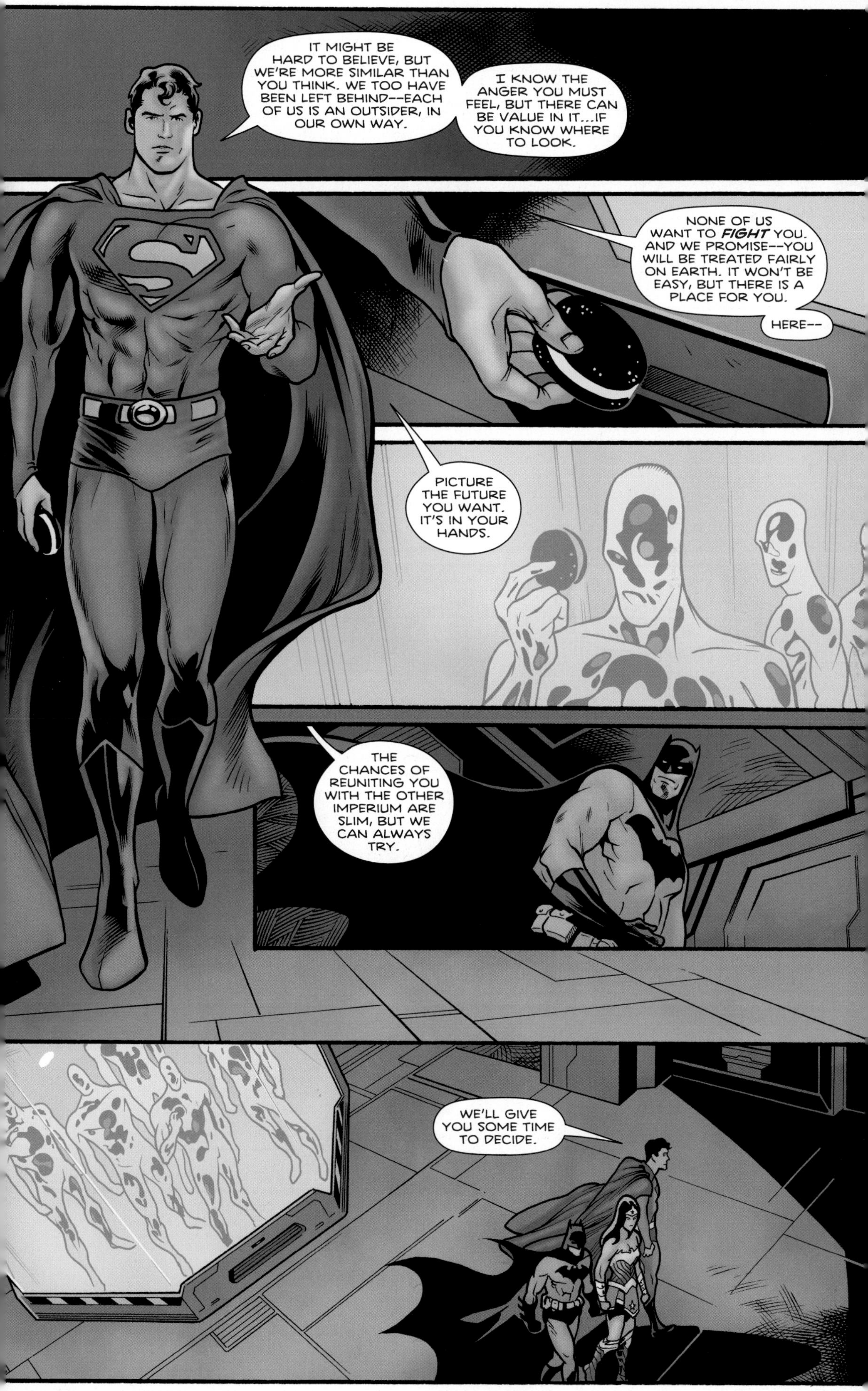
IT MIGHT BE HARD TO BELIEVE, BUT WE'RE MORE SIMILAR THAN YOU THINK. WE TOO HAVE BEEN LEFT BEHIND--EACH OF US IS AN OUTSIDER, IN OUR OWN WAY.
I KNOW THE ANGER YOU MUST FEEL, BUT THERE CAN BE VALUE IN IT...IF YOU KNOW WHERE TO LOOK.
NONE OF US WANT TO ***FIGHT*** YOU. AND WE PROMISE--YOU WILL BE TREATED FAIRLY ON EARTH. IT WON'T BE EASY, BUT THERE IS A PLACE FOR YOU.
HERE--
PICTURE THE FUTURE YOU WANT. IT'S IN YOUR HANDS.
THE CHANCES OF REUNITING YOU WITH THE OTHER IMPERIUM ARE SLIM, BUT WE CAN ALWAYS TRY.
WE'LL GIVE YOU SOME TIME TO DECIDE.

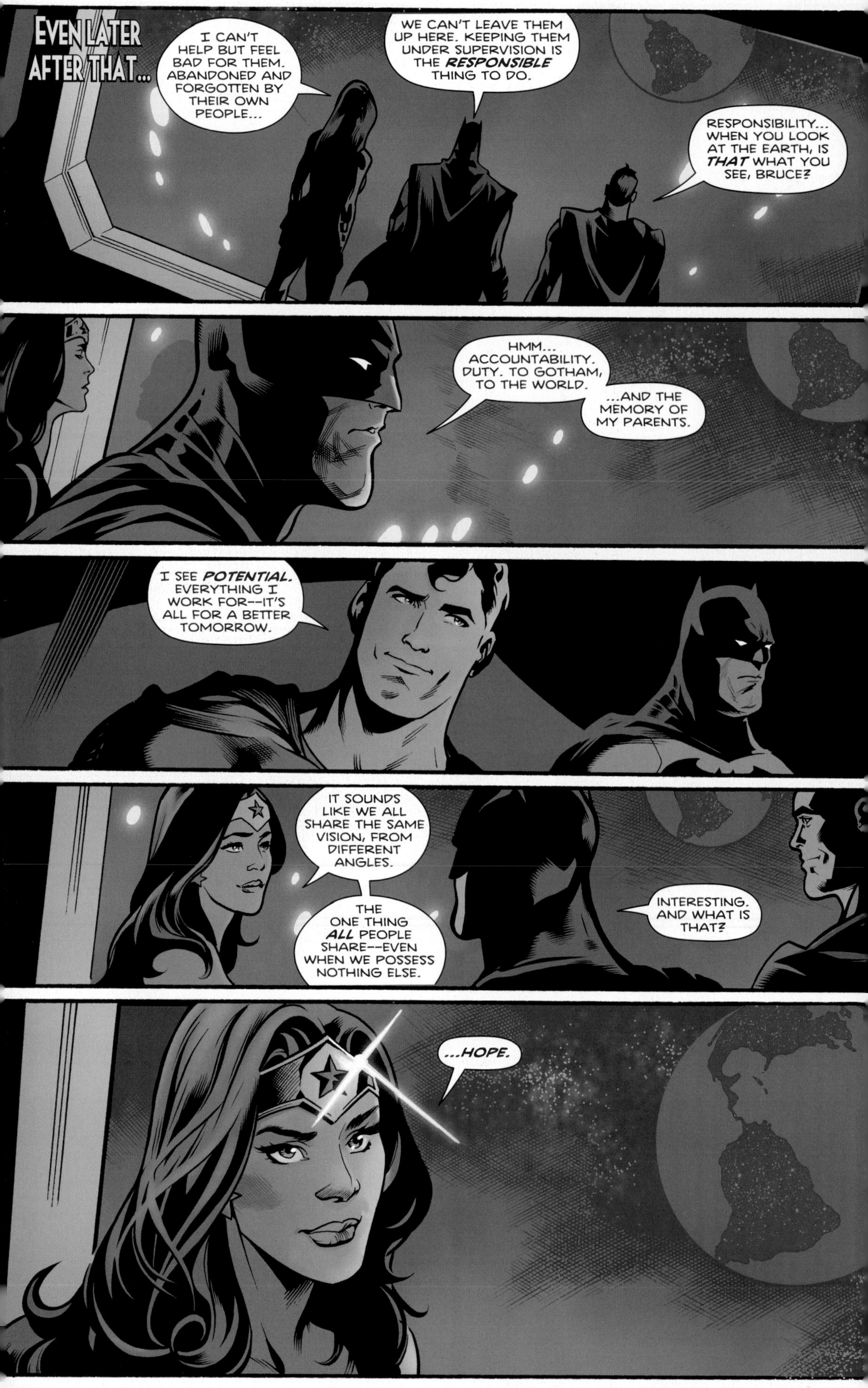
EVEN LATER AFTER THAT...
I CAN'T HELP BUT FEEL BAD FOR THEM. ABANDONED AND FORGOTTEN BY THEIR OWN PEOPLE...
WE CAN'T LEAVE THEM UP HERE. KEEPING THEM UNDER SUPERVISION IS THE RESPONSIBLE THING TO DO.
RESPONSIBILITY... WHEN YOU LOOK AT THE EARTH, IS THAT WHAT YOU SEE, BRUCE?
HMM... ACCOUNTABILITY. DUTY. TO GOTHAM, TO THE WORLD.
...AND THE MEMORY OF MY PARENTS.
I SEE POTENTIAL. EVERYTHING I WORK FOR--IT'S ALL FOR A BETTER TOMORROW.
IT SOUNDS LIKE WE ALL SHARE THE SAME VISION, FROM DIFFERENT ANGLES.
THE ONE THING ALL PEOPLE SHARE--EVEN WHEN WE POSSESS NOTHING ELSE.
INTERESTING. AND WHAT IS THAT?
...HOPE.

***Wonder Woman* #794** cover art by
Yanick Paquette & Nathan Fairbairn

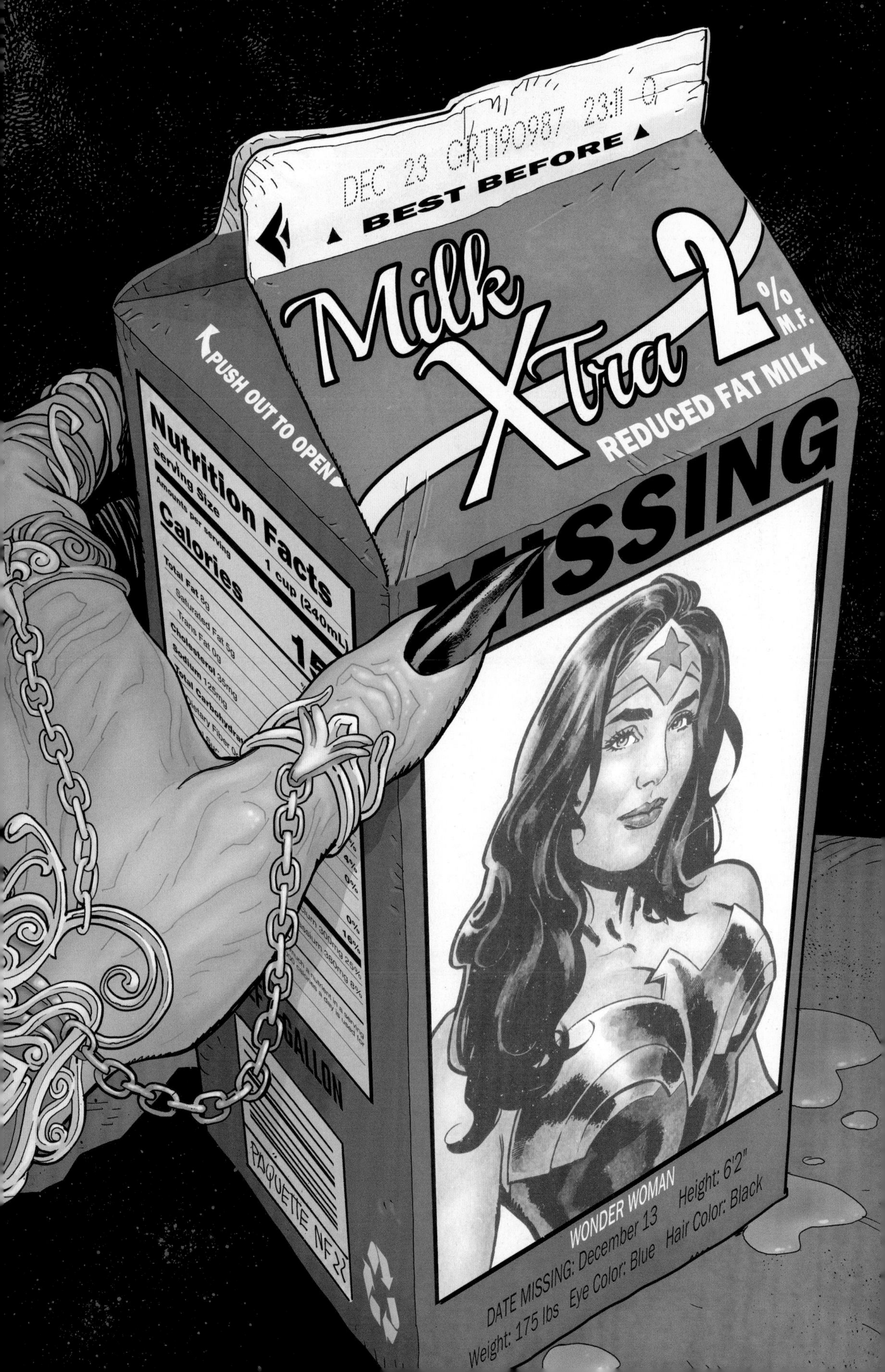
DEC 23 GRT190987 23:11
BEST BEFORE
Milk Xtra 2% M.F.
REDUCED FAT MILK
PUSH OUT TO OPEN
Nutrition Facts
Serving Size 1 cup (240mL)
Amounts per serving
Calories
MISSING
WONDER WOMAN
DATE MISSING: December 13 Height: 6'2"
Weight: 175 lbs Eye Color: Blue Hair Color: Black
PAQUETTE NF22

***Wonder Woman* #794** variant
cover art by Jen Bartel

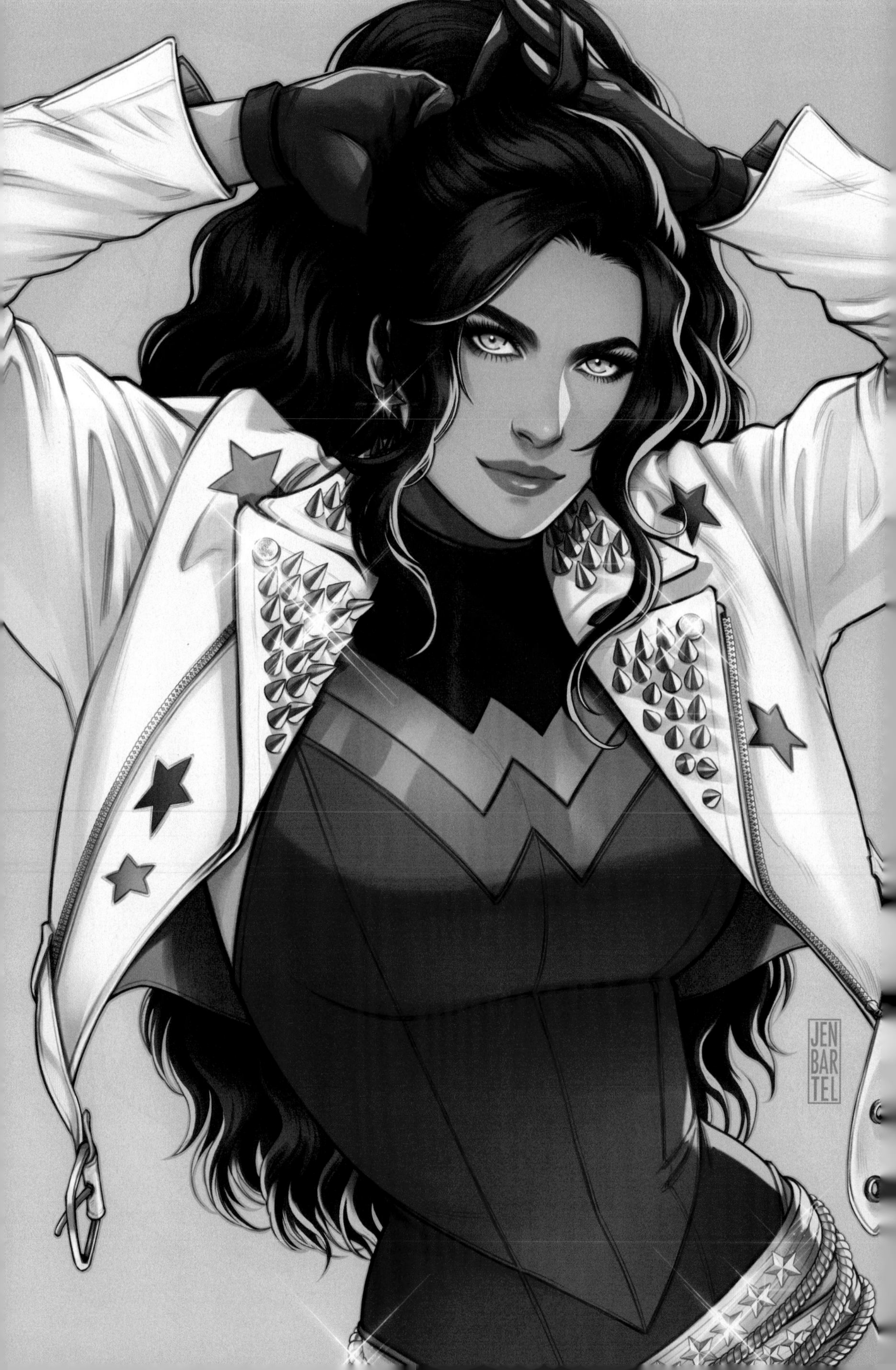
JEN BARTEL

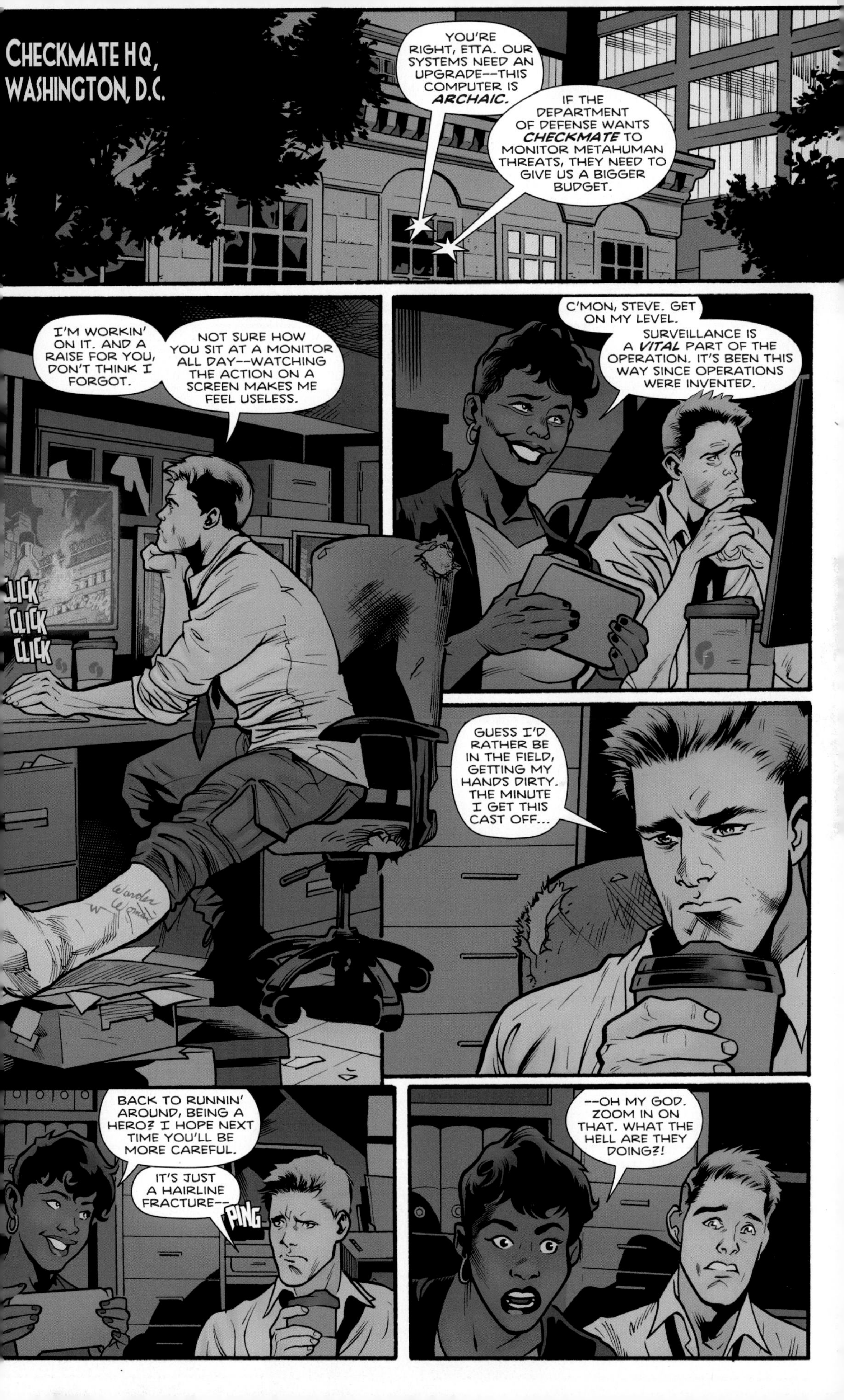
CHECKMATE HQ, WASHINGTON, D.C.
YOU'RE RIGHT, ETTA. OUR SYSTEMS NEED AN UPGRADE--THIS COMPUTER IS ARCHAIC.
IF THE DEPARTMENT OF DEFENSE WANTS CHECKMATE TO MONITOR METAHUMAN THREATS, THEY NEED TO GIVE US A BIGGER BUDGET.
I'M WORKIN' ON IT. AND A RAISE FOR YOU, DON'T THINK I FORGOT.
NOT SURE HOW YOU SIT AT A MONITOR ALL DAY--WATCHING THE ACTION ON A SCREEN MAKES ME FEEL USELESS.
CLICK CLICK CLICK
C'MON, STEVE. GET ON MY LEVEL.
SURVEILLANCE IS A VITAL PART OF THE OPERATION. IT'S BEEN THIS WAY SINCE OPERATIONS WERE INVENTED.
GUESS I'D RATHER BE IN THE FIELD, GETTING MY HANDS DIRTY. THE MINUTE I GET THIS CAST OFF...
BACK TO RUNNIN' AROUND, BEING A HERO? I HOPE NEXT TIME YOU'LL BE MORE CAREFUL.
IT'S JUST A HAIRLINE FRACTURE--
PING
--OH MY GOD. ZOOM IN ON THAT. WHAT THE HELL ARE THEY DOING?!

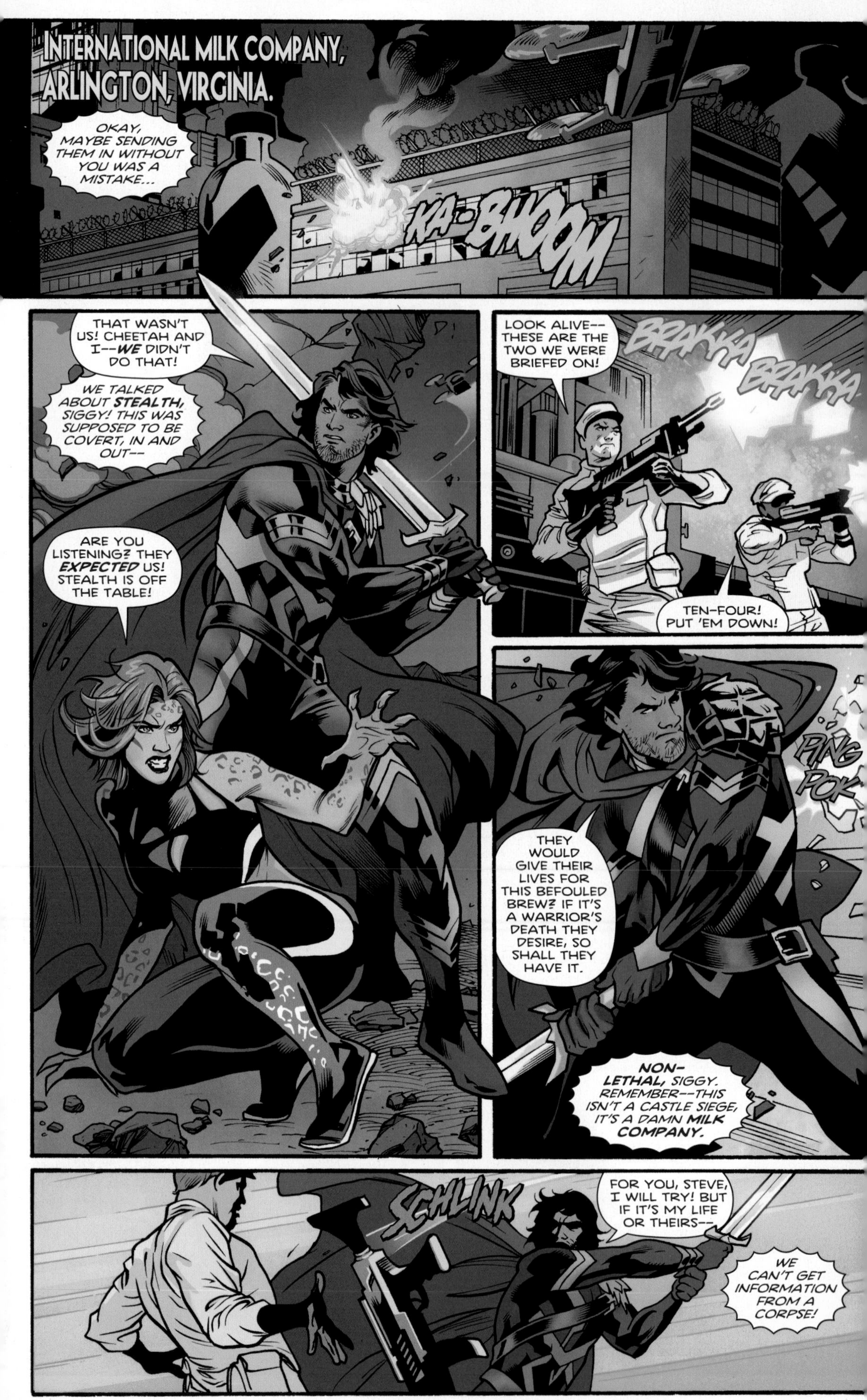
INTERNATIONAL MILK COMPANY, ARLINGTON, VIRGINIA.
OKAY, MAYBE SENDING THEM IN WITHOUT YOU WAS A MISTAKE...
KA-BHOOM
THAT WASN'T US! CHEETAH AND I--WE DIDN'T DO THAT!
WE TALKED ABOUT STEALTH, SIGGY! THIS WAS SUPPOSED TO BE COVERT, IN AND OUT--
ARE YOU LISTENING? THEY EXPECTED US! STEALTH IS OFF THE TABLE!
LOOK ALIVE-- THESE ARE THE TWO WE WERE BRIEFED ON!
BRAKKA BRAKKA
TEN-FOUR! PUT 'EM DOWN!
PING POK
THEY WOULD GIVE THEIR LIVES FOR THIS BEFOULED BREW? IF IT'S A WARRIOR'S DEATH THEY DESIRE, SO SHALL THEY HAVE IT.
NON-LETHAL, SIGGY. REMEMBER--THIS ISN'T A CASTLE SIEGE, IT'S A DAMN MILK COMPANY.
SCHLINK
FOR YOU, STEVE, I WILL TRY! BUT IF IT'S MY LIFE OR THEIRS--
WE CAN'T GET INFORMATION FROM A CORPSE!

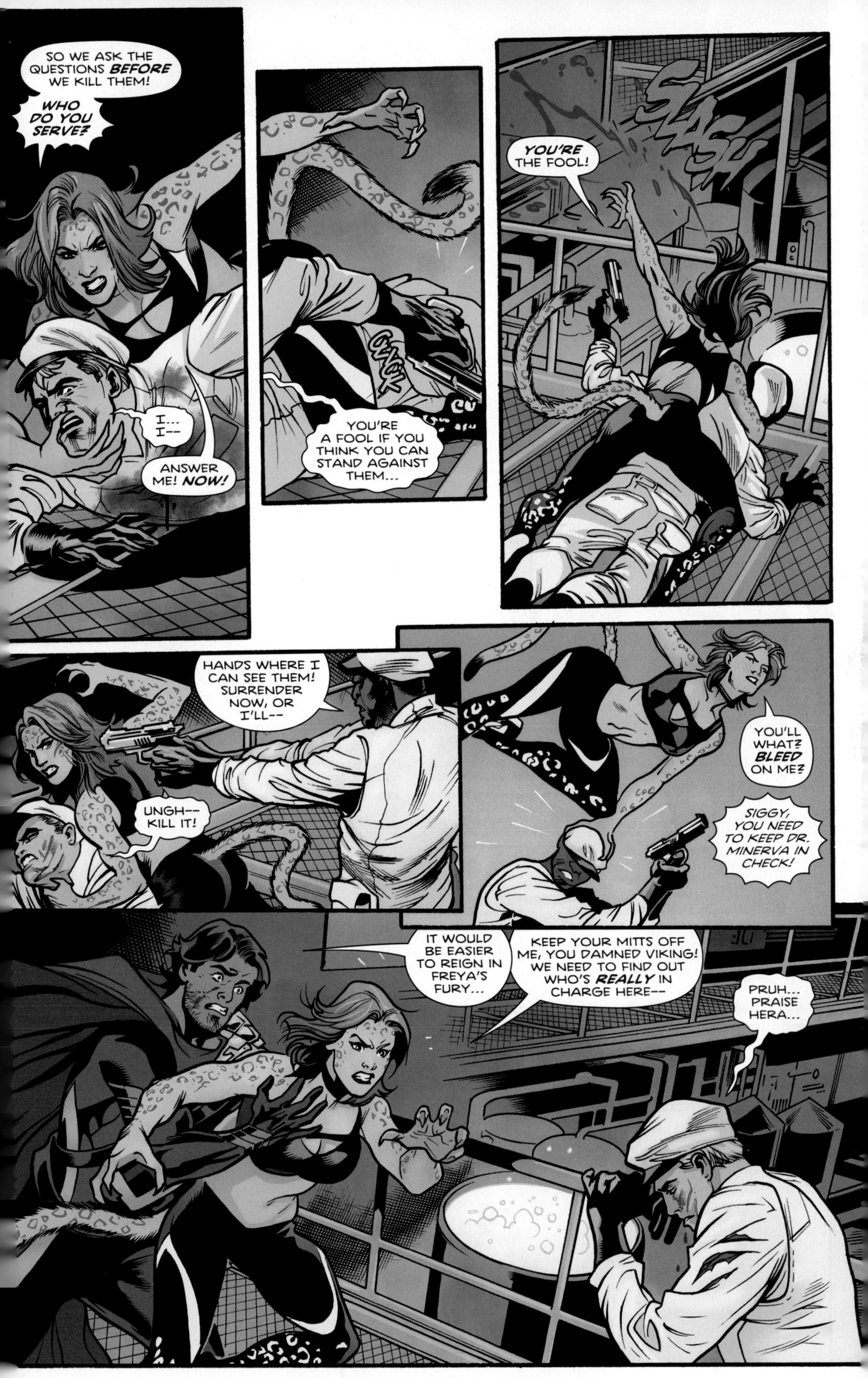
SO WE ASK THE QUESTIONS BEFORE WE KILL THEM!
WHO DO YOU SERVE?
I... I--
ANSWER ME! NOW!
CRACK
YOU'RE A FOOL IF YOU THINK YOU CAN STAND AGAINST THEM...
SLASH
YOU'RE THE FOOL!
HANDS WHERE I CAN SEE THEM! SURRENDER NOW, OR I'LL--
UNGH-- KILL IT!
YOU'LL WHAT? BLEED ON ME?
SIGGY, YOU NEED TO KEEP DR. MINERVA IN CHECK!
IT WOULD BE EASIER TO REIGN IN FREYA'S FURY...
KEEP YOUR MITTS OFF ME, YOU DAMNED VIKING! WE NEED TO FIND OUT WHO'S REALLY IN CHARGE HERE--
PRUH... PRAISE HERA...

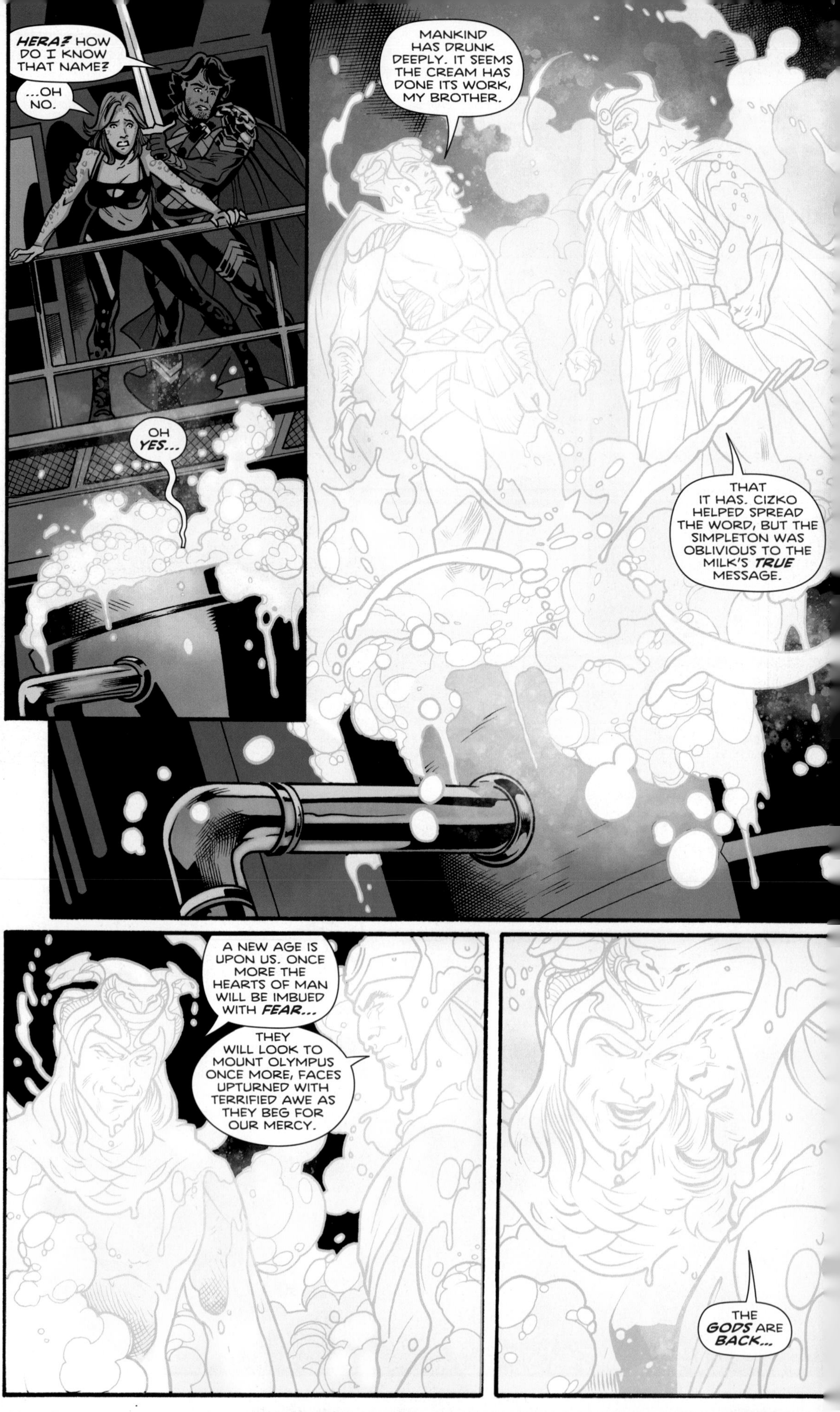
HERA? HOW DO I KNOW THAT NAME?
...OH NO.
OH YES...
MANKIND HAS DRUNK DEEPLY. IT SEEMS THE CREAM HAS DONE ITS WORK, MY BROTHER.
THAT IT HAS. CIZKO HELPED SPREAD THE WORD, BUT THE SIMPLETON WAS OBLIVIOUS TO THE MILK'S TRUE MESSAGE.
A NEW AGE IS UPON US. ONCE MORE THE HEARTS OF MAN WILL BE IMBUED WITH FEAR...
THEY WILL LOOK TO MOUNT OLYMPUS ONCE MORE, FACES UPTURNED WITH TERRIFIED AWE AS THEY BEG FOR OUR MERCY.
THE GODS ARE BACK...

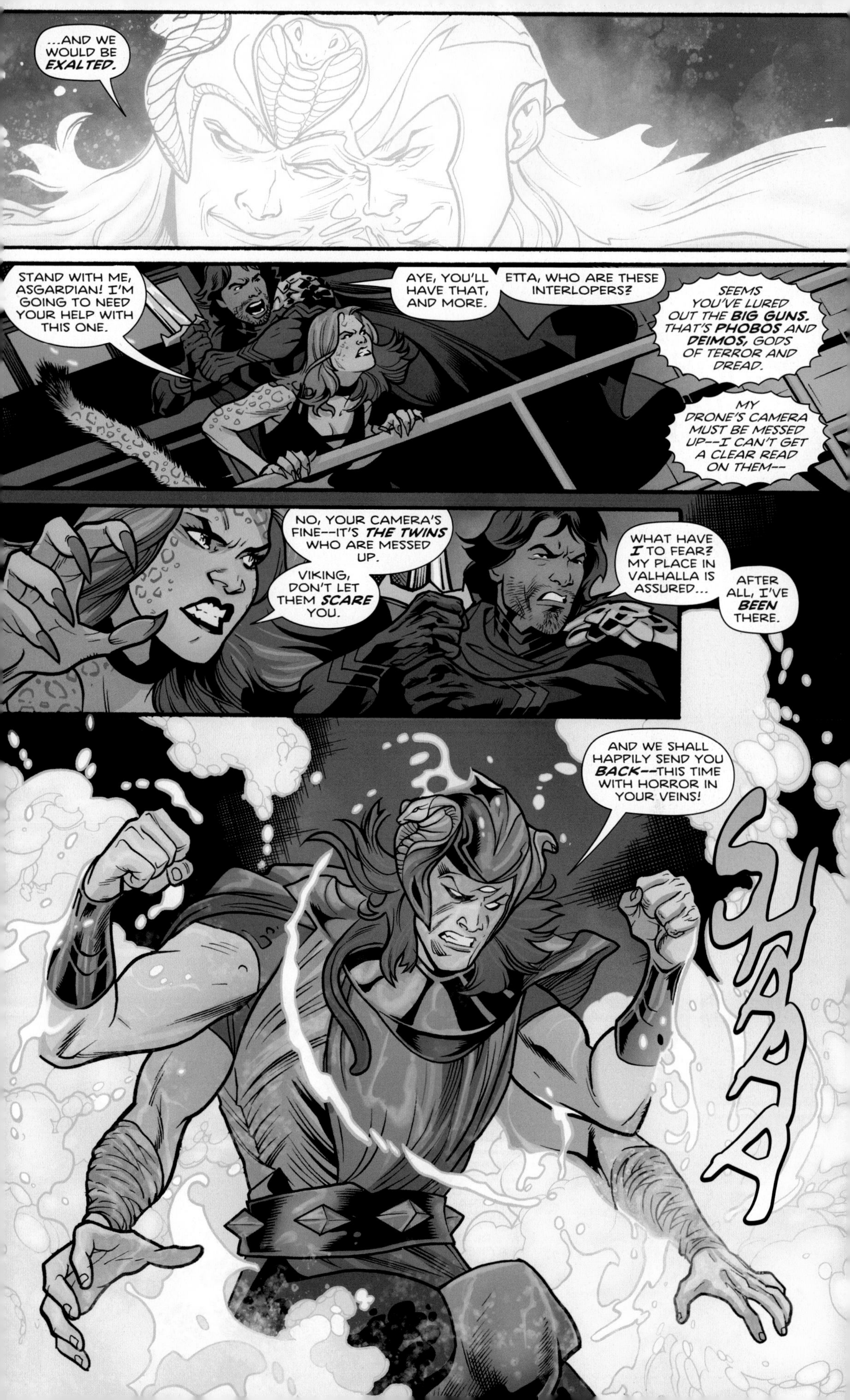

...AND WE WOULD BE ***EXALTED.***
STAND WITH ME, ASGARDIAN! I'M GOING TO NEED YOUR HELP WITH THIS ONE.
AYE, YOU'LL HAVE THAT, AND MORE.
ETTA, WHO ARE THESE INTERLOPERS?
*SEEMS YOU'VE LURED OUT THE **BIG GUNS.** THAT'S **PHOBOS** AND **DEIMOS,** GODS OF TERROR AND DREAD.*
MY DRONE'S CAMERA MUST BE MESSED UP--I CAN'T GET A CLEAR READ ON THEM--
NO, YOUR CAMERA'S FINE--IT'S ***THE TWINS*** WHO ARE MESSED UP.
VIKING, DON'T LET THEM ***SCARE*** YOU.
WHAT HAVE ***I*** TO FEAR? MY PLACE IN VALHALLA IS ASSURED...
AFTER ALL, I'VE ***BEEN*** THERE.
AND WE SHALL HAPPILY SEND YOU ***BACK***--THIS TIME WITH HORROR IN YOUR VEINS!
SHAAA

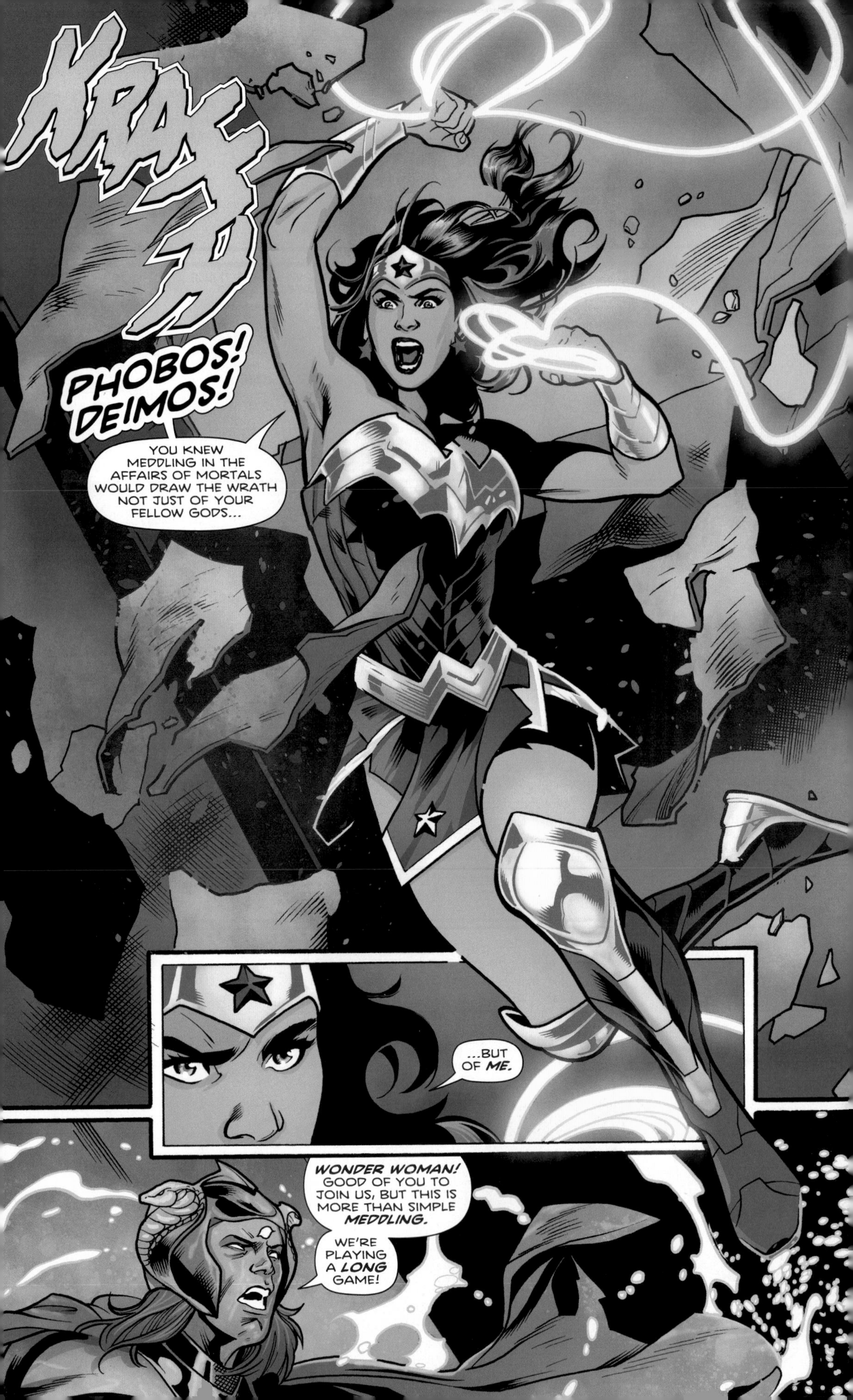
KRAK
PHOBOS! DEIMOS!
YOU KNEW MEDDLING IN THE AFFAIRS OF MORTALS WOULD DRAW THE WRATH NOT JUST OF YOUR FELLOW GODS...
...BUT OF ME.
WONDER WOMAN! GOOD OF YOU TO JOIN US, BUT THIS IS MORE THAN SIMPLE MEDDLING.
WE'RE PLAYING A LONG GAME!

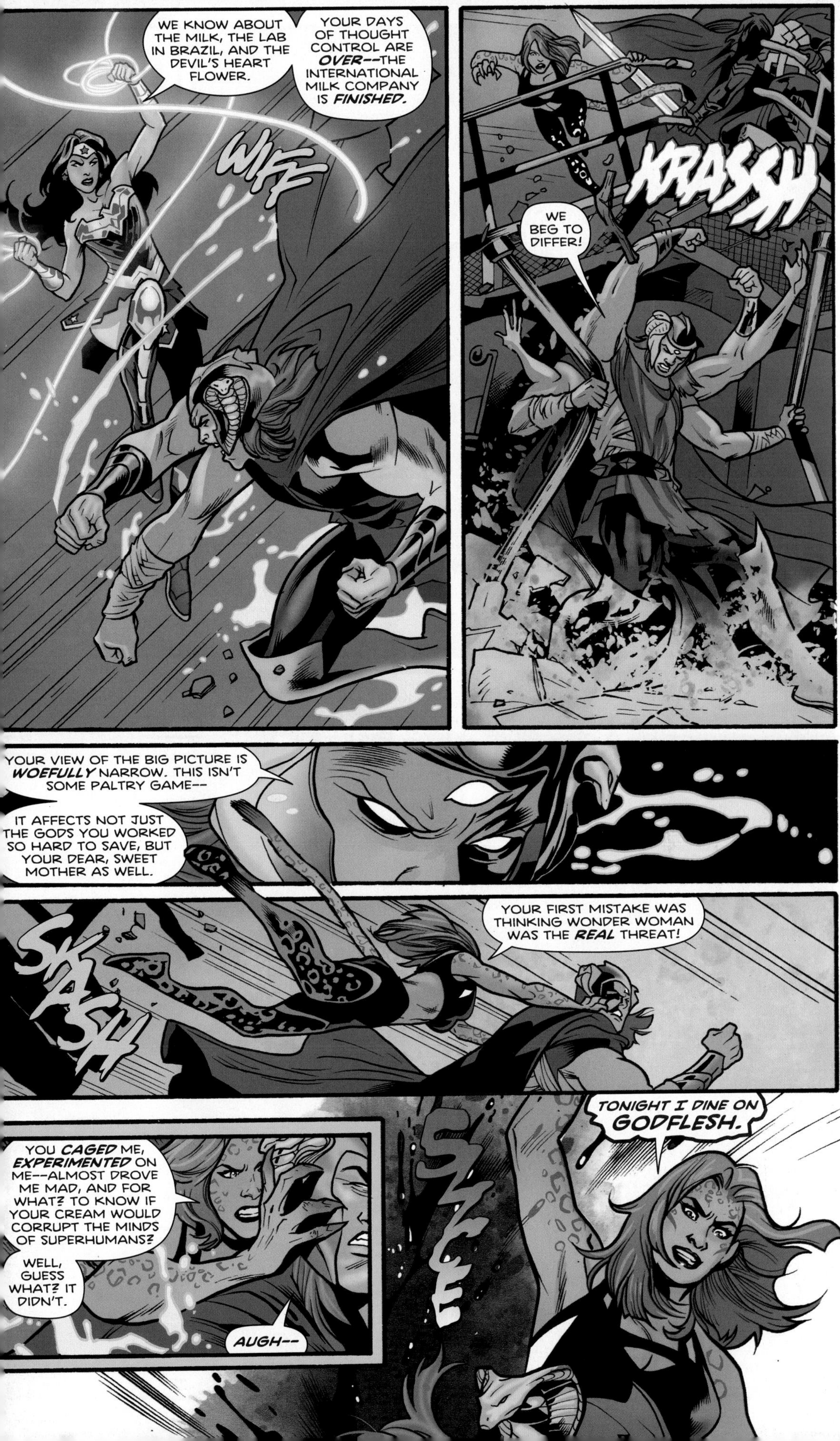

WE KNOW ABOUT THE MILK, THE LAB IN BRAZIL, AND THE DEVIL'S HEART FLOWER.
YOUR DAYS OF THOUGHT CONTROL ARE OVER--THE INTERNATIONAL MILK COMPANY IS FINISHED.
WIFF
KRASSH
WE BEG TO DIFFER!
YOUR VIEW OF THE BIG PICTURE IS WOEFULLY NARROW. THIS ISN'T SOME PALTRY GAME--
IT AFFECTS NOT JUST THE GODS YOU WORKED SO HARD TO SAVE, BUT YOUR DEAR, SWEET MOTHER AS WELL.
SHASH
YOUR FIRST MISTAKE WAS THINKING WONDER WOMAN WAS THE REAL THREAT!
YOU CAGED ME, EXPERIMENTED ON ME--ALMOST DROVE ME MAD, AND FOR WHAT? TO KNOW IF YOUR CREAM WOULD CORRUPT THE MINDS OF SUPERHUMANS?
WELL, GUESS WHAT? IT DIDN'T.
AUGH--
SMACK
TONIGHT I DINE ON GODFLESH.

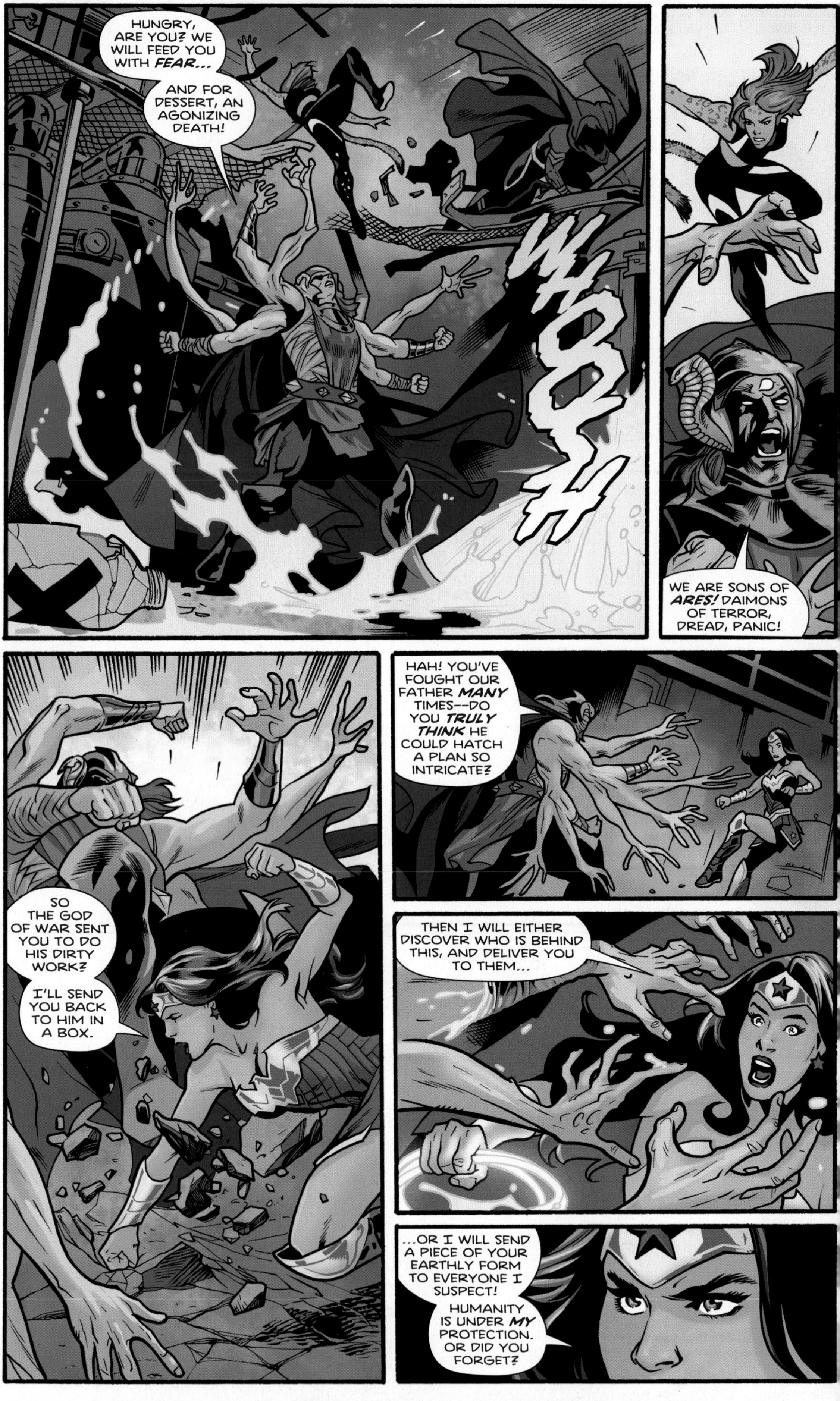
HUNGRY, ARE YOU? WE WILL FEED YOU WITH FEAR...
AND FOR DESSERT, AN AGONIZING DEATH!
WHOOSH
WE ARE SONS OF ARES! DAIMONS OF TERROR, DREAD, PANIC!
SO THE GOD OF WAR SENT YOU TO DO HIS DIRTY WORK?
I'LL SEND YOU BACK TO HIM IN A BOX.
HAH! YOU'VE FOUGHT OUR FATHER MANY TIMES--DO YOU TRULY THINK HE COULD HATCH A PLAN SO INTRICATE?
THEN I WILL EITHER DISCOVER WHO IS BEHIND THIS, AND DELIVER YOU TO THEM...
...OR I WILL SEND A PIECE OF YOUR EARTHLY FORM TO EVERYONE I SUSPECT!
HUMANITY IS UNDER MY PROTECTION. OR DID YOU FORGET?

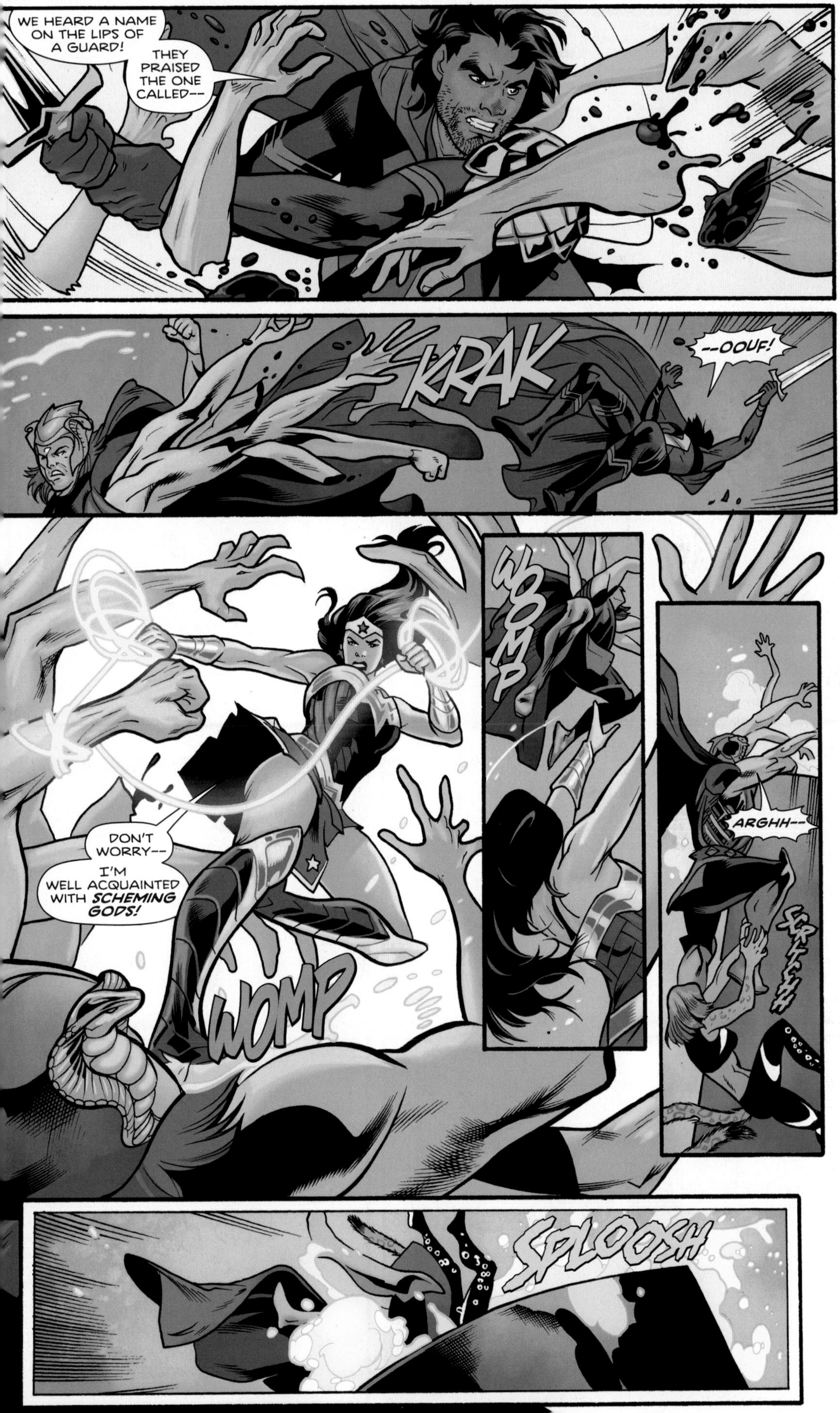
WE HEARD A NAME ON THE LIPS OF A GUARD!
THEY PRAISED THE ONE CALLED--
KRAK
--OOUF!
DON'T WORRY--
I'M WELL ACQUAINTED WITH *SCHEMING GODS!*
WOMP
WOMP
ARGHH--
SCRITCHH
SPLOOSH

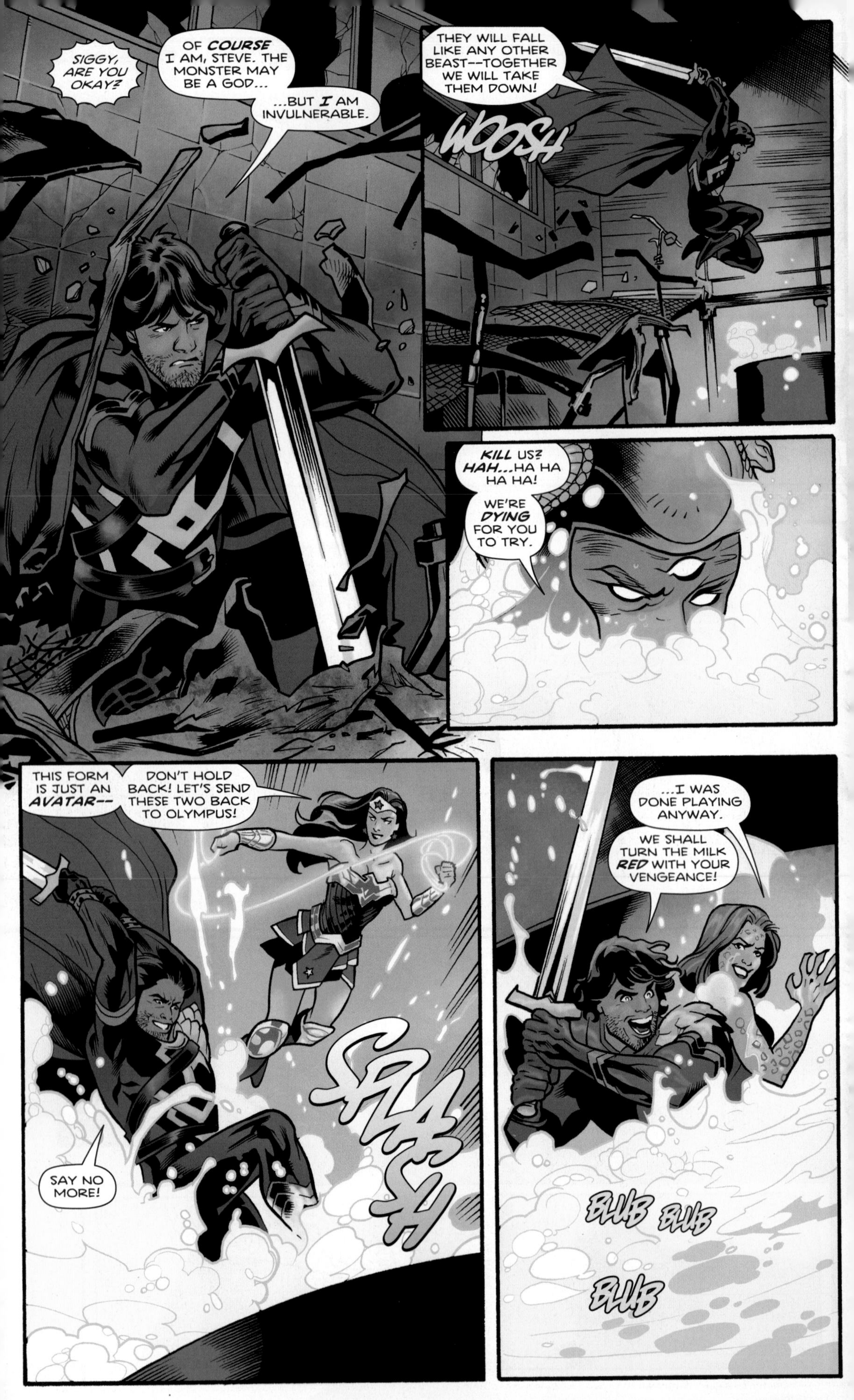
SIGGY, ARE YOU OKAY?
OF COURSE I AM, STEVE. THE MONSTER MAY BE A GOD...
...BUT I AM INVULNERABLE.
THEY WILL FALL LIKE ANY OTHER BEAST--TOGETHER WE WILL TAKE THEM DOWN!
WOOSH
KILL US? HAH...HA HA HA HA!
WE'RE DYING FOR YOU TO TRY.
THIS FORM IS JUST AN AVATAR--
DON'T HOLD BACK! LET'S SEND THESE TWO BACK TO OLYMPUS!
SAY NO MORE!
SPLASH
...I WAS DONE PLAYING ANYWAY.
WE SHALL TURN THE MILK RED WITH YOUR VENGEANCE!
BLUB BLUB
BLUB

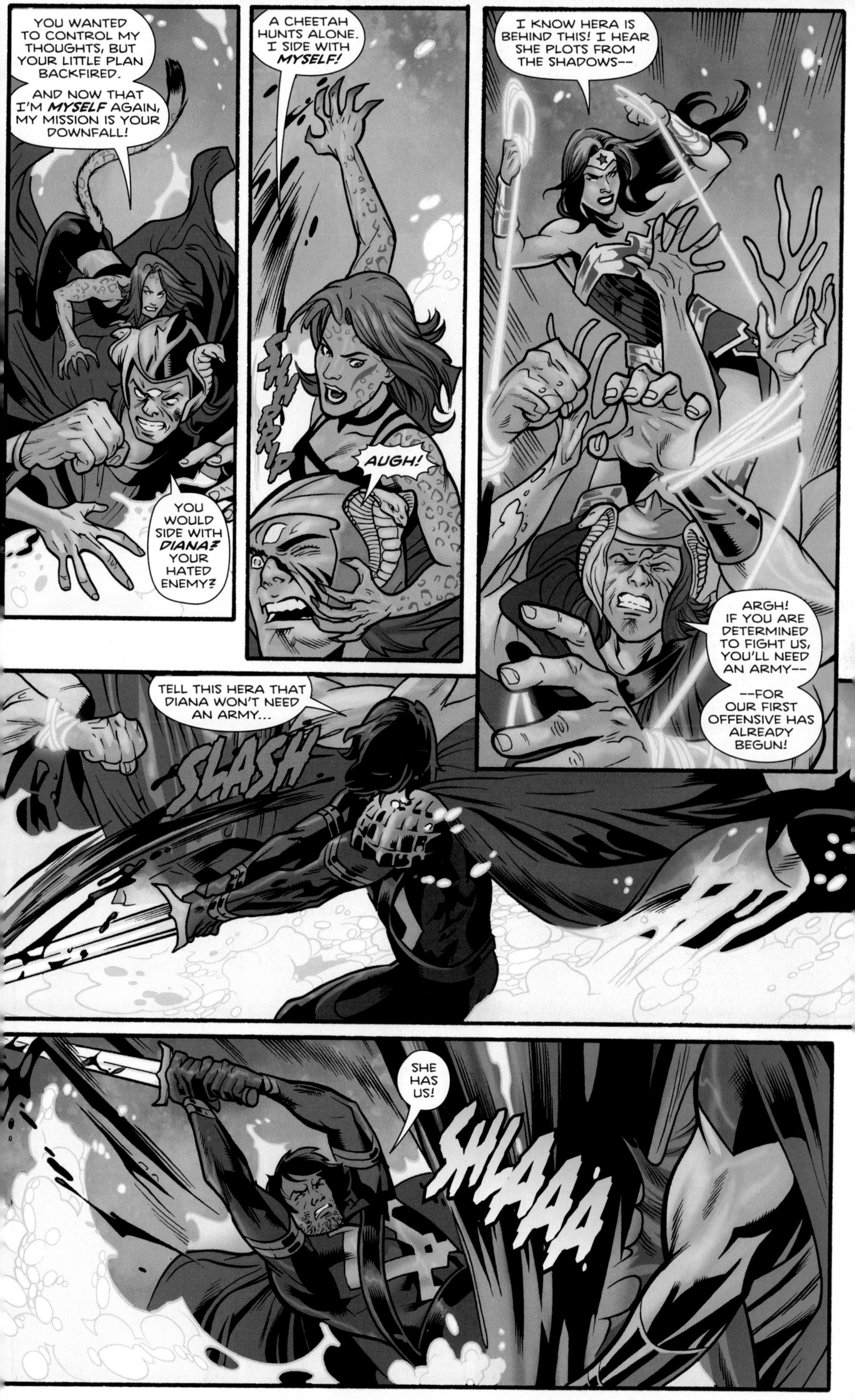
YOU WANTED TO CONTROL MY THOUGHTS, BUT YOUR LITTLE PLAN BACKFIRED.
AND NOW THAT I'M *MYSELF* AGAIN, MY MISSION IS YOUR DOWNFALL!
YOU WOULD SIDE WITH *DIANA?* YOUR HATED ENEMY?
A CHEETAH HUNTS ALONE. I SIDE WITH *MYSELF!*
SHHRRIP
AUGH!
I KNOW HERA IS BEHIND THIS! I HEAR SHE PLOTS FROM THE SHADOWS--
ARGH! IF YOU ARE DETERMINED TO FIGHT US, YOU'LL NEED AN ARMY--
--FOR OUR FIRST OFFENSIVE HAS ALREADY BEGUN!
TELL THIS HERA THAT DIANA WON'T NEED AN ARMY...
SLASH
SHE HAS US!
SHLAAA

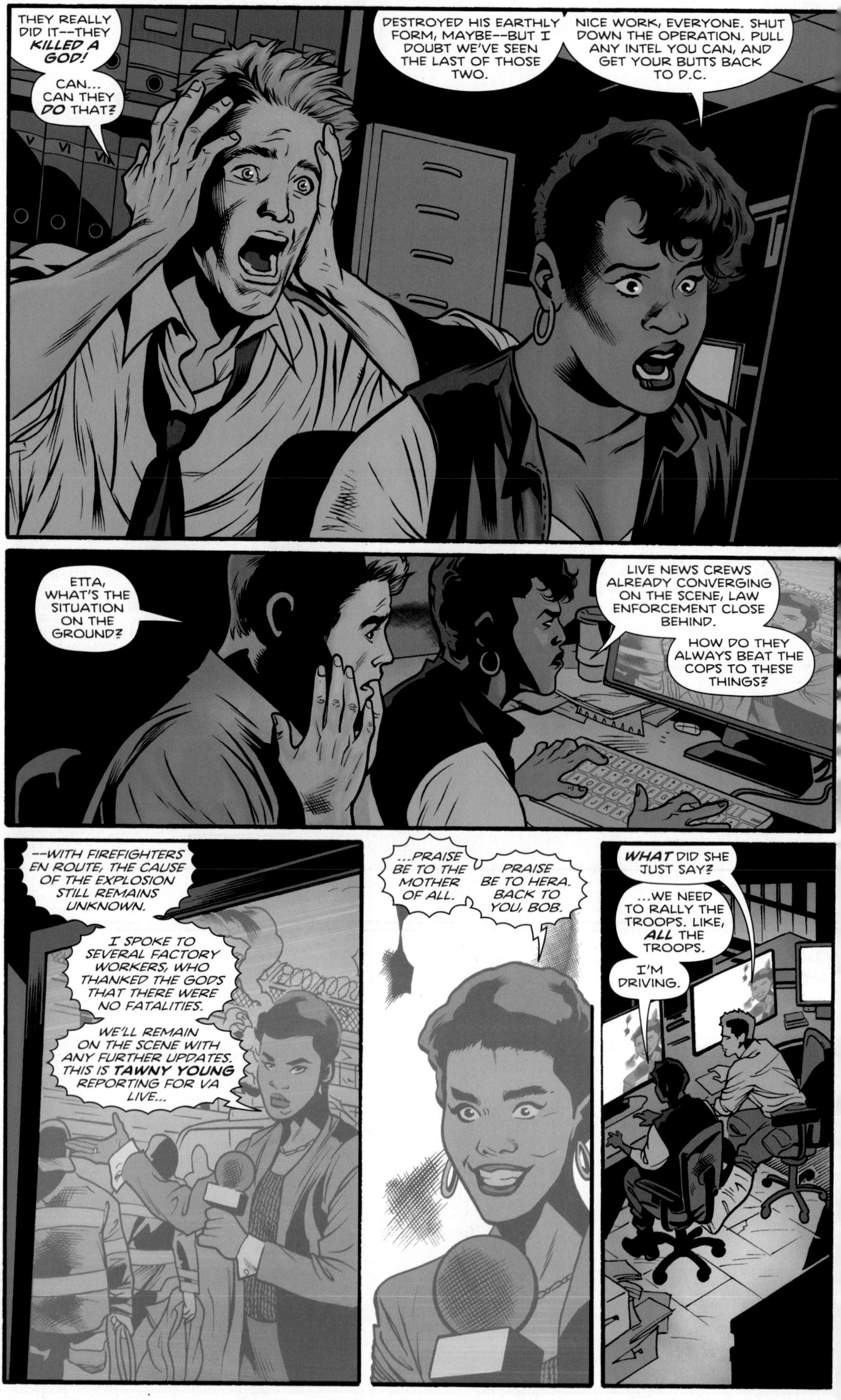
THEY REALLY DID IT--THEY KILLED A GOD!
CAN... CAN THEY DO THAT?
DESTROYED HIS EARTHLY FORM, MAYBE--BUT I DOUBT WE'VE SEEN THE LAST OF THOSE TWO.
NICE WORK, EVERYONE. SHUT DOWN THE OPERATION. PULL ANY INTEL YOU CAN, AND GET YOUR BUTTS BACK TO D.C.
ETTA, WHAT'S THE SITUATION ON THE GROUND?
LIVE NEWS CREWS ALREADY CONVERGING ON THE SCENE, LAW ENFORCEMENT CLOSE BEHIND.
HOW DO THEY ALWAYS BEAT THE COPS TO THESE THINGS?
--WITH FIREFIGHTERS EN ROUTE, THE CAUSE OF THE EXPLOSION STILL REMAINS UNKNOWN.
I SPOKE TO SEVERAL FACTORY WORKERS, WHO THANKED THE GODS THAT THERE WERE NO FATALITIES.
WE'LL REMAIN ON THE SCENE WITH ANY FURTHER UPDATES. THIS IS TAWNY YOUNG REPORTING FOR VA LIVE...
...PRAISE BE TO THE MOTHER OF ALL.
PRAISE BE TO HERA. BACK TO YOU, BOB.
WHAT DID SHE JUST SAY?
...WE NEED TO RALLY THE TROOPS. LIKE, ALL THE TROOPS.
I'M DRIVING.

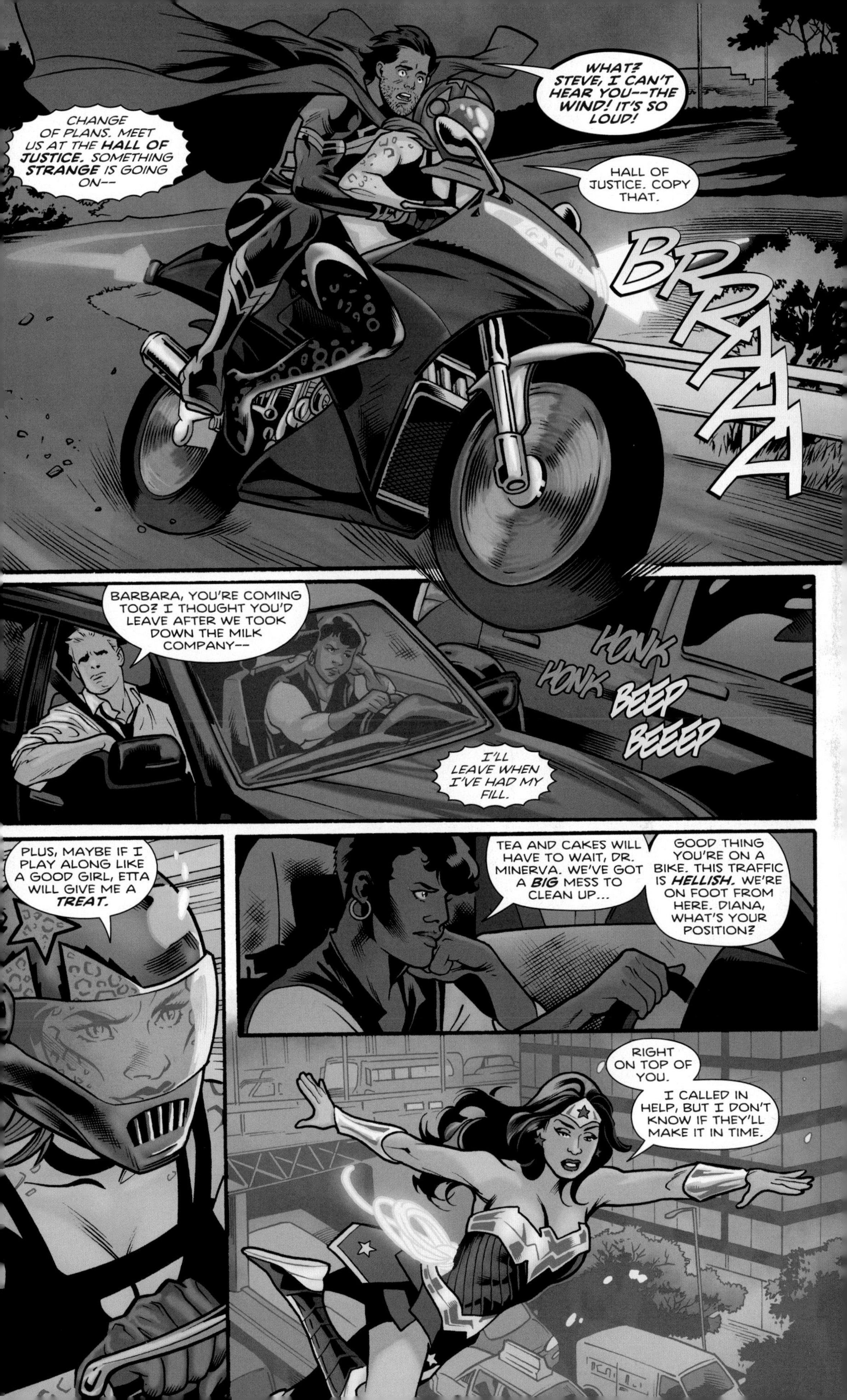
CHANGE OF PLANS. MEET US AT THE HALL OF JUSTICE. SOMETHING STRANGE IS GOING ON--
WHAT? STEVE, I CAN'T HEAR YOU--THE WIND! IT'S SO LOUD!
HALL OF JUSTICE. COPY THAT.
BRRAAA
BARBARA, YOU'RE COMING TOO? I THOUGHT YOU'D LEAVE AFTER WE TOOK DOWN THE MILK COMPANY--
HONK HONK BEEP BEEEP
I'LL LEAVE WHEN I'VE HAD MY FILL.
PLUS, MAYBE IF I PLAY ALONG LIKE A GOOD GIRL, ETTA WILL GIVE ME A TREAT.
TEA AND CAKES WILL HAVE TO WAIT, DR. MINERVA. WE'VE GOT A BIG MESS TO CLEAN UP...
GOOD THING YOU'RE ON A BIKE. THIS TRAFFIC IS HELLISH. WE'RE ON FOOT FROM HERE. DIANA, WHAT'S YOUR POSITION?
RIGHT ON TOP OF YOU.
I CALLED IN HELP, BUT I DON'T KNOW IF THEY'LL MAKE IT IN TIME.

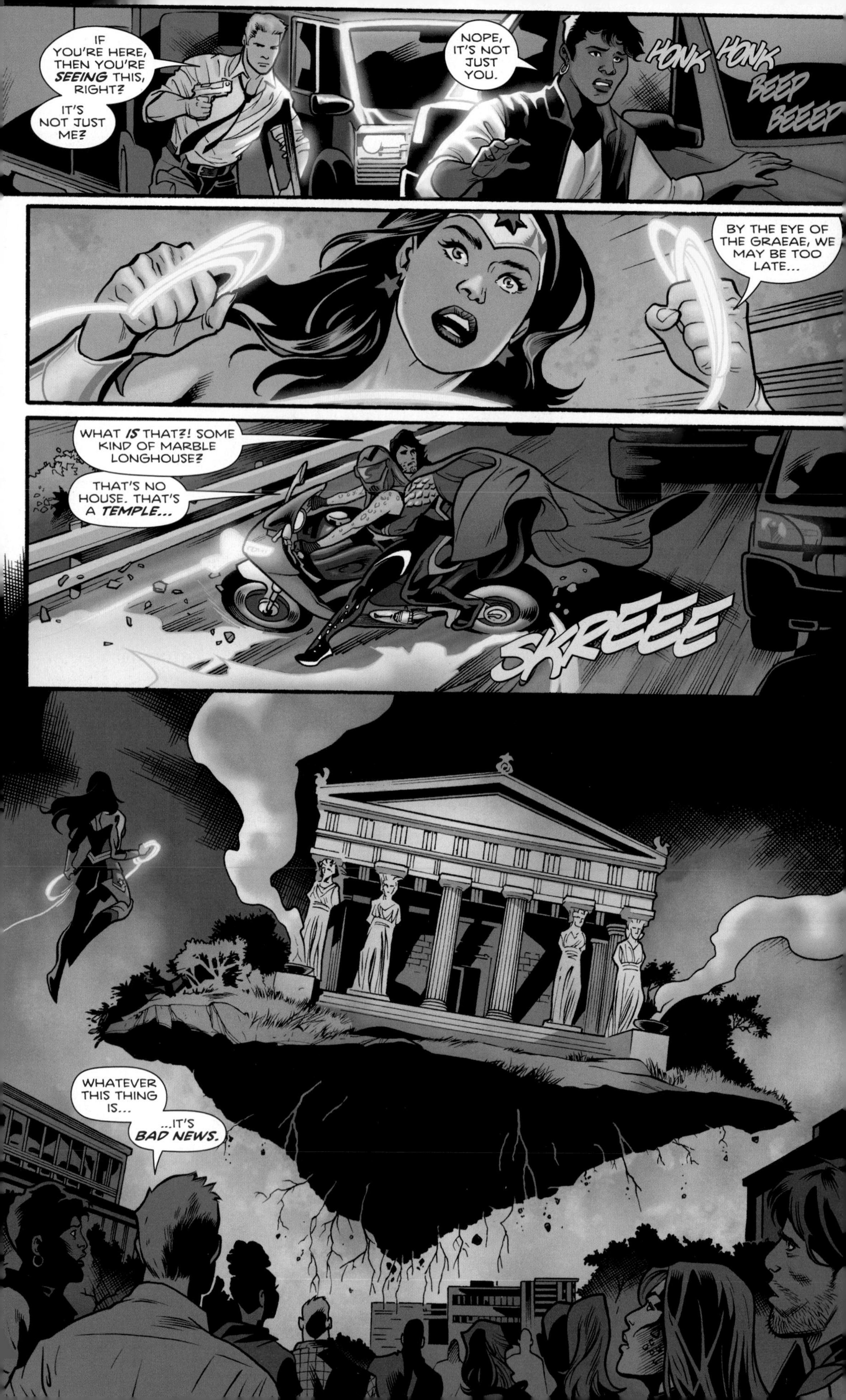
IF YOU'RE HERE, THEN YOU'RE SEEING THIS, RIGHT?
IT'S NOT JUST ME?
NOPE, IT'S NOT JUST YOU.
HONK HONK BEEP BEEEP
BY THE EYE OF THE GRAEAE, WE MAY BE TOO LATE...
WHAT IS THAT?! SOME KIND OF MARBLE LONGHOUSE?
THAT'S NO HOUSE. THAT'S A TEMPLE...
SKREEE
WHATEVER THIS THING IS...
...IT'S BAD NEWS.

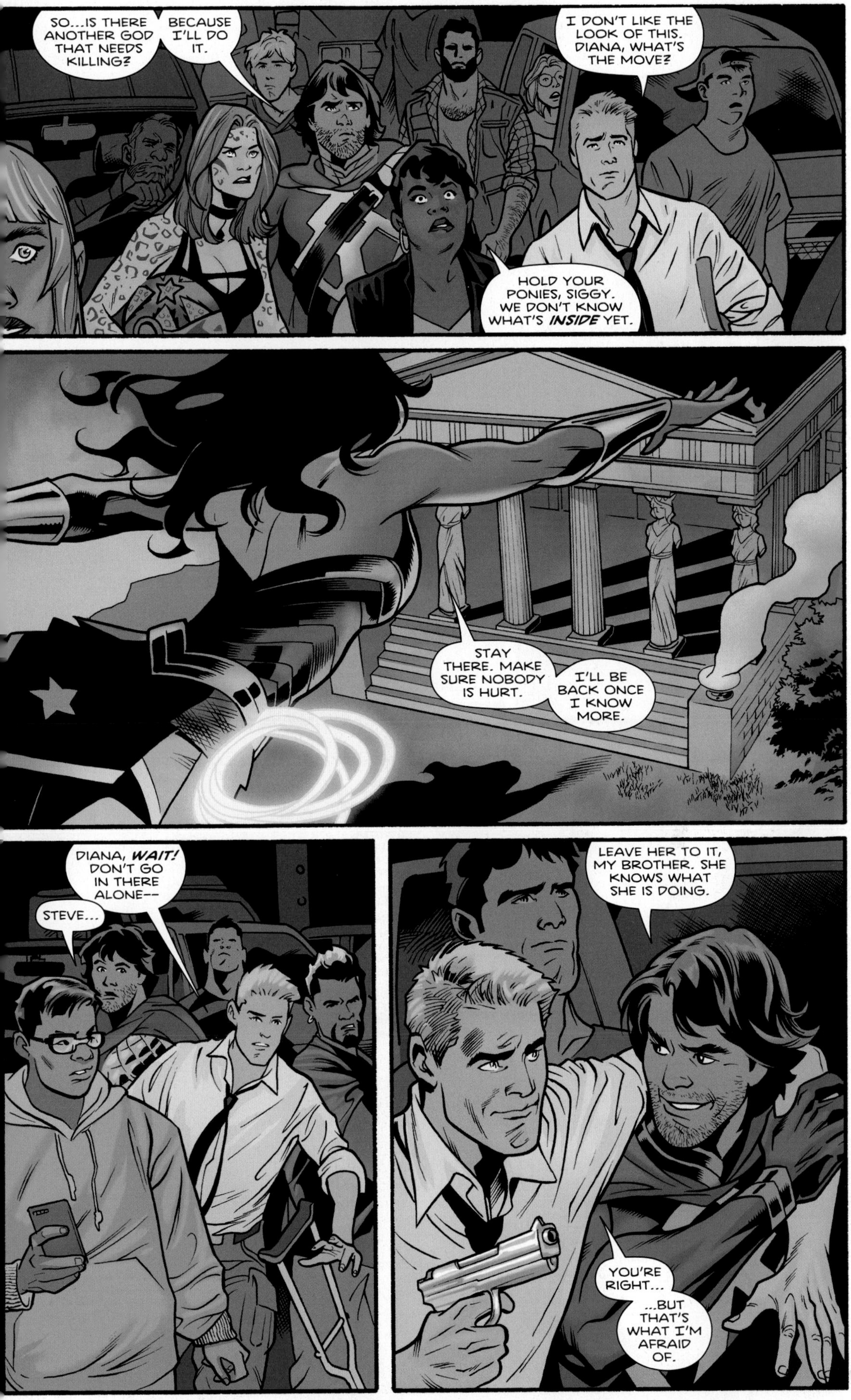

SO...IS THERE ANOTHER GOD THAT NEEDS KILLING?
BECAUSE I'LL DO IT.
I DON'T LIKE THE LOOK OF THIS. DIANA, WHAT'S THE MOVE?
HOLD YOUR PONIES, SIGGY. WE DON'T KNOW WHAT'S INSIDE YET.
STAY THERE. MAKE SURE NOBODY IS HURT.
I'LL BE BACK ONCE I KNOW MORE.
DIANA, WAIT! DON'T GO IN THERE ALONE--
STEVE...
LEAVE HER TO IT, MY BROTHER. SHE KNOWS WHAT SHE IS DOING.
YOU'RE RIGHT...
...BUT THAT'S WHAT I'M AFRAID OF.

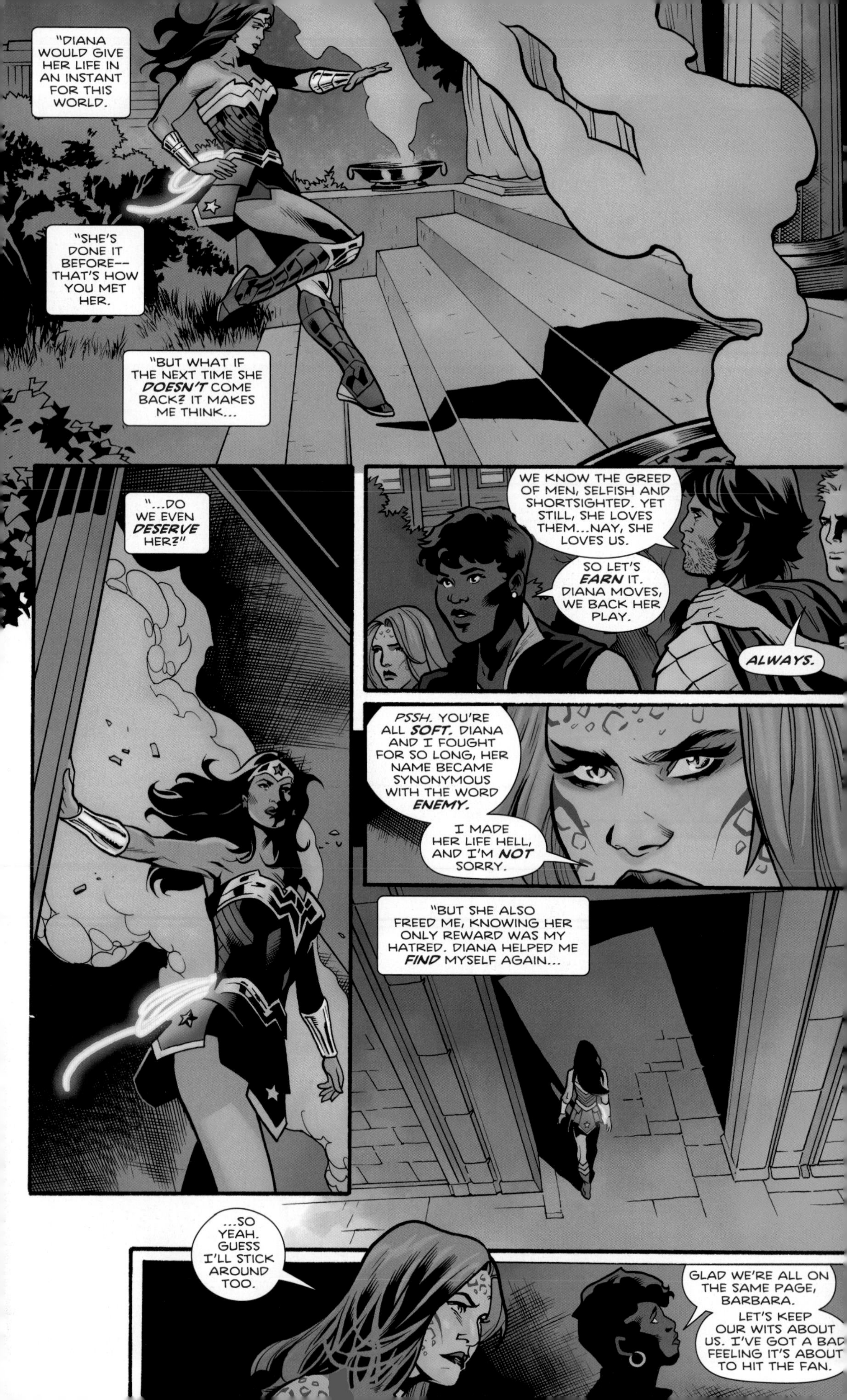
"DIANA WOULD GIVE HER LIFE IN AN INSTANT FOR THIS WORLD.
"SHE'S DONE IT BEFORE--THAT'S HOW YOU MET HER.
"BUT WHAT IF THE NEXT TIME SHE DOESN'T COME BACK? IT MAKES ME THINK...
"...DO WE EVEN DESERVE HER?"
WE KNOW THE GREED OF MEN, SELFISH AND SHORTSIGHTED. YET STILL, SHE LOVES THEM...NAY, SHE LOVES US.
SO LET'S EARN IT. DIANA MOVES, WE BACK HER PLAY.
ALWAYS.
PSSH. YOU'RE ALL SOFT. DIANA AND I FOUGHT FOR SO LONG, HER NAME BECAME SYNONYMOUS WITH THE WORD ENEMY.
I MADE HER LIFE HELL, AND I'M NOT SORRY.
"BUT SHE ALSO FREED ME, KNOWING HER ONLY REWARD WAS MY HATRED. DIANA HELPED ME FIND MYSELF AGAIN...
...SO YEAH. GUESS I'LL STICK AROUND TOO.
GLAD WE'RE ALL ON THE SAME PAGE, BARBARA.
LET'S KEEP OUR WITS ABOUT US. I'VE GOT A BAD FEELING IT'S ABOUT TO HIT THE FAN.

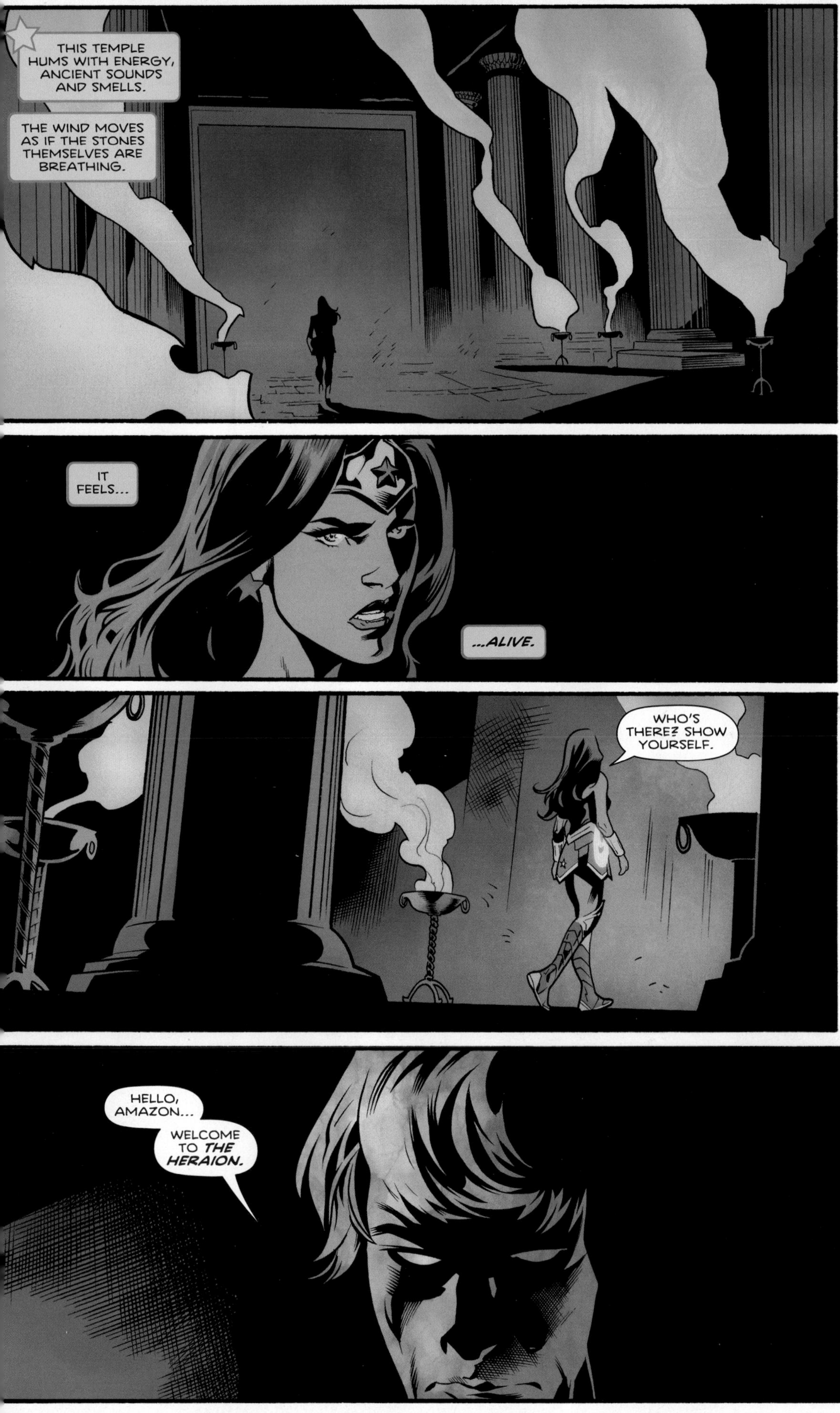
THIS TEMPLE HUMS WITH ENERGY, ANCIENT SOUNDS AND SMELLS.
THE WIND MOVES AS IF THE STONES THEMSELVES ARE BREATHING.
IT FEELS...
...ALIVE.
WHO'S THERE? SHOW YOURSELF.
HELLO, AMAZON...
WELCOME TO THE HERAION.

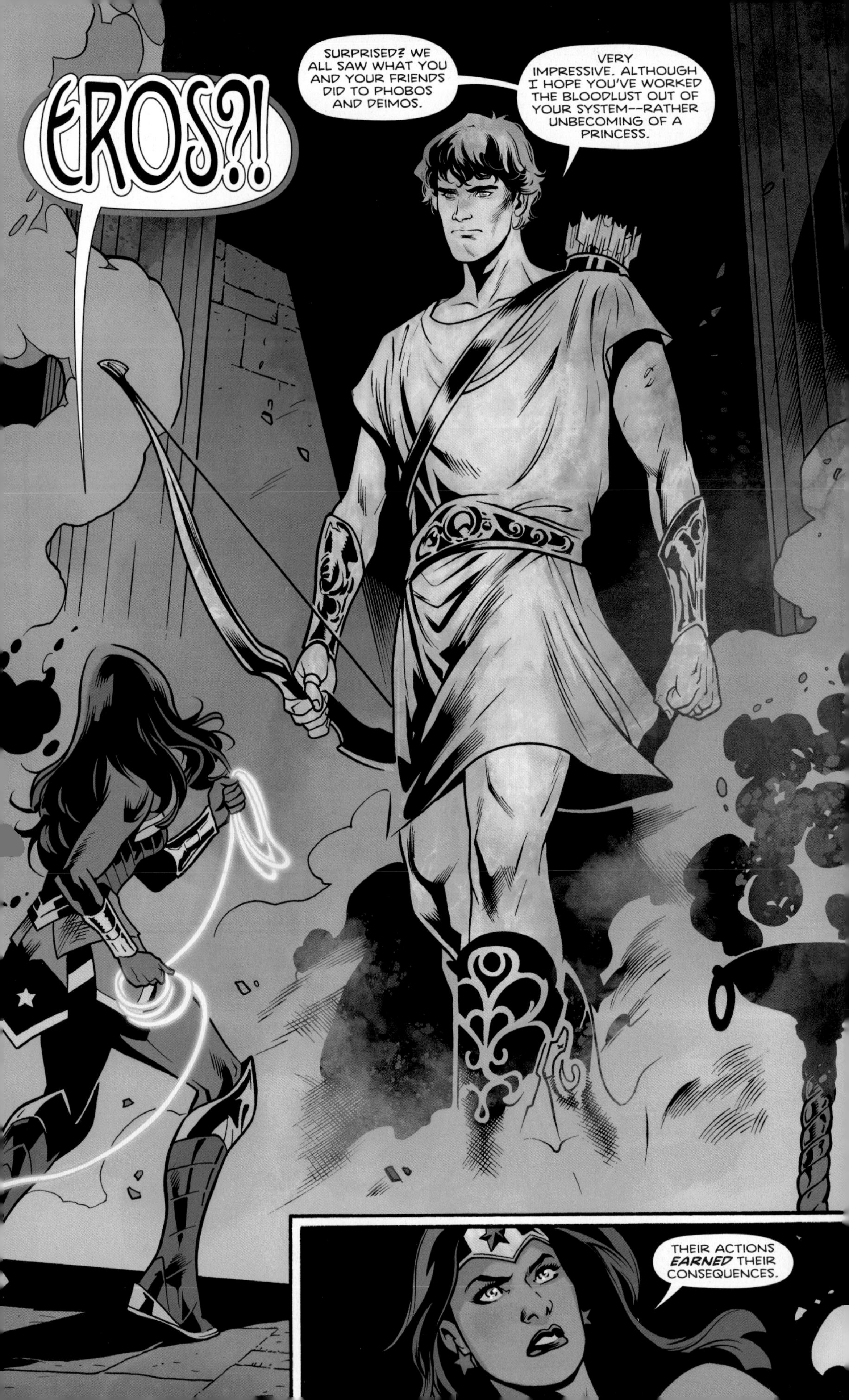
EROS?!
SURPRISED? WE ALL SAW WHAT YOU AND YOUR FRIENDS DID TO PHOBOS AND DEIMOS.
VERY IMPRESSIVE. ALTHOUGH I HOPE YOU'VE WORKED THE BLOODLUST OUT OF YOUR SYSTEM--RATHER UNBECOMING OF A PRINCESS.
THEIR ACTIONS EARNED THEIR CONSEQUENCES.

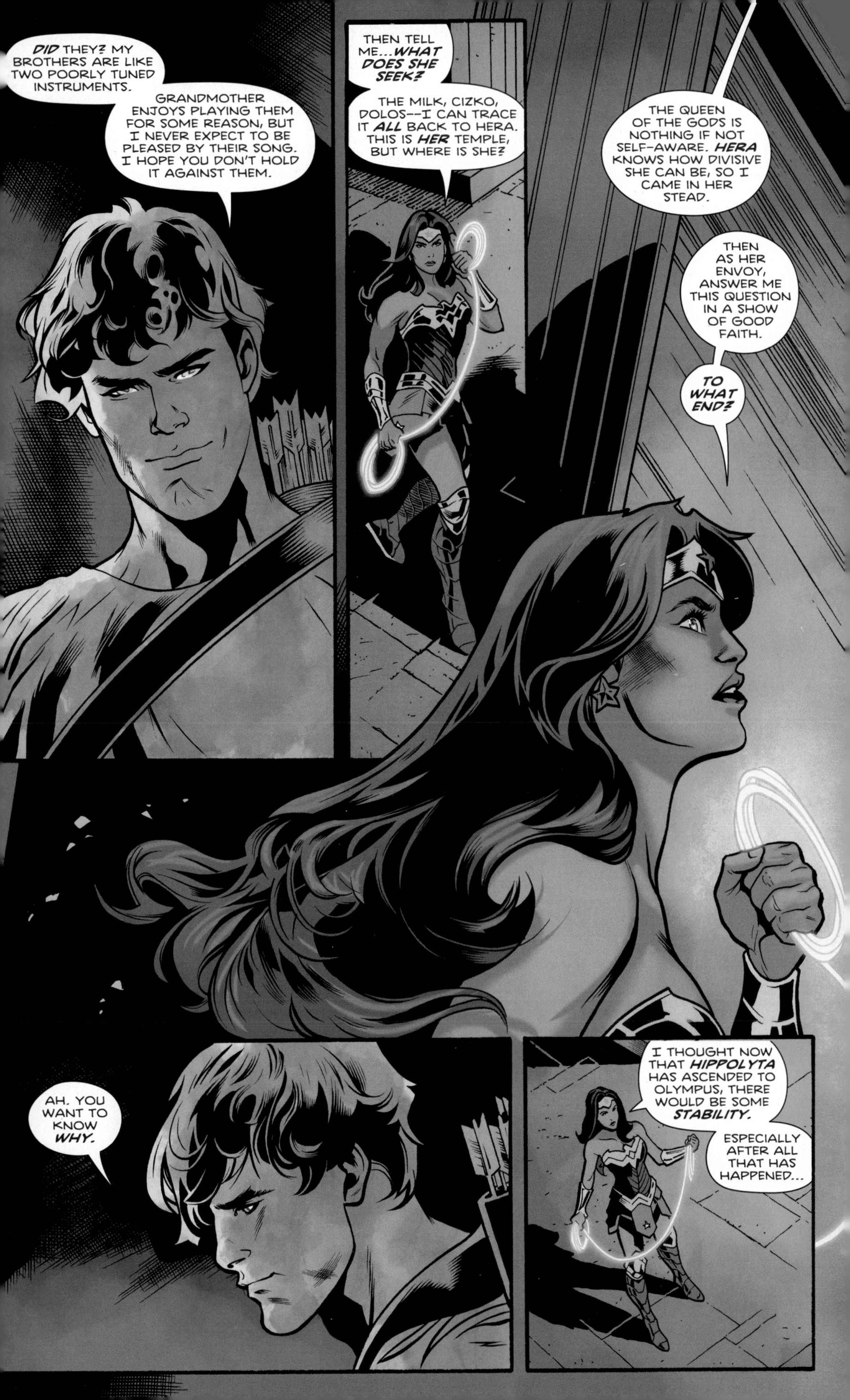
DID THEY? MY BROTHERS ARE LIKE TWO POORLY TUNED INSTRUMENTS.
GRANDMOTHER ENJOYS PLAYING THEM FOR SOME REASON, BUT I NEVER EXPECT TO BE PLEASED BY THEIR SONG. I HOPE YOU DON'T HOLD IT AGAINST THEM.
THEN TELL ME...WHAT DOES SHE SEEK?
THE MILK, CIZKO, DOLOS--I CAN TRACE IT ALL BACK TO HERA. THIS IS HER TEMPLE, BUT WHERE IS SHE?
THE QUEEN OF THE GODS IS NOTHING IF NOT SELF-AWARE. HERA KNOWS HOW DIVISIVE SHE CAN BE, SO I CAME IN HER STEAD.
THEN AS HER ENVOY, ANSWER ME THIS QUESTION IN A SHOW OF GOOD FAITH.
TO WHAT END?
AH. YOU WANT TO KNOW WHY.
I THOUGHT NOW THAT HIPPOLYTA HAS ASCENDED TO OLYMPUS, THERE WOULD BE SOME STABILITY.
ESPECIALLY AFTER ALL THAT HAS HAPPENED...

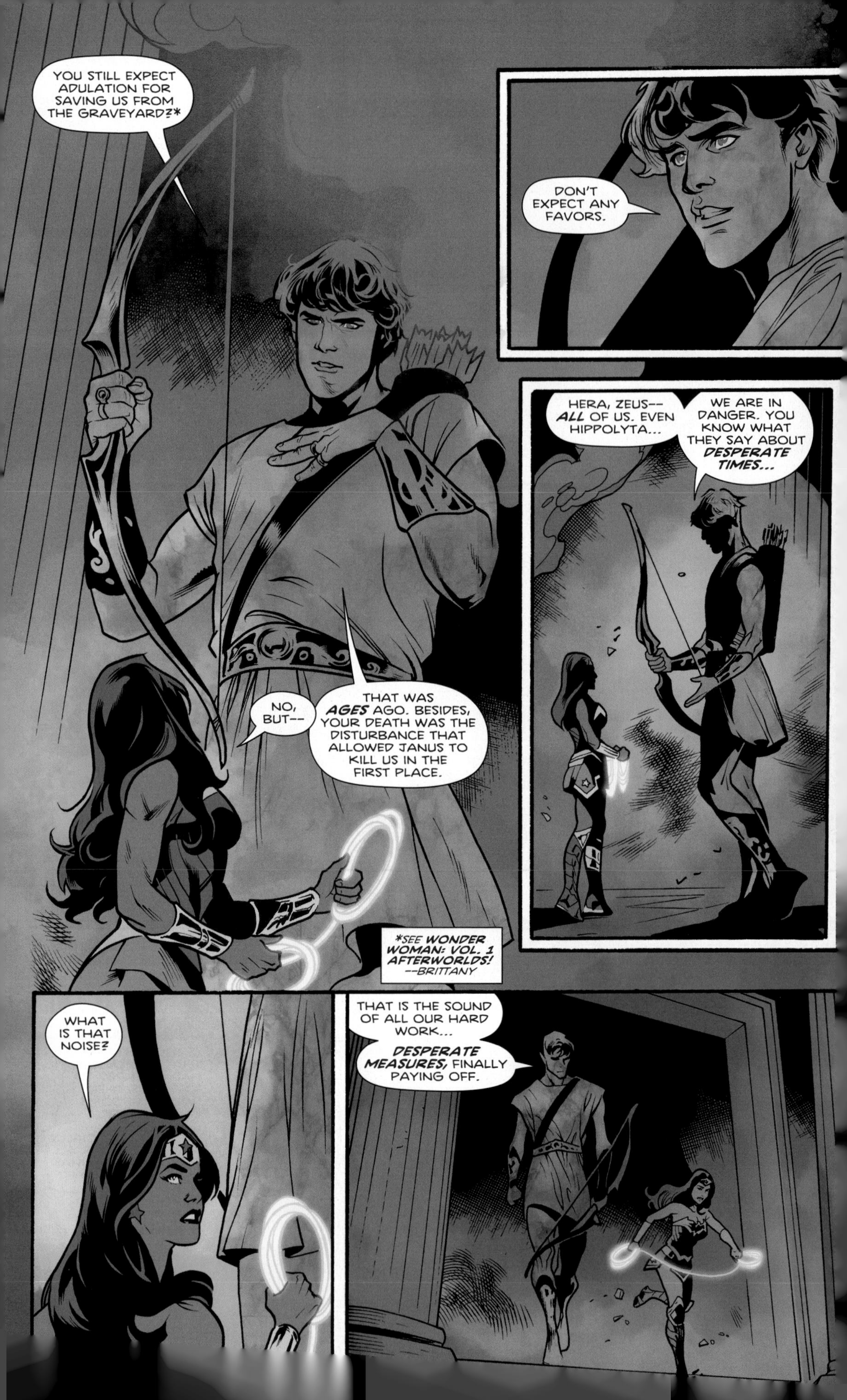
YOU STILL EXPECT ADULATION FOR SAVING US FROM THE GRAVEYARD?*
DON'T EXPECT ANY FAVORS.
NO, BUT--
THAT WAS AGES AGO. BESIDES, YOUR DEATH WAS THE DISTURBANCE THAT ALLOWED JANUS TO KILL US IN THE FIRST PLACE.
HERA, ZEUS-- ALL OF US. EVEN HIPPOLYTA...
WE ARE IN DANGER. YOU KNOW WHAT THEY SAY ABOUT DESPERATE TIMES...
*SEE WONDER WOMAN: VOL. 1 AFTERWORLDS! --BRITTANY
WHAT IS THAT NOISE?
THAT IS THE SOUND OF ALL OUR HARD WORK...
DESPERATE MEASURES, FINALLY PAYING OFF.

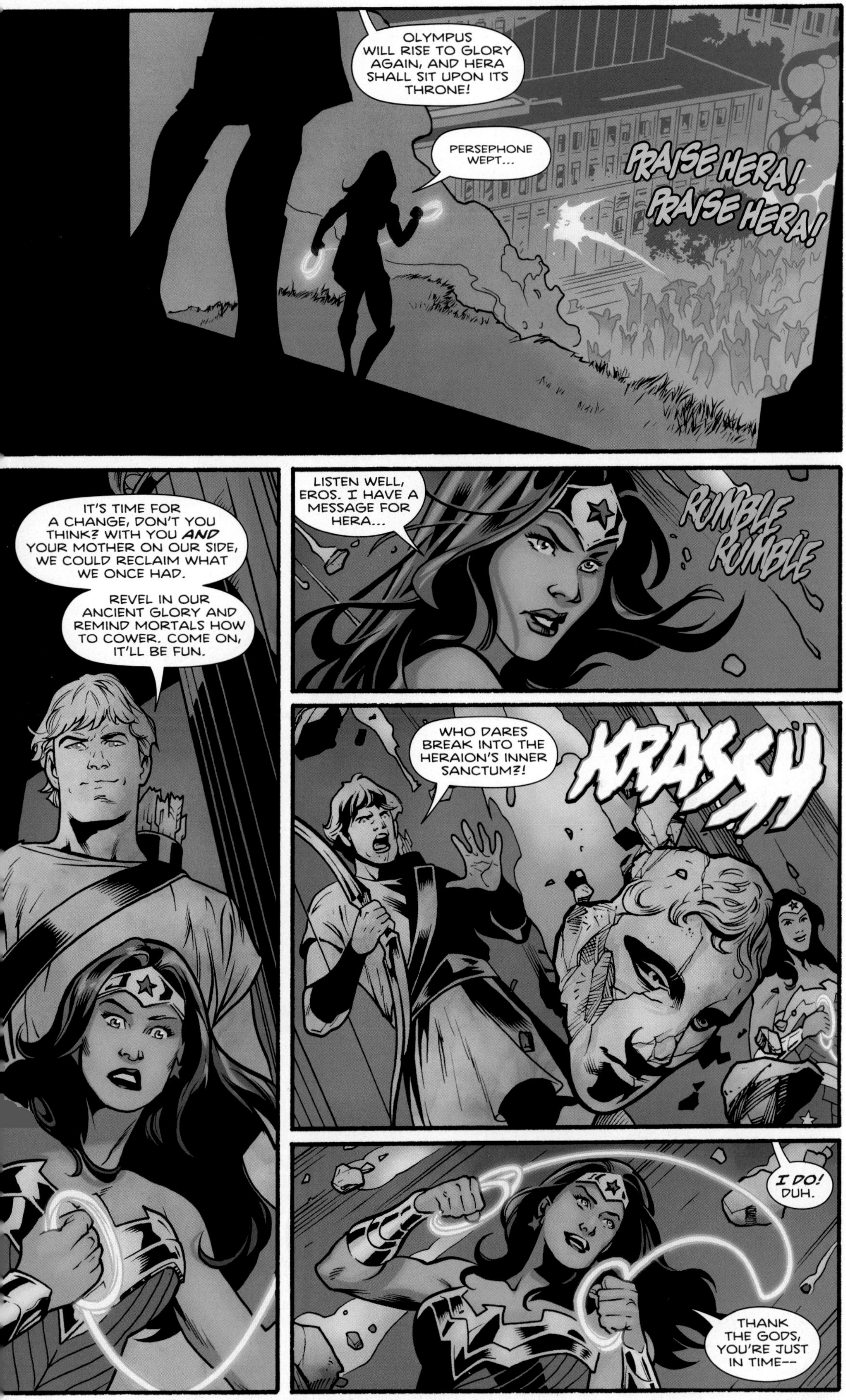
OLYMPUS WILL RISE TO GLORY AGAIN, AND HERA SHALL SIT UPON ITS THRONE!
PERSEPHONE WEPT...
PRAISE HERA! PRAISE HERA!
IT'S TIME FOR A CHANGE, DON'T YOU THINK? WITH YOU AND YOUR MOTHER ON OUR SIDE, WE COULD RECLAIM WHAT WE ONCE HAD.
REVEL IN OUR ANCIENT GLORY AND REMIND MORTALS HOW TO COWER. COME ON, IT'LL BE FUN.
LISTEN WELL, EROS. I HAVE A MESSAGE FOR HERA...
RUMBLE RUMBLE
WHO DARES BREAK INTO THE HERAION'S INNER SANCTUM?!
KRASSH
I DO! DUH.
THANK THE GODS, YOU'RE JUST IN TIME--

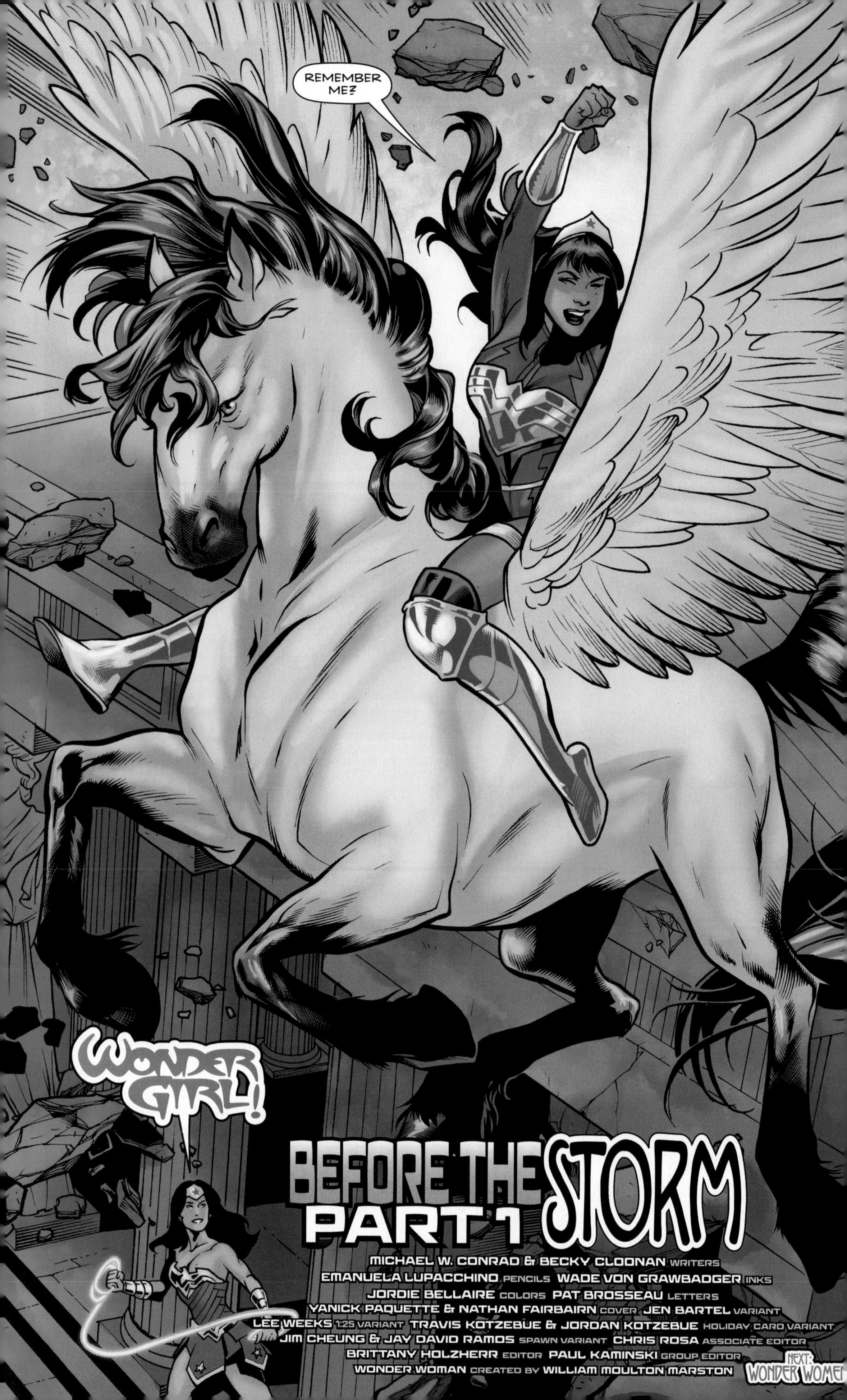
REMEMBER ME?
WONDER GIRL!
BEFORE THE STORM
PART 1
MICHAEL W. CONRAD & BECKY CLOONAN WRITERS
EMANUELA LUPACCHINO PENCILS WADE VON GRAWBADGER INKS
JORDIE BELLAIRE COLORS PAT BROSSEAU LETTERS
YANICK PAQUETTE & NATHAN FAIRBAIRN COVER JEN BARTEL VARIANT
LEE WEEKS 1:25 VARIANT TRAVIS KOTZEBUE & JORDAN KOTZEBUE HOLIDAY CARD VARIANT
JIM CHEUNG & JAY DAVID RAMOS SPAWN VARIANT CHRIS ROSA ASSOCIATE EDITOR
BRITTANY HOLZHERR EDITOR PAUL KAMINSKI GROUP EDITOR
WONDER WOMAN CREATED BY WILLIAM MOULTON MARSTON
NEXT: WONDER WOME

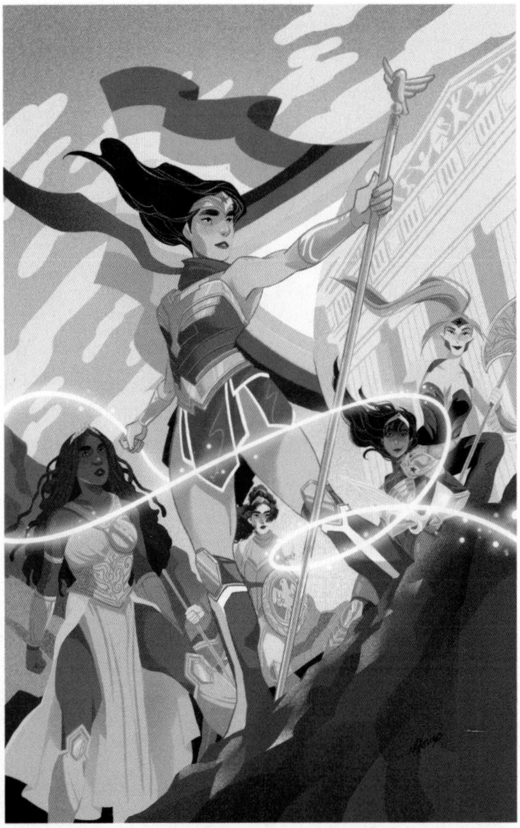

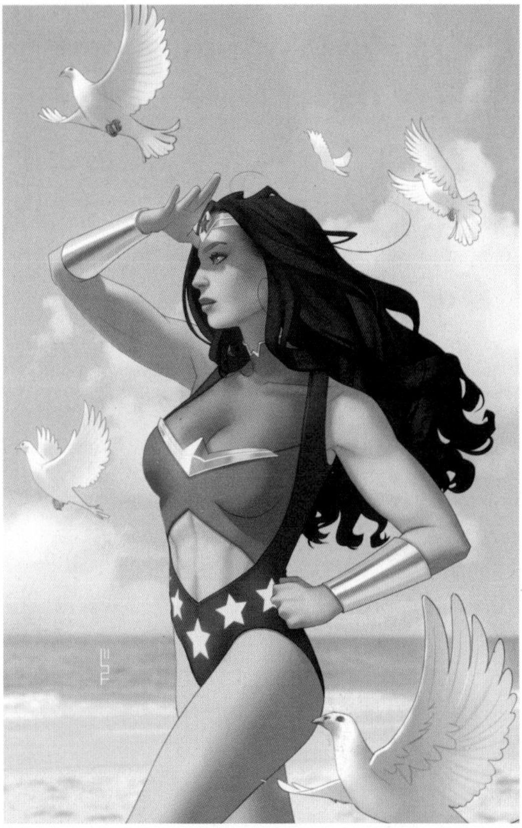

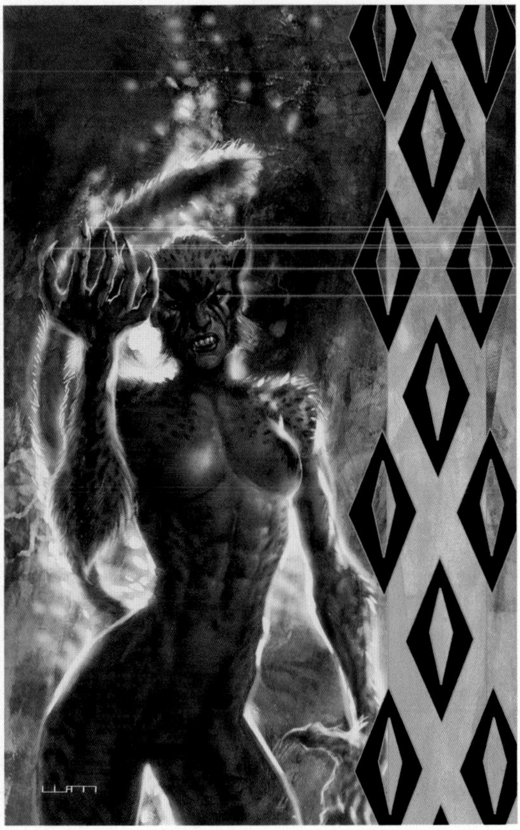

***Wonder Woman* #788**
Pride variant cover art by Nicole Goux

***Wonder Woman* #790**
Swimsuit variant cover art
by W. Scott Forbes

***Wonder Woman* #791**
1:25 variant cover art by Liam Sharp

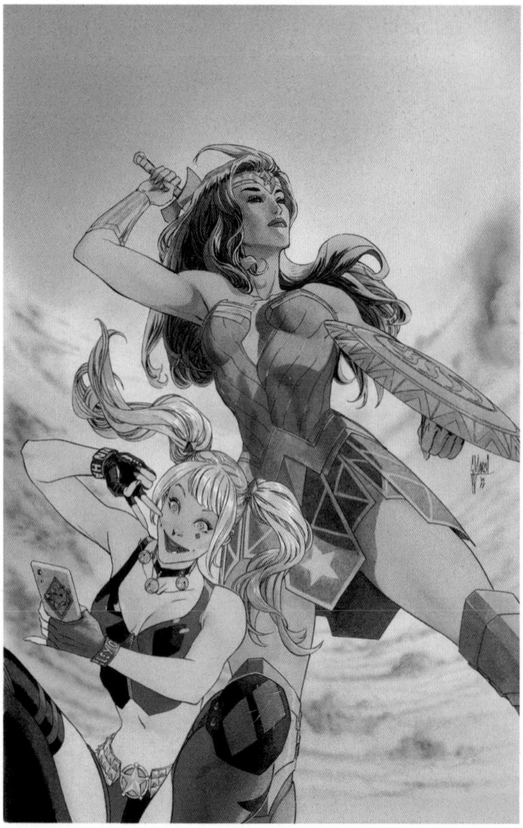

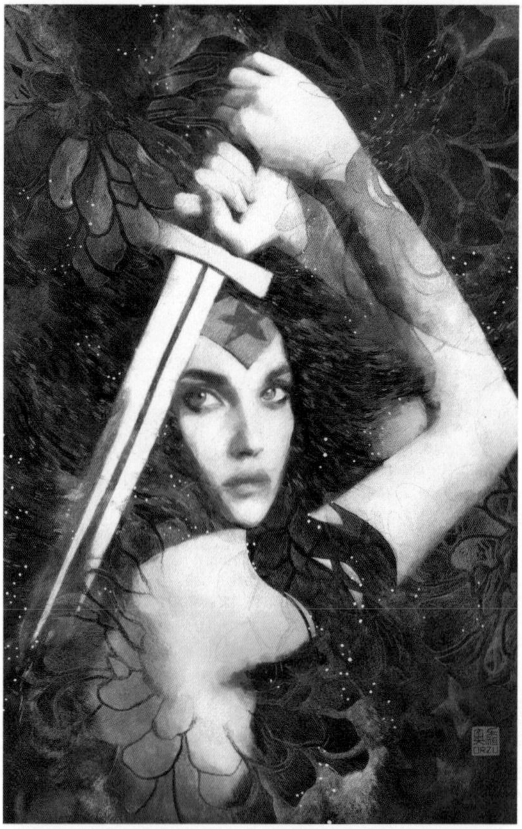

***Wonder Woman* #791**
Harley Quinn 30th Anniversary variant cover art by Guillem March

***Wonder Woman* #792**
variant cover art by Zu Orzu

***Wonder Woman* #792**
1:50 Cheetah Costume variant cover art by Crystal Kung

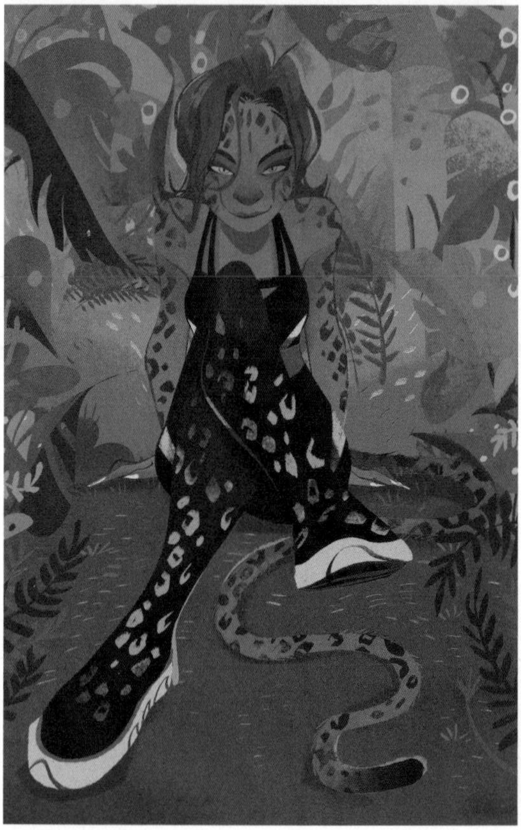

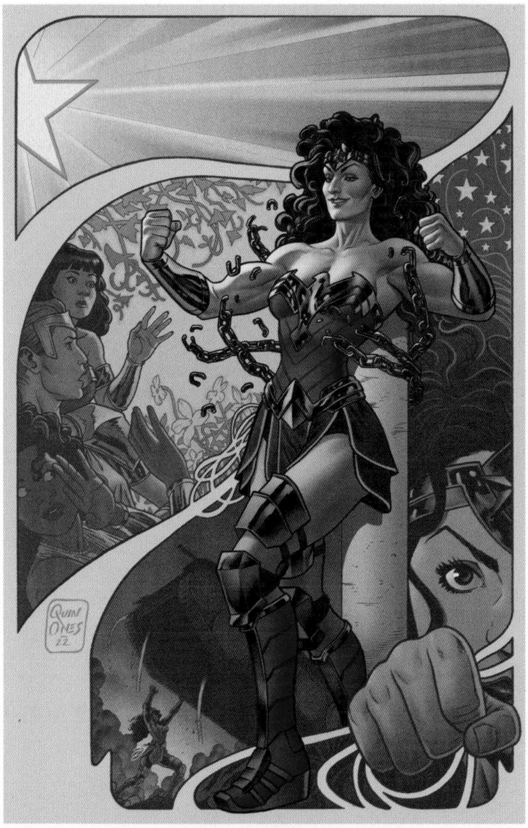

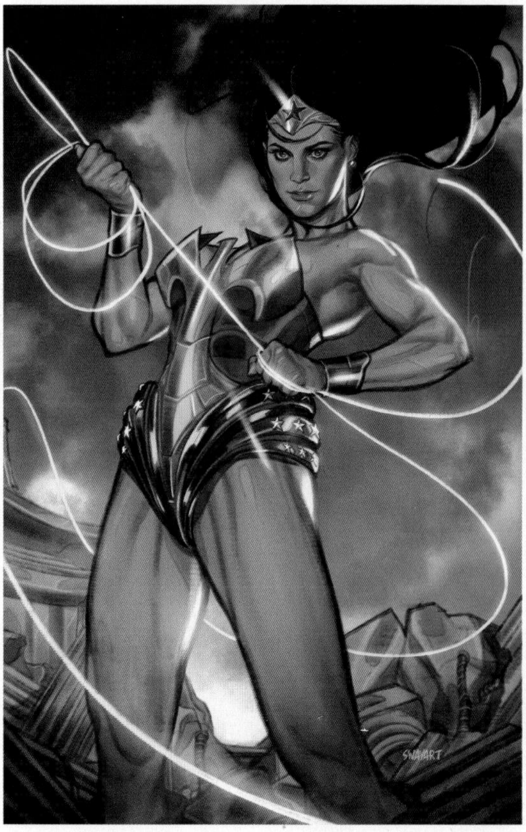
SWAAART

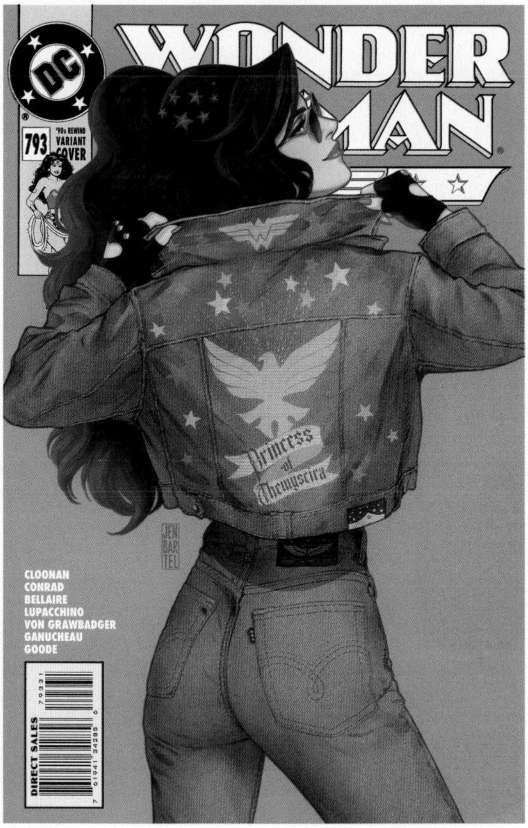
DC
WONDER
MAN
793
'90s REWIND
VARIANT
COVER
Princess
of
Themyscira
JEN
BAR
TEL
CLOONAN
CONRAD
BELLAIRE
LUPACCHINO
VON GRAWBADGER
GANUCHEAU
GOODE
DIRECT SALES

***Wonder Woman* #793**
1:25 variant cover art by Joe Quinones

***Wonder Woman* #793**
Nubia 50th Anniversary variant cover art by Joshua "Sway" Swaby

***Wonder Woman* #793**
'90s Rewind variant cover art by Jen Bartel

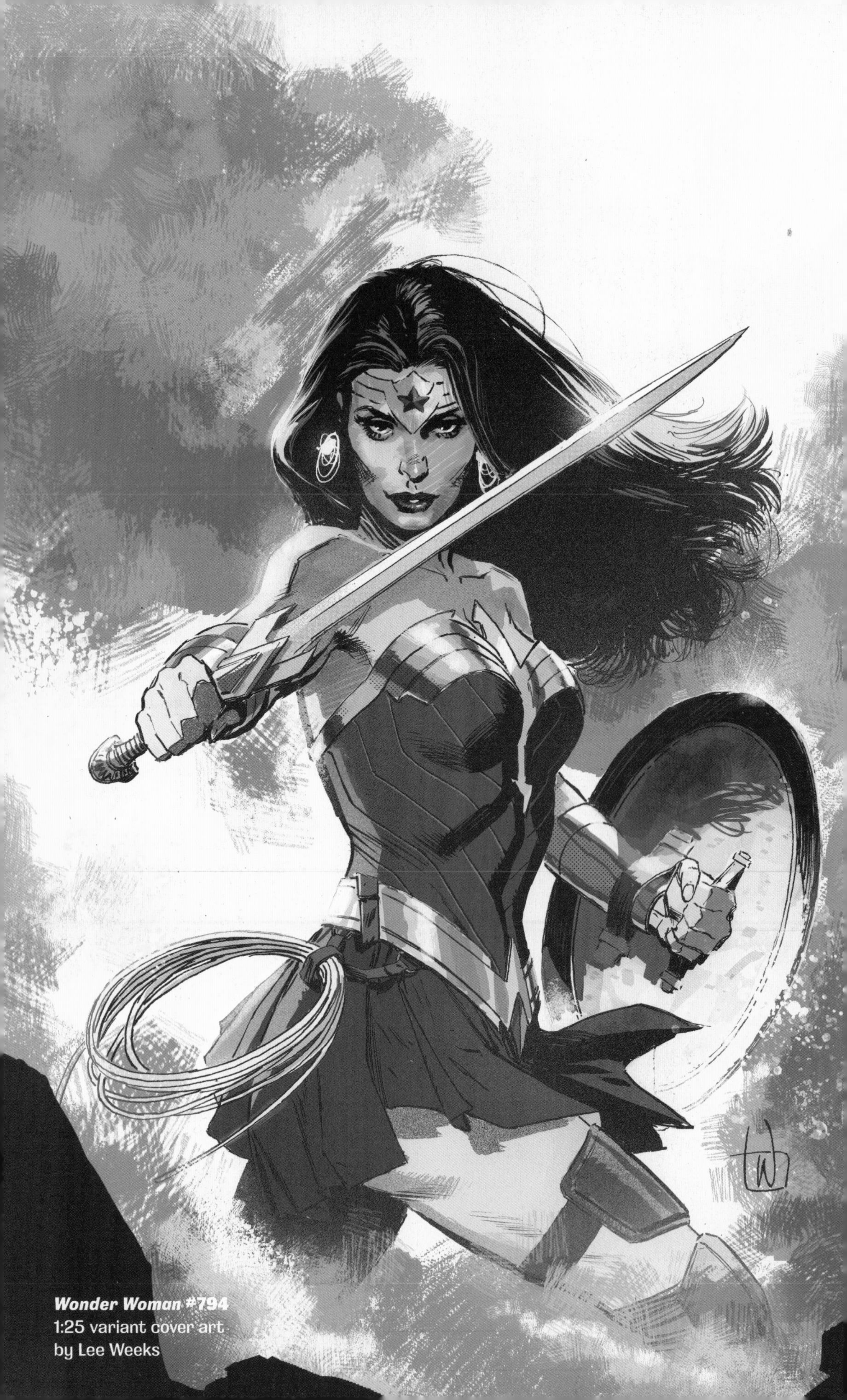

***Wonder Woman* #794**
1:25 variant cover art
by Lee Weeks